Accounting

7th Edition

by John A. Tracy, CPA, and Tage C. Tracy, CPA

for dummies®
A Wiley Brand

Accounting For Dummies®, 7th Edition

Published by: **John Wiley & Sons, Inc.**, 111 River Street, Hoboken, NJ 07030-5774, www.wiley.com

Copyright © 2022 by John Wiley & Sons, Inc., Hoboken, New Jersey

Published simultaneously in Canada

For general information on our other products and services, please contact our Customer Care Department within the U.S. at 877-762-2974, outside the U.S. at 317-572-3993, or fax 317-572-4002. For technical support, please visit https://hub.wiley.com/community/support/dummies.

Wiley publishes in a variety of print and electronic formats and by print-on-demand. Some material included with standard print versions of this book may not be included in e-books or in print-on-demand. If this book refers to media such as a CD or DVD that is not included in the version you purchased, you may download this material at http://booksupport.wiley.com. For more information about Wiley products, visit www.wiley.com.

Library of Congress Control Number: 2021950434

ISBN 978-1-119-83752-7 (pbk); ISBN 978-1-119-83753-4 (ebk); ISBN 978-1-119-83754-1 (ebk)

SKY10031811_120721

Contents at a Glance

Table of Contents

Introduction

You may know individuals who make their living as accountants. You may be thankful that they're the accountants and you're not. You may prefer to leave accounting to the accountants and think that you don't need to know anything about accounting. This attitude reminds us of the old Greyhound Bus advertising slogan: "Leave the Driving to Us." Well, if you could get around everywhere you wanted to go on the bus, that would be no problem. But if you have to drive most places, you'd better know something about cars. Throughout your life, you do lots of "financial driving," and you should know something about accounting.

Sure, accounting involves numbers. So does watching your car mileage, knowing your blood pressure, keeping track of your bank balance, negotiating the interest rate on your home mortgage, monitoring your retirement fund, and bragging about your kid's grade point average. You deal with numbers all the time. Accountants provide *financial* numbers, and these numbers are very important in your financial life. Knowing nothing about financial numbers puts you at a serious disadvantage. In short, financial literacy requires a working knowledge of accounting, which this book provides.

About This Book

Here are some advantages this book offers over other accounting texts:

>> We explain accounting in plain English, and we keep jargon and technical details to a minimum.

>> We carefully follow a step-by-step approach in explaining topics.

>> We include only topics that nonaccountants should understand. We avoid topics that only practicing accountants have to know.

>> We include candid discussions of sensitive accounting topics that go unmentioned in many books.

>> We combine our vast experience of both theoretical accounting (that is, how it is taught in the classroom) with actual practiced accounting (how accounting is applied in real-world businesses) to provide a deeper, more robust, and practical approach to understanding accounting.

>> We've set up the book so you can read the chapters in any order you please. You can tailor your reading plan to give priority to the chapters of most interest to you and read other chapters as time permits.

We should mention one thing: This book is *not* an accounting textbook. Introductory accounting textbooks are dry as dust and overly detailed. However, textbooks have one useful feature: They include exercises and problems. If you have the time, you can gain additional insights and test your understanding of accounting by working the exercises and short problems in coauthor John's book *Accounting Workbook For Dummies* (Wiley).

A quick note: Sidebars (shaded boxes of text) dig into the details of a given topic, but they aren't crucial to understanding it. Feel free to skip them. You can also pass over the text accompanied by the Technical Stuff icon, as it offers some interesting but nonessential information about accounting.

Finally, within this book, you may note that some web addresses break across two lines of text. If you're reading this book in print and want to visit one of these webpages, simply key in the address exactly as it's noted in the text, pretending the line break doesn't exist. If you're reading this as an ebook, you have it easy — just click the web address to be taken directly to the webpage.

Foolish Assumptions

We've written this book with a wide audience in mind. You should find yourself more than once in the following list of potential readers:

>> **Business managers (at all levels):** Trying to manage a business without a good grip on financial statements can lead to disaster. How can you manage the financial performance of your business if you don't understand your financial statements in the first place?

>> **Business buyers and sellers:** Anyone thinking of buying or selling a business should know how to read its financial statements and how to "true up" these accounting reports that serve as a key point of reference for setting a market value on the business.

>> **Entrepreneurs:** As budding business managers, they need a solid grasp of accounting basics.

- >> **Active investors:** Investors in marketable securities, real estate, and other ventures need to know how to read financial statements, both to stay informed about their investments and to spot any signs of trouble.

- >> **Passive investors:** Many people let the pros manage their money by investing in mutual funds or using investment advisors to handle their money; even so, they need to understand the investment performance reports they get, which use plenty of accounting terms and measures.

- >> **Accountants, bookkeepers, and controllers:** Strengthening their knowledge of accounting should improve their effectiveness and value to the organization and advance their careers.

- >> **People who want to take control of their personal finances:** Many aspects of managing your personal finances involve the accounting vocabulary and accounting-based calculation methods.

- >> **Anyone interested in following economic, business, and financial news:** Articles in *The Wall Street Journal* and other financial news sources are heavy with accounting terms and measures.

- >> **Administrators and managers of government and not-for-profit entities:** Making profit is not the goal of these entities, but they have to stay within their revenue limits and keep on a sound financial footing.

- >> **Politicians at local, state, and federal levels:** These folks pass many laws having huge financial consequences, and the better they understand accounting, the better informed their votes should be (we hope).

- >> **Investment bankers, institutional lenders, and loan officers:** These folks should already know, but you would be amazed at how many times we've come across these types of professionals that still don't have a complete understanding of accounting.

- >> **Business and finance professionals:** This includes lawyers and financial advisors, of course, but even clergy counsel members of their flock on financial matters occasionally.

Icons Used in This Book

The following icons can help you find information quickly and easily.

REMEMBER

This icon points out accounting ideas that are particularly deserving of your attention. These concepts are the undergirding and building blocks of accounting — concepts that you should be very clear about and that clarify your understanding of accounting principles in general.

This icon calls your attention to useful advice on practical financial topics. It saves you the cost of buying a highlighter.

Taking special note of Warning material can steer you around a financial road hazard and keep you from blowing a fiscal tire. In short — watch out!

We use this icon sparingly. It refers to specialized accounting stuff that's heavy going, which only a CPA could get really excited about. However, you may find these topics interesting enough to return to them when you have the time. Feel free to skip these points and stay with the main discussion.

Beyond the Book

This book is packed with useful information, but if you're looking for a compact overview of the most important points, check out the online Cheat Sheet. Go to www.dummies.com and search for "Accounting For Dummies Cheat Sheet" in the Search box. You'll find FAQs on financial statements, accounting tips for business managers, and definitions of key accounting terms. We also want to note that all of the figures presented in this book have been prepared in Excel and can be obtained free of charge by reaching out to us and requesting a copy of the workbook file at tagetracy@cox.net.

Where to Go from Here

There's no law against starting on page 1 and reading through to the last page. However, you may first want to scan the book's Contents at a Glance and see which chapters pique your interest.

Perhaps you're an investor who's interested in finding out more about financial statements and the key financial statement ratios for investors. In that case, you might start with Chapters 6, 7, and 8, which explain the three primary financial statements of businesses, and finish with Chapter 11, on reading a financial report. (And don't overlook Chapter 20.)

Or maybe you're a small-business owner/manager with a basic understanding of your financial statements, but you need to improve how you use accounting information for making key profit decisions and for planning and controlling your cash flow. You might jump right into Chapters 15 and 17, which explain analyzing profit behavior and budgeting cash flows.

1
Opening the Books on Accounting

Discover how accountants are the financial information gatekeepers in the economy and why accounting is so important for for-profit businesses, nonprofit organizations, and government agencies.

Find out how a business or other entity prepares its financial statements, its tax returns, and the reports to its managers. Know how to make sure these documents conform to established standards.

Get the lowdown on bookkeeping — the record-keeping part of accounting — to ensure that the financial information of a business is timely, complete, accurate, and reliable, especially the numbers reported in financial statements and tax returns.

Understand why safeguarding company assets is an integral part of an accountant's job and how the digital age, the cloud, and technology are transforming the world of accounting.

Look at the various types of business legal entities, see how accounting differs for each one, and get some helpful hints on when different legal structures are best used.

» Grasping how all economic activity requires accounting

» Understanding the accounting function's primary roles

» Watching an accounting department in action

» Shaking hands with business financial statements

» Realizing accounting is both an art form and science

Chapter **1**

Accounting in Today's New Economy

There was a captive audience present when I (coauthor John) taught Accounting 101 because, then as well as now, all business school students have to take this course. In contrast, very few arts and science students elect the course, which is unfortunate. Accounting 101 teaches about business, including the nature of profit (which most people don't fully understand) and the fundamentals of capitalism.

The course is a very good training ground for becoming *financially literate*. Accounting is the language of business, finance, investing, and taxes. To be financially literate, you need to know basic accounting. These days, there's a big push to improve financial literacy, and a basic accounting course offers a useful framework for understanding and thinking about financial issues. Financial literacy is important to help ensure financial security for you and your family as you go through life and eventually enter into retirement.

In one sense, this book is the accounting course you never took. For business grads, the book presents an opportune review of topics you've gotten rusty on. We dare say that even accounting majors can glean many insights from this book. You don't need a college education to gain from this book, however. Like all the *For Dummies* books, this book delivers useful information in a plain-talking manner, with a light touch to keep it interesting.

As you go through life, you come face to face with a flood of accounting-generated information — more than you would ever imagine. Regrettably, much of this information isn't intuitive, and it doesn't come with a user's manual. In short, most of the accounting information you encounter isn't readily clear.

One main reason for learning some accounting is to understand its vocabulary and valuation methods so you can make more intelligent use of the information. Accountants are financial scorekeepers. In playing or watching any game, you need to know how the score is kept. The purpose of this book is to make you a knowledgeable spectator of and sometimes a participant in the accounting game.

REMEMBER

Let us point out another reason you should know accounting basics — the *defensive* reason. Many people in the cold, cruel financial world are on the prowl to take advantage of your lack of savvy about accounting. These unscrupulous characters treat you as a lamb waiting to be fleeced. An important defense against such tactics is to know some accounting, which helps you ask the right questions and understand the crucial points on which con artists want to keep you in the dark.

Checking Your Preconceptions about Accounting

You probably fall in with the majority of people who have preconceptions about accounting — which in fact may be way off the mark. For instance, most people think that you have to be good at math to understand accounting. Accounting deals with numbers, that's for sure, but by no means does it require calculus or other math — just arithmetic. Accountants make calculations and compare numbers. That's about it. We've never heard of an accountant taking the first derivative of an accounting equation or doing any other calculus computation.

The problem is that many people — perhaps even you — are number-phobic. They avoid anything to do with digits. They wouldn't think of doing their annual income tax return. Accountants deal in numbers. But be aware that every accounting number has a name or label attached. There are no naked numbers in accounting. The basic unit of information in accounting is the *account,* which consists of both

>> A name

>> Its amount or value

The vocabulary of accounting consists of accounts. Accountants communicate in terms of accounts.

Another preconception is that accountants have their heads buried in a torrent of details. Accountants have no choice; they have to be detail-oriented. At the same time, they have to see how the details fit into the overall scheme of things. The avalanche of details is condensed into accounting reports that disclose relatively few *aggregate* accounts. One reason for learning accounting is to understand what these collective accounts include.

Thinking about where assets come from

We explain later that accountants decide how to record transactions, which are economic exchanges (see the later section "Focusing on Transactions"). Many people aren't aware of the double duty of accountants in recording transactions. Accountants look at things from two points of view — the give and the take of the transaction. This is called *double-entry* accounting, which we explain in Chapter 3. The following example illustrates the two-sided nature of accounting.

Suppose a business reports $1,000,000 in total assets at the end of its most recent year. Most people, quite naturally, focus on the makeup of its assets (how much cash, for example). But the composition of its assets is only half the financial picture of a business. You've heard the expression that there are two sides to every story. Well, in accounting, there are two sides to the financial condition of a business.

Accounting deals with assets, of course. Accountants are equally concerned with the sources of the assets. In this example, the $1,000,000 in assets comes from three sources: $300,000 liabilities; $500,000 capital; and $200,000 surplus. You probably have a good idea of what liabilities are. *Capital* is money invested in the business by the owners. *Surplus* is profit that has been earned and not distributed to the owners. The sum of all three sources taken together equals the *total assets* of the business. The books are in balance.

Asking about profit

Businesses are profit motivated, so a natural question is "How much profit did the business earn over the last year?" Suppose the business had $120,000 surplus at the beginning of the year, and the business didn't distribute any of its profit to its owners during the year. Therefore, the business earned $80,000 profit for the year: $120,000 surplus at start of year → $200,000 surplus at end of year = $80,000 gain in surplus, which is the profit for the year.

REMEMBER

One popular misconception is that earning profit increases cash by the same amount. Unfortunately, it's not as simple as that. Earning profit involves many assets and several liabilities. Cash is the main asset but not the only one affected by earning profit. One purpose of learning accounting is to understand the financial "fallout" from making profit. Profit consists of changes in assets and liabilities that, taken all together, increase the surplus of the business. The cash result from making profit is either higher or lower than the amount of profit. Isn't this interesting?

Sorting out stereotypes of accountants

We recently saw a cartoon in which the young son of clowns is standing in a circus tent and is dressed as a clown, but he's holding a briefcase. He's telling his clown parents that he's running away to join a CPA firm. This cartoon plays off the stereotype of a CPA (certified public accountant) as a boring "bean counter" who wears a green eyeshade, has no sense of humor, and possesses the personality of an undertaker (no offense to morticians). Maybe you've heard the joke that an accountant with a personality is one who looks at *your* shoes when he's talking to you instead his own shoes.

Like most stereotypes, there's an element of truth in this image of accountants. As a CPA and accounting professor for more than 40 years (coauthor John) and a financial and accounting consultant for more than 36 years (coauthor Tage), we've met and known a large number of accountants. Most accountants are not as gregarious as used-car salespeople (though some are). Accountants certainly are more detail-oriented than your average person, and they're a little more comfortable with complex calculations. Accountants are very good at one thing: Examining both sides of financial transactions — the give and the take, what was gotten and what was given. Accountants know better than anyone that, as economists are fond of saying, there's no such thing as a free lunch.

Because accountants work with numbers and details, you hear references to accountants as bean counters, digit heads, number nerds, and other names we don't dare mention here. Accountants take these snide references in stride and with good humor. Actually, accountants rank among the most respected professionals in many polls. Many people and businesses rely on their accountants for business, financial, and even investment advice. Accountants are much more than preparers of your tax returns.

If you walked down a busy street in Chicago, Denver, New York, or Los Angeles, we doubt that you could pick out the accountants. We have no idea whether accountants have higher or lower divorce rates, whether they go to church more frequently, whether most are Republicans or Democrats, or whether they generally sleep well at night. We do think overall that accountants are more honest in paying their income taxes, although we have no proof of this. (And yes, we know of a couple of accountants who tried to cheat on their federal income tax returns.)

Providing Vital Financial Information

In a nutshell, accountants "keep the books" of businesses — and of not-for-profit (NFP) and government entities also — by following systematic methods to record the financial activities of the entity. All this recordkeeping is done for one primary purpose: to create the database necessary for the preparation of complete, accurate, reliable, and timely financial reports, tax returns, and other types of financial communications. In *financial reports,* accounting information is presented in the form of *financial statements* that are packaged with other information such as explanatory footnotes and a letter from top management. Accountants design financial reports for *nonaccountants,* such as business owners, lenders, and investors.

Financial reports are sent to people who have a stake in the outcomes of the activities. If you own stock in Microsoft, for example, or you have money in a mutual fund, you receive regular financial reports. If you invest your hard-earned money in a private business or a real estate venture, or if you save money in a credit union, you receive regular financial reports. If you're a member of a nonprofit association or organization, you're entitled to receive regular financial reports. We hope you carefully read these financial reports, but if you don't — or if you do yet don't understand what you're reading — it could be that you don't understand the language of accounting.

One important reason for studying accounting is to make sense of the financial statements in the financial reports you get. We guarantee that Warren Buffett knows accounting and how to read financial statements. We sent him a copy of our book *How to Read a Financial Report* (John Wiley & Sons, Inc.). In his reply, he said he planned to recommend it to his "accounting challenged" friends.

Recognizing users of accounting information

People who use accounting information fall into two broad groups: *insiders (internal users)* and *outsiders (external users)*.

>> Business managers are insiders; they have the authority and responsibility to run a business. They need a good understanding of accounting terms and the methods used to measure profit and put values on assets and liabilities. Accounting information is indispensable for planning and controlling the financial performance and condition of the business. Likewise, administrators of NFP and governmental entities need to understand the accounting terminology and measurement methods in their financial statements.

>> The rest of us are outsiders. We aren't privy to the day-to-day details of a business or organization. We have to rely on financial reports from the entity to know what's going on. Therefore, we need to have a good grip on the financial statements included in the financial reports. For all practical purposes, financial reports are the only source of financial information we get directly from a business or other organization.

By the way, the employees of a business — even though they obviously have a stake in the success of the business — don't necessarily receive its financial reports. Only the investors in the business and its lenders are entitled to receive the financial reports. Of course, a business *could* provide this information to employees who aren't shareowners, but generally speaking, most businesses do not. The financial reports of public businesses are in the public domain, so their employees can easily secure a copy. However, most businesses don't automatically mail financial reports to all employees.

In your personal financial life, a little accounting knowledge is a big help for understanding investing in general, how investment performance is measured, and many other important financial topics. With some basic accounting knowledge, you'll sound much more sophisticated when speaking with your banker or broker. We can't promise you that learning accounting will save you big bucks on your income taxes, but it can't hurt and will definitely help you understand what your tax preparer is talking about.

REMEMBER

This is *not* a book on bookkeeping and recordkeeping systems. We offer a brief explanation of procedures for capturing, processing, and storing accounting information in Chapter 3. Even experienced bookkeepers and accountants should find some useful nuggets in that chapter. However, this book is directed to *users* of accounting information. We focus on the end products of accounting, particularly financial statements, and not on how information is accumulated. When buying a new car, you're interested in the finished product, not details of the manufacturing process that produced it.

Using accounting in your personal financial life

We're sure you know the value of learning personal finance and investing fundamentals. (Given the big push these days on improving financial literacy, we recommend *Personal Finance For Dummies* and *Investing For Dummies* by Eric Tyson, MBA, both published by Wiley.) A great deal of the information you use in making personal finance and investment decisions is *accounting information.* However, we do have one knock on books in these areas: They don't make clear that you need a solid understanding of financial statements to make good use of the financial information.

REMEMBER

We've noticed that a sizable percent of the populace bash the profit motive and seem to think businesses should not make a profit. We would remind you, however, that you have a stake in the financial performance of the business you work for, the government entities you pay taxes to, the churches and charitable organizations you donate money to, the retirement plan you participate in, the businesses you buy from, and the healthcare providers you depend on. The financial performance and viability of these entities has a direct bearing on your personal financial life and well-being.

We're all affected by the profit performance of businesses, even though we may not be fully aware of just how their profit performance affects our jobs, investments, and taxes. For example, as an employee, your job security and your next raise depend on the business's making a profit. If the business suffers a loss, you may be laid off or asked to take a reduction in pay or benefits. Business managers get paid to make profit happen. If the business fails to meet its profit objectives or suffers a loss, its managers may be replaced (or at least not get their bonuses). As authors, we hope our publisher continues to make a profit so we can keep receiving our royalty checks.

Your investments in businesses, whether direct or through retirement accounts and mutual funds, suffer if the businesses don't turn a profit. We hope the stores we trade with make profit and continue in business. The federal government and most states depend on businesses making profit so they can collect income taxes from them.

Accounting extends into many nooks and crannies of your life. You're doing accounting when you make entries in your checkbook and when you fill out your federal income tax return. When you sign a mortgage on your home, you should understand the accounting method the lender uses to calculate the interest amount charged on your loan each period. Individual investors need to understand accounting basics in order to figure their return on invested capital. And it goes without saying that every organization, profit–motivated or not, needs to know how it stands financially.

Seeing accounting at work

Accounting methods must fit the nature of the entity being accounted for and how the entity carries out its purpose. Accounting is not a case of one size fits all. Here's a quick sweep of the radar screen to give you an idea of different types of entities that accounting methods are adapted to:

>> Accounting for profit-motivated businesses and accounting for nonprofit organizations (such as hospitals, homeowners' associations, churches, credit unions, and colleges)

>> Income tax accounting while you're living and estate tax accounting after you die

>> Accounting for farmers who grow their products, accounting for miners who extract their products from the earth, accounting for producers who manufacture products, and accounting for retailers who sell products that others make

>> Accounting for businesses and professional firms that sell services rather than products, such as the entertainment, transportation, and healthcare industries

>> Accounting where periodic financial statements are legally mandated (public companies are the primary example) and accounting where such formal accounting reports are not legally required

>> Accounting that mainly adheres to historical cost (businesses) and accounting that records changes in market value (mutual funds, for example)

>> Accounting in the private sector of the economy and accounting in the public (government) sector

>> Accounting for going-concern businesses that will be around for some time and accounting for businesses in bankruptcy that may not be around tomorrow

Accounting is necessary in a free–market capitalist economic system. It's equally necessary in a centralized, government–controlled socialist economic system. All economic activity requires information. The more developed the economic system, the more the system depends on information. Much of the information comes from the accounting systems used by the businesses, institutions, individuals, and other players in the economic system.

Some of the earliest records of history are the accounts of wealth and trading activity. The need for accounting information was a main incentive in the development of the number system we use today. The history of accounting is quite interesting (but beyond the scope of this book).

Accounting's Two Primary Roles

We aim to make this section of the book as easy to understand as possible by stating what should be obvious. That is, the accounting function in most businesses has two primary purposes:

>> First, the accounting function and systems established must be able to produce complete, accurate, reliable, and timely ("CART") financial information on which businesses can base sound decisions.

   In today's intensely competitive global economy that is now supported by a broad ranging technology infrastructure that delivers information in split seconds, it has never been more important for accounting systems and the entire accounting function to produce and deliver vital financial information on a timely basis for review and management action.

>> Second, a business's accounting function must be developed, implemented, managed, and periodically revised and updated to always be in the mindset of safeguarding company assets. Here, we are not just talking about preventing theft of liquid or hard assets such as an employee who may be embezzling cash or stealing inventory. Rather, the accounting function is now one of the critical gatekeepers associated with helping protect company intellectual property, shelter invaluable customer data and databases, preserve the integrity of critical financial information, control and direct the distribution of confidential financial operating results to the appropriate parties, and assist with critical risk management and insurance protection strategies, just to name a few.

As you progress through the rest of this book, it becomes abundantly clear that the accounting function has evolved into something much more than a bunch of bean counters, working with debits and credits, producing financial statements, and trying desperately to meet the annual income tax reporting deadlines. If the last 24 months has taught us anything, it is that the speed at which economic business models are now formulated, launched, disrupted, expanded, contracted, and potentially eliminated from the global market is in warp drive. Massive volumes of raw confidential business data are now considered one of the most valuable assets a company owns and monetizes to generate profits (aided by huge technological advancements). As such, accounting's role in producing CART financial information in coordination with helping protect this data has never been more critical. Throughout this book, we provide examples and make references to accounting in the new, digital age; we start by diving into the digitization of accounting in Chapter 4 and a new era of risks.

Taking a Peek behind the Scenes

Every business and not-for-profit entity needs a reliable bookkeeping system (see Chapter 3). *Accounting* is a much broader term than *bookkeeping.* For one thing, accounting encompasses the problems in measuring the financial effects of economic activity. Furthermore, accounting includes the function of *financial reporting* to those who need the information. Business managers and investors and many other people depend on financial reports for information about the performance and condition of the entity.

Bookkeeping — also called *recordkeeping* — refers to the process of capturing, accumulating, organizing, storing, protecting, and accessing the financial information base of the entity. Of course, the financial information base should be complete, accurate, reliable, and timely. Every recordkeeping system needs quality controls built into it, which are called *internal controls* or *internal accounting controls.* When an error creeps into the system, it can be difficult to root out and correct. Data-entry controls are particularly important. The security of online and computer-based accounting systems has become a top priority of both for-profit businesses and not-for-profit entities. So-called cyber threats are a serious problem and can bring a big business to its knees, which we discuss further in Chapter 4.

REMEMBER

Accountants design the internal controls for the recordkeeping system, which serve to minimize errors in recording the large number of activities that an entity engages in over a specific time period. The internal controls that accountants design are also relied on to detect and deter theft, embezzlement, fraud, and dishonest behavior of all kinds. In accounting, internal controls are the ounce of prevention that's worth a pound of cure.

Most people don't realize the importance of the accounting department in keeping a business operating without hitches and delays. That's probably because accountants oversee many of the back-office functions in a business — as opposed to sales, for example, which is frontline activity, out in the open and in the line of fire. Go into any retail store, and you're in the thick of sales activities. But have you ever seen a company's accounting department in action?

Folks may not think much about these back-office activities, but they would sure notice if those activities didn't get done. On payday, a business had better not tell its employees, "Sorry, but the accounting department is running a little late this month; you'll get your checks later." And when a customer insists on up-to-date information about how much they owe the business, the accounting department can't very well say, "Oh, don't worry, just wait a week or so, and we'll get the information to you then."

Typically, the accounting department is responsible for the following:

>> **Payroll:** The total wages and salaries earned by every employee every pay period, which are called *gross wages* or *gross earnings,* have to be calculated. Based on detailed private information in personnel files and earnings-to-date information, the correct amounts of income tax, Social Security tax, and several other deductions from gross wages have to be determined.

Actually, a good deal of information has to be reported to employees each pay period, regarding withholdings and employee benefits. Retirement, vacation, sick pay, and other benefits earned by the employees have to be updated every pay period. Many employees do not get a payroll check. Instead, their money is sent electronically to the employee's bank account. The total amounts of withheld income tax and Social Security taxes, plus the employment taxes imposed on the employer, have to be paid to federal and state government agencies on time.

In short, payroll is a complex and critical function that the accounting department performs, often with the assistance of the human resource department. *Note:* Many businesses outsource payroll functions to companies that specialize in this area.

>> **Cash receipts:** All cash received from sales and from all other sources — whether via good old-fashioned cash or checks, credit cards, debit cards, electronic payments such as wire transfers or ACH, or other more modern payment vehicles such as PayPal — has to be carefully identified and recorded, not only in the cash account but also in the appropriate account for the source of the cash received. The accounting department makes sure that the cash is deposited in the appropriate checking accounts of the business and that an adequate amount of coin and currency is kept on hand for making change for customers. Accountants balance the checkbook of the business and control which persons have access to incoming cash receipts. (In larger organizations, the *treasurer* may be responsible for some of these cash-flow and cash-handling functions.)

>> **Cash disbursements:** A business writes many other checks or processes numerous electronic payments (such as Automated Clearing House or ACH payments, wire transfers, and so on) during the course of a year — to pay for

a variety of purchases, to pay property taxes, to pay on loans, and to distribute some of its profit to the owners of the business, for example. The accounting department prepares all these checks for the signatures of the business officers who are authorized to sign checks. The accounting department keeps all the supporting business documents and files to know when the checks should be paid, makes sure that the amount to be paid is correct, and forwards the checks for signature. More and more businesses are switching to electronic methods of payments, which avoids the need for actually writing checks and mailing the checks. Electronic payments must be carefully protected to guard against hackers who would like to divert payments to themselves.

>> **Procurement and inventory:** Accounting departments usually are responsible for keeping track of all purchase orders that have been placed for *inventory* (products to be sold by the business) and all other assets and services that the business buys, from light bulbs to forklifts. A typical business makes many purchases during the course of a year, many of them on credit, which means that the items bought are received today but paid for later. So this area of responsibility includes keeping files on all liabilities that arise from purchases on credit so that cash payments can be processed on time. The accounting department also keeps detailed records on all products held for sale by the business and, when the products are sold, records the cost of the goods sold.

>> **Costing:** Costs are not as obvious as you might think. Tell someone that the cost of a new car is so many dollars, and most people accept the amount without question. Business owners and managers know better. Many decisions have to be made regarding which factors to include in the manufacturing cost of a product or in the purchase costs of products sold by retailers such as Costco and Walmart. Tracking costs is a major function of accounting in all businesses.

>> **Property accounting:** A typical business owns many different substantial long-term assets that go under the generic name *property, plant, and equipment* — including office furniture and equipment, retail display cabinets, computers, machinery and tools, vehicles (autos and trucks), buildings, and land. Except for relatively small-cost items, such as screwdrivers and pencil sharpeners, a business maintains detailed records of its property, both for controlling the use of the assets and for determining personal property and real estate taxes. The accounting department keeps these property records.

>> **Tax compliance:** The task of managing multiple tax accounting, reporting, and compliance functions usually falls on the shoulders of the accounting department. This extends well beyond simply completing annual income tax

returns because most businesses must deal with a slew of other tax reporting and compliance matters, including sales/use, property, excise, payroll, and multiple other forms of taxation, at multiple levels including federal, state, county, local, and municipal.

>> **Liabilities accounting:** An entity must keep track of all relevant details about every liability it owes — from short-term purchases on credit to long-term notes payable. No entity can lose track of a liability and not pay it on time (or negotiate an extension) without hurting its credit rating.

REMEMBER

In most businesses and other entities, the accounting department is assigned other functions as well, but this list gives you a pretty clear idea of the back-office functions that the accounting department performs. Quite literally, a business could not operate if the accounting department did not do these functions efficiently and on time. And to repeat one point, to do these back-office functions well, the accounting department must design a good bookkeeping system and make sure that it's complete, accurate, reliable, and timely.

Focusing on Transactions

REMEMBER

The recordkeeping function of accounting focuses on *transactions*, which are economic exchanges between a business or other entity and the parties with which the entity interacts and makes deals. A good accounting system captures and records every transaction that takes place without missing a beat. Transactions are the lifeblood of every business, the heartbeat of activity that keeps it going. Understanding accounting, to a large extent, means understanding how accountants record the financial effects of transactions.

The financial effects of many transactions are clear-cut and immediate. On the other hand, figuring out the financial effects of some transactions is puzzling and dependent on future developments. The financial effects of some transactions can be difficult to determine at the time of the original transaction because the outcome depends on future events that are difficult to predict. We bring up this point because most people seem to think that accounting for transactions is a cut-and-dried process. Frankly, recording some transactions is more in the nature of "let's make our best assessment, cross our fingers, and wait and see what happens." The point is that recording the financial effects of some transactions is tentative and conditional on future events.

Separating basic types of transactions

A business is a whirlpool of transactions. Accountants categorize transactions into three broad types:

>> **Profit-making transactions** consist of *revenue* and *expenses* as well as gains and losses outside the normal sales and expense activities of the business. We explain earlier in this chapter that one way to look at profit is as an increase in retained earnings (surplus). Another way of defining *profit* is as the amount of total revenue for the period minus all expenses for the period. Both viewpoints are correct.

   Included in this group of transactions are transactions that take place before or after the recording of revenue and expenses. For example, a business buys products that will be held for future sale. The purchase of the products is not yet an expense. The expense is not recorded until the products are sold. The purchase of products for future sale must, of course, be recorded when the purchase takes place.

>> **Investing transactions** refers to the acquisition (and eventual disposal) of *long-term operating assets* such as buildings, heavy machinery, trucks, office furniture, and so on. Some businesses also invest in *financial assets* (bonds, for example). These are not used directly in the operations of the business; the business could get along without these assets. These assets generate investment income for the business. Investments in financial assets are included in this category of transactions.

>> **Financing transactions** refers to raising capital and paying for the use of the capital. Every business needs assets to carry on its operations, such as a working balance of cash, inventory of products held for sale, long-term operating assets (as described in the preceding bullet point), and so on. Broadly speaking, the capital to buy these assets comes from two sources: debt and equity. *Debt* is borrowed money, on which interest is paid. *Equity* is ownership capital. The payment for using equity capital depends on the ability of the business to earn profit and have the cash flow to distribute some or all of the profit to its equity shareholders.

REMEMBER

Profit-making transactions, also called *operating activities*, are high frequency. During the course of a year, even a small business has thousands of revenue and expense transactions. (How many cups of coffee, for example, does your local coffee store sell each year? Each sale is a transaction.) In contrast, investing and financing transactions are generally low frequency. A business does not have a high volume of these types of transactions, except in very unusual circumstances.

Knowing who's on the other side of transactions

Another way to look at transactions is to look at the *counterparties* of the transactions; this term refers to the persons or entities that the business enters into an economic exchange with. A business interacts with a variety of counterparties. A business is the hub of transactions involving the following persons and entities:

» Its **customers,** who buy the products and services that the business sells; also, a business may have other sources of income, such as investments in financial assets (bonds, for example)

» Its **employees,** who provide services to the business and are paid wages and salaries and are provided with benefits, such as retirement plans, medical insurance, workers' compensation, and unemployment insurance

» **Independent contractors,** who are hired on a contract basis to perform certain services for the business; these services can be anything from hauling away trash and repairing plumbing problems to advising the business on technical issues and auditing by a CPA firm

» Its **vendors and suppliers,** who sell a wide range of things to the business, such as products for resale, electricity and gas, insurance coverage, telephone and internet services, and so on

» **Government entities,** which are the federal, state, and local agencies that collect income taxes, sales taxes, payroll taxes, and property taxes from or through the business

» **Sellers of the various long-term operating assets** used by the business, including building contractors, machinery and equipment manufacturers, and auto and truck dealers

» Its **debt sources of capital,** who loan money to the business, charge interest on the amount loaned, and are due to be repaid at definite dates in the future

» Its **equity sources of capital,** the individuals and financial institutions that invest money in the business as owners and who expect the business to earn profit on the capital they invest

Recording events

Certain other events that have a financial impact on the business have to be recorded as well. They're called *events* because they're not based on give-and-take bargaining — unlike the something-given-for-something-received nature of economic exchanges. Events such as the following have an economic impact on a business and are recorded:

>> A business may lose a lawsuit and be ordered to pay damages. The liability to pay the damages is recorded.

>> A business may suffer a flood loss that is uninsured. The waterlogged assets may have to be written down, meaning that the recorded values of the assets are reduced to zero if they no longer have any value to the business. For example, products that were being held for sale to customers (until they floated down the river) must be removed from the inventory asset account.

>> A business may decide to abandon a major product line and downsize its workforce, requiring that severance compensation be paid to the laid-off employees.

As we explain in more detail in Chapter 3, at the end of the year, the accountant conducts a special survey to ensure that all events and developments during the year that should be recorded have been recorded so that the financial statements and tax returns for the year are complete and correct.

Taking the Financial Pulse of a Business

We devote a good deal of space in this book to explaining *financial statements*. In Chapter 2, we explain the fundamental information components of financial statements, and then Part 2 gets into the nitty-gritty details. Here, we simply want to introduce you to the primary kinds of financial statements so you know from the get-go what they are and why they're so crucial.

REMEMBER

Financial statements are prepared at the end of each accounting period. A period may be one month, one quarter (three calendar months), or one year. Financial statements report *summary amounts*, or *totals*. Accountants seldom prepare a complete listing of the details of all the activities that took place during a period or the individual items making up a total amount. Business managers may need to search through a detailed list of all the specific transactions that make up a total amount, and when they want to drill down into the details, they ask the accountant for the more detailed information. But this sort of detailed listing is *not* a financial statement — although it may be very useful to managers.

The outside, nonmanager investors in a business receive summary-level financial statements. For example, investors see the total amount of sales revenue for the period but not how much was sold to each and every customer. Financial statements are based on the assumption that you, the reader, are not a manager of the business (see the earlier section "Recognizing users of accounting information").

The managers of the business should make good use of their financial statements, but they also need more detailed information beyond what's in the business's financial statements.

Meeting the balance sheet (statement of financial condition)

One type of financial statement is a "Where do we stand at the end of the period?" type of report. This is called the *statement of financial condition* or, more commonly, the *balance sheet*. The date of preparation is given in the header, or title, at the top of this financial statement. We present and explain a typical balance sheet in Chapter 2. Our purpose here is simply to present the basic content in a balance sheet.

A balance sheet summarizes the two opposite aspects of a business, which you could think of as the financial yin and yang of the business:

>> **Assets:** One side of the balance sheet lists the *assets* of the business, which are the economic resources owned and being used in the business. The asset *values* reported in the balance sheet are the amounts recorded when the assets were originally acquired — although we should mention that an asset is written down below its historical cost when the asset has suffered a loss in value. (And to complicate matters, some assets are written up to their current fair values.) Some assets have been on the books only a few weeks or a few months, so their reported historical values are current. The values for other assets, on the other hand, are their costs when they were acquired many years ago.

>> **Sources of assets:** On the other side of the balance sheet is a breakdown of where the assets came from, or their *sources*. Assets do not materialize out of thin air. Assets arise from three basically different sources:

- **Creditors:** Businesses borrow money in the form of interest-bearing loans that must be paid back at a later date, and they buy things on credit that are paid for later. So part of total assets can be traced to creditors, which are the *liabilities* of a business.

- **Owners:** Every business needs to have owners invest capital (usually money) in the business.

- **Profit:** Businesses retain part or all of their annual profits, increasing the *surplus* of the business. We use this term earlier in "Thinking about where assets come from." In most balance sheets, surplus is called *retained earnings* or an equivalent title. From here on, we stick with the title *retained earnings*.

  One final definition: The total of owners' capital invested in the business and its retained earnings is labeled *owners' equity*.

Given the basic sources of assets, the financial condition of a business is condensed as follows:

$$\$Assets = \$Liabilities + \$Capital + \$RetainedEarnings$$

The dollar signs are to remind you that for each item, there's a dollar amount that goes with it. This depiction of financial condition is referred to as the *accounting equation*. It stresses the point that the total amount of all assets equals the total amount of liabilities and owners' equity. One side cannot be heavier than the other side. An imbalance signals accounting errors in recording the transactions of the business.

Looking at the accounting equation, you can see why the statement of financial condition is called the *balance sheet*; the equal sign means the two sides balance or are equal in total amounts.

Suppose a business reports $2.5 million total assets (without going into the details of which particular assets the business holds). Knowing that total assets are on the books at $2.5 million, we also know that the total of its liabilities, plus the capital invested by its owners, plus its retained profit adds up to $2.5 million.

Continuing with this example, suppose that the total amount of the liabilities of the business is $1.0 million. This means that the total amount of *owners' equity* in the business is $1.5 million, which equals total assets less total liabilities. This amount is also called the *net worth* of the business; to be more accurate, it should be called the *recorded net worth* of the business (which does not necessarily equal the present market value of the business). Without more information, we don't know how much of total owners' equity is traceable to capital invested by the owners in the business and how much is the result of profit retained in the business. But we do know that the total of these two sources of owners' equity is $1.5 million.

Double-entry bookkeeping is a centuries-old, very clever method for keeping the accounting equation in balance. We discuss double-entry bookkeeping in Chapter 3. Basically, double-entry bookkeeping simply means that both sides of transactions are recorded. For example, if one asset goes up, another asset goes down — or, alternatively, either a liability or owners' equity element goes up. In accounting, *double-entry* means *two-sided*, not that transactions are recorded twice.

Reporting profit and loss

REMEMBER

Everyone (including managers, lenders, and owners) is interested in whether the business enjoyed a profit or suffered a loss for the year. Suppose you have in your hands the balance sheet of a business showing the end of last year and the end of the year just ended. You can calculate profit or loss for the most recent year by computing the increase in retained earnings and adding the amount of distributions from profit during the year. Suppose the business's retained earnings increased $5.0 million during the year and it paid out $2.0 million cash from profit to its owners. Therefore, its profit for the year is $7.0 million.

Oh, you want to know its revenue and expenses for the year — not just the profit for the year. In fact, the standard practice in financial reporting is to present a financial statement that discloses the total revenue and total expenses for the period and ends with the profit (or loss) on the bottom line of the statement. The *income statement* summarizes sales revenue and other income, which are offset by the expenses and losses during the period. Deducting expenses from revenue and income leads down to the well-known *bottom line*, which is the final net profit or loss for the period and is called *net income* or *net loss* (or some variation of these terms). Alternative titles for this financial statement are the *statement of operations* and the *statement of earnings*. Inside a business, but not in its external financial reports, the income statement is commonly called the *P&L* (profit and loss) report.

TIP

Of course, the bottom line of the income statement should be the same amount that could be computed by adding the change in retained earnings and distributions to owners during the year from the profit.

Reporting cash flows and changes in owners' equity

Cash is king, as business managers and investors will tell you. More than a quarter of a century ago, the rule-making authority in financial accounting said a business should report a *statement of cash flows* to supplement the income statement and balance sheet. This financial statement summarizes the business's cash inflows and outflows during the period.

A highlight of this statement is the cash increase or decrease from profit (or loss) for the period. This key amount in the cash flow statement is called *cash flow from operating activities.* We explain the statement of cash flows in Chapters 2 and 8. Be warned early on that many argue that this cash flow figure is more important than bottom-line profit for the period. Well, we'll see about that!

REMEMBER

It becomes clear throughout this book that we harp on and emphasize the importance of the statement of cash flows because it offers critical financial information about how a business generates and consumes cash. What we have found over our vast experience is that while most parties (internal and external — both are equally guilty) jump right to the income statement to identify the growth in top-line sales revenue or how much bottom-line profit was generated, or focus on the balance sheet to evaluate the company's financial strength, the statement of cash flows tends to get passed over relatively quickly. *Why?* you may ask. It usually comes down to either the party being lazy, having a lack of understanding (as to the purpose of this statement), or believing that the statement of cash flows is overly complex and is not particularly important. All are poor excuses because, in order to truly understand accounting and a company's financial statements, the statement of cash flows should never be overlooked!

Also, it's common for many businesses to include a summary of changes in their owners' equity accounts during the year. Typically it's called a *statement of changes in stockholders' equity.* We could argue that it's not a full-fledged financial statement, but there's little point in arguing semantics here — although the other three financial statements (balance sheet, income statement, and cash flows statement) are "full-size" statements. Larger, public corporations are required to present this statement, whereas smaller, private businesses have more leeway in deciding whether to include such a summary. We explain the statement of changes in stockholders' equity in Chapter 2.

Remembering management's role

We explain more about the three primary financial statements (balance sheet, income statement, and statement of cash flows) in Chapter 2. They constitute the hard core of a financial report to those persons outside a business who need to stay informed about the business's financial affairs. These individuals have invested capital in the business, or the business owes them money; therefore, they have a financial interest in how well the business is doing.

To keep informed about what's going on and the financial position of the business, the managers of a business also use these three key financial statements. These statements are essential in helping managers control the performance of a business, identify problems as they come up, and plan the future course of a business. Managers also need other information that isn't reported in the three basic financial statements. (In Chapter 13, we explain these additional reports.)

The three primary financial statements constitute a business's financial center of gravity. The president and chief executive officer of a business (plus other top-level officers) are responsible for seeing that the financial statements are prepared according to applicable financial reporting standards and according to established accounting principles and methods.

WARNING

If a business's financial statements are later discovered to be seriously in error or deliberately misleading, the business and its top executives can be sued for damages suffered by lenders and investors who relied on the financial statements. For this reason, business managers must understand their responsibility for the financial statements and the accounting methods used to prepare the statements. In a court of law, managers can't plead ignorance.

We've met more than one business manager who doesn't have a clue about his or her financial statements. This situation is a little scary; a manager who doesn't understand financial statements is like an airplane pilot who doesn't understand the instrument readouts in the cockpit. Such a manager *could* run the business and "land the plane safely," but knowing how to read the instrument panels along the way is much more prudent.

Business managers at all levels need to understand financial statements and the accounting methods used to prepare them. Also, lenders to a business, investors in a business, business lawyers, government regulators of business, entrepreneurs, anyone thinking of becoming an entrepreneur and starting a business, and, yes, even economists should know the basics of financial statement accounting. We've noticed that even experienced business journalists, who ought to know better, sometimes refer to the balance sheet when they're talking about profit performance. The bottom line is found in the income statement, not the balance sheet!

Accounting as a Form of Art

Throughout this book, you read references to accounting being more of a form of art than an exact science. We are not implying that accountants and the profession of accounting don't have to follow specific rules, standards, and guidelines; as you see in Chapter 2, a very robust set of rules and authoritative organizations have been established to provide guidance to accountants in plying their trade.

However, it should be noted that accounting is by no means an exact science because accountants are constantly having to use estimates, complete complex financial analyses, and evaluate data (that always seems to be a moving target) when preparing financial information, reports, and statements. Further, economic conditions are constantly changing and evolving at what seems like the speed of light these days (such as with Covid-19's impact in 2020 and beyond), making the accountant's job even more challenging. You would be amazed at how even the slightest change in an assumption or data point used, such as increasing the interest rate used to calculate the estimated current value of future obligations, can impact the overall financial results of a business.

To reiterate one of our primary goals, the purpose of the concepts and topics presented in this book is not to provide a detailed overview of technical accounting rules or guidelines, such as the theory behind accounting for capital asset leases or applying Black–Scholes to account for stock option expense, but rather to offer a 10,000-foot overview of accounting and key concepts every business must address, starting with the following fundamental statement.

REMEMBER

To produce accurate financial information, every business must develop, implement, maintain, and manage a properly functioning accounting system that at its foundation relies on establishing, implementing, and adhering to agreed-upon accounting policies, procedures, and controls applied on a consistent basis and in accordance with generally accepted accounting principles (GAAP).

These generally accepted accounting principles are "a set of rules that encompass the details, complexities, and legalities of business and corporate accounting." These rules are established by various accounting organizations, boards, and groups, with the primary group being the Financial Accounting Standards Board (FASB), which uses GAAP as the foundation for its comprehensive set of approved accounting methods and practices.

There you have it — when producing financial information, businesses should adhere to GAAP as established by FASB. Seems simple enough, but as you work through the remainder of this book, it should become abundantly clear that GAAP is more or less a series of guidelines that businesses can use to provide a certain amount of leeway when actual financial information is produced. Or maybe the best way to think of it is referring to this quote from Captain Barbossa from the *Pirates of the Caribbean* franchise: "And thirdly, the code (translation to accounting — GAAP) is more what you'd call *guidelines* than actual *rules.*" Yes, very good guidelines but guidelines nonetheless that provide accountants with a reasonable amount of leeway when preparing financial information.

Chapter **2**

Introducing Financial Statements

C hapter 1 presents a brief introduction to the three primary business financial statements: the income statement, the balance sheet, and the statement of cash flows. In this chapter, you get more tidbits about these three *financials*, as they're sometimes called. Then, in Part 2, you really get the goods. Remember when you were learning to ride a bicycle? Chapter 1 is like getting on the bike and learning to keep your balance. In this chapter, you put on your training wheels and start riding. Then, when you're ready, the chapters in Part 2 explain all 21 gears of the financial statements bicycle, and then some.

For each financial statement, we introduce its basic information components. The purpose of financial statements is to communicate information that is useful to the readers of the financial statements, to those who are entitled to the information. Financial statement readers include the managers of the business and its lenders and investors. These constitute the primary audience for financial statements. (Beyond this primary audience, others are also interested in a business's financial statements, such as its labor union or someone considering buying the business.) Think of yourself as a shareholder in a business. What sort of information would you want to know about the business? The answer to this question should be the touchstone for the accountant in preparing the financial statements.

The financial statements explained in this chapter are for businesses. Business financial statements serve as a useful template for not-for-profit (NFP) entities and other organizations (social clubs, homeowners' associations, retirement communities, and so on). In short, business financial statements are a good reference point for the financial statements of non-business entities. There are differences but not as many as you may think. As we go along in this and the following chapters, we point out the differences between business and non-business financial statements.

Toward the end of this chapter, we briefly discuss accounting standards and financial reporting standards. Notice here that we distinguish accounting from financial reporting:

>> *Accounting standards* deal primarily with how to record transactions for measuring profit and for putting values on assets, liabilities, and owners' equity.

>> *Financial reporting standards* focus on additional aspects such as the structure and presentation of financial statements, disclosure in the financial statements and elsewhere in the report, and other matters.

We use the term *financial accounting* to include both types of standards.

REMEMBER

The philosophy behind the need for standards is that all businesses should follow uniform methods for measuring and reporting profit performance and reporting financial condition. Consistency in financial accounting across all businesses is the name of the game. We won't bore you with a lengthy historical discourse on the development of accounting and financial reporting standards in the United States. The general consensus (backed by law) is that businesses should use consistent accounting methods and terminology. General Motors and Microsoft should use the same accounting methods; so should Wells Fargo and Apple. Of course, businesses in different industries have different types of transactions, but the same types of transactions should be accounted for in the same way. That is the goal.

Setting the Stage for Financial Statements

This chapter focuses on the basic *information components* of each financial statement reported by a business. The first step is to get a good idea of the information content reported in financial statements. The second step is to become familiar with more details about the "architecture," rules of classification, and other features of financial statements (see Part 2).

Offering a few preliminary comments about financial statements

Realistic examples are needed to illustrate and explain financial statements. But this presents a slight problem. The information content of a business's financial statements depends on whether it sells products, services, or both (for instance, Apple sells both products and services); invests in other businesses; and so on. For example, the financial statements of a movie theater chain are different from those of a bank, which are different from those of an airline, which are different from an automobile manufacturer's, which are different from — well, you name it.

The classic example used to illustrate financial statements involves a business that sells both products and services, and sells on credit to its customers. Therefore, the assets in the example include *receivables* from the business's sales on credit and *inventory* of products it has purchased or manufactured that are awaiting future sale. Keep in mind, however, that many businesses that sell products do not sell on credit to their customers. Many retail businesses sell only for cash (or accept credit or debit cards that are near cash). Such businesses do not have a receivables asset.

REMEMBER

The financial statements of a business do not present a "history" of the business. Financial statements are, to a large extent, limited to the recent profit performance and financial condition of the business. A business may add some historical discussion and charts that aren't strictly required by financial reporting standards. (Public corporations that have their ownership shares and debt traded in open markets are subject to various disclosure requirements under federal law, including certain historical information.)

The illustrative financial statements that follow in this part and Part 2 do not include a historical narrative of the business. Nevertheless, whenever you see financial statements, we encourage you to think about the history of the business. To help you out in this regard, here are some particulars about the business example we use in this chapter:

>> It sells products and services to other businesses (not on the retail level).

>> It sells on credit, and its customers take approximately a month or so before they pay.

>> It holds a fairly large stock of products awaiting sale.

>> It owns a wide variety of long-term operating assets that have useful lives from 3 to 30 years or longer (building, machines, tools, computers, office furniture, goodwill, intellectual property, and so on).

>> It has been in business for many years and has made a profit most years.

>> It borrows money for part of the total assets it needs.

>> It's organized as a corporation and pays federal and state income taxes on its annual taxable income.

>> It has never been in bankruptcy and is not facing any immediate financial difficulties.

The following sections present the company's annual income statement for the year just ended, its balance sheet at the end of the year, and its statement of cash flows for the year.

Looking at other aspects of reporting financial statements

TIP

Dollar amounts in financial statements are typically rounded off, either by not presenting the last three digits (when rounded to the nearest thousand) or by not presenting the last six digits (when rounded to the nearest million). We strike a compromise on this issue: We show the last three digits for each item as 000, which means that we rounded off the amount but still show all digits. Many smaller businesses report their financial statement dollar amounts to the last dollar or even the last penny, for that matter. Keep in mind that having too many digits in a dollar amount makes it hard to comprehend.

The financial statements in this chapter are more in the nature of an outline. Actual financial statements use only one- or two-word account titles on the assumption that you know what all these labels mean. What you see in this chapter, on the other hand, are the basic information components of each financial statement. We explain the full-blown, classified, detailed financial statements in Part 2. (We know you're eager to get to those chapters.) In this chapter, we offer descriptions for each financial statement element rather than the terse and technical account titles you find in actual financial statements. Also, we strip out subtotals that you see in actual financial statements because they aren't necessary at this point.

REMEMBER

Oops! We forgot to mention a few things about financial reports. Financial reports are rather stiff and formal. No slang or street language is allowed, and we've never seen a swear word in one. Financial statements would get a G in the movies rating system. Seldom do you see any graphics or artwork in a financial statement itself, although you do see a fair amount of photos and graphics on other pages in the financial reports of public companies. And there's virtually no humor in financial reports. However, we might mention that Warren Buffett, in his annual letter to the stockholders of Berkshire Hathaway, includes some wonderful humor to make his points.

The Income Statement

First on the minds of financial report readers is the profit performance of the business. The *income statement* is the all-important financial statement that summarizes the profit-making activities of a business over a period of time. Figure 2-1 shows the basic information content of an external income statement for our company example. *External* means that the financial statement is released outside the business to those entitled to receive it — primarily its shareowners and lenders. Internal financial statements stay within the business and are used mainly by its management; they aren't circulated outside the business because they contain competitive and confidential information.

Presenting the components of the income statement

Figure 2-1 presents the major ingredients, or information packets, in the income statement for a technology company that sells products and services. As you may expect, the income statement starts with *sales revenue* on the top line. There's no argument about this, although in the past, certain companies didn't want to disclose their annual sales revenue (to hide the large percent of profit they were earning on sales revenue).

Sales revenue is the total amount that has been or will be received from the company's customers for the sales of products and services to them. Simple enough, right? Well, not really. The accounting profession is currently reexamining the technical accounting standards for recording sales revenue, and this has proven to be a challenging task. Our business example, like most businesses, has adopted a certain set of procedures for the timeline of recording its sales revenue.

Recording expenses involves much more troublesome accounting problems than revenue problems for most businesses. Also, there's the fundamental question regarding which information to disclose about expenses and which information to bury in larger expense categories in the external income statement. We say much more about expenses in later chapters. At this point, direct your attention to the five kinds of expenses in Figure 2-1. Expenses are deducted from sales revenue to determine the final profit for the period, which is referred to as the *bottom line.* Actually, the preferred label is *net income,* as you see in the figure.

TIP

The five expense categories you see in Figure 2-1 should almost always be disclosed in external income statements. These constitute the minimum for adequate disclosure of expenses. The *cost of goods sold* or *cost of sales* (for service companies) is just what it says: the cost of the products sold or services delivered to customers. The cost of the products or services delivered should be matched against the revenue from the sales, of course.

QW Example Tech., Inc.
Income Statement
for the Fiscal Year Ending
12/31/2020

Description		Amount
Total amount of revenue from sales of products and services during the year, including discounts and returns	R	$71,064,000
Total costs of goods sold that are included in sales revenue, including the costs of manufacturing the products, purchasing the products, direct labor costs, and other directly variable costs of sales	CoGS	($26,891,000)
Gross profit (sometimes referred to as gross margin): Total sales revenue less total costs of goods sold	GP	$44,173,000
Selling, general, and administrative expenses, which is the total amount of operating expenses of the business for the year (excluding other expenses listed separately in the income statement)	OpE	($36,678,000)
Net income before interest, taxes, and other expenses	NetI	$7,495,000
Total interest expense charged to a business for the year on the amount of its interest-bearing debt	Int	($350,000)
Total other expenses (or income) incurred or earned by the business during the year that is not in the normal course of operations	OtE	($250,000)
Total amount of federal, state, and local income taxes paid or payable to the authorities for the taxable year	Tax	($2,413,000)
Net income (or loss) earned during the year: Sometimes referred to as net earnings or net profit	Net	$4,482,000

FIGURE 2-1: Income statement information components for a technology company that sells products and services.

Only one conglomerate operating expense has to be disclosed. In Figure 2-1, it's called *selling, general, and administrative expenses,* which is a popular title in income statements. This is an all-inclusive expense total that mixes together many kinds of expenses, including administrative employee wages and benefit costs, advertising expenses, depreciation of assets, and so on. But it doesn't include interest expenses, income tax expenses, or other expenses; these three expenses are generally reported separately in an income statement.

The cost of goods sold or cost of sales expense and the selling, general, and administrative expenses take the biggest bites out of sales revenue. The other three expenses (interest, income tax, and other expenses) are relatively small as a percent of annual sales revenue but are important enough in their own right to be reported separately. And though you may not need this reminder, *bottom-line profit* (net income) is the amount of sales revenue in excess of the business's total expenses. If either sales revenue or any of the expense amounts are wrong, then profit is wrong.

REMEMBER

A service business does not sell products; therefore, it doesn't have the traditional cost of goods sold expense (as it is not selling any tangible goods). In place of cost of goods sold, a service business often simply refers to the direct costs as *costs of sales*, which generally capture labor expenses for wages, payroll taxes, benefits, and other expenses that directly vary with sales revenue. Most service businesses are labor intensive; they have relatively large labor costs as a percent of sales revenue. Service companies differ in how they report their operating expenses. For example, United Airlines breaks out the cost of aircraft fuel and landing fees. The largest expense of the insurance company State Farm is payments on claims. The movie chain AMC reports film exhibition costs separate from its other operating expenses. We offer these examples to remind you that accounting should always be adapted to the way the business operates and makes profit. In other words, accounting should follow the business model.

Income statement pointers

TIP

Most businesses break out one or more expenses instead of disclosing just one very broad category for all selling, general, and administrative expenses. For example, Apple, in its 2020 consolidated income statement, discloses research and development expenses separate from its selling, general, and administrative expenses. A business could disclose expenses for advertising and sales promotion, salaries and wages, research and development (as does Apple), and delivery and shipping — though reporting these expenses varies quite a bit from business to business. Businesses do not disclose the compensation of top management in their external financial reports, although this information can be found in the proxy statements of public companies that are filed with the Securities and Exchange Commission (SEC). In summary, the extent of details disclosed about operating expenses in externally reported financial reports varies quite a bit from business to business. Financial reporting standards are rather permissive on this point.

Inside most businesses, a profit statement is called a *P&L (profit and loss) report.* These internal profit performance reports to the managers of a business include more detailed information about expenses and about sales revenue — a good deal more! Reporting just five expenses to managers (as shown in Figure 2-1) would not do. Chapter 13 explains P&L reports to managers.

Sales revenue refers to sales of products or services to customers. In some income statements, you also see the term *income,* which generally refers to amounts earned by a business from sources other than sales. For example, a real estate rental business receives rental income from its tenants. (In the example in this chapter, the business has only sales revenue.)

The income statement gets the most attention from business managers, lenders, and investors (not that they ignore the other two financial statements). The much-abbreviated versions of income statements that you see in the financial press, such as in *The Wall Street Journal,* report the top line (sales revenue and income) and the bottom line (net income) and not much more. Refer to Chapter 6 for more information on income statements.

The Balance Sheet

A more accurate name for a balance sheet is *statement of financial condition* or *statement of financial position,* but the term *balance sheet* has caught on, and most people use this term. The most important thing is not the "balance" but rather the information reported in this financial statement.

In brief, a balance sheet summarizes on the one hand the assets of the business and on the other hand the sources of the assets. However, looking at assets is only half the picture. The other half consists of the liabilities and owner equity of the business. Cash is listed first, and other assets are listed in the order of their nearness to cash. Liabilities are listed in order of their due dates (the earliest first, and so on). Liabilities are listed ahead of owners' equity. We discuss the ordering of the components in a balance sheet in Chapter 7.

Presenting the components of the balance sheet

Figure 2-2 shows the building blocks of a typical balance sheet for a business that sells products and services on credit. As mentioned, one reason the balance sheet is called by this name is that its two sides balance, or are equal in total amounts. In this example, the $27.172 million total assets equals the $27.172 million total liabilities and owners' equity. The balance or equality of total assets on the one side of the scale and the sum of liabilities plus owners' equity on the other side of the scale is expressed in the *accounting equation,* which we discuss in Chapter 1. *Note:* The balance sheet in Figure 2-2 shows the essential elements in this financial statement. In a financial report, the balance sheet includes additional features and frills, which we explain in Chapter 7.

QW Example Tech., Inc.
Balance Sheet
for the Fiscal Year Ending
12/31/2020

Description	Amount
Assets:	
Cash and equivalents	$11,281,000
Trade accounts receivables: Sales made on credit and expected to be collected	$8,883,000
Inventory: Unsold product stated at purchase cost or manufacturing cost	$1,733,000
Prepaid expenses	$325,000
Long-term assets such as machinery, equipment, buildings, computers, etc., stated at cost less cumulative amount of depreciation expense recorded over the years	$4,350,000
Other long-term assets such as intellectual property, goodwill, investments, notes receivable, and other assets, stated at cost or net realizable value	$600,000
Total Assets	$27,172,000
Liabilities and Owners' Equity:	
Trade accounts payables and accrued liabilities: Non-interest-bearing liabilities from purchases made on credit and for unpaid outstanding expenses	$4,213,000
Notes and loans payable: Interest-bearing liabilities or debt owed by the business to third parties, both short-term and long-term	$7,000,000
Total Liabilities	$11,213,000
Owners or shareholders' equity: Capital invested in business plus retained profits less amounts paid for distributions or dividends	$15,959,000
Total Liabilities and Owners' Equity	$27,172,000

© John Wiley & Sons, Inc.

FIGURE 2-2: Balance sheet information components for a technology business that sells products and services on credit.

Take a quick walk through the balance sheet. For a technology company that sells products and services on credit, assets are reported in the following order: First is cash, then receivables, then cost of products held for sale, and finally the long-term operating assets of the business. Moving to the other side of the balance sheet, the liabilities section starts with the trade liabilities (from buying on credit) and liabilities for unpaid expenses. Following these operating liabilities is the interest-bearing debt of the business. Owners' equity sources are then reported below liabilities. So a balance sheet is a composite of assets on one hand and a composite of liabilities and owners' equity sources on the other hand.

CHAPTER 2 **Introducing Financial Statements** 37

REMEMBER

A balance sheet is a reflection of the fundamental two-sided nature of a business (expressed in the *accounting equation,* which we discuss in Chapter 1). In the most basic terms, assets are what the business owns, and liabilities plus owners' equity are the sources of the assets. The sources have claims against the assets. Liabilities and interest-bearing debt have to be paid, of course, and if the business were to go out of business and liquidate all its assets, the residual after paying all its liabilities would go to the owners.

A company that sells services doesn't have an inventory of products being held for sale. A service company may or may not sell on credit. Airlines don't sell on credit, for example. If a service business doesn't sell on credit, it won't have two of the sizable assets you see in Figure 2-2: receivables from credit sales and inventory of products held for sale. Generally, this means that a service-based business doesn't need as much total assets compared with a products-based business with the same size sales revenue.

The smaller amount of total assets of a service business means that the other side of its balance sheet is correspondingly smaller. In plain terms, this means that a service company doesn't need to borrow as much money or raise as much capital from its equity owners.

As you may suspect, the particular assets reported in the balance sheet depend on which assets the business owns. We include six basic types of assets in Figure 2-2. These are the hardcore assets that a business selling products or services on credit would have. It's possible that such a business could lease (or rent) virtually all its long-term operating assets instead of owning them, in which case the business would report no such assets. In this example, the business owns these so-called *fixed assets.* They're *fixed* because they are held for use in the operations of the business and are not for sale, and their usefulness lasts several years or longer.

Balance sheet pointers

So where does a business get the money to buy its assets? Most businesses borrow money on the basis of interest-bearing notes or other credit instruments for part of the total capital they need for their assets. Also, businesses buy many things on credit and, at the balance sheet date, owe money to their suppliers, which will be paid in the future.

These operating liabilities are never grouped with interest-bearing debt in the balance sheet. The accountant would be tied to the stake for doing such a thing. Liabilities are not intermingled with assets — this is a definite no-no in financial reporting. You can't subtract certain liabilities from certain assets and report only the net balance.

Could a business's total liabilities be greater than its total assets? Well, not likely — unless the business has been losing money hand over fist. In the vast majority of cases, a business has more total assets than total liabilities. Why? For two reasons:

>> Its owners have invested money in the business.

>> The business has earned profit over the years, and some (or all) of the profit has been retained in the business. Making profit increases assets; if not all the profit is distributed to owners, the company's assets rise by the amount of profit retained.

WARNING

In the company example (see Figure 2-2), owners' equity is about $16 million, or $15.959 million to be more exact. Sometimes this amount is referred to as *net worth* because it equals total assets minus total liabilities. However, net worth can be misleading because it implies that the business is worth the amount recorded in its owners' equity accounts. The market value of a business, when it needs to be known, depends on many factors. The amount of owners' equity reported in a balance sheet, which is called the business's *book value*, is not irrelevant in setting a market value on the business, but it usually isn't the dominant factor. The amount of owners' equity in a balance sheet is based on the history of capital invested in the business by its owners and the history of its profit performance and distributions from profit.

TIP

A balance sheet could be whipped up anytime you want — say, at the end of every day. In fact, some businesses (such as banks and other financial institutions) need daily balance sheets, but few businesses prepare balance sheets that often. Typically, preparing a balance sheet at the end of each month is adequate for general management purposes — although a manager may need to look at the business's balance sheet in the middle of the month. In external financial reports (those released outside the business to its lenders and investors), a balance sheet is required at the close of business on the last day of the income statement period. If its annual or quarterly income statement ends, say, September 30, then the business reports its balance sheet at the close of business on September 30.

The profit *for the most recent period* is found in the income statement; periodic profit is not reported in the balance sheet. The profit reported in the income statement is before any distributions from profit to owners. The cumulative amount of profit over the years that hasn't been distributed to the business's owners is reported in the owners' equity section of the company's balance sheet.

TIP

By the way, notice that the balance sheet in Figure 2-2 is presented in a top-and-bottom format instead of a left-and-right format. Either the vertical (portrait) or horizontal (landscape) mode of display is acceptable. You see both layouts in financial reports. Of course, the two sides of the balance sheet should be kept together, either on one page or on facing pages in the financial report. You can't put assets up front and hide the other side of the balance sheet in the rear of the financial report.

The Statement of Cash Flows

To survive and thrive, business managers confront three financial imperatives:

>> **Make an adequate profit (or at least break even, for a not-for-profit entity).** The income statement reports whether the business made a profit or suffered a loss for the period.

>> **Keep the financial condition in good shape.** The balance sheet reports the financial condition of the business at the end of the period.

>> **Control cash flows.** Management's control over cash flows is reported in the *statement of cash flows,* which presents a summary of the business's sources and uses of cash during the same period as the income statement.

This section introduces you to the statement of cash flows. (We coauthored *Cash Flow For Dummies,* published by Wiley, which you may want to take a peek at for more information.) Financial reporting standards require that the statement of cash flows be reported when a business reports an income statement.

Presenting the components of the statement of cash flows

Successful business managers tell you that they have to manage both profit and cash flow; you can't do one and ignore the other. Business managers have to deal with a two-headed dragon in this respect. Ignoring cash flow can pull the rug out from under a successful profit formula.

REMEMBER

Figure 2-3 shows the basic information components of the statement of cash flows for the business example we've been using in this chapter. The cash activity of the business during the period is grouped into five sections:

>> First, almost all statements of cash flow start where the income statement left off — that is, by presenting the net profit or loss for the period. You'll notice

that the net profit at the bottom of the income statement in Figure 2-1 agrees with the net profit at the top of the statement of cash flows in Figure 2-3 (which it should).

» Second, all non-cash expenses such as depreciation and amortization expenses are called out, which get added back to net profit. This should make sense given that the expenses are "non-cash."

» The third figure reconciles net income for the period with the cash flow from the business's profit-making activities, or *operating activities,* including increases and decreases in current assets (for example, trade accounts receivables and inventory) and current liabilities (for example, trade accounts payables and accrued liabilities).

» The fourth figure summarizes the company's *investing* transactions during the period, or more specifically, what long-term assets the company purchased or invested in.

» And finally the fifth figure reports the company's *financing* transactions, or more specifically, whether the company raised cash from securing a loan or selling stock or whether the company used cash to repay loans or issue a dividend.

The net increase or decrease in cash from the five types of cash activities during the period is added to or subtracted from the beginning cash balance to get the cash balance at the end of the year.

In the example, the business earned a $4.482 million profit (net income) during the year (see Figure 2-1), which included non-cash expenses of $1.739 million (primarily for depreciation expense) that need to be added back to properly reconcile cash changes during the period. The cash result of its operating activities was to increase its cash by $1.372 million, which you see in the first part of the statement of cash flows (see Figure 2-3). The actual cash inflows from revenues and outflows for expenses run on a different timetable from when the sales revenue and expenses are recorded for determining profit. We give a more comprehensive explanation of the differences between cash flows and sales revenue and expenses in Chapter 8.

The next part of the statement of cash flows sums up the long-term investments the business made during the year, such as constructing a new production plant or replacing machinery and equipment. If the business sold any of its long-term assets, it reports the cash inflows from these divestments in this section of the statement of cash flows. The cash flows of other investment activities (if any) are reported in this part of the statement as well. As you can see in Figure 2-3, the business invested $750,000 in new long-term operating assets (trucks, equipment, tools, and computers).

QW Example Tech., Inc. Statement of Cash Flows for the Fiscal Year Ending 12/31/2020	
Description	Amount
Net income (loss): Statement of cash flows starts with the net income or loss generated by the company for the like reporting period	$4,482,000
Non-cash expenses: Addback all non-cash expenses incurred by the business for items such as depreciation expense, amortization expense, and others	$1,739,000
Change in cash from operating activities: Increase or decrease in current assets and current liabilities impacting cash from normal operating activities during the period	$1,372,000
Change in cash from investing activities: Increase or decrease in cash resulting from making investments in or disposals of long-term capital/operating assets (equipment, patents, etc.)	($750,000)
Change in cash from financing activities: Increase or decrease in cash resulting from transactions with lenders and owners including new loans, repayment of loans, new equity, distributions or dividends paid to owners, and others	$3,650,000
Change in cash during the period	$10,493,000
Cash at beginning of period	$788,000
Cash at end of period	$11,281,000

FIGURE 2-3: Information components of the statement of cash flows.

© John Wiley & Sons, Inc.

The final part of the statement sums up the dealings between the business and its sources of capital during the period — borrowing money from lenders and raising capital from its owners. Cash outflows to pay debt are reported in this section, as are cash distributions from profit paid to the owners of the business. The final part of the example statement shows that the result of these transactions was to increase cash by $3.650 million. (By the way, in this example, the business did make a dividend payment to the shareholders from profit. It probably could have been larger, but it wasn't — which is an important point that we discuss in the later section "Why no (or limited) cash distribution from profit?")

As you see in Figure 2-3, the net result of the five types of cash activities was a $10.493 million increase during the year. The increase is added to the cash balance at the start of the year to get the cash balance at the end of the year, which is $11.281 million. We should make one point clear: The $10.493 cash increase during the year (in this example) is never referred to as a cash flow *bottom line* or any such thing.

The term *bottom line* is reserved for the final line of the income statement, which reports net income — the final amount of profit after all expenses are deducted.

Statement of cash flows pointers

When I (coauthor John) started in public accounting, the cash flow statement wasn't required in financial reports. In 1987, the American rulemaking body for financial accounting standards (the Financial Accounting Standards Board) made it a required statement. Relatively speaking, this financial statement hasn't been around that long — only about 35 years at the time of this writing. How has it gone? Well, in our humble opinion, this financial statement is a disaster for financial report readers.

Statements of cash flows of most businesses are frustratingly difficult to read and far too technical. The average financial report reader understands the income statement and balance sheet. Certain items may be hard to fathom, but overall, the reader can make sense of the information in the two financial statements. In contrast, trying to follow the information in a statement of cash flows — especially the first section of the statement — can be a challenge even for a CPA. (More about this issue is in Chapter 8.)

Imagine you have a highlighter in your hand and the three basic financial statements of a business in front of you. What are the most important numbers to mark? *Bottom-line profit* (net income) in the income statement is one number you'd mark for sure. Another key number is *cash flow from operating activities* in the statement of cash flows. You don't have to understand the technical steps of how the accountant gets this cash flow number, but pay attention to how it compares with the profit number for the period. (We explain this point in more detail in Chapter 11.)

Cash flow is almost always different from net income. The sales revenue reported in the income statement does not equal cash collections from customers during the year, and expenses do not equal cash payments during the year. Cash collections from sales minus cash payments for expenses gives cash flow from a company's profit-making activities; sales revenue minus expenses gives the net income earned for the year. Sorry, mate, but that's how the cookie crumbles.

A Note about the Statement of Changes in Shareowners' Equity

Many business financial reports include a *fourth* financial statement — or at least it's called a "statement." It's really a summary of the changes in the constituent elements of owners' equity (stockholders' equity of a corporation). The corporation is one basic type of legal structure that businesses use. In Chapter 5, we explain the alternative legal structures available for conducting business operations. We don't show a statement of changes in owners' equity here. We show an example in Chapter 9, in which we explain the preparation of a financial report for release.

When a business has a complex owner's equity structure, a separate summary of changes in the components of owners' equity during the period is useful for the owners, the board of directors, and the top-level managers. On the other hand, in some cases, the only changes in owners' equity during the period were earning profit and distributing part of the cash flow from profit to owners. In this situation, there isn't much need for a summary of changes in owners' equity. The financial statement reader can easily find profit in the income statement and cash distributions from profit (if any) in the statement of cash flows. For details, see the later section "Why no (or limited) cash distribution from profit?"

Gleaning Important Information from Financial Statements

The whole point of reporting financial statements is to provide important information to people who have a financial interest in the business — mainly its investors and lenders. From that information, investors and lenders are able to answer key questions about the financial performance and condition of the business. We discuss a few of these key questions in this section. In Chapters 11, 12, and 20, we discuss a longer list of questions and explain financial statement analysis, including using ratios to evaluate financial results.

How's profit performance?

Investors use two important measures to judge a company's annual profit performance. Here, we use the data from Figures 2-1 and 2-2 for the company. Of course, you can do the same ratio calculations for a product or service business. For convenience, the dollar amounts here are expressed in thousands:

>> **Return on sales = profit as a percent of annual sales revenue:**

$4.482 million bottom-line annual profit (net income) ÷ $71.064 million annual sales revenue = 6.3%

>> **Return on equity = profit as a percent of owners' equity:**

$4.482 million bottom-line annual profit (net income) ÷ $15.959 million owners' equity = 28.1%

Profit looks pretty thin compared with annual sales revenue. The company earns only 6.3 percent return on sales. In other words, 93.7 cents out of every sales dollar goes for expenses, and the company keeps only 6.3 cents for profit. (Many businesses earn 10 percent or higher return on sales.) However, when profit is compared with owners' equity, things look much better. The business earns more than 28 percent profit on its owners' equity. We'd bet you don't have many investments earning 28 percent per year.

Is there enough cash?

Cash is the lubricant of business activity. Realistically, a business can't operate with a zero cash balance. It can't wait to open the morning mail to see how much cash it will have for the day's needs (although some businesses try to operate on a shoestring cash balance). A business should keep enough cash on hand to keep things running smoothly even when there are interruptions in the normal inflows of cash. A business has to meet its payroll on time, for example. Keeping an adequate balance in the checking account serves as a buffer against unforeseen disruptions in normal cash inflows.

At the end of the year, the company in our example has $11.281 million cash on hand (refer to Figure 2-2). This cash balance is available for general business purposes. (If there are restrictions on how the business can use its cash balance, the business is obligated to disclose the restrictions.) Is $11.281 million enough? Interestingly, businesses do not have to comment on their cash balance. We've never seen such a comment in a financial report.

The business has $4.213 million in operating liabilities that will come due for payment over the next one to three months (see Figure 2-2). Therefore, it has enough cash to pay these liabilities. But it has just barely enough cash on hand to pay its operating liabilities and its $7.0 million interest-bearing debt. Lenders don't expect a business to keep a cash balance more than the amount of debt; this condition would defeat the very purpose of lending money to the business, which is to have the business put the money to good use and be able to pay interest on the debt.

Lenders are more interested in the ability of the business to control its cash flows so that when the time comes to pay off loans, it will be able to do so. They know that the other, non-cash assets of the business will be converted into cash flow. Receivables will be collected, and products held in inventory will be sold, and the sales will generate cash flow. So you shouldn't focus just on cash; you should look at the other assets as well.

Taking this broader approach, the business has $11.281 million in cash, $8.883 million in trade accounts receivables, and $1.733 million in inventory, which adds up to $21.897 million in cash and cash potential. Relative to its $11.213 million in total liabilities ($4.213 million in operating liabilities plus $7.0 million of debt), the business looks like it's in pretty good shape. On the other hand, if it turns out that the business isn't able to collect its receivables and isn't able to sell its products, the business would end up in deep doo-doo.

TIP

One other way to look at a business's cash balance is to express its cash balance in terms of how many days of sales the amount represents. In the example, the business has an ending cash balance equal to 58 days of sales, calculated as follows:

$71.064 million annual sales revenue ÷ 365 days = $194,696 sales per day

$11.281 million cash balance ÷ $194,696 sales per day = 58 days

The business's cash balance equals almost two months of sales activity, which most lenders and investors would consider adequate.

Can you trust financial statement numbers?

Whether the financial statements are correct depends on the answers to two basic questions:

>> Does the business have a reliable accounting system in place and employ competent accountants?

>> Has its management manipulated the business's accounting methods or deliberately falsified the numbers?

WARNING

We'd love to tell you that the answer to the first question is always yes and that the answer to the second question is always no. But you know better, don't you? A recent survey of 400 chief financial officers and financial executives revealed that they think that about 20 percent of corporations distort their earnings reports (income statements) — even though the companies stay within the boundaries of accepted accounting standards. We would estimate that for most businesses, you should take their financial statements with a grain of salt and keep in mind that the numbers could be manipulated in the range of 10 to 20 percent higher or lower. Even though most people think accounting is an exact science, it isn't. There's a fair amount of play in the numbers, as we discuss later in this book.

Furthermore, there are lots of crooks and dishonest persons in the business world who think nothing of manipulating the accounting numbers and cooking the books. Also, organized crime is involved in many businesses. And we have to tell you that in our experience, many businesses don't put much effort into keeping their accounting systems up to speed, and they skimp on hiring competent accountants. In short, there's a risk that the financial statements of a business could be incorrect and seriously misleading.

To increase the credibility of their financial statements, many businesses hire independent CPA auditors to examine their accounting systems and records and to express opinions on whether the financial statements conform to established standards. In fact, some business lenders insist on an annual audit by an independent CPA firm as a condition of making a loan. The outside, non-management investors in a privately owned business could vote to have annual CPA audits of the financial statements. Public companies have no choice; under federal securities laws, a public company is required to have annual audits by an independent CPA firm.

WARNING

Two points: CPA audits are not cheap, and these audits aren't always effective in rooting out financial reporting fraud by managers. Unfortunately, there have been many cases of CPA auditors failing to detect serious financial fraud that had been going on for years, right under their auditing noses. Cleverly concealed fraud is very difficult to uncover, unless you stumble over it by accident. CPAs are supposed to apply *professional skepticism* in doing their audits, but this doesn't always lead to discovery of fraud.

Why no (or limited) cash distribution from profit?

Distributions from profit by a business C corporation (see Chapter 5 to understand the different forms of business legal entities) are called *dividends* (because the total amount distributed is divided up among the stockholders). Cash distributions from profit to owners are included in the final section of the statement of cash flows (refer to Figure 2-3). In our example, the business made a cash distribution in the form of a dividend from profit of $400,000 — even though it earned $4.482 million of net income (see Figure 2-1), or just 8.9 percent of profits. Why so low?

It's clear that the company has plenty of cash available to issue a dividend, as not only did it generate $4.482 million in net profit, but it also generated another $3.111 million in cash from non-cash expenses and operating activities ($1.739 million plus $1.372 million; see Figure 2-3). Should the business have distributed, say, at least half of its cash flow from profit, or roughly $3.8 million, to its owners? If you owned 20 percent of the ownership shares of the business, you would have received 20 percent, or roughly $760,000, of the dividend. But you got almost no cash return on your investment in the business. Your shares should be worth more because the profit for the year increased the company's owners' equity, but you didn't see any of this increase in your wallet.

REMEMBER

Deciding whether to make cash distributions from profit to shareowners is in the hands of the directors of a business corporation. Its shareowners elect the directors, and in theory the directors act in the best interests of the shareowners. So, evidently, the directors thought the business had better use for the $3.8 million cash flow from profit than distributing some of it to shareowners. In our example, the company does indeed have something big planned for the use of its cash hoard of $11.281 million, as it has earmarked funds to support buying a complimentary business in future years. Generally, the main reason for not making cash distributions from profit is to finance the growth of the business — to use all the cash flow from profit for expanding the assets needed by the business at the higher sales level (which is the case here). Ideally, the directors of the business would explain their decision not to distribute any money from profit to the shareowners. But generally, no such comments are made in financial reports.

Complying with Accounting and Financial Reporting Standards

When an independent CPA audits the financial report of a business, there's no doubt regarding which accounting and financial reporting standards the business uses to prepare its financial statements and other disclosures. The CPA explicitly states which standards are being used in the auditor's report. What about unaudited financial reports? Well, the business could clarify which accounting and financial reporting standards it uses, but you don't see such disclosure in all cases.

When the financial report of a business is not audited and does not make clear which standards are being used to prepare its financial report, the reader is entitled to assume that appropriate standards are being used. However, a business may be way out in left field (or out of the ballpark) in the "guideposts" it uses for recording profit and in the preparation of its financial statements. A business may make up its own "rules" for measuring profit and preparing financial statements. In this book, we concentrate on authoritative standards, of course.

Imagine the confusion that would result if every business were permitted to invent its own accounting methods for measuring profit and for putting values on assets and liabilities. What if every business adopted its own individual accounting terminology and followed its own style for presenting financial statements? Such a state of affairs would be a Tower of Babel.

REMEMBER

The goal is to establish broad-scale uniformity in accounting methods for all businesses. The idea is to make sure that all accountants are singing the same tune from the same hymnal. The authoritative bodies write the tunes that accountants have to sing.

Looking at who makes the standards

Who are the authoritative bodies that set the standards for financial accounting and reporting? In the United States, the highest-ranking authority in the private (nongovernment) sector for making pronouncements on accounting and financial reporting standards — and for keeping these standards up to date — is the Financial Accounting Standards Board (FASB). This rulemaking body has developed a *codification* of all its pronouncements. This is where accountants look to first.

Outside the United States, the main authoritative accounting-standards setter is the International Accounting Standards Board (IASB), which is based in London. The IASB was founded in 2001. More than 8,000 public companies have their securities listed on the several stock exchanges in the European Union (EU) countries. In many regards, the IASB operates in a manner similar to the Financial Accounting Standards Board (FASB) in the United States, and the two have very similar missions. The IASB has already issued many standards, which are called International Financial Reporting Standards. Without going into details, FASB and IASB are not in perfect harmony (even though congruence of their standards was the original goal of the two organizations).

Also, in the United States, the federal Securities and Exchange Commission (SEC) has broad powers over accounting and financial reporting standards for companies whose securities (stocks and bonds) are publicly traded. Actually, because it derives its authority from federal securities laws that govern the public issuance and trading in securities, the SEC outranks the FASB. The SEC has on occasion overridden the FASB but not very often.

TIP

Consider taking the time to Google the acronyms of these three authoritative sources of financial accounting standards. You'll find which particular financial accounting standards and problem areas are under active review and development. In late 2015, for instance, lease accounting and revenue accounting were under active review and transition to new standards, to say nothing about a host of other financial accounting problems (for example, how to account for derivatives).

Knowing about GAAP

The authoritative standards and rules that govern financial accounting and reporting by businesses in the United States are called *generally accepted accounting principles (GAAP)*. The financial statements of an American business should be in full compliance with GAAP regarding reporting its cash flows, profit-making activities, and financial condition — *unless* the business makes very clear that it has prepared its financial statements using some other basis of accounting or has deviated from GAAP in one or more significant respects.

WARNING

If GAAP are not the basis for preparing a business's financial statements, the business should make very clear which other basis of accounting it's using and avoid using titles for its financial statements that are associated with GAAP. For example, if a business uses a simple cash receipts and cash disbursements basis of accounting — which falls way short of GAAP — it should not use the terms *income statement* and *balance sheet*. These terms are part and parcel of GAAP, and their use as titles for financial statements implies that the business is using GAAP.

There are upwards of 7,000 public companies in the United States and easily more than a million privately owned businesses. Now, are we telling you that all these businesses should use the same accounting methods, terminology, and presentation styles for their financial statements? Putting it in such a stark manner makes us suck in our breath a little. The ideal answer is that all businesses *should* use the same rulebook of GAAP. However, the rulebook permits alternative accounting methods for some transactions. Furthermore, accountants have to interpret the rules as they apply GAAP in actual situations. The devil is in the detail.

WARNING

In the United States, GAAP constitute the gold standard for preparing financial statements of business entities. The presumption is that any deviations from GAAP would cause misleading financial statements. If a business honestly thinks it should deviate from GAAP — in order to better reflect the economic reality of its transactions or situation — it should make very clear that it has not complied with GAAP in one or more respects. If deviations from GAAP are not disclosed, the business may have legal exposure to those who relied on the information in its financial report and suffered a loss attributable to the misleading nature of the information.

GAAP also include requirements for *disclosure,* which refers to the following:

>> The types of information that have to be included with the financial statements

>> How information is classified and presented in financial statements (mainly in the form of footnotes)

The SEC makes the disclosure rules for public companies. Disclosure rules for private companies are controlled by GAAP. Chapter 10 explains the disclosures that are required in addition to the three primary financial statements of a business (the income statement, balance sheet, and statement of cash flows).

Divorcing public and private companies

Traditionally, GAAP and financial reporting standards were viewed as equally applicable to public companies (generally large corporations) and private companies (generally smaller). For some time, private companies have argued that some of the standards issued by the FASB are too complex and burdensome for private companies to apply. Although most accountants don't like to admit it, there's always been a de facto divergence in actual financial reporting practices by private companies compared with the more rigorously enforced standards for public companies. For example, a surprising number of private companies still do not include a statement of cash flows in their financial reports, even though this has been a GAAP requirement for 30 years.

REMEMBER

Although it's hard to prove one way or the other, our view is that the financial reports of private businesses generally measure up to GAAP standards in all significant respects. At the same time, however, there's little doubt that the financial reports of some private companies fall short. In fact, in the invitation to comment on the proposal to establish an advisory committee for private company accounting standards, the FASB said, "Compliance with GAAP standards for many for-profit private companies is a choice rather than a requirement because private companies can often control who receives their financial information." Recently, a Private Company Council (PCC) was established; it's separate from the FASB but subject to oversight by the FASB.

Private companies do not have many of the accounting problems of large, public companies. For example, many public companies deal in complex derivative instruments, issue stock options to managers, provide highly developed defined-benefit retirement and health benefit plans for their employees, enter into complicated intercompany investment and joint venture operations, have complex organizational structures, and so on. Most private companies don't have to deal with these issues.

Finally, we should mention in passing that the AICPA, the national association of CPAs, has started a project to develop an *Other Comprehensive Basis of Accounting* for privately held small and medium-sized entities. Oh my! What a time we live in regarding accounting standards. The upshot seems to be that we're drifting toward separate accounting standards for larger public companies versus smaller private companies — and maybe even a third branch of standards for small and medium-sized companies.

Following the rules and bending the rules

An often-repeated story concerns three persons interviewing for an important accounting position. They're asked one key question: "What's 2 plus 2?" The first candidate answers, "It's 4," and is told, "Don't call us. We'll call you." The second candidate answers, "Well, most of the time the answer is 4, but sometimes it's 3, and sometimes it's 5." The third candidate answers, "What do you want the answer to be?" Guess who gets the job. This story exaggerates, of course, but it does have an element of truth.

The point is that interpreting GAAP is not cut-and-dried. Many accounting standards leave lots of wiggle room for interpretation. *Guidelines* would be a better word to describe many accounting rules. Deciding how to account for certain transactions and situations requires seasoned judgment and careful analysis of the rules. Furthermore, many estimates have to be made. Deciding on accounting methods requires, above all else, *good faith*.

WARNING

A business may resort to "creative" accounting to make profit for the period look better or to make its year-to-year profit less erratic than it really is (which is called *income smoothing*). Like lawyers who know where to find loopholes, accountants can come up with inventive interpretations that stay within the boundaries of GAAP. We warn you about these creative accounting techniques — also called *massaging the numbers* — at various points in this book. Massaging the numbers can get out of hand and become accounting fraud, also called *cooking the books*. Massaging the numbers has some basis in honest differences for interpreting the facts. Cooking the books goes way beyond interpreting facts; this fraud consists of *inventing* facts and good old-fashioned chicanery.

Chapter **3**

Safeguarding Company Assets

W
e think it's safe to say that most folks are not enthusiastic bookkeepers. Let's hope you reconcile or balance your checkbook against your bank statement every month (most likely electronically these days) and somehow manage to pull together all the records you need for your annual federal income tax return. But if you're like us, you stuff your bills in a drawer or bury them in your cellphone somewhere, and just drag them out once a month when you pay them. And when's the last time you prepared a detailed listing of all your assets and liabilities (even though a listing of assets is a good idea for fire insurance purposes)? Personal computer programs are available to make bookkeeping for individuals more organized, but you still have to enter lots of data into the program, and in our experience, most people don't put forth the effort.

Individuals can get along quite well without much bookkeeping — but the exact opposite is true for a business. First of all, a business needs a good bookkeeping system simply to operate day to day. An army marches on its stomach. A business marches on data and information, without which it literally couldn't make it through the day.

In addition to facilitating day-to-day operations, a company's bookkeeping system serves as the source of information for preparing its periodic financial statements, tax returns, reports to managers, and a variety of other demands. The completeness, accuracy, reliability, and timeliness (the acronym CART that you see referenced time and again throughout this book) of these reports is critical to the business's survival. If its accounting records are incomplete or inaccurate, its financial statements, tax returns, and management reports are incomplete or inaccurate. And inaccuracy simply won't do. In fact, inaccurate and incomplete bookkeeping records could be construed as evidence of deliberate fraud (or at least of incompetence). Suppose, for instance, that the Internal Revenue Service decides to audit a business. The business won't get very far with the excuse that it doesn't have records to back up the deductions in its tax returns.

Obviously, then, business management has to be sure that their company's bookkeeping and accounting system is dependable and up to snuff. This chapter shows you what bookkeepers and accountants do, mainly so you have a clear idea of what it takes to be sure that the information coming out of the accounting system is complete, accurate, reliable, and timely for all the demands on the system. We stress that strong internal accounting controls are absolutely necessary.

Separating the Duties of Bookkeepers and Accountants

REMEMBER

It's useful to distinguish between bookkeeping and accounting because they aren't completely interchangeable:

>> *Bookkeeping* refers mainly to the recordkeeping aspects of accounting and is heavily weighted toward processing transactions (for example, billing a customer, paying a vendor, and so on); it's essentially the process (some would say the drudgery) of preparing documents or managing computer-based digital data entries for recording all the detailed information regarding the transactions and other activities of a business (or other organization, venture, or project).

>> The term *accounting* is much broader, going into the realm of designing the bookkeeping system, establishing controls to make sure the system is working well, and analyzing and verifying the recorded information. Accountants give orders; bookkeepers follow them. And we might add that accountants are paid better than bookkeepers.

Bookkeepers spend most of their work time keeping the recordkeeping process running smoothly according to the system established by the business — and they also spend a fair amount of time dealing with problems that inevitably arise in recording so much information. Accountants, on the other hand, have a different focus. You can think of accounting as what goes on before and after bookkeeping. Accountants are in charge of preparing reports based on the information accumulated by the bookkeeping process: financial statements, tax returns, and various confidential reports to managers.

TIP

Measuring profit performance is a critical task for accountants — a task that depends on the accuracy and completeness of the information recorded by the bookkeeper. The accountant decides how to measure sales revenue and expenses (as well as any special gains and losses) to determine the profit or loss for the period. The tough questions about profit — how to measure it in our complex and advanced economic environment — can't be answered through bookkeeping alone. We discuss accounting problems in Chapter 9.

These are the important differences between bookkeeping and accounting. Bookkeeping has two main jobs:

>> Recording the financial effects and other relevant details of the wide variety of transactions and other activities of the entity

>> Generating a *constant* stream of documents and electronic interactions and outputs to keep the business operating every day

Bookkeeping builds up the financial database of the entity. This is a perpetual, nonstop process for a business of any size. A business does bookkeeping every day.

Accounting, on the other hand, focuses on the *periodic* preparation of three main types of output: reports to managers, tax returns (income tax, sales tax, payroll tax, and so on), and financial statements and reports. These outputs are done according to established timetables. For example, external financial reports are prepared every quarter (3 months) and at the end of the year (12 months). Tax returns have their own timetables, as dictated by the tax laws and regulations. Accountants have much more choice in deciding how often to prepare financial reports to managers. The managers of some businesses require daily or even hourly financial reports; in other businesses, quarterly reports are adequate to keep on top of things.

REMEMBER

In this book, we explain the fundamentals of financial reporting to the "outside," or non-management creditors and investors of a business. The main focus is on the financial statements sent to them (see Chapters 6 through 10). This field of accounting is referred to as *financial accounting* (although it might be better called *external financial accounting*). The externally reported financial statements are useful to managers as well, but managers need considerably more detailed information than is reported in the external financial statements of a business. Much of this management information is confidential and not for circulation outside the business. We offer a limited discussion of accounting to managers in Part 4.

Pedaling through the Bookkeeping Cycle

If anything, bookkeeping is a very repetitive process. Certain basic steps are done in virtually every bookkeeping system. The steps are done in a certain order, although the specific methods and procedures of each step vary from business to business. For example, entering the data for a sale could be done by scanning bar codes in a grocery store, or it could require an in-depth legal interpretation for a complex order from a customer for an expensive piece of equipment. We briefly explain the basic steps in this section. (See also the later section "Double-Entry Accounting," which explains how the books are kept in balance by using debits and credits for recording transactions.)

Getting to the end of the period

Although the means and specific procedures regarding how the bookkeeping process is carried out vary from business to business, all businesses walk through the following steps during the accounting period. These basic four steps take up most of the time spent on recordkeeping:

1. **Prepare original *source documents* or *electronic references* for all transactions, operations, and other events of the business.**

    When buying products, a business gets a *purchase invoice* (or its electronic equivalent) from the supplier. When borrowing money from the bank, a business signs a *note payable,* a copy of which the business keeps. When a customer uses a credit card to buy a retailer's product, the business gets the *credit card receipt* (or an electronic alternative) as evidence of the transaction. When preparing payroll, a business depends on *salary rosters* and *time tracking systems.* All these key business forms serve as sources of information for the bookkeeping system — in other words, information the bookkeeper uses in recording the financial effects of the activities of the business.

2. **Determine the *financial effects* of the transactions, operations, and other events of the business.**

    The activities of the business have financial effects that must be recorded: The business is better off, worse off, or at least "different off" as the result of its transactions. Examples of typical business transactions include paying employees, making sales to customers, borrowing money from the bank, and buying products that will be sold to customers. The bookkeeping process begins by determining the relevant information about each transaction. The chief accountant (controller) of the business establishes the rules and methods for measuring the financial effects of transactions. Of course, the bookkeeper should comply with these rules and methods.

3. **Make *original entries* of financial effects in journals, with appropriate references to source documents.**

   Using source documents or electronic files, the bookkeeper makes the first, or original, entry for every transaction into a journal; this information is later recorded in accounts (see the next step). A *journal* is a chronological record of transactions in the order in which they occur — like a very detailed personal diary.

   Here's a simple example that illustrates recording a transaction in a journal: A retail bookstore, expecting a big demand from its customers, purchases, on credit, 100 copies of *Accounting For Dummies,* 7th Edition, from the publisher, Wiley. The books are received and placed on the shelves. (One hundred copies is a lot to put on the shelves, but our relatives promised to rush down and buy several copies each.) The bookstore now owns the books and also owes Wiley $1,500, which is the cost of the 100 copies. Here we look only at recording the purchase of the books, not recording subsequent sales of the books and paying the bill to Wiley.

   The bookstore has established a specific inventory asset account called "Inventory–Trade Paperbacks" for books like this one. And the purchase liability to the publisher should be entered in the account "Accounts Payable–Publishers." Therefore, the original journal entry for this purchase records an increase in the inventory asset account of $1,500 and an increase in the liability accounts payable of $1,500. Notice the balance in the two sides of the transaction: An asset increases $1,500 on the one side, and a liability increases $1,500 on the other side. All is well (assuming there are no mistakes).

   In ancient days, bookkeepers had to record journal entries by hand, and even today there's nothing wrong with a good hand-entry (manual) bookkeeping system. But bookkeepers now can use online, real-time computer systems that take over many of the tedious chores of bookkeeping (see Chapter 4). Unfortunately, so much keyboard typing has replaced hand cramps with carpal tunnel syndrome for some bookkeepers, but at least the work gets done more quickly and with fewer errors!

   Summing up, a journal entry records the whole transaction in one place at one time. All changes caused by the transaction are chronicled in one entry. However, making journal entries does not provide a running balance for the individual assets, liabilities, and other financial components of a business (or other entity) — which leads to the next step in the bookkeeping process.

4. **Post the financial effects of transactions in the accounts changed by the transactions.**

Journal entries are the sources for recording changes caused by transactions in the *accounts* of the entity. An account is a separate record or file for each asset, each liability, and so on. The pluses and minuses of the transaction are recorded in the accounts changed by the transaction. In this way, a running balance is kept for each. Recording the effects of transactions from journal entries to accounts is called *posting*.

Think of each account as an address. The changes recorded in the original journal entries are "delivered," or posted to the accounts. A business (or other entity) establishes an official *chart*, or list of accounts, that is used for posting transactions. The original journal entry records the whole transaction in one place; then, in the second step called *posting*, each change is recorded in the separate accounts affected by the transaction.

TIP

We can't exaggerate the importance of entering transaction data correctly and in a timely manner — both in original journal entries and in the posting step. The prevalence of data-entry errors is one important reason that most retailers use cash registers that read bar-coded information on products; this approach more accurately captures the necessary information and speeds up the entry of the information. One way of stressing this point is the well-known data-processing expression "garbage in, garbage out."

Finishing up for the period

After doing the four bookkeeping procedures we explain in the preceding section, the business is ready to finish the process. At the end of the period, certain steps are necessary to make the business's accounts ready for the preparation of its financial statements (and other accounting reports such as tax returns). We continue the numbering from the preceding section, so we start with Step 5:

5. **Perform *end-of-period procedures* — the critical steps for getting the accounting records up to date and ready for the preparation of management accounting reports, tax returns, and financial statements.**

A *period* is a stretch of time — from one day (even one hour) to one month to one quarter (three months) to one year — that is determined by the needs of the business. A year is the longest period of time that a business would wait to prepare its financial statements. Most businesses need accounting reports and financial statements at the end of each quarter, and many need monthly financial statements.

TECHNICAL STUFF

Before accounting reports can be prepared at the end of the period, the bookkeeper needs to bring the accounts of the business up to date and to complete the bookkeeping process. Generally these end-of-period procedures consist mainly of making *adjusting entries* in the accounts of the business. One such end-of-period adjusting entry, for example, is recording depreciation expense for the period (see Chapters 6 and 7 for more on depreciation). Another is taking an actual count and making a critical inspection of the business's inventory so that the inventory records can be adjusted to recognize any shoplifting, employee theft, and other inventory shrinkage.

The accountant needs to be heavily involved in end-of-period procedures and be sure to check for errors in the business's accounts. Data-entry clerks and bookkeepers may not fully understand the unusual nature of some business transactions and may have entered transactions incorrectly. One reason for establishing internal controls (discussed in the later section "Enforcing Strong Internal Controls") is to keep errors to a minimum. Ideally, accounts should contain very few errors at the end of the period, but the accountant can't make any assumptions and should make a final check for any errors that may have fallen through the cracks.

6. **Compile the *adjusted trial balance,* which is the accountant's basis for preparing management reports, tax returns, and financial statements.**

After all the end-of-period procedures have been completed, the bookkeeper compiles a comprehensive listing of all accounts, which is often called the *adjusted trial balance.* Modest-sized businesses maintain hundreds of accounts for their various assets, liabilities, owners' equity, revenue, and expenses. Larger businesses keep thousands of accounts, and very large businesses may keep more than 10,000 accounts.

In contrast, external financial statements and tax returns contain a relatively small number of accounts. For example, a typical external balance sheet reports only 25 to 35 accounts (maybe even fewer). Apple's consolidated September 26, 2020, end-of-fiscal year balance sheet contains just 27 accounts, including totals. (Apple's 2020 10-K annual report to the Securities and Exchange Commission includes more accounts.) The annual income tax return (Form 1120) for business corporations contains a relatively small number of accounts.

The accountant takes the adjusted trial balance and telescopes similar accounts into one summary amount that is reported in a financial report or tax return. For example, a business may keep hundreds of separate inventory accounts, every one of which is listed in the adjusted trial balance. The accountant collapses all these accounts into one summary inventory account that's presented in the balance sheet of the business. In grouping the accounts, the accountant should comply with established financial reporting standards and income tax requirements.

7. **Close the books** — bring the bookkeeping for the fiscal year just ended to a close and get things ready to begin the bookkeeping process all over again for the coming fiscal year.

Books is the common term for a business's complete set of accounts. (Well, okay, we should include journal entries in the definition of *books,* but you get the point.) A business's transactions are a constant stream of activities that doesn't end tidily on the last day of the year, which can make preparing financial statements and tax returns challenging. The business has to draw a clear line of demarcation between activities for the year (the 12-month accounting period) ended and the year yet to come by *closing the books* for one year and starting with fresh books for the next year.

TIP

Most medium-sized and larger businesses prepare an internal *accounting manual* or set of policies and procedures that spells out in great detail the specific accounts and procedures for recording transactions. A business should regularly review its chart of accounts and accounting rules and policies and make revisions. Companies do not take this task lightly; discontinuities in the accounting system can be major shocks and have to be carefully thought out. Nevertheless, bookkeeping and accounting systems can't remain static for very long. If these systems were never changed, bookkeepers would still be sitting on high stools making entries with quill pens and bottled ink in leather-bound ledgers.

Managing Accounting Systems

In our experience, too many business managers and owners ignore their bookkeeping and accounting systems or take them for granted — unless something goes wrong. They assume that if the books are in balance, everything is okay, and that you can simply hit a print report icon or button to produce qualify financial information. The later section "Double-Entry Accounting" covers exactly what it means to have "books in balance" — it does *not* necessarily mean that everything is okay.

To determine whether your bookkeeping system is up to snuff, check out this section, which provides a checklist of the most important elements of a good system.

Categorize financial information: The chart of accounts

Suppose that you're the accountant for a corporation and you're faced with the daunting task of preparing the annual federal income tax return for the business.

The Internal Revenue Service (IRS) requires that you report the following expenses (and this list contains just the minimum!):

>> Advertising

>> Bad debts

>> Charitable contributions

>> Compensation of officers

>> Cost of goods sold

>> Depreciation

>> Employee benefit programs

>> Interest

>> Pensions and profit-sharing plans

>> Rents

>> Repairs and maintenance

>> Salaries and wages

>> Taxes and licenses

You must provide additional information for some of these expenses. For example, the cost of goods sold expense is determined in a schedule that also requires inventory cost at the beginning of the year, purchases during the year, cost of labor during the year (for manufacturers), other costs, and inventory cost at year-end.

Where do you start? Well, if it's March 1 and the corporate tax return deadline is March 15, you start by panicking — unless you were smart enough to think ahead about the kinds of information your business would need to report. In fact, when your accountant first designs your business's accounting system, they should dissect every report to managers, the external financial statements, and the tax returns, breaking down all the information into basic account categories such as those we just listed.

REMEMBER

For each category of information that you need to include in an accounting report, you need an *account* (or a group of accounts), which is a record of the activities in that category. An account is basically a focused history of a particular dimension of a business. Individuals can have accounts, too — for example, your checkbook (physical or digital) is an account of the cash inflows and outflows and the balance of your checking account (assuming that you remember to record all activities and reconcile your checkbook against your bank statement). We doubt that you keep a written account of the coin and currency in your wallet, pockets, glove compartment, and sofa cushions, but a business needs to keep track of all its cash, no matter where it is. An account serves as the source of information for preparing financial statements, tax returns, and reports to managers.

The term *general ledger* refers to the complete set of accounts established and maintained by a business. The *chart of accounts* is the formal index of these accounts — the complete listing and classification of the accounts used by the business to record its transactions. *General ledger* usually refers to the actual accounts and often to the balances in those accounts at some particular time. The chart of accounts, even for a relatively small business, contains more than 100 accounts. Larger business organizations need thousands of accounts. The larger the number, the more likely that the accounts are given number codes according to some scheme — for example, all assets may be in the 100 to 300 range; all liabilities, in the 400 to 500 range; and so on.

TIP

As a business manager, you should make sure that the controller (chief accountant) or perhaps an outside CPA consultant reviews the chart of accounts periodically to determine whether the accounts are up to date and adequate for the business's needs. Over time, income tax rules change, business economic models evolve, the company goes into new lines of business, the company adopts new employee benefit plans, and so on. Most businesses are in constant flux, and the chart of accounts has to keep up with these changes.

Standardize source documents and data-entry procedures for recording activities

Just like you need a constant circulation of blood to live, businesses need a constant flow of paperwork and electronic activity. Even in this age of the internet and the cloud, electronic communication, and computers, a business generates and depends on lots of documentation (either hard paperwork or digitized documents in PDFs). And much of this documentation is used in the accounting process. Placing an order to buy products, selling a product to a customer, determining the earnings of an employee for the month — virtually every business transaction needs some documentation, generally called *source documents.* When you pay a bill, for example, don't you want a "hard copy" to examine before you write the check?

Source documents serve as legal evidence of the terms and conditions agreed upon by the business and the other person or organization that it's dealing with. Both parties receive some kind of source document. For example, for a sale at a cash register, the customer gets a sales receipt, and the business keeps a running record of all the transactions in the register, which can be printed out later if need be.

Clearly, an accounting system needs to standardize the forms and procedures for processing and recording all normal, repetitive transactions and should control the generation and handling of these source documents. From the bookkeeping point of view, these business forms and documents are important because they provide the input information needed for recording transactions in the business's accounts. Sloppy paperwork leads to sloppy accounting records, and sloppy accounting records just won't do when the time comes to prepare tax returns and financial statements.

TIP

If you're the owner of a small business, you probably want to check out an office supply store or, better yet, online documentation websites to see the kinds of forms that you can buy right off the shelf or download with the stroke of a key. You can find many of the basic forms and documents that you need for executing and recording business transactions. Also, computer accounting software systems today include templates for most business forms and source documents needed by a business.

Hire competent personnel

A business shouldn't be penny-wise and pound-foolish. What good is meticulously collecting source documents if the information on those documents isn't entered into your system correctly? You shouldn't try to save a few bucks by hiring the lowest-paid people you can find. Bookkeepers and accountants, like all other employees in a business, should have the skills and knowledge needed to perform their functions. Here are some guidelines for choosing the right people to enter and control the flow of your business's data and for making sure that those people *remain* the right people:

>> **College degree:** Many accountants in business organizations have a college degree with a major in accounting. However, as you move down the accounting department, you find that more and more employees do not have a college degree and perhaps don't even have any courses in accounting — they learned bookkeeping methods and skills through on-the-job training or possibly from vocational schools. Although these employees may have good skills and instincts, our experience has been that they tend to do things by the book, so you want to at least think twice about a potential employee who has no college-based accounting background.

TIP

>> **Professional credentials:** When hiring higher-level accountants in a business organization, you want to determine whether they should be certified public accountants (CPAs). Larger businesses insist on this credential, along with a specific number of years' experience in public accounting.

Until recently, the only other main professional accounting credential was the CMA, or certified management accountant, sponsored by the Institute of Management Accountants (IMA). The CMA credential is American born and bred. In contrast, the Chartered Global Management Accountant (CGMA) designation is co-sponsored by the American Institute of CPAs and the British Chartered Institute of Management Accountants. Unlike the CPA license, the CMA and CGMA designations recognize professional achievement and experience, but the government doesn't regulate these credentials. (We discuss the CPA in Chapter 1.)

Note: For bookkeepers, the American Institute of Professional Bookkeepers sponsors the Certified Bookkeeper designation. For more information, go to www.AIPB.org.

In our opinion, a business is prudent to require the CPA, CGMA, or CMA credential for its chief accountant (who usually holds the title of *controller*). Alternatively, a business could regularly consult with a CPA in public practice for advice on its accounting system and on accounting problems that come up.

More and more, businesses are turning to experts in recognizing fraud, embezzlement, and cybercrime for advice and to investigate suspicious situations. Even relatively small businesses are vulnerable to these threats. One mark of expertise that you could look for is the *Certified in Financial Forensics (CFF)* credential sponsored by the American Institute of Certified Public Accountants (AICPA).

>> **Continuing education:** Bookkeepers and accountants need continuing education to keep up with changes in the income tax law and financial reporting requirements as well as changes in how the business operates. Ideally, bookkeepers and accountants should be able to spot needed improvements and implement these changes in order to make accounting reports to managers more useful. Fortunately, many short-term courses, online programs, and the like are available at very reasonable costs for keeping up on the latest accounting developments. Many continuing education courses are available on the internet, but you should be cautious and check out the standards of an internet course. Although each state is slightly different, states require that CPAs in public practice take 30 to 40 hours per year of continuing education to keep their licenses.

>> **Integrity:** Possibly the most important quality to look for is also the hardest to judge. Bookkeepers and accountants need to be honest people because of the control they have over your business's financial records. Conduct a careful background check when hiring new accounting personnel. After you hire them, periodically (and discreetly) check whether their lifestyles match their salaries, but be careful not to invade their privacy. Small-business owners and managers have closer day-in and day-out contact with their accountants and

bookkeepers, which can be a real advantage — they get to know their accountants and bookkeepers on a personal level. Even so, we could tell you many true stories about long-time, "trusted" bookkeepers who made off with some of the family fortune.

Get involved in end-of-period procedures

REMEMBER

Suppose that all transactions during the year have been recorded correctly. Therefore, the business is ready to prepare its financial statements from those accounts, isn't it? Not so fast! As we explain earlier in "Finishing up for the period" (see Step 5), certain additional procedures are necessary at the end of the period to make sure that the accounts are correct and complete for preparing financial statements and income tax returns for the year. Two main things must be done at the end of the period:

>> **Record normal, routine *adjusting entries.*** For example, depreciation expense isn't a transaction as such and therefore isn't included in the flow of transactions recorded in the day-to-day bookkeeping process. (Chapter 6 explains depreciation expense.) Similarly, certain other expenses and income may not have been associated with a specific transaction and therefore haven't been recorded. In many businesses, there's a normal lag in recording certain transactions, such as billing customers for services already provided. These "catch up" entries should be recorded. Year-end adjusting entries are necessary to have correct balances for determining profit for the period. The purpose is to make the revenue, income, expense, and loss accounts up to date and correct for the year.

>> ***Make a careful sweep of all matters*** **to check for other developments that may affect the accuracy of the accounts.** For example, the company may have discontinued a product line. The remaining inventory of these products may need to be removed from the inventory asset account, with a corresponding loss recorded in the period. Or the company may have settled a long-standing lawsuit, and the amount of damages needs to be recorded. Layoffs and severance packages are another example of what the chief accountant needs to look for before preparing reports.

Lest you think of accounting as dry and dull, let us tell you that end-of-period accounting procedures can stir up controversy of the heated-debate variety. These procedures require that the accountant make decisions and judgment calls that upper management may not agree with. For example, the accountant may suggest recording major losses that would put a big dent in profit for the year and cause the business to report a loss. The outside CPA auditor (assuming that the business has an independent audit of its financial statements) often gets in the middle of the argument. These kinds of debates are precisely why business managers need to know some accounting: to hold up their end of the argument and participate in the great sport of yelling and name-calling — strictly on a professional basis, of course.

REMEMBER

This also touches on a concept that you may hear from time to time — that accounting is just as much of an art form as a science. What we mean by this is that while accounting is a technical profession that has a large amount of authoritative content to work with and provides guidance, the actual application of accounting concepts, rules, and regulations (in the real world where internal management pressures can be significant) is often fairly subjective.

Leave good audit trails

Good accounting systems leave good audit trails. An *audit trail* is a clear-cut, well-marked path of the sequence of events leading up to an entry in the accounts, starting with the source documents and following through to the final posting in the accounts; an auditor can "re-walk" the path. Even if a business doesn't have an outside CPA do an annual audit, the accountant has frequent occasion to go back to the source documents and either verify certain information in the accounts or reconstruct the information in a different manner. Suppose that a salesperson is claiming some suspicious-looking travel expenses; the accountant would probably want to go through all of this person's travel and entertainment reimbursements for the past year.

WARNING

If the IRS comes in for a field audit of your income tax return, you'd better have good audit trails to substantiate all your expense deductions and sales revenue for the year. The IRS has rules about saving source documents for a reasonable period of time and having a well-defined process for making bookkeeping entries and keeping accounts. Think twice before throwing away or deleting source documents too soon. Also, ask your accountant to demonstrate and lay out for your inspection the audit trails for key transactions, such as cash collections, sales, cash disbursements, and inventory purchases. Even computer-based accounting systems recognize the importance of audit trails. Well-designed computer programs provide the ability to backtrack through the sequence of steps in the recording of specific transactions.

Keep alert for unusual events and developments

WARNING

Business managers should encourage their accountants to stay alert to anything out of the ordinary that may require attention. Suppose that the accounts receivable balance for a customer is rapidly increasing — that is, the customer is buying more and more from your company on credit but isn't paying for these purchases quickly. Maybe the customer has switched more of his company's purchases to your business and is buying more from you only because he's buying less from other businesses. But maybe the customer is planning to stiff your business and take off without paying his debts. Or maybe the customer is planning to go into bankruptcy soon and is stockpiling products before the company's credit rating heads south.

Don't forget internal time bombs: A bookkeeper's reluctance to take a vacation could mean that they don't want anyone else looking at the books.

To some extent, accountants have to act as the eyes and ears of the business. Of course, that's one of the main functions of a business manager as well, but the accounting staff can play an important role.

Design truly useful reports for managers

We've seen too many off-the-mark accounting reports to managers — reports that are difficult to decipher and not very useful or relevant to the manager's decision-making needs and control functions. These bad reports waste the manager's time, one of the most serious offenses in management accounting.

Part of the problem lies with the managers themselves. As a business manager, have you told your accounting staff what you need to know, when you need it, and how to present it in the most efficient manner? When you stepped into your position, you probably didn't hesitate to rearrange your office, and maybe you even insisted on hiring your own support staff. Yet you most likely lie down like a lap-dog regarding your accounting reports. Maybe you assume that the reports have been done a certain way and that arguing for change is no use.

REMEMBER

On the other hand, accountants bear a good share of the blame for poor management reports. Accountants should proactively study the manager's decision-making responsibilities and provide the information that is most useful, presented in the most easily digestible manner. To a certain extent, this is what we mean when we say "reliable" (in the acronym CART). While financial information may be accurate, reliability speaks to the concept of producing and reporting financial information in a way that truly benefits a business manager and assists them in making informed business decisions. Don't assume that accuracy automatically equates to reliability.

In designing the chart of accounts, the accountant should keep in mind the type of information needed for management reports. To exercise control, managers need much more detail than what's reported on tax returns and external financial statements. And as we explain in Chapter 15, expenses should be regrouped into different categories for management decision-making analysis. A good chart of accounts looks to both the external and the internal (management) needs for information.

TIP

So what's the answer for a manager who receives poorly formatted reports? Demand a report format that suits your needs! See Chapter 15 for a useful profit report model, and show it to your accountant as well.

Enforcing Strong Internal Controls

REMEMBER

Any accounting system worth its salt should establish and vigorously enforce effective *internal controls* — basically, additional forms and procedures over and above what's needed strictly to move operations along. These additional procedures serve to deter and detect errors (honest mistakes) and all forms of dishonesty by employees, customers, suppliers, and even managers themselves. Unfortunately, many businesses pay only lip service to internal controls; they don't put into place good internal controls, or they don't seriously enforce their internal controls (they just go through the motions).

Internal controls are like highway truck weigh stations, which make sure that a truck's load doesn't exceed the limits and that the truck has a valid plate. You're just checking that your staff is playing by the rules. For example, to prevent or minimize shoplifting, many retailers use video surveillance as well as tags that set off the alarms if the customer leaves the store with the tag still on the product. Likewise, a business should implement certain procedures and forms to prevent (as much as possible) theft, embezzlement, kickbacks, fraud, and simple mistakes by its own employees and managers.

The Sarbanes-Oxley Act of 2002 (often referred to as SOX) applies to public companies that are subject to the federal Securities and Exchange Commission (SEC) jurisdiction. Congress passed this law mainly in response to Enron and other massive financial reporting fraud disasters. The act, which is implemented through the SEC and the Public Company Accounting Oversight Board (PCAOB), requires that public companies establish and enforce a special module of internal controls over external financial reporting.

Although Sarbanes-Oxley applies legally only to public companies, the accounting profession has taken the position that requirements of the law are relevant to all businesses. As a matter of fact, independent CPA auditors in their audit report state whether they think the internal controls over financial reporting are adequate for preventing misleading financial statements.

INTERNAL CONTROLS AGAINST MISTAKES AND THEFT

Accounting is characterized by lots of documentation — forms and procedures (digital or hard copy) are plentiful. Most business managers and employees have their enthusiasm under control when it comes to the documentation and procedures that the accounting department requires. One reason for this attitude, in our experience, is that nonaccountants fail to appreciate the need for accounting controls.

These *internal controls* are designed to minimize errors in bookkeeping that processes a great deal of detailed information and data. Equally important, controls are necessary to deter employee fraud, embezzlement, and theft as well as fraud and dishonest behavior against the business from the outside. Every business is a target for fraud and theft, such as customers who shoplift; suppliers who deliberately ship less than the quantities invoiced to a business and hope that the business won't notice the difference (called *short-counts*); and even dishonest managers themselves, who may pad expense accounts or take kickbacks from suppliers or customers.

For these reasons, a business should take steps to avoid being an easy target for dishonest behavior by its employees, customers, and suppliers. Every business should institute and enforce certain control measures, many of which are integrated into the accounting process. Following are five common examples of internal control procedures:

- Requiring a second signature or electronic approval on cash disbursements over a certain dollar amount

- Matching up receiving reports based on actual counts and inspections of incoming shipments with purchase orders before approving checks for payment to suppliers

- Requiring both a sales manager's and another high-level manager's approval for *write-offs* of customers' overdue receivable balances (that is, closing the accounts on the assumption that they won't be collected), including a checklist of collection efforts that were undertaken

- Having auditors or employees who do not work in the warehouse take surprise counts of products stored in the company's warehouse and compare the counts with inventory records

- Requiring mandatory vacations by every employee, particularly bookkeepers and accountants, during which time someone else does that person's job (because a second person may notice irregularities or deviations from company policies)

I (coauthor Tage) have decades of experience working closely with small businesses, and I've found that many small-business owners tend to think they're immune to embezzlement and fraud by their loyal and trusted employees. These are personal friends, after all. Yet many small businesses are hit hard by fraud and can least afford the consequences. Most studies of fraud in small businesses have found that the average loss is well into six figures! You know, even in a friendly game of poker with our buddies, we always cut the deck before dealing the cards around the table. Your business, too, should put checks and balances in place to discourage dishonest practices and to uncover any fraud and theft as soon as possible.

And then there's the growing specter of hacks into the information databases of businesses. These intrusions are referred to as *cyber threats, hacks,* and *ransomware.* Hackers have broken into the computer information systems of many major companies, getting around the inadequate controls the businesses had in place. Interestingly, hackers haven't shown interest in accounting information per se. Rather, the hackers are after Social Security numbers, credit scores, home addresses, passwords, email addresses — mainly personal and private information. In addition, there's been a growing trend with ransomware where the perpetrator hacks a computer system to paralyze a company from operating, thus causing significant financial damage (and demanding a ransom payment to restore order).

We don't know of a computer database break-in for the purpose of manipulating or destroying accounting information — but a hacker could alter accounting information after breaking into a company's information system. The topic of cybercrime is beyond the scope of this book, other than to warn you about this serious threat that requires a whole new set of internal controls. A new class of forensic professionals has emerged who advise and assist businesses in coming to grips with cyber threats. These specialists include both accountants and IT (information technology) experts.

Double-Entry Accounting

Businesses and nonprofit entities use *double-entry accounting.* But we've never met an individual who used double-entry accounting in personal bookkeeping. Instead, individuals use single-entry accounting. For example, when you write a check, process an electronic payment, or make a payment on your credit card balance, you undoubtedly make an entry in your checkbook to decrease your bank balance. And that's it. You make just one entry — to decrease your checking account balance. It wouldn't occur to you to make a second, companion entry to decrease your credit card liability balance. Why? Because you don't keep a liability account for what you owe on your credit card. You depend on the credit card company to make an entry to decrease your balance.

REMEMBER

Businesses and nonprofit entities have to keep track of their liabilities as well as their assets. And they have to keep track of *all* sources of their assets. (Some part of their total assets comes from money invested by their owners, for example.) When a business writes a check or processes an ACH payment to pay one of its liabilities, it makes a two-sided (or double) entry — one to decrease its cash balance in the bank and the second to decrease the liability. This is double-entry accounting in action. Double-entry does *not* mean a transaction is recorded twice; it means both sides of the transaction are recorded at the same time.

TIP

The two-sided nature of business accounting is summarized in the *accounting equation,* which puts assets on one side (almost always on the left) and the sources of assets on the opposite side, as follows:

$$\$Assets = \$Liabilities + \$Capital + \$Retained\ Earnings$$

The equal sign means that for every dollar of assets, there's a dollar from one of the sources of assets on the right side of the accounting equation. Assets do not materialize out of nothing. Assets come from somewhere. There are three fundamental sources of assets: liabilities, capital invested in the business by its owners, and retained earnings (accumulated profit that has been earned but not distributed to its owners by the entity). Combining a business's capital and retained earnings gives you its *owners' equity,* or the *net worth* of the business.

The accounting equation is a condensed version of the balance sheet. The *balance sheet* is the financial statement that summarizes a business's assets on the one side and its liabilities plus its owners' equity on the other side. As we just mentioned, liabilities and owners' equity are the sources of the business's assets. Each source has different types of claims on the assets, which we explain in Chapter 7.

One main function of the bookkeeping/accounting system is to record all transactions of a business — every single last one. If you look at transactions through the lens of the accounting equation, there's a beautiful symmetry in transactions (well, beautiful to accountants at least). All transactions have a natural balance. The sum of financial effects on one side of a transaction equals the sum of financial effects on the other side. Thus, the name of the balance sheet — because in theory, the balance sheet should always be, well, in balance.

Suppose a business buys a new delivery truck for $65,000 and pays by check (how old-fashioned is that?). The truck asset account increases by the $65,000 cost of the truck, and cash in the bank decreases $65,000. Here's another example: A company borrows $2 million from its bank. Its cash in the bank increases by $2 million, and the liability for its note payable to the bank increases by the same amount.

Just one more example: Suppose a business suffers a loss from a tornado because some of its assets were not insured (dumb!). The assets destroyed by the tornado are written off (decreased to zero balances), and the amount of the loss decreases the owners' equity by the same amount. The loss works its way through the income statement but ends up as a decrease in retained earnings.

TIP

Virtually all business recordkeeping systems use *debits and credits* for making sure that both sides of transactions are recorded and for keeping the two sides of the accounting equation in balance. A change in an account is recorded as either a debit or a credit according to the rules in Table 3-1.

TABLE 3-1

Bookkeeping Rules for Debits and Credits

Account Type	Increase	Decrease
Asset accounts	Debit	Credit
Liability accounts	Credit	Debit
Owners' equity accounts	Credit	Debit

An increase in an asset is tagged as a debit; an increase in a liability or owners' equity account is tagged as a credit. Decreases are just the reverse. Following this scheme, the total of debits must equal the total of credits in recording every transaction. In brief: *Debits have to equal credits.* Isn't that clever? Well, the main point is that the method works. Debits and credits have been used for centuries. (A book published in 1494 describes how business traders and merchants of the day used debits and credits in their bookkeeping.)

Note: Sales revenue and expense accounts also follow debit and credit rules. Revenue increases owners' equity (and thus is a credit), and an expense decreases owners' equity (and thus is a debit).

Following the rules of debits and credits, asset accounts have debit balances, and liabilities and owners' equity accounts have credit balances. (Yes, a balance sheet account can have a wrong-way balance in unusual situations, such as cash having a credit balance because the business has written more checks than it has money for in its checking account.) The total of accounts with debit balances should equal the total of accounts with credit balances. When the total of debit balance accounts equals the total of credit balance accounts, the *books are in balance.*

WARNING

Even when the books are in balance, errors are still possible. The bookkeeper may have recorded debits or credits in the wrong accounts, or may have entered wrong amounts, or may have missed recording some transactions altogether. Having balanced books simply means that the total of accounts with debit balances equals the total of accounts with credit balances. The important thing is whether the books (the accounts) have *correct* balances, which depends on whether all transactions and other developments have been recorded correctly.

Juggling the Books to Conceal Embezzlement and Fraud

WARNING

Fraud and illegal practices occur in large corporations and in one-owner/manager-controlled small businesses — and in every size business in between. Some types of fraud are more common in small businesses, including *sales skimming* (not recording all sales revenue, to deflate the taxable income of the business and its owner) and the recording of personal expenses through the business (to make these expenses deductible for income tax). Some kinds of fraud are committed mainly by large businesses, including paying bribes to foreign officials and entering into illegal conspiracies to fix prices or divide the market. The purchasing managers in any size business can be tempted to accept kickbacks and under-the-table payoffs from vendors and suppliers.

Some years ago, my (coauthor John's) wife and I hosted a Russian professor who was a dedicated Communist. I asked him what surprised him the most on his first visit to the United States. Without hesitation, he answered, *"The Wall Street Journal."* I was puzzled. He then explained that he was amazed to read so many stories about business fraud and illegal practices in the most respected capitalist newspaper in the world. Many financial reporting fraud stories are on the front pages today, as they were when we wrote the previous editions of this book. And there are a number of stories of companies that agreed to pay large fines for illegal practices (usually without admitting guilt).

None of this is news to you. You know that fraud and illegal practices happen in the business world. Our point in bringing up this unpleasant topic is that fraud and illegal practices require manipulation of a business's accounts. For example, if a business pays a bribe, it doesn't record the amount in a bald-faced account called "bribery expense." Rather, the business disguises the payment by recording it in a legitimate expense account (such as "repairs and maintenance expense" or "legal expense"). If a business records sales revenue before sales have taken place (a not-uncommon type of financial reporting fraud), it does not record the false revenue in a separate account called "fictional sales revenue." The bogus sales are recorded in the regular sales revenue account.

Here's another example of an illegal practice. *Money laundering* involves taking money from illegal sources (such as drug dealing) and passing it through a business to make it look legitimate — to give the money a false identity. This money can hardly be recorded as "revenue from drug sales" in the accounts of the business. Also, if an employee embezzles money from the business, he has to cover his tracks by making false entries in the accounts or by not making entries that should be recorded.

REMEMBER

Manipulating accounts to conceal fraud, illegal activities, and embezzlement is generally called *juggling the accounts*. Another term you've probably heard is *cooking the books*. Although this term is sometimes used in the same sense of juggling the accounts, *cooking the books* typically refers to deliberate accounting fraud in which the main purpose is to produce financial statements that tell a better story than is supported by the facts. Now here's an irony: When crooks commit accounting fraud, they also need to know the real story, so they keep two sets of books — one for the fraud numbers and one for the real numbers.

WARNING

When the accounts have been juggled or the books have been cooked, the financial statements of the business are distorted, incorrect, and misleading. Lenders, other creditors, and the owners who have capital invested in the business rely on the company's financial statements. Also, a business's managers and board of directors (the group of people who oversee a business corporation) may be misled — assuming that they're not a party to the fraud — and may also have liability to third-party creditors and investors for their failure to catch the fraud. Creditors and investors who end up suffering losses have legal grounds to sue the managers and directors (and perhaps the independent auditors who did not catch the fraud) for damages suffered.

We think that most persons who engage in fraud also cheat on their federal income taxes; they don't declare the ill-gotten income. Needless to say, the IRS is on constant alert for fraud in federal income tax returns, both business and personal returns. The IRS has the authority to come in and audit the books of the business and also the personal income tax returns of its managers and investors. Conviction for income tax evasion is a felony, we might point out.

Chapter **4**

Accounting in the Digital Age

Over the past ten years, the rate of change in technological advancements clearly has been nothing short of mind-numbing. The computing power now possessed in a mobile format (cellphones, tablets, laptops, and yes, even watches and glasses) that allows for real-time access to data, information, articles, content, videos, and just about everything else has transformed how businesses operate, assess financial performances, manage employees, and interact with customers. These technology trends have been further amplified and accelerated by the Covid pandemic that hit the world in early 2020 (and is still present as we write this book). The move toward remote working and learning has pushed what was once a luxury or nice-to-have (that is, I can work from home once a week) to a must-have (employees demanding that employers provide work-from-home or remote-working solutions).

Nowhere is this trend more prevalent than in the heavy data processing and financial transaction side of businesses, including information technology operations (such as IT or MIS), financial analysis and planning, and accounting. This chapter is dedicated to covering critical topics related to performing and managing the accounting function in the digital age by evaluating the topics from two perspectives:

>> First, what are the latest technological trends or tools that are available to businesses to assist with managing the accounting functions more efficiently?

>> Second, what risks are present with these technological trends or tools, and how does the accounting function need to adapt or evolve to manage these risks?

Noting a Few Foundational Accounting Concepts Related to Technology

REMEMBER

Before we dive into the latest and greatest technological trends and tools, we draw your attention to these base accounting concepts that never go out of style and always remain the foundation of accounting:

>> **CART:** Every accounting system, whether 100 percent automated or still being maintained in the dark ages on green ledger sheets, should always strive to produce *complete, accurate, reliable,* and *timely* financial information on which to base sound business decisions. This has been, is, and will always be the primary goal and objective of accounting systems.

>> **SGA:** Accounting systems, whether maintained in the cloud or on the ground, must be designed, controlled, and managed to ensure that company assets are always safeguarded. Never has this been more important because SGA, which stands for *safeguarding assets,* relates to making sure physical assets are properly insured or access is restricted from theft, and more importantly, invaluable company digital data (such as vital customer sales and operating information) is protected from both criminals and competitors.

>> **GIGO or DIGO:** The old saying of *garbage in, garbage out* is more important now than ever before. This is why we offer the acronym DIGO, which stands for *data in, garbage out.* The tendency in the modern accounting era is to assume that if the data flowing into the accounting system has been digitized and/or is supported by blockchain-enabled digital ledgers, then the data is more apt to be correct and free of errors. Don't make this rookie mistake; errors are just as likely to occur with digitized business transactions and records, but if the flow of these records (through the accounting and financial information reporting system) is left unchecked, they can pollute a financial

reporting system very quickly and create even more damage if the output reaches decision-makers who ultimately base decisions on erroneous information.

>> **Art versus science:** The profession of accounting is governed by numerous organizations (for example, the Financial Accounting Standards Board, or FASB) that have for decades assisted with documenting guidelines, policies, and procedures for accountants to utilize when preparing company financial information (that is, GAAP — generally accepted accounting principles). Further, colleges, universities, trade schools, and other institutions attempt to educate accountants to apply the GAAP in a consistent manner. But don't forget that accounting still remains a profession that incorporates a significant number of opinions, subjectivity, and for lack of a better term, creativity (the art side of the equation) that technology most likely will never be able to replace.

REMEMBER

The advances made in technology and the digital economy have had a profound and positive impact on the accounting function. These advances have made life so much easier on so many fronts for accountants; one of the single biggest benefits has been allowing accountants to shift their focus and efforts from wasting time on processing data, paperwork, and financial transactions to being able to analyze and interpret accounting and financial reports and data. This is undoubtedly a huge benefit but one that can be achieved only by keeping in mind two critical concepts:

>> Data integrity has been, is, and will always be of utmost importance; in today's rapid-paced global economic environment, DIGO (data in, garbage out) is not acceptable and it can be fatal to a business.

>> Developing and implementing proper accounting controls, policies, and procedures to protect the security of all financial data and information has reached an entirely new level given the risks associated with digitizing source documents. As we note in the next section, security, security, and security are the critical buzzwords with accounting systems and software.

REMEMBER

As you work your way through the remainder of this chapter, we want to reinforce that the current technology-based tools available to accountants are absolutely wonderful to have and use, and they have, without question, made accounting systems more efficient. But these technology-based tools have added an entirely new layer of financial and operational management risks that must be proactively managed to achieve our two primary goals of CART and SGA. Remember the old saying "The more things change, the more things stay the same"? This certainly applies to the business accounting function today, tomorrow, or 20 years from now.

Using Accounting Software in the Cloud and on the Ground

It's possible, though not likely, that a very small business would keep its books the old-fashioned way: Record all transactions and do all the other steps of the bookkeeping cycle with pen and paper and by making handwritten entries using the old green ledger sheets. However, even a small business has a relatively large number of transactions that have to be recorded in journals and accounts, to say nothing about the end-of-period steps in the bookkeeping cycle (covered in Chapter 3).

When mainframe computers were introduced in the 1950s and 1960s, one of their very first uses was for accounting chores. However, only large businesses could afford these electronic behemoths. Smaller businesses didn't use computers for accounting until some years after personal computers came along in the 1980s. A bewildering array of computer software packages is available today for small, medium, and large businesses. Some larger corporations develop and utilize their own computer-based accounting systems (that is, they write their own code), but more and more large companies are utilizing ERP (enterprise resource planning) systems to support their accounting requirements. Indeed, we identified over 1,000 accounting software systems listed on the Software Advice website; check out the current numbers at www.softwareadvice.com/accounting.

Many businesses do their accounting work in-house, on the ground at their own locations. They use on-the-premises computers, develop or buy accounting software, and control their own backup files. They may use an outside firm to handle certain accounting chores, particularly payroll. Alternatively, a business can do some or most of its accounting in the cloud. The term *cloud* refers to large-scale offsite computer servers that a business connects with over the internet. The cloud can be used simply as the backup storage location for the company's accounting records. Cloud servers have the reputation of being very difficult to break into by hackers. Cloud providers offer a variety of accounting and business software and services that are too varied to discuss here. In short, a business can do almost all its accounting in the cloud. Of course, the business still needs very strong controls over the transmission of accounting information to and from the cloud. More and more businesses are switching to the cloud for doing more and more of their accounting tasks.

This has become an increasing trend during the Covid pandemic, when many businesses were forced to close their offices and staff worked from home. Having data in the cloud has made it much more accessible to all who are responsible for that information and others who need access to it for strategic or other purposes. Most experts expect the trend of going to the cloud to continue.

Except for larger entities that employ their own accounting software and information technology experts, other businesses find that they need the consultation of outside IT (information technology) experts in choosing, implementing, upgrading, and replacing accounting software.

REMEMBER

If we were giving a talk to owners/managers of small to medium-sized businesses, we would offer the following words of advice about accounting software:

>> Choose your accounting software carefully. It's hard to pull up stakes and switch to another software package. Changing even just one module, such as payroll or inventory, in your accounting software can be quite difficult.

>> In evaluating accounting software, you and your accountant should consider three main factors: ease of use, whether it has the particular features and functionalities you need, and the likelihood that the vendor will continue in business and be around to update and make improvements in the software.

>> In real estate, the prime concern is "location, location, location." The watchwords in accounting software are "security, security, security." You need very tight controls over all aspects of using the accounting software and over who is authorized to make changes in any of the modules of the accounting software.

>> Even when using advanced, sophisticated accounting software, a business must design the specialized reports it needs for its various managers and make sure that these reports are generated correctly from the accounting database.

>> Never forget "garbage in, garbage out" (see the previous section). Data-entry errors can be a serious problem in computer-based accounting systems. Here's a personal example: My (coauthor John's) retirement fund manager entered the birthdate of my spouse incorrectly. Because of a common transposition error, my spouse was recorded as 27 years younger than me. This mistake would have caused us grief with the IRS and resulted in our receiving much less monthly retirement income than we were entitled to. Fortunately, we had already calculated the correct amount, and after many telephone calls, we got this straightened out.

It's next to impossible to eliminate data-entry errors altogether. Even barcode readers make mistakes, and barcode tags themselves may have been tampered with. A business should adopt strong controls to minimize these input errors as well as strong internal controls for the verification of data entry.

>> Make sure your accounting software leaves good audit trails (which you need for management control) for your CPA when they audit your financial statements and for the IRS when it decides to audit your income tax returns. The lack of good audit trails looks very suspicious to the IRS.

>> Online accounting systems that permit remote input and access over the internet or a local area network with multiple users present special security problems. Think twice before putting any part of your accounting system online (and if you do, institute airtight controls).

TIP

Smaller businesses and even many medium-sized businesses don't have the budget to hire full-time information system and information technology (IT) specialists. They use consultants to help them select accounting software packages, install software, and get it up and running. Like other computer software, accounting programs are frequently revised and updated. A consultant can help keep a business's accounting software up to date, correct flaws and security weaknesses in the program, and take advantage of its latest features.

Controlling and Protecting Money Flows in the Electronic Age

For most businesses, the most targeted asset for theft is good old-fashioned cash. The reason is simple: It's the most liquid asset for criminals to steal and dispose of. Types of cash can range significantly:

>> A small amount of currency that resides in a cash register at a retailer

>> Currency that a bank keeps on hand in a bank teller's drawer

>> Millions of dollars of cash that sits in a bank account (or accounts) of a major corporation

>> Cryptocurrencies that are kept in a virtual wallet (although there is doubt as to whether cryptocurrencies are in fact cash)

Needless to say, the use of physical cash has been significantly reduced over the years as other forms of electronic payments replace the need to exchange physical cash. Per a report issued by the Federal Reserve Bank of San Francisco in 2020, consumers used cash in 26 percent of all transactions in 2019, down from 30 percent in 2017. Looking out further (although the exact numbers are not available yet), it is anticipated that the use of cash will see another major decrease because of Covid, given the explosion in direct-to-consumer business models and direct delivery companies such as Amazon, Grubhub, and others.

The reason we highlight these trends is not to state the obvious but rather to emphasize that while the form in which payments are made is changing (from cash to electronic), the sheer volume of electronic payments has exploded over the past ten years. Per a study offered by the CPA Practice Advisor, global digital payments are anticipated to reach $6.6 trillion by 2021, a 40 percent increase in just two years. So basically, every operating business has had to adapt and evolve to the changing landscape to process and receive electronic payments. This, in turn, has driven the requirement of companies to ensure they develop and implement proper policies and procedures to safeguard company assets because criminals are going to follow the cash; if they can't steal it from a retail store, they'll devise systems to steal money electronically.

All companies need to process payments on two fronts:

>> For cash inflows, companies must ensure that customers can remit payments for the goods or services purchased in the most efficient and friendly manner possible.

>> For cash outflows, companies must devise systems to ensure their vendors, suppliers, and employees are paid in an accurate and timely fashion.

For large businesses (think of Walmart and Amazon), the ebb and flow of payment processing (both inflows and outflows) can range in the tens of thousands of transactions daily, so these organizations have developed extremely sophisticated systems to track these payment flows. For small to medium-sized businesses, processing electronic payments is just as important and valuable to the organization to which they devised specific strategies and third-party relationships to assist with managing payment flows (and controlling risks). Find out more about digitally protecting money flows in the following sections.

Processing payroll

Most businesses rely on third-party payroll processing organizations (for example, ADP) to manage the task of paying employees. There are so many advantages to using third-party payroll processing organizations that the reasons are almost too many to list, but the primary pluses are centered in the following:

>> Ease in complying with federal and state payroll tax regulations by expert third parties

>> Processing direct deposit of payroll to the employees' bank account (to avoid issuing actual checks)

>> External control of sensitive employee pay information by a third party

>> Direct online access to payroll records when pay rates, withholdings, and so on need to be changed

Long gone are the days of calling in payroll to your account rep on a semi-monthly basis; these days, you simply log on and update employee pay information in real time.

Controlling bank accounts

Bank account information needs to be provided to your customers (so they can process electronic payments to your business) and to vendors and suppliers (so they can receive payments from your business). With so much bank account information floating around in the cyberworld, it can be very helpful to set up unique bank accounts used for specific fund control purposes.

For example, a company may have a unique bank account set up for the sole purpose of receiving customer payments. This account is monitored every day and the excess funds are "swept" or consolidated into the company's primary operating account. The same concept holds for payroll accounts as well as vendor payment accounts because these may be funded with just enough money to cover the payments being made. The idea is to avoid concentrating funds in an account that may have more risk of being accessed from unwanted third parties or criminals. If a loss is realized, the loss can be minimized with only a limited amount of funds exposed at any time. The idea is to receive and sweep (customer payments) and remit and fund (vendor/supplier payments).

Surveying bank forms of electronic payments

Let's begin with processing payments via the traditional banking route, which includes using a wide range of options:

>> Completing transfers via bank wires (domestic or international)

>> Processing ACH (Automated Clearing House) transfers

>> Processing bank transfers (you and your vendor both use the same bank so you can transfer funds internally, within the bank)

>> Using bank-provided vendor pay-bill systems (a vendor wants to be paid with a check, which you process electronically online through the bank so it generates and distribute the physical check, alleviating the need for checks to be generated in-house)

REMEMBER

Other forms of bank payments are available as well, but the general idea here is to leverage the extensive knowledge and security the bank has set up and implemented to process electronic payments in a tightly controlled and secure environment. Banks are highly regulated and operate in an industry that demands the highest level of trust from the public. Banks have, over the decades, devised payment processing systems that are some of the securest in the world, so why not utilize this expertise to protect your hard-earned cash?

Checking out non-bank forms of electronic payments

It seems that every day a new form of electronic payment is being devised. These include using credit cards, debit cards, PayPal, Apple Pay, Amazon Pay, Venmo, and similar types of electronic payment services. The reasons companies use these types of electronic payment services vary widely:

>> A customer paying with a credit card to earn "points" (for travel or cash back)

>> A business paying with a credit card to create separation between its bank and the vendor (and use the financing "float")

>> A large company such as Amazon making sure that every form of customer payment can be accepted to maximize the sales opportunity (to eliminate any reason for the customer to terminate the sale)

The point is that non-bank forms of electronic payments are here to stay, and you can expect them to continue to increase in use as the world moves rapidly toward a cashless economy.

From a business perspective, it's almost impossible to build payment systems that don't incorporate the use of non-bank forms of payments because this has simply become the norm in today's economy. This doesn't mean that non-bank payments have no risk. Plenty of traps and problems may arise when using non-bank forms of electronic payments, including these:

>> Having to absorb merchant fees when accepting customer payments electronically (for example, Visa or PayPal charge the merchant 2.5 percent to process the payment)

>> Controlling consumer personal information (like credit card numbers) that could possibly be hacked and exposed

>> Having to reconcile cash receipts from multiple electronic payment providers against your sales records (to match and properly apply cash receipts)

>> Maintaining agreements with multiple electronic payment providers

REMEMBER

The management and accounting issue is straightforward: The benefit of processing payments electronically must be analyzed and compared with the associated risks and costs. This may seem like a relatively simple cost–benefit analysis (on the surface), where the benefits of ease of customer payment are apparent, but the costs need to be thoroughly understood because they relate to not just a stated "processing fee" but also the risks a company takes with managing large amounts of data (and the company's responsibility to protect this data).

Using enhanced accounting controls

One important point we want to make on the electronic payments front is the need for businesses to develop, implement, and execute enhanced accounting controls, policies, and procedures to proactively manage this new environment. Here, we offer four examples of how companies have developed enhanced controls:

>> **Using real-time reconciliations:** A direct-to-consumer company may generate hundreds of thousands of dollars of sales during a peak holiday season such as Black Friday. When this happens, literally hundreds of individual sales are processed with most payments coming from credit cards, debit cards, PayPal, and other sources. To ensure that all customer sales are matched with customer payments, real-time reconciliations (daily or even more frequently) are performed to ensure that all payments are received and recorded correctly.

>> **Offloading data risks:** Companies may rely on front-end or consumer-facing computer platforms such as Shopify to act as a retail storefront on the web. On top of a company like Shopify providing a well-developed and sophisticated platform (which you don't have to create), Shopify can assist with processing the electronic payments so that vital customer personal information such as a full credit card number is maintained by Shopify (and protected with their security systems); your company doesn't have to maintain it. And since you don't maintain this information, the risk of data hacks or breaches is reduced, lowering your financial risk and exposure.

>> **Monitoring frequency:** In the old days, a bank account could be reviewed and reconciled once a month. Not so today, as bank activity and transactions are constantly monitored for unusual or suspicious activity on a daily, hourly, or even real-time basis. Working closely with your bank and merchant account provider to develop systems to actively monitor financial transactions represents a big win for both parties.

>> **Securing cyber-insurance:** Specific forms of insurance are now widely available for purchase to assist with the financial losses that may arise from data breaches, hacks, and so on. Simply put, a cyber-insurance policy, also referred to as "cyber-risk insurance" or "cyber-liability insurance" coverage, is a financial product that enables businesses to transfer the costs involved with recovery from a cyber-related security breach or similar events. Twenty years ago, this type of insurance was a "nice to have" item. Today, it's a must-have.

CONSIDERING THE FUTURE OF CRYPTOCURRENCIES

We would be remiss if we didn't include a brief discussion on the use of cryptocurrencies, such as Bitcoin and Ethereum (two of the more popular choices) and associated blockchain technology. The first item to consider is whether cryptocurrencies are even a currency; today, they are not considered currency but are referred to as an asset class (more appropriate in today's environment). Given that cryptocurrencies do not represent legal tender of a government or country, have highly volatile price environments, are subject to technology risks (because they basically represent ownership of a series of digits), are not widely accepted as a form of payment, don't have the global economic markets of well-established currencies (such as the U.S. dollar), and may be subject to significant government regulations, it's difficult, at the time of this book's publication, to classify cryptocurrencies as actual currencies on par with the U.S. dollar, Japanese yen, Chinese yuan, and the European euro. Rather, cryptocurrencies are still functioning at the capacity of a speculative asset class that is rapidly evolving in the new digital-based economy.

However, cryptocurrencies in one form or another will most likely find their footing down the road to become more widely accepted, stable, and able to operate within an equitable market (for buying, selling, and trading), thus eventually becoming a potential additional non-bank form of electronic payments (covered earlier in this chapter). Here's some advice on the cryptocurrency front:

- Educate yourself thoroughly on the pros and cons of using this form of electronic payment.

- Tread lightly to start; the cryptocurrency space most likely will remain volatile for the foreseeable future.

Managing the Accounting Function in the On-Demand World

To close this chapter, we cover a variety of items related to managing the accounting function in a world that now is built on accessing large amounts of data or information, efficiency in storing this data or information, speed in accessing the information, and widespread availability to the information. The topics highlighted in the following sections present a basic overview or sampling of the types of changes that are occurring at breakneck speed as the old days of the green eye-shaded bean counter give way to a tech-enabled financial information provider with access to vital information at the touch of a button.

Source documentation

In the olden days, most source documentation was stored in a "hard format" (such as paper-based storage systems that required large amounts of space). Not so today because the transition to paperless storage systems is now the norm rather than the exception. Companies actively maintain accounting records such as customer sales orders and invoices, shipping or packing slips, purchase orders, vendor/supplier invoices, employee wage records, third-party contracts, and the list goes on and on in a digital format. Basically, anything that was paper-based is now being stored in an electronic format (such as a PDF, JPEG, or PNG) or computer coded.

The good news is that the storage of source documentation is much more efficient, cheaper, and more readily accessible. The bad news is that with so much source documentation available electronically, if proper security and access controls have not been implemented, the risk of vital documents being accessed by unauthorized personnel or outside parties has become much more elevated (see the next section).

Data rooms

Data rooms or internal data centers are virtual locations where basically all digitized documentation resides. Companies such as Dropbox specialize in helping companies organize and safeguard almost any type of digital company data, ranging from simple customer orders or copies of vendor invoices to confidential company formation documentation, third-party agreements, and the like. Businesses have the option to outsource digital documentation storage to a company like Dropbox or manage this process internally by maintaining their own computer systems. Either way, convenience, security, and accessibility represent advantages of using data rooms because controls can be built in to give different parties access to different levels of company documentation. For example, a company may want to give its human resources manager access to employee contracts and pay records (in a specific subfolder maintained in the data room) but would not want to provide this person access to critical financing documentation.

WARNING

Well-developed and managed (we cannot emphasize this point enough) data rooms are now the norm, but a word of caution is warranted. Proactive management of data rooms is essential to ensure that only authorized personnel have access to the correct folder or subfolder of source documentation.

Financial reporting

Review and control of input and output is more important now than ever before. With online, cloud-based accounting systems, it can be tempting to simply push a button for a pre-formatted report, and voilà, just like that, out comes a financial report such as an income statement or balance sheet for review with the management team. We cannot tell you how many times we've seen underqualified or inexperienced parties access the accounting system, produce a financial report, and think they have become an expert because the accounting system is just so easy to use. Worse yet, they then distribute it to a third party without thinking about it twice. (Translation: This is a fatal error.)

REMEMBER

The problem is parties who are not qualified accountants or financial professionals may not understand that critical adjustments and/or financial transactions must be captured in the accounting system to ensure that CART (complete, accurate, reliable, and timely) financial reports are ready and available for management review. We cannot emphasize enough that tight controls must be maintained by a business to ensure that critical financial reports and statements are released at the appropriate time, after review by qualified parties, and distributed only to the right parties, supported by a reliable analysis (to assist with understanding the financial results).

Flash reports and KPIs

The real-time economy we live and operate in has resulted in an explosion of what are referred to as flash reports (targeted, high-frequency, compressed reports) that generally focus on highlighting a company's KPIs (key performance indicators). For example, a direct-to-consumer company may launch a new social media advertising campaign on Instagram over a three-hour period during a holiday shopping window and wants to have access to sales data from different advertising strategies instantaneously (in other words, a quick flash report). This real situation happens every day.

REMEMBER

What is important to remember about this type of reporting is that the financial and operational data doesn't always originate from the accounting system but may come from a consumer-facing sales technology platform or other type of company technology management system. Here, the accounting function needs to "extend" beyond the base accounting system to develop and implement controls that ensure that the financial information being reported from another source technology platform is consistent with the financial transactions being captured and reported in the accounting system. Again, we cannot tell you how many horror stories have resulted from two different technology systems not being properly monitored and reconciled to ensure consistency and accuracy of financial reporting. These days, financial information is seemingly anywhere and everywhere and easily accessible, which runs the risk of creating an exponential increase in reporting errors and mistakes (if proper controls and security have not been established).

Accounting and financial analysis tools

Countless financial and accounting technology tools, resources, platforms, systems, and the like are available today to assist companies with managing their business. These tools range from the likes of the ever-popular Excel or Google Docs to very specific software platforms that sit on top of accounting systems to help generate periodic financial statements. It would be pointless to attempt to list every financial or accounting technology-based tool available; by the time we prepared the list, a quarter of the systems would be gone, replaced by new solutions.

REMEMBER

These tools are very valuable to the accounting and financial groups within a business but must be managed closely for a couple of reasons:

>> First, the business financial information contained in these tools (such as an Excel spreadsheet used to house a company's financial forecasts) tends to be very confidential and needs to be tightly controlled.

>> Second, these tools often are very easy to use, update, change, edit, and so on (by multiple parties), and when changes are made, audit trails (the what and why and how of changes) are often sacrificed.

Disciplined accounting management of these tools is just as important as with the company's primary accounting system used to capture transactional and financial data.

» Comparing partnerships, limited
liability companies, and sole
proprietorships

» Expanding on business corporations
and classes of stock

Chapter **5**

Recognizing the Legal and Accounting Entity

The enterprise being accounted for is called the *accounting entity*. An accounting entity can be a business, a not-for-profit (NFP) association, a church, a social club, a government organization, or what have you. There are many kinds of accounting entities. In this chapter, we focus on profit-motivated business entities, although other types of accounting entities are interesting creatures that have unique features and accounting issues. But let's get back to business here.

Chapter 3 explains the accounting equation and notes that this accounting axiom is echoed in the balance sheet of a business — assets on one side, liabilities plus owners' equity on the other. This chapter, along with Chapter 18, which dives into capitalizing a business, explains the right side of the balance sheet, emphasizing owners' equity. Every business entity has an owners' equity structure of some sort. Financial report readers should definitely know which configuration of owners' equity the business uses.

Asset titles in a balance sheet are largely self-explanatory (although there are some unusual titles, to be sure). Without knowing much accounting, you can get a good sense about the assets listed in a balance sheet — although you may not be certain about the values reported for the assets. Also, you'd probably get a good sense of the liabilities reported in a balance sheet, but you might hit a wall when you got to the owners' equity section.

A business may have only one type of ownership, or it may have two or more classes of ownership. There isn't a one-size-fits-all model of owners' equity. Owners' equity starts with the business securing capital — persuading individuals, investors, or other legal entities to invest some of their hard-earned money to the business. Chapter 18 gives you the details on raising capital.

The obvious reason for investing in a business rather than putting your money in a safer type of investment is the potential for greater rewards. As one of the owners of a business, you're entitled to your fair share of the business's profit, as are the other owners, of course. You may not get as big a piece of the profit pie as you're expecting. There could be claims that rank ahead of you, and you may not see *any* profit after all these claims are satisfied. The manner in which the profit is divided among owners depends on the business's legal structure of its owners' equity.

This chapter explains how the legal form of a business dictates whether it pays income taxes at the legal entity level or at the individual ownership level. In one type of legal structure, the business pays income taxes at the entity level *and* its owners pay a second layer of income taxes if they receive a dividend from the business's profit. In this case, Uncle Sam gets two bites of the profit apple, which obviously is not desirable.

TIP

We're not lawyers, but we certainly appreciate the need for lawyers. We don't offer legal advice in this chapter; however, we do mention in several places the need to consult a lawyer, especially in founding a new business. Nor do we offer tax advice here. The publisher of this book (John Wiley & Sons, Inc.) offers several income tax books under the general imprint of J.K. Lasser that we recommend for your attention.

Being Aware of the Legal Roots of Business Entities

REMEMBER

One of the most important aspects of our legal system, from the business and economic point of view, is that the law enables *entities* to be created for conducting business activities. These entities are separate and distinct from the individual owners of the business. Business entities have many of the rights of individuals. Business entities can own property and enter into contracts, for example. In starting a business venture, one of the first things the founders have to do is select which type of legal structure to use — which usually requires the services of a lawyer who knows the laws of the state in which the business is organized.

A business may have just one owner or multiple owners. A one-owner business may choose to operate as a sole proprietorship or can operate as a corporation; a multi-owner business must choose to be a corporation, a partnership, or a limited liability company (LLC). There are millions of entities of each type in the American economy. There are other types of legal entities as well — see the sidebar "Limiting liability: Professional corporations and LLPs" later in this chapter.

No legal structure is inherently better than another; which one is right for a particular business is something that the business's founders need to decide at the time of starting the business. In the following sections, we provide a summary of the five basic types of business legal entities that are most commonly utilized in the United States to operate for-profit businesses. We should clarify that other legal forms are available for governmental and nonprofit organizations, but for the purposes of our analysis, we focus on for-profit businesses only. As previously noted, no one legal entity is inherently better than another; the legal entity choice really comes down to the company's business plan, desires of the owners, and need to raise capital. Our discussion progresses from the simplest business legal entity form to more complex forms.

Sole proprietorship

The simplest and least costly type of business legal entity is the sole proprietorship ("SP"). This type of business legal entity is just like it sounds: A single person starts a business and has no other partners, investors, or shareholders. Basically, any United States citizen can start an SP with a business idea and a valid Social Security number. Of course, local regulations may apply that require a business permit or license to be obtained, but in general, SPs are the easiest to start (as well as being very inexpensive because limited legal fees should be incurred).

WARNING

On the downside, it should be noted that SPs do not offer any legal protection or shield (from being considered a separate business entity such as a corporation or LLC) from potential legal action because there is no distinction made between the individual owner and the SP using this business legal form. Further, SPs cannot raise equity capital from another party; by definition, this would terminate the SP status (because more than one owner would be present). SPs are best designed for micro or very small businesses that have relatively simply business plans and low operating risks (from a liability standpoint).

Partnerships

Partnerships generally come in two forms — general partnerships and limited partnerships. As the name indicates, partnerships infer that multiple owners or "partners" are equity stakeholders in the operating entity. The number and type of partners can vary significantly by the type of business entity, how much capital is required, the type of industry the business operates within, and so on:

>> A general partnership is treated as a separate business legal entity by the taxing authorities, but it should be noted that similar to SPs in the previous section, there is no legal liability shield; each general partner has unlimited personal liability. This represents a significant risk with general partnerships and an advantage of corporations and LLCs (covered later in this chapter).

>> Limited partnerships are usually operated by a general partner with the limited partners providing equity capital only. The advantage of a limited partnership is that the limited partners can generally limit their financial exposure to just their initial investment, assuming they maintain a passive role in the investment with no active management involvement (because the limited partnership structure provides a liability shield to these investors).

Partnerships are relatively easy to set up but do require additional support from legal counsel to ensure any governing documents (as to how the partnership will be operated and managed) are set up correctly. This creates added expenses to form the partnership, but we want to emphasize that making sure the partnership is set up correctly from day one is well worth the added costs. Partnerships can raise capital from multiple sources, but some limitations may discourage investments from certain parties. In general, partnerships are often utilized to target certain business opportunities, often in real estate development or passive asset investment activities.

S corporations

S corporations are the simplest form of a corporation offering liability protection (because the S corporation is viewed as a separate entity for legal purposes). S corporations are relatively easy and inexpensive to form; although legal counsel is generally retained to help form an S corporation, the initial governing documents of the S corporation, including the articles of incorporation and bylaws, tend to be boilerplate and relatively straightforward to prepare. In addition, S corporations are treated as "pass through" entities for income taxation purposes, which means that profits and losses from the entity are allocated to the owners on a prorated basis and taxed only once, at the individual owner level (avoiding double-taxation risks associated with C corporations). Here we have a legal entity that offers a liability shield and tax advantages, and is relatively easy and cheap to form (all positives).

 The primary downsides to operating as an S corporation are based in the equity flexibility:

WARNING

- » S corporations can have only one class of stock (all shareholders are treated equally with voting and profit distribution rights), whereas LLCs and C corporations, covered later in this chapter, can have multiple classes of ownership or stocks (with different rights).

- » S corporations are limited to having only individuals, trusts, and estates as shareholders, whereas other legal entities such as LLCs or C corporations are restricted from investing in the S corporation (translation, no institutional investors).

- » S corporations are limited to 100 domestic individual shareholders (no foreigners).

Given these restrictions, S corporations are generally utilized by small and medium-sized businesses that are closely held and don't need to access large tranches of equity capital from sophisticated funding sources.

Limited liability companies (LLCs)

Limited liability companies (LLCs) have become quite popular over the past two decades because they offer a significant amount of attractive features to business operators and external investors. Investors in LLCs are generally referred to as "members" that own units as opposed to shareholders that own stock. The advantages of an LLC are centered in the liability shield, income tax management, and capital raising flexibility:

- » LLCs provide a liability shield to the equity owners (similar to corporations) that limits, in most cases, the risk of loss to their actual investment.

- » LLCs can take advantage of various income tax rules and regulations to allocate profits and losses in the most advantageous manner possible.

- » LLCs can secure capital from almost any qualified investor or party, ranging from an individual to another LLC to a C corporation, and can structure different types or tranches of equity, such as common and preferred (thus providing it more flexibility when raising capital).

WARNING

The biggest drawbacks to forming an LLC is centered in the fact that the company must draft an operating agreement that spells out how the entity will be managed and operated. This can be a lengthy, somewhat complex, and expensive document to prepare, requiring qualified legal counsel advice and support — and that can get expensive. This type of legal entity is more expensive to form and complex to operate; it's best utilized for businesses that will require larger amounts of capital from different sources (and looking for different protections) and that will be operating more diversified and complex business models.

C corporations

The final type of legal entity we summarize is the C corporation. When you look at Wall Street and listed publicly traded companies (as well as the largest privately owned businesses), they are almost always structured as C corporations. The clear benefits of C corporations are centered on the liability shield as well as maximum flexibility when raising capital:

>> As with LLCs and S corporations (covered earlier in this chapter), C corporations offer a liability shield because they are viewed as a separate legal entity.

>> C corporations have almost no restrictions on what types of parties or groups from which they can raise funding, and that may include venture capitalists, pension funds, private equity groups, LLCs, foreign businesses, hedge funds, and so on.

>> C corporations can offer multiple classes of equity, including different classes of common stock (with different voting rights), preferred stock or equities, common stock options or warrants, and a variety of other types of equity. In fact, you may find a large C corporation that has two classes of common stock outstanding, a half dozen preferred stock classes, and a wide range of stock options and warrants.

WARNING

However, C corporations also have a couple of drawbacks:

>> These entities tend to have much more complex equity structures, which can be confusing to understand and also very expensive (from a legal and regulatory perspective) to maintain.

>> The income tax benefits associated with the pass-through nature of taxable income and losses is not available to the C corporation, which exposes it to potential double-taxation risks. For example, if the C corporation earned a $1 billion taxable profit, its federal income tax expense would be $210 million (based on 2020 income tax rates of 21 percent). If the C corporation then elected to issue a dividend to the shareholders, the dividend would be subject to income tax at the recipient's effective income tax rate. Hence, the risk of double taxation, once at the company taxable income level and again at the individual recipient level.

C corporations are best utilized by the largest and most complex business organizations that have significant capital requirements and also diverse business operations (that may span the globe).

Going It Alone: Sole Proprietorships

A *sole proprietorship* is basically the business arm of an individual who has decided not to carry on their business activity as a separate legal entity (as a corporation, partnership, or limited liability company). This is the default when you don't establish a separate legal entity.

REMEMBER

A sole proprietorship is not a separate entity; it's like the front porch of a house — attached to the house but a distinct area. You may be a sole proprietor of a business without knowing it! An individual may do house repair work on a part-time basis or be a full-time barber who operates on their own. Both activities are included in the broad definition of sole proprietorships. Whenever you regularly provide services for a fee, sell things at a flea market, or engage in any business activity whose primary purpose is to make profit, you're a sole proprietor. If you carry on business activity to make profit or income, the IRS requires that you file a separate Schedule C, "Profit or Loss From Business," with your annual individual income tax return. Schedule C summarizes your income and expenses from your sole proprietorship business.

WARNING

As the sole owner (proprietor), you have *unlimited liability,* meaning that if your business can't pay all its liabilities, the creditors to whom your business owes money can come after your personal assets. Many part-time entrepreneurs may not know this or may put it out of their minds, but this is a big risk to take. We have friends who are part-time business consultants, and they operate their consulting businesses as sole proprietorships. If they're sued for giving bad advice, all their personal assets are at risk — though they may be able to buy malpractice insurance to cover these losses.

Obviously, a sole proprietorship has no other owners to prepare financial statements for, but the proprietor should still prepare these statements to know how their business is doing. Banks usually require financial statements from sole proprietors who apply for loans.

TIP

One other piece of advice for sole proprietors: You don't have to separate invested capital from retained earnings like corporations do and keep two separate accounts. But you should still keep these two accounts for owners' equity — not only for the purpose of tracking the business, but for the benefit of any future buyers of the business as well.

Differentiating Partnerships and Limited Liability Companies

Suppose you're starting a new business with one or more other owners, but you don't want it to be a corporation. You can choose to create a *partnership* or a *limited liability company*, which are the main alternatives to the corporate form of business.

REMEMBER

A partnership is also called a *firm*. You don't see this term used to refer to a corporation or limited liability company nearly as often as you see it refer to a partnership. The term *firm* connotes an association of a group of individuals working together in a business or professional practice.

Looking at important features

Compared with the relatively rigid structure of corporations, the partnership and limited liability company forms of legal entities allow the division of management authority, profit sharing, and ownership rights among the owners to be very flexible. Here are the key features of these two legal structures:

>> **Partnerships:** Partnerships avoid the double-taxation feature that corporations are subject to. Partnerships also differ from corporations with respect to owners' liability. A partnership's owners fall into two categories:

- **General partners** are subject to *unlimited liability*. If a business can't pay its debts, its creditors can reach into general partners' personal assets. General partners have the authority and responsibility to manage the business. They're roughly equivalent to the president and other high-level managers of a business corporation. The general partners usually divide authority and responsibility among themselves, and often they elect one member of their group as the senior general partner or elect a small executive committee to make major decisions.

- **Limited partners** escape the unlimited liability that the general partners have hanging around their necks. Limited partners are not responsible, as individuals, for the liabilities of the partnership entity. These junior partners have ownership rights to the business's profit, but they don't generally participate in the high-level management of the business. A partnership must have one or more general partners; not all partners can be limited partners.

  Many large partnerships copy some of the management features of the corporate form — for example, a senior partner who serves as chair of the general partners' executive committee acts in much the same way as the chair of a corporation's board of directors.

In most partnerships, an individual partner can't sell his interest to an outsider without the consent of all the other partners. You can't just buy your way into a partnership; the other partners have to approve your joining the partnership. In contrast, you can buy stock shares and thereby become part owner of a corporation without the approval of the other stockholders.

>> **Limited liability company (LLC):** The LLC is an alternative type of business entity. An LLC is like a corporation regarding limited liability, and it's like a partnership regarding the flexibility of dividing profit among the owners. An LLC can elect to be treated either like a partnership or as a corporation for federal income tax purposes. Usually, a tax expert should be consulted on this choice.

The key advantage of the LLC legal form is its flexibility — especially regarding how profit and management authority are determined. For example, an LLC permits the founders of the business to put up, say, only 10 or 20 percent of the money to start a business venture while keeping all management authority in their hands. The other investors share in profit but not necessarily in proportion to their invested capital.

LLCs have much more flexibility than corporations, but this flexibility can have a downside. The owners must enter into a very detailed agreement that spells out the division of profit, the division of management authority and responsibility, their rights to withdraw capital, and their responsibilities to contribute new capital as needed. These schemes can get very complicated and difficult to understand, and they may end up requiring a lawyer to untangle them. If the legal structure of an LLC is too complicated and too far off the beaten path, the business may have difficulty explaining itself to a lender when applying for a loan, and it may have difficulty convincing new shareholders to put capital into the business.

Understanding profit allocation

A partnership treats salaries paid to partners (at least to its general partners) as distributions from profit. In other words, profit is determined *before* the deduction of partners' salaries. LLCs are more likely to treat salaries paid to owner-managers as an expense (like a corporation). We should warn you that the accounting for compensation and services provided by the owners in an LLC and the partners in a partnership gets rather technical and is beyond the scope of this book.

The partnership or LLC agreement specifies how to divide profit among the owners. Whereas owners of a corporation receive a share of profit directly proportional to the number of common stock shares they own, a partnership or LLC doesn't have to divide profit according to how much each owner invested. Invested capital is only one of three factors that generally play into profit allocation in partnerships and LLCs:

- » **Treasure:** Owners may be rewarded according to how much of the *treasure* — invested capital — they contributed. So if Jane invested twice as much as Joe did, her cut of the profit may be twice as much as Joe's.

- » **Time:** Owners who invest more time in the business may receive more of the profit. Some partners or owners, for example, may generate more billable hours to clients than others, and the profit-sharing plan reflects this disparity. Some partners or owners may work only part-time, so the profit-sharing plan takes this factor into account.

- » **Talent:** Regardless of capital and time, some partners bring more to the business than others. Maybe they have better business contacts, or they're better *rainmakers* (they have a knack for making deals happen), or they're celebrities whose names alone are worth a special share of the profit. Whatever it is that they do for the business, they contribute much more to the business's success than their capital or time suggests.

LIMITING LIABILITY: PROFESSIONAL CORPORATIONS AND LLPs

Professional partnerships — physicians, CPAs, lawyers, and so on — may choose to become *professional corporations (PCs)*, which are a special type of legal structure that state laws offer to professionals who otherwise would have to operate under the specter of unlimited partnership liability. States also permit *limited liability partnerships (LLPs)* for qualified professionals (such as doctors, lawyers, CPAs, and dentists), in which all the partners have limited liability.

These types of legal entities were recently created in reaction to large damage awards in malpractice lawsuits against partners. The professionals pleaded for protection from the unlimited liability of the partnership form of organization that they had traditionally used. Until these new types of professional legal entities came along, the code of professional ethics of the various professions required that practitioners operate as a partnership (or as sole practitioners).

Today, most professional associations are organized as PCs or LLPs. They function very much as partnerships do but without the unlimited liability feature — which is like having the best of both worlds.

TIP

A partnership needs to maintain a separate capital (ownership) account for each partner. The total profit of the entity is allocated into these capital accounts, as spelled out in the partnership agreement. The agreement also specifies how much money each partner can withdraw from his capital account. For example, partners may be limited to withdrawing no more than 80 percent of their anticipated share of profit for the coming year, or they may be allowed to withdraw only a certain amount until they've built up their capital accounts.

Incorporating a Business

The law views a *corporation* as a real, live person. Like an adult, a corporation is treated as a distinct and independent individual who has rights and responsibilities. (A corporation can't be sent to jail, but its officers can be put in the slammer if they're convicted of using the corporate entity for carrying out fraud.) A corporation's "birth certificate" is the legal form that is filed with the Secretary of State of the state in which the corporation is created (incorporated). A corporation must also have a legal name, like an individual. Some names cannot be used, such as the State Department of Motor Vehicles; you need to consult a lawyer on this point.

The corporate legal form offers several important advantages. A corporation has *unlimited life*; it stays alive until the shareowners vote to terminate the entity. The ownership interests in a corporation, specifically the shares of stock issued by the corporation, are generally *transferable*. You can sell your shares to another person or bequeath them in your will to your grandchildren. You don't need the approval of the other shareholders to transfer ownership of your shares. Each ownership share most often has one vote in the election of directors of a business corporation (generally speaking). In turn, the directors hire and fire the key officers of the corporation. This provides a practical way to structure the management of a business. Or looking at it from a different perspective, the shareholders elect the board of directors, the board of directors appoint company officers (such as the CEO or chief executive officer), and the company officers hire management.

Just as a child is separate from his or her parents, a corporation is separate from its owners. The corporation is responsible for its own debts. The bank can't come after you if your neighbor defaults on their loan, and the bank can't come after you if the corporation you've invested money in goes belly up. If a corporation doesn't pay its debts, its creditors can seize only the corporation's assets, not the assets of the corporation's owners, with certain exceptions:

» If fraud or the willful intent to deceive is undertaken by company officers or board members, these parties may be subject to direct personal losses.

>> When certain taxes are held in trust (for example, payroll taxes withheld from employee wages) by the corporation, if these taxes are not paid, the IRS or state taxing authorities can "pierce" the corporate legal entity and attempt to collect any unpaid payroll taxes directly from the company's officers, board of directors, and/or material investors (that are in the know).

The general rule for corporations is that its creditors can seize the corporation's assets only in the event of a dispute, but every rule has exceptions, which we emphasize with the preceding two scenarios.

REMEMBER

This important legal distinction between the obligations of the business entity and its individual owners is known as *limited liability* — that is, the liability of the owners is limited. Even if the owners have deep pockets, they have no legal exposure for the unpaid debts of the corporation (again, with exceptions). The legal fence between a corporation and its owners is sometimes called the *corporate shield* because it protects the owners from being held responsible for the debts of the corporation.

So when you invest money in a corporation as an owner, you know that the most you can lose is the amount you put in. You may lose every dollar you put in, but the corporation's creditors can't reach through the corporate entity to grab your assets to pay off the liabilities of the business. (But you should check with your lawyer on this issue — just to be sure.)

Issuing stock shares

When raising equity capital, a corporation issues ownership shares to persons who invest money in the business. These ownership shares are documented by stock certificates, which state the name of the owner and how many shares are owned. The corporation has to keep a register of how many shares everyone owns, of course. (An owner can be an individual, another corporation, or any other legal entity.) Actually, many public corporations use an independent agency to maintain their ownership records. In some situations, stock shares are issued in *book entry form*, which means you get a formal letter (not a fancy engraved stock certificate) attesting to the fact that you own so many shares. Your legal ownership is recorded in the official books or stock registry of the business.

The owners of a corporation are called *stockholders* because they own stock shares issued by the corporation. The stock shares are *negotiable*, meaning the owner can sell them at any time to anyone willing to buy them without having to get the approval of the corporation or other stockholders. *Publicly owned corporations* are those whose stock shares are traded in public markets, such as the New York Stock Exchange and Nasdaq. There's a ready market for the buying and selling of the stock shares.

The stockholders of a private business have the right to sell their shares, although they may enter into a binding agreement restricting this right. For example, suppose you own 20,000 of the 100,000 stock shares issued by the business. Therefore, you have 20 percent of the voting power in the business (one share has one vote). You may agree to offer your shares to the other shareowners before offering the shares to someone outside the present group of stockholders. Or you may agree to offer the business itself the right to buy back the shares. (A corporation can buy back some of its own stock shares; it can cannibalize itself, so to speak.) In these ways, the continuing stockholders of the private business control who owns the stock shares of the business.

Distinguishing different classes of stock shares

TIP

Before you invest in stock shares, you should ascertain whether the corporation has issued just one class of stock shares. A *class* is one group, or type, of stock shares, all having identical rights; every share is the same as every other share. A corporation can issue two or more different classes of stock shares. For example, a business may offer Class A and Class B stock shares, where Class A stockholders are given the vote in elections for the board of directors, but Class B stockholders do not get a vote.

State laws generally are liberal when it comes to allowing corporations to issue different classes of stock shares. A whimsical example is that holders of one class of stock shares could get the best seats at the annual meetings of the stockholders. But whimsy aside, differences between classes of stock shares are significant and affect the value of the shares of each class of stock.

Two classes of corporate stock shares, common stock and preferred stock, are fundamentally different. Here are two basic differences:

>> **Preferred stock:** Preferred stockholders are promised a certain amount of cash dividends each year and/or are provided other "preferences" (see Chapter 18). If the corporation is in default on paying preferred stock dividends, certain additional rights kick into gear. For example, as a rule preferred stockholders do not have a vote on corporate matters. However, if their dividends are not paid, the preferred stockholders could gain a seat on the board of directors.

» **Common stock:** Common stockholders have the most risk. A business that ends up in deep financial trouble is obligated to pay off its liabilities first and then its preferred stockholders. By the time the common stockholders get their turn, the business may have no money left to pay them. The corporation makes no cash dividend promises to its common stockholders. Each year, the board of directors must decide how much, if any, cash dividends to distribute to its common stockholders.

You may think that common stock doesn't seem too attractive. But consider the following points:

» Preferred stock shares usually are promised a *fixed* (limited) dividend per year and typically don't have a claim to any profit beyond the stated amount of dividends. (Some corporations issue *participating* preferred stock, which gives the preferred stockholders a contingent right to more than just their basic amount of dividends or, under certain situations, allows the preferred stock to be converted into common stock.)

» As we mention earlier, preferred stockholders may not have equal voting rights, unless they don't receive dividends for one period or more or other terms of their preferred investment are violated. In other words, preferred stock shareholders usually don't participate in electing a public corporation's board of directors or vote on other critical issues facing the corporation. However, we should note that for privately held companies that have raised equity capital in the form of preferred stock, active voting participation is usually present to ensure the investors have a say in the company's management.

The advantages of common stock, therefore, are the ability to vote in corporation elections and the unlimited *upside potential:* After a corporation's obligations to its preferred stockholders are satisfied, the rest of the profit it has earned accrues to the benefit of its common stock.

Here are some important things to understand about common stock shares:

» Each stock share is equal to every other stock share in its class. This way, ownership rights are standardized, and the main difference between two stockholders is how many shares each owns.

» The only time a business must return stockholders' capital to them is when the majority of stockholders vote to liquidate the business (in part or in total). Other than this, the business's managers don't have to worry about the stockholders withdrawing capital.

>> A stockholder can sell their shares at any time, without the approval of the other stockholders. However, as we mention earlier, the stockholders of a privately owned business may agree to certain restrictions on this right when they first became stockholders in the business.

>> Stockholders can put themselves in key management positions, or they may delegate the task of selecting top managers and officers to the *board of directors*, which is a small group of persons selected by the stockholders to set the business's policies and represent stockholders' interests.

Now, don't get the impression that if you buy 100 shares of IBM, you can get yourself elected to its board of directors. On the other hand, if Warren Buffett bought 100 million shares of IBM, he could very well get himself on the board. The relative size of your ownership interest is key. If you put up more than half the money in a business, you can put yourself on the board and elect yourself president of the business. The stockholders who own 50 percent plus one share constitute the controlling group that decides who goes on the board of directors.

WARNING

The all-stocks-are-created-equal aspect of corporations is a practical and simple way to divide ownership, but its inflexibility can be a hindrance. Suppose the stockholders want to delegate to one individual extraordinary power or to give one person a share of profit out of proportion to their stock ownership. The business can make special compensation arrangements for key executives and ask a lawyer for advice on the best way to implement the stockholders' intentions. Nevertheless, state corporation laws require that certain voting matters be settled by a majority vote of stockholders. If enough stockholders oppose a certain arrangement, the other stockholders may have to buy them out to gain a controlling interest in the business. (The LLC legal structure permits more flexibility in these matters. We talk about this type of legal structure earlier in this chapter.)

Determining the market value of stock shares

If you want to sell your stock shares, how much can you get for them? There's a world of difference between owning shares of a public corporation and owning shares of a private corporation. *Public* means there's an active market in the stock shares of the business; the shares are *liquid*. You can convert the shares into cash in a flash by calling your stockbroker or going online to sell them. You can check a daily financial newspaper — such as *The Wall Street Journal* — for the current market prices of many large publicly owned corporations. Or you can go to one of many websites (such as http://finance.yahoo.com) that provide current market prices. But stock shares in privately owned businesses aren't publicly traded, so how can you determine the value of your shares in such a business?

Well, we don't mean to sidestep the question, but stockholders of a private business don't worry about putting a precise market value on their shares — until they're serious about selling their shares or when something else happens that demands putting a value on the shares. When you die, the executor of your estate has to put a value on the shares you own (excuse us — the shares you *used to* own) for estate tax purposes. If you divorce your spouse, then as part of the divorce settlement, a value is needed for the stock shares you own. When the business itself is put up for sale, a value is put on the business; dividing this total value by the number of stock shares issued by the business gives the value per share.

Other than during events like these, which require that a value be put on the stock shares, the shareowners of a private business get along quite well without knowing a definite value for their shares. This doesn't mean they have no idea of the value of their business and what their shares are worth. They read the financial statements of their business, so they know its profit performance and financial condition. In the backs of their minds, they should have a reasonably good estimate regarding how much a willing buyer might pay for the business and the price they would sell their shares for. So even though they don't know the exact market value of their stock shares, they aren't completely in the dark.

TIP

Space doesn't permit an extended discussion of business valuation methods here, but generally speaking, the value of ownership shares in a private business depends heavily on its recent profit performance and its current financial condition disclosed in its latest financial report. The financial statements may have to be *trued up*, as they say, to bring some of the historical cost values in the balance sheet up to current replacement values.

REMEMBER

Business valuation is highly dependent on the specific circumstances of each business. The present owners may be very eager to sell out, and they may be willing to accept a low price instead of taking the time to drive a better bargain. The potential buyers of the business may see opportunities that the present owners don't see or aren't willing to pursue. Even Warren Buffett, who has a well-deserved reputation for knowing how to value a business, admits that he's made some real blunders along the way.

Watching out for dilution of share value

WARNING

Watch out for developments that cause a *dilution effect* on the value of your stock shares — that is, that cause each stock share to drop in value. Keep in mind that sometimes the dilution effect may be the result of a good business decision, so even though your share of the business has decreased in the short term, the long-term profit performance of the business (and therefore your investment) may benefit. But you need to watch for these developments closely. The following situations cause a dilution effect:

>> **A business issues additional stock shares at the going market value but doesn't really need the additional capital — the business is in no better profit-making position than it was before issuing the new stock shares.** For example, a business may issue new stock shares in order to let a newly hired chief executive officer buy them. The immediate effect may be a dilution in the value per share. Over the long term, however, the new CEO may turn the business around and lead it to higher levels of profit that increase the stock's value.

>> **A business issues new stock shares at a discount below its stock shares' current value.** For example, the business may issue a new batch of stock shares at a price lower than the current market value to employees who take advantage of an employee stock-purchase plan. Selling stock shares at a discount, by itself, has a dilution effect on the market value of the shares. But in the grand scheme of things, the stock-purchase plan may motivate its employees to achieve higher productivity levels, which can lead to superior profit performance of the business.

Now here's one for you: The main purpose of issuing additional stock shares is to deliberately dilute the market value per share. For example, a publicly owned corporation doubles its number of shares by issuing a two-for-one *stock split*. Each shareholder gets one new share for each share presently owned, without investing any additional money in the business. As you would expect, the market value of the stock drops in half — which is exactly the purpose of the split because the lower stock price is better for stock market trading (according to conventional wisdom).

Recognizing conflicts between stockholders and managers

Stockholders are primarily concerned with the profit performance of the business; the dividends they receive and the value of their stock shares depend on it. Managers' jobs depend on living up to the business's profit goals. But whereas stockholders and managers have the common goal of optimizing profit, they have certain inherent conflict of interests:

>> **The more money that managers make in wages and benefits, the less stockholders see in bottom-line net income.** Stockholders obviously want the best managers for the job, but they don't want to pay more than they have to. In many corporations, top-level managers, for all practical purposes, set their own salaries and compensation packages.

WHERE DOES PROFIT GO IN A CORPORATION?

Suppose that a private business earned $1.32 million net income for the year just ended and has issued 400,000 capital stock shares. Divide net income by the number of shares, and you come up with *earnings per share* of $3.30. Suppose the business paid $400,000 cash dividends during the year, or $1.00 per share. The retained earnings account thus increased $2.30 per share (earnings per share minus dividends per share). Although the stockholders don't have the cash to show for it, their investment is better off by $2.30 per share, or $920,000 in total ($2.30 per share increase × 400,000 shares = $920,000). The retention of $920,000 profit shows up in the balance sheet as an increase in retained earnings on the one hand and as a $920,000 increase in the *net assets* on the other hand. Net assets equals total assets minus total liabilities. The stockholders hope that the business will use the increase in its net assets to improve future profit, which hopefully will lead to higher cash dividends.

Now, suppose the business is a public company that is 1,000 times larger. It earned $1.32 billion on its 400 million capital stock shares and distributed $400 million in cash dividends. You may think that the market value should increase $2.30 per share, because this is the amount per share that the business earned and retained in the business and did not distribute to its shareholders. Your thinking is quite logical: Profit is an increase in the net assets of a business (assets less liabilities, which is also called *net worth*). The business is $2.30 per share "richer" at the end of the year than it was at the start of the year, due to the profit it earned and retained.

Yet it's entirely possible that the market price of the stock shares actually *decreased* during the year. Market prices are governed by psychological, political, and economic factors that go beyond the information in the financial reports of a business. Financial statements are only one of the information sources that stock investors use in making their buy-and-sell decisions. Chapters 11, 12, and 20 explain how stock investors use the information in financial reports.

REMEMBER

Most public business corporations establish a compensation committee consisting of outside directors that sets the salaries, incentive bonuses, and other forms of compensation of the top-level executives of the organization. An *outside director* is one who has no management position in the business and who therefore should be more objective and should not be beholden to the chief executive of the business. This is good in theory, but it doesn't work out all that well in practice — mainly because the top-level executive of a large public business typically has the dominant voice in selecting the persons to serve on its board of directors. Being a director of a large public corporation is a prestigious position, to say nothing of the annual fees that are fairly substantial at most corporations.

>> **The question of who should control the business can be tough to answer.** Managers are hired for their competence and are intimately familiar with the business; stockholders may have no experience relevant to running the business, but their money makes the business tick. In ideal situations, the two sides respect each other's contributions to the business and use this tension constructively. Of course, the real world is far from ideal, and in some companies, managers control the board of directors rather than the other way around.

WARNING

As an investor, be aware of these issues and how they affect the return on your investment in a business. If you don't like the way your business is run, you can sell your shares and invest your money elsewhere. (However, if the business is privately owned, there may not be a ready market for its stock shares, which puts you between a rock and a hard place.)

2

Exploring Financial Statements

Get to know the ins and outs of the *income statement,* which summarizes the profit-making activities of the business and its bottom-line profit or loss for the period.

Understand how the *balance sheet* reports the financial condition of the business at a point in time — specifically on the last day of the profit period.

Expand your knowledge of what's included in the *statement of cash flows,* which reports the amount of cash produced from profits or consumed from losses, and how businesses identify and secure other sources of cash during the period and what the business did with this money (that is, what they used the cash for).

Make sure you're up to speed on the topic of *adequate disclosure* in external financial reports to the creditors and investors of a business. Business financial reports should reveal all the information that the creditors and investors are entitled to know.

Chapter **6**

Reporting Profit or Loss in the Income Statement

I n this chapter, we lift up the hood and explain how the profit engine runs. Making a profit is the main financial goal of a business. (Not-for-profit organizations and government entities don't aim to make profit, but they should break even and avoid a deficit.) Accountants are the profit scorekeepers in the business world and are tasked with measuring the most important financial number of a business. We should warn you right here that measuring profit is a challenge in most situations because determining the correct amounts for revenue and expenses (and for special gains and losses, if any) is no walk in the park.

REMEMBER

We want to point out that of the three primary financial statements (the balance sheet, the income statement, and the statement of cash flows), the income statement is the financial statement that tends to be the most easily "manipulated" and the most targeted to, shall we say, embellish. The reason for this is that most external parties tend to focus their review or analysis first on the income statement with such items as "How fast are top-line sales growing?" and "How much profit did the company generate?" which are critical performance points of interest. We should emphasize that most companies make a concerted effort to prepare complete, accurate, reliable, and timely financial statements, including the income statement, that do not contain material misstatements, but as you find throughout this book, it does pay to raise an eyebrow every now and then when a company's financial performance seems just a bit off or too good to be true.

For all businesses, managers have the demanding tasks of generating sales and controlling expenses, whereas accountants have the tough and essential job of measuring revenue and expenses and preparing financial reports that summarize the profit-making activities in a fair and reasonable fashion. Also, accountants are called on to help business managers analyze profit for decision-making, which we explain in Chapters 15 and 16. And accountants prepare profit forecasts for management, which we cover in Chapter 17.

This chapter explains how profit-making activities are reported in a business's external financial reports to its owners, investors, creditors, and lenders. Revenue and expenses change the financial condition of the business, a fact often overlooked when reading a profit report. Keep in mind that recording revenue and expenses (and gains and losses) and then reporting these profit-making activities in external financial reports are governed by authoritative accounting standards, which we discuss in Chapter 2.

Presenting Typical Income Statements

REMEMBER

At the risk of oversimplification, we would say that businesses make profit in three basic ways:

>> **Selling products** (with allied services) and controlling the cost of the products sold and other operating costs (for example, an auto manufacturer)

>> **Selling services** and controlling the cost of providing the services and other operating costs (such as a CPA or legal firm)

>> **Investing** in assets that generate investment income and market value gains and controlling operating costs (banks, for example)

Obviously, this list isn't exhaustive, but it captures a large swath of business activity. In this chapter, we show you typical externally reported income statements for the three types of businesses. Products range from automobiles to computers to food to clothes. The customers of a company that sells products may be final consumers in the economic chain, or a business may sell to other businesses. Services range from transportation to entertainment to consulting, such as CPA or law firms. Investment businesses range from mutual funds to credit unions to banks to real estate development companies.

Looking at businesses that sell products

Figure 6-1 presents a classic profit report for a technology-based *product-oriented* business that also sells software and services; this report, called the *income statement*, would be sent to its outside, or external, owners, investors, creditors, and/ or lenders. (The report could just as easily be called the *net income statement* because the bottom-line profit term preferred by accountants is *net income*, but the word *net* is dropped from the title, and it's most often called the income statement.) Alternative titles for the external profit report include *earnings statement, operating statement, statement of operating results,* and *statement of earnings.* **Note**: Profit reports prepared for managers that stay inside a business are usually called *P&L* (profit and loss) statements, but this moniker isn't used much in external financial reporting.

QW Example Tech., Inc. Sales of Both Products & Software Services for the Fiscal Year Ending 12/31/2020		
Income Statement For the Twelve-Month Period Ending (All Numbers in Thousands)	FYE 12/31/2019	FYE 12/31/2020
Sales Revenue, Net	$53,747	$71,064
Costs of Goods Sold	$23,314	$26,891
Gross Profit	$30,433	$44,173
Selling, General, & Administrative Expenses	$29,286	$36,678
Operating Income (Loss)	$1,147	$7,495
Other Expenses (Income):		
Other Expenses & (Income)	$250	$250
Interest Expense	$400	$350
Total Other Expenses (Income)	$650	$600
Net Profit (Loss) Before Income Taxes	$497	$6,895
Income Tax Expense (Benefit)	$174	$2,413
Net Income (Loss)	$323	$4,482
Earnings Per Share (Fully Diluted)	$0.32	$2.76
Confidential — Property of QW Example Tech., Inc.		

FIGURE 6-1: Typical income statement for a technology business.

The heading of an income statement identifies the business (which in this example is incorporated — thus the "Inc." following the name), the financial statement title ("Income Statement"), and the time period summarized by the statement ("for the Fiscal Year Ending December 31, 2019, and Fiscal Year Ending December 31, 2020"). We explain the legal organization structures of businesses in Chapter 5.

You may be tempted to start reading an income statement at the bottom line. But this financial report is designed for you to read from the top line (sales revenue) and proceed down to the last — the bottom line (net income). Each step down the ladder in an income statement involves the deduction of an expense. In Figure 6-1, five expenses are deducted from the sales revenue amount, and four profit lines are given: gross profit, operating earnings, net profit before income tax, and net income:

>> **Gross profit (also called gross margin)** = sales revenue minus the cost of goods (products) sold expense but before operating and other expenses are considered

>> **Operating earnings (or loss)** = profit (or loss) before interest, other expenses, and income tax expenses are deducted from gross profit

>> **Profit (or loss) before income tax** = profit (or loss) after deducting interest and other expenses from operating earnings but before income tax expense

>> **Net income** = final profit for period after deducting all expenses from sales revenue, which is commonly called the "bottom line"

Although you see income statements with fewer than four profit lines, you seldom see an income statement with more.

Terminology in income statements varies somewhat from business to business, but you can usually determine the meaning of a term from its context and placement in the income statement.

TIP

Notice in Figure 6-1 that below the net income line, the *earnings per share* (EPS) amount is reported. This important number equals net income divided by the number of ownership shares that the business corporation has issued and that are being held by its shareholders. All public corporations whose stock shares are traded in stock markets must report this key metric. EPS is compared to the current market price of the stock to help judge whether the stock is over- or underpriced. Private companies aren't required to report EPS, but they may decide to do so. If a private business decides to report its EPS, it should follow the accounting standard for calculating this number. We discuss the calculation of EPS in Chapter 12.

REMEMBER

The standard practice for most businesses is to report two-year comparative financial statements in side-by-side columns — for the period just ended and for the same period one year ago. Indeed, some companies present three-year comparative financial statements. Two-year or three-year financial statements may be legally required, such as for public companies whose debt and ownership shares are traded in a public market. For ease of presentation, we have included only one additional year of the income statement (for the Fiscal Year Ending December 31, 2019) for comparison purposes.

Looking at businesses that sell services

Figure 6-2 presents a typical income statement for a *service-oriented* business — in this example, one that operates a small-business consulting company.

Local Sample Service Co, Inc. Sales of Services for the Fiscal Year Ending 12/31/2020	
Unaudited Income Statement <u>For the Twelve-Month Period Ending</u>	FYE <u>12/31/2020</u>
Sales Revenue, Net	$4,252,000
Costs of Sales	$2,625,000
Gross Profit	$1,627,000
Selling, General, & Administrative Expenses	$1,310,000
Operating Income (Loss)	$317,000
Other Expenses (Income):	
Other Expenses & (Income)	$5,000
Interest Expense	$11,000
Total Other Expenses (Income)	$16,000
Net Profit (Loss) Before Income Taxes	$301,000
Income Tax Expense (Benefit)	$800
Net Income (Loss)	$300,200
Earnings Per Share (Fully Diluted)	$3.00
Confidential — Property of Local Sample Service Co, Inc.	

FIGURE 6-2: Typical income statement for a business that sells services.

© *John Wiley & Sons, Inc.*

If a business sells services and doesn't sell products, it doesn't have a traditional cost of goods sold expense (which reflects the costs of tangible products sold) but rather will often report a more generic costs of sales expense. In Figure 6-2, we present a simple income statement for a small consulting firm. You will notice that a gross profit line is present, similar to our technology company example in Figure 6-1. Although not always required, almost all service-based businesses incur some type of direct expenses that vary with sales revenue. In our example, the direct expenses recorded as costs of sales include salaries, wages, employee benefits, travel, and similar types of expenses that are incurred as a direct result of generating consulting sales revenue (the staff bills to customers at different hourly rates). So it makes sense and is prudent for service businesses to properly reflect these direct expenses as costs of sales to properly calculate and present a gross profit. This represents the first profit line reported in the service business income statement.

In Figure 6-2, the second profit line is *operating earnings* (or *operating income*), which is profit before interest, other, and income tax expenses. The service business example in Figure 6-2 discloses five broad types of expenses, similar to our technology company example. In comparing the income statement examples in Figures 6-1 and 6-2, we want to draw your attention to two items:

» First, you will notice a reference to "other expenses" in the income statement, which sits below operating income but above net profit before income taxes. It's becoming increasingly common for businesses of all sizes, shapes, and forms to report "other" expenses below the operating income line to properly disclose expenses that may be unique, unusual, and/or nonrecurring in nature. While this may be true, quite often businesses attempt to dump various expenses (for lack of a better term) in the "other" category to give the appearance that operating income is actually higher or stronger than it may actually be. We discuss this accounting tactic later in this book, but we want to call it to your attention here, given that it's becoming more widely used.

» Second, you will notice that the income tax expense for our service business is very low — only $800. The reason for this is that most small, service-oriented businesses tend to operate as an S corporation, partnership, or LLC/LLP, which (as discussed in Chapter 5) function as tax flow-through entities. That is, the income tax expense is not incurred at the company level, but rather the net taxable income is passed through to the owners of the company and they pay income tax expense at their personal level.

TIP

The premise of financial reporting is that of *adequate disclosure,* but you find many variations in the reporting of expenses. A business — whether a product or service company or an investment company — has fairly wide latitude regarding the number of expense lines to disclose in its external income statement. A CPA auditor (assuming that the company's financial report is audited) may not be satisfied that just three expenses provide enough detail about the operating activities of the business. Accounting standards do not dictate that particular expenses must be disclosed (other than cost of goods sold expense).

Public companies must disclose certain expenses in their publicly available filings with the federal Securities and Exchange Commission (SEC). Filing reports to the SEC is one thing; in their reports to shareholders, most businesses are relatively stingy regarding how many expenses are revealed in their income statements.

Looking at investment businesses

Figure 6-3 presents an income statement for an investment business. Notice that this income statement discloses three types of revenue: interest and dividends that were earned, gains from sales of investments during the year, and unrealized gains of the market value of its investment portfolio. Instead of gains, the business could've had realized and unrealized losses during a down year, of course. Generally, investment businesses are either required or are under a good deal of pressure to report their three types of investment return. Investment companies might not borrow money and thus have no interest expense. Or they might. We show interest expense in Figure 6-3 for the investment business example.

REMEMBER

We should mention in passing that public investment companies, such as mutual funds and exchange traded securities (ETS), are heavily regulated by the SEC as well as other types of investment entities that raise capital in public offerings. Our purpose in showing the income statement for an investment business (Figure 6-3) is simply for comparison with businesses that sell products and those that sell services (see Figures 6-1 and 6-2).

Typical Investment Company, Inc. Investment Business for the Fiscal Year Ending 12/31/2020	
Unaudited Income Statement For the Twelve-Month Period Ending	**FYE** 12/31/2020
Interest and Dividends	$15,000,000
Realized Gain (Loss) from Investments	$2,500,000
Unrealized Gain (Loss) on Investments	$12,500,000
Total Return on Investments	$30,000,000
Selling, General, & Administrative Expenses	$22,500,000
Operating Income (Loss)	$7,500,000
Interest Expense	$2,500,000
Net Profit (Loss) Before Income Taxes	$5,000,000
Income Tax Expense	$1,500,000
Net Income (Loss)	$3,500,000
Earnings Per Share (Fully Diluted)	$14.00

Confidential — Property of Typical Investment Company, Inc.

FIGURE 6-3:
Typical income statement for an investment business.

© John Wiley & Sons, Inc.

Taking Care of Housekeeping Details

REMEMBER

We want to point out a few things about income statements that accountants assume everyone knows but, in fact, are not obvious to many people. (Accountants do this often: They assume that the people using financial statements know a good deal about the customs and conventions of financial reporting, so they don't make things as clear as they could.)

>> **Minus signs are missing.** Expenses are deductions from sales revenue, but hardly ever do you see minus signs in front of expense amounts to indicate that they're deductions. Forget about minus signs in income statements and in other financial statements as well. Sometimes parentheses are put around a deduction to signal that it's a negative number, but that's the most you can expect to see.

>> **Your eye is drawn to the bottom line.** Putting a double underline under the final (bottom-line) profit number for emphasis is common practice but not universal. Instead, net income may be shown in bold type. You generally don't see anything as garish as a fat arrow pointing to the profit number or a big smiley encircling the profit number.

>> **Profit isn't usually called** *profit.* As you see in Figures 6-1, 6-2, and 6-3, bottom-line profit is called *net income.* Businesses use other terms as well, such as *net earnings* or just *earnings.* (Can't accountants agree on anything?) In this book, we use the terms *net income* and *profit* interchangeably, but when showing a formal income statement, we stick to "net income."

>> **You don't get details about sales revenue.** The sales revenue amount in an income statement of a product or service company is the combined total of all sales during the year; you can't tell how many different sales were made, how many different customers the company sold products or services to, or how the sales were distributed over the 12 months of the year. (Public companies are required to release quarterly income statements during the year, and they include a special summary of quarter-by-quarter results in their annual financial reports; private businesses may or may not release quarterly sales data.) Sales revenue does not include sales and excise taxes that the business collects from its customers and remits to the government. Further, sales revenue is usually reported as a "net" figure, which includes gross sales less any deductions for sales returns, discounts, allowances, and the like.

Note: In addition to sales revenue from selling products and/or services, a business may have income from other sources. For instance, a business may have earnings from investments in marketable securities. In its income statement, investment income goes on a separate line and is not commingled with sales revenue. (The businesses featured in Figures 6-1 and 6-2 do not have investment income.)

>> **Gross profit matters.** The *cost of goods sold* expense of a business that sells products is the cost of products sold to customers, the sales revenue of which is reported on the *sales revenue* line. The idea is to match up the sales revenue of goods sold with the cost of goods sold and show the *gross profit* (also called *gross margin*), which is the profit before other expenses are deducted. The other expenses could in total be more than gross profit, in which case the business would have a net loss for the period. (By the way, a bottom-line loss usually has parentheses around it to emphasize that it's a negative number.)

>> **Operating costs are lumped together.** The broad category *selling, general, and administrative expenses* (refer to Figure 6-1) consists of a variety of costs of operating the business and making sales. Here are some examples:

- Personnel compensation or wages and direct burden (such as retirement benefits, health insurance, payroll taxes paid by the business, vacation or paid days off, and other forms of direct burden) for staff that are part of the company's overhead (and not directly associated with costs of goods sold).

- Marketing, advertising (social media, traditional print, and so on), selling, and promotional expenditures

- Insurance premiums for general liability, property, cybersecurity, errors and omissions, and others

- Rent paid for using assets and/or property taxes on buildings and land

- Cost of utilities (such as gas and electric)

- Travel, lodging, meals, and entertainment costs

- Telecommunication and internet charges

- Depreciation of operating assets that are used more than one year (including buildings, land improvements, cars and trucks, computers, office furniture, tools and machinery, and shelving)

- Professional services such as legal, accounting, taxation, strategic consulting, and so on

HOW BIG IS A BIG BUSINESS, AND HOW SMALL IS A SMALL BUSINESS?

One key measure of the size of a business is the number of employees it has on its payroll. Could the business shown in Figure 6-1 have 500 employees? Probably not. This would mean that the annual sales revenue per employee would be only a little over $142,000 ($71.064 million annual sales revenue divided by 500 employees), which is relatively low for a technology company. But the annual wage per employee in many industries today is over $50,000 and much higher in some industries. Much more likely, the number of full-time employees in this business is closer to 140. This number of employees yields roughly $507,000 sales revenue per employee, which means that the business could probably afford an average annual wage of $75,000 per employee or higher.

Public companies generally disclose their numbers of employees in their annual financial reports, but private businesses generally don't. U.S. accounting standards do not require that the total number and total compensation of employees be reported in the external financial statements of a business or in the footnotes to the financial statements.

The definition of a "small business" isn't uniform. Generally, the term refers to a business with fewer than 100 full-time employees, but in some situations, it refers to businesses with fewer than 20 employees or even fewer than 10 full-time employees. Say a business has 20 full-time employees on its payroll who earn an average of $40,000 in annual wages (a relatively low amount). This costs $800,000 for its annual payroll before figuring in employee benefits (such as Social Security taxes, 401(k) matching retirement plans, health insurance, and so on). Product businesses need to earn annual gross profit equal to two or three times their basic payroll expense.

As with sales revenue, you don't get much detail about operating expenses in a typical income statement as it's presented to the company's debtholders and shareholders. A business may disclose more information than you see in its income statement — mainly in the footnotes that are included with its financial statements. (We explain footnotes in Chapter 10.) Public companies have to include more detail about the expenses in their filings with the SEC, which are available to anyone who looks up the information.

Being an Active Reader

The worst thing you can do when presented with an income statement is to be a passive reader. You should be inquisitive. An income statement is not fulfilling its purpose unless you grab it by its numbers and start asking questions.

For example, you should be curious regarding the size of the business (see the nearby sidebar "How big is a big business, and how small is a small business?"). Another question to ask is "How does profit compare with sales revenue for the year?" Profit (net income) equals what's left over from sales revenue after you deduct all expenses. The business featured in Figure 6-1 produced $4.482 million profit from its $71.064 million sales revenue for the year, which equals 6.3 percent. (The service business did a little better at roughly 7 percent; see Figure 6-2.) This ratio of profit to sales revenue means expenses absorbed 93.7 percent of sales revenue. Although it may seem rather thin, a 6.3 percent profit margin on sales is quite acceptable for many businesses. (Some businesses consistently make a bottom-line profit of 10 to 20 percent of sales, and others are satisfied with a 1 or 2 percent profit on sales revenue.) Profit ratios on sales vary widely from industry to industry.

REMEMBER

Accounting standards are relatively silent regarding which expenses have to be disclosed on the face of an income statement or elsewhere in a financial report. For example, the amount a business spends on advertising doesn't have to be disclosed. (In contrast, the rules for filing financial reports with the SEC require disclosure of certain expenses, such as repairs and maintenance expenses. Keep in mind that the SEC rules apply only to public businesses.)

In the technology business example in Figure 6-1, expenses such as professional fees, corporate labor overhead costs, and advertising expenditures are buried in the all-inclusive *selling, general, and administrative expenses* line. (If the business manufactures the products it sells instead of buying them from another business, a good part of its annual labor cost is included in its *cost of goods sold* expense.) Some companies disclose specific expenses such as advertising and marketing costs, research and development costs, and other significant expenses. In short, income statement expense–disclosure practices vary from business to business.

Another set of questions you should ask in reading an income statement concerns the *profit performance* of the business. Refer again to the technology company's profit performance report (Figure 6-1). Profitwise, how did the business do? Underneath this question is the implicit question "Relative to *what?*" Generally speaking, four sorts of benchmarks are used for evaluating profit performance:

>> Broad, industrywide performance averages

>> Immediate competitors' performances

>> The business's own performance in recent years

>> The company's internal forecast for the like period

Deconstructing Profit

Now that you've had the opportunity to read an income statement (see Figures 6-1, 6-2, and 6-3), we want to ask a question: What *is* profit? Our guess is that you'll answer that profit is revenue less expenses. In an accounting class, you'd get only a "C" grade for this answer. Your answer is correct, as far as it goes, but it doesn't go far enough. This answer doesn't strike at the core of profit. It doesn't tell us what profit consists of or the substance of profit.

In this section, we explain the anatomy of profit. Having read the technology company's income statement, you now know that the business earned net income for the year ending December 31, 2020 (see Figure 6-1). Where's the profit? If you had to put your finger on the profit, where would you touch?

Recording profit works like a pair of scissors: You have the positive revenue blade and the negative expenses blade. Revenue and expenses have opposite effects. This leads to two questions: What is a revenue? And what is an expense?

Figure 6-4 summarizes the financial natures of revenue and expenses in terms of impacts on assets and liabilities. Notice the symmetrical framework of revenue and expenses. It's beautiful in its own way, don't you think? In any case, this summary framework is helpful for understanding the financial effects of revenue and expenses.

Revenue and expense effects on assets and liabilities

Here's the gist of the two-by-two matrix shown in Figure 6-4. In recording a sale, the bookkeeper increases a revenue account. The revenue account accumulates sale after sale during the period. So at the end of the period, the total sales revenue for the period is the balance in the account. This amount is the cumulative end-of-period total of all sales during the period. All sales revenue accounts are combined for the period, and one grand total is reported in the income statement on the top line. As each sale (or other type of revenue event) is recorded, either an asset account is increased or a liability account is decreased.

TIP

We're sure you follow that revenue increases an asset. For example, if all sales are made for cash, the company's cash account increases accordingly. On the other hand, you may have trouble understanding that certain revenue transactions are recorded with a decrease in a liability. Here's why: Customers may pay in advance for a product or service to be delivered later (examples are prepaying for theater tickets and making a down payment for future delivery of products). In recording such advance payments from customers, the business increases cash, of course, and increases a liability account usually called *deferred revenue*. The term *deferred* simply means postponed. When the product or service is delivered to the customer — and not before then — the bookkeeper records the amount of revenue that has now been earned *and* decreases the deferred revenue liability by the same amount.

Recording expenses is rather straightforward. When an expense is recorded, a specific expense account is increased, and either an asset account is decreased or a liability account is increased the same amount. For example, to record the cost of goods sold, the expense with this name is increased, say, $35,000, and in the same entry, the inventory asset account is decreased $35,000. Alternatively, an expense entry may involve a liability account instead of an asset account. For example, suppose the business receives a $10,000 bill from its CPA auditor that it will pay later. In recording the bill from the CPA, the audit expense account is increased $10,000, and a liability account called *accounts payable* is increased $10,000.

TECHNICAL
STUFF

The summary framework of Figure 6-4 has basically no exceptions. Recording revenue and expenses (as well as gains and losses) always follow these rules with really only one significant exception. That exception lies in the requirement for companies to record employee compensation expense related to the issuance of stock options. In this situation (which usually applies only to publicly traded companies), an expense is recorded as noted in Figure 6-4, but the offset is not to increase a liability but rather an increase in shareholders' equity is realized. We mention this as employee stock option expense has become an important accounting issue over the past five years and is something to keep in mind. But for simplicity purposes, we assume the logic summarized in Figure 6-4 will hold for the remainder of our discussion.

So where does this leave you for understanding profit? Profit itself doesn't show up in Figure 6-4, does it? Profit depends on amounts recorded for revenue and expenses, of course, as we show in the next section.

Comparing three scenarios of profit

Figure 6-5 presents three scenarios of profit in terms of changes in the assets and liabilities of a business. In all three cases, the business makes the same amount of profit: $10, as you see in the abbreviated income statements on the right side. (We keep the numbers small, but you can think of $10 million instead of $10 if you prefer.)

To find the amount of profit, first determine the amount of revenue and expenses for each case. In all three cases, total expenses are $90, but the changes in assets and liabilities differ:

>> In Case 1, revenue consists of $100 asset increases; no liability was involved in recording revenue.

>> In Case 2, revenue was from $100 decreases in a liability.

>> In Case 3, you see both asset increases and liability decreases for revenue.

REMEMBER

Revenue and expenses are originally recorded as increases or decreases in different asset and liability accounts. Cash is just one asset. We explain the other assets and the liabilities in the later section "Pinpointing the Assets and Liabilities Used to Record Revenue and Expenses."

Case A

	Asset	Liability	Income Statement	Amount
Revenue	$100	$0	Revenue	$100
Expense	($60)	$30	Expenses	$90
			Net Profit	$10

Case B

	Asset	Liability	Income Statement	Amount
Revenue	$0	($100)	Revenue	$100
Expense	($60)	$30	Expenses	$90
			Net Profit	$10

Case C

	Asset	Liability	Income Statement	Amount
Revenue	$50	($50)	Revenue	$100
Expense	($45)	$45	Expenses	$90
			Net Profit	$10

© John Wiley & Sons, Inc.

FIGURE 6-5: Comparing asset and liability changes for three profit scenarios.

Some businesses make sales for cash; cash is received at the time of the sale. In recording these sales, a revenue account is increased and the cash account is increased. Some expenses are recorded at the time of cutting a check to pay the expense. In recording these expenses, an appropriate expense account is increased and the cash asset account is decreased. However, for most businesses, the majority of their revenue and expense transactions do not simultaneously affect cash.

For most businesses, cash comes into play before or after revenue and expenses are recorded. For example, a business buys products from its supplier that it will sell sometime later to its customers. The purchase is paid for before the goods are sold. No expense is recorded until products are sold. Here's another example: A business makes sales on credit to its customers. In recording credit sales, a sales revenue account is increased and an asset account called *accounts receivable* is increased. Later, the receivables are collected in cash. The amount of cash actually collected through the end of the period may be less than the amount of sales revenue recorded.

REMEMBER

Cash inflow from revenue is almost always different from revenue for the period. Furthermore, cash outflow for expenses is almost always different from expenses for the period. The lesson is this: Do not equate revenue with cash inflow, and do not equate expenses with cash outflows. The net cash flow from profit for the period — revenue inflow minus expense outflow — is bound to be higher or lower than the accounting-based measure of profit for the period. The income statement does not report cash flows!

This chapter lays the foundation for Chapter 8, where we explain cash flow from profit. Cash flow is an enormously important topic in every business. We are sure even Apple, with its huge treasure of marketable investments, worries about its cash flow.

Folding profit into retained earnings

REMEMBER

After profit is determined for the period, which means that all revenue and expenses have been recorded for the period, the profit amount is entered as an increase in *retained earnings*. Doing this keeps the accounting equation in balance. For Case 1 in Figure 6-5, for example, the changes in the accounting equation for the period are as follows:

+$40 Assets = +$30 Liabilities + $10 Retained Earnings

The $40 increase on the asset side is balanced by the $30 increase in liabilities and the $10 increase in retained earnings on the opposite side of the accounting equation. The books are in balance.

In most situations, not all annual profit is distributed to owners; some is retained in the business. Unfortunately, the retained earnings account sounds like an asset in the minds of many people. It isn't! It's a source-of-assets account, not an asset account. It's on the right side of the accounting equation; assets are on the left side.

The technology business in Figure 6-1 earned $4.482 million profit for the year. Therefore, during the year, its retained earnings increased this amount because net income is captured in this owners' equity account. You know this for sure, but what you can't tell from the income statement is how the assets and liabilities of the business were affected by its sale and expense activities during the period. The technology company's $4.482 million net income resulted in some mixture of changes in its assets and liabilities, such that its owners' equity increased $4.482 million. Could be that its assets increased $3.0 million and its liabilities decreased $1.482 million, but you can't tell this from the income statement.

TIP

The financial gyrations in assets and operating liabilities from profit-making activities are especially important for business managers to understand and pay attention to because they have to manage and control the changes. It would be dangerous to assume that making a profit has only beneficial effects on assets and liabilities. One of the main purposes of the statement of cash flows, which we discuss in Chapter 8, is to summarize the financial changes caused by the profit activities of the business during the year.

Pinpointing the Assets and Liabilities Used to Record Revenue and Expenses

The sales and expense activities of a business involve cash inflows and outflows, as we are sure you know. What you may not know, however, is that the profit-making activities of a business that sells products or services on credit involves four other basic assets and three basic types of liabilities. Cash is the pivotal asset. You may have heard the old saying that "all roads lead to Rome." In like manner, revenue and expenses, sooner or later, lead to cash. But in the meantime, other asset and liability accounts are used to record the flow of profit activity. This section explains the main assets and liabilities used in recording revenue and expenses.

Making sales: Accounts receivable and deferred revenue

REMEMBER

Many businesses allow their customers to buy their products or services on credit, or "on the cuff," as they said in the old days. The customer buys now and pays later. To record credit sales, a business uses an asset account called *accounts receivable*. Recording a credit sale increases sales revenue and increases accounts receivable. The business records now and collects later. The immediate recording of credit sales is one aspect of the *accrual basis of accounting*. When the customer pays the business, cash is increased and accounts receivable is decreased. In most cases, a business doesn't collect all of its credit sales by the end of the year, so it reports a balance for its accounts receivable in its end-of-period balance sheet (see Chapter 7).

In contrast to making sales on credit, some businesses collect cash before they deliver their products or services to customers. An example of this is found in software companies that operate SaaS business models (software as a service). A company such as Microsoft will sell you a one-year subscription to use its Office product that provides you the right to use the software (per the terms of their agreement). Another example is when you buy and pay for an airline ticket days or weeks ahead of your flight. When a business receives advance payments from customers, it increases cash (of course) and increases a liability account called *deferred revenue*. Sales revenue isn't recorded until the product or service is delivered to the customer. When delivered sales revenue is increased, the liability account is decreased, which reflects that part of the liability has been "paid down" by delivery of the product or service.

REMEMBER

Increases or decreases in the asset *accounts receivable* and the liability account *deferred revenue* affect cash flow during the year from the profit-making activities of the business. We explain cash flow in Chapter 8. Until then, keep in mind that the balance of accounts receivable is money waiting in the wings to be collected in the near future, and the balance in deferred revenue is the amount of money collected in advance from customers. These two accounts appear in the balance sheet, which we discuss in Chapter 7.

Selling products: Inventory

The *cost of goods sold* is one of the primary expenses of businesses that sell products. (In Figure 6-1, notice that this expense equals roughly 38 percent of the sales revenue for the year.) This expense is just what its name implies: the cost that a business pays for the products or services it sells to customers. A business makes profit by setting its sales prices high enough to cover the costs of products and services sold, the costs of operating the business, interest on borrowed money, and income taxes (assuming that the business pays income tax), with something left over for profit.

When the business acquires products (by purchase or manufacture), the cost of the products goes into an *inventory* asset account (and, of course, the cost is either deducted from the cash account or added to a liability account, depending on whether the business pays cash or buys on credit). When a customer buys that product, the business transfers the cost of the products sold from the inventory asset account to the *cost of goods sold* expense account because the products are no longer in the business's inventory; the products have been delivered to the customer.

In the first layer in the income statement of a product company, the cost of goods sold expense is deducted from the sales revenue for the goods sold. Almost all businesses that sell products report the cost of goods sold as a separate expense in their income statements, as you see in Figure 6-1. Most report this expense as shown in Figure 6-1 so that *gross profit* is reported. But some product companies simply report cost of goods sold as one expense among many and do not call attention to gross profit. Actually, you see many variations on the theme of reporting gross profit. Some businesses use the broader term "cost of sales," which includes cost of goods sold as well as other costs that might include direct wages and employee benefits, third-party logistical services, and others.

REMEMBER

A business that sells products needs to have a stock of those products on hand for ready sale to its customers. When you drive by an auto dealer and see all the cars, SUVs, and pickup trucks waiting to be sold, note that these products are inventory. The cost of unsold products (goods held in inventory) is not yet an expense; only after the products are actually sold does the cost get recorded as an expense.

In this way, the cost of goods sold expense is correctly matched against the sales revenue from the goods sold. Correctly matching expenses against sales revenue is the essential starting point of accounting for profit.

Prepaying operating costs: Prepaid expenses

Prepaid expenses are the opposite of unpaid expenses. For example, a business purchases property insurance and general liability insurance (in case a customer who slips on a wet floor or is insulted by a careless salesperson sues the business). Insurance premiums must be paid ahead of time, before coverage starts. The premium cost is allocated to expense in the actual periods benefited. At the end of the year, the business may be only halfway through the insurance coverage period, so it should allocate only half the premium cost as an expense. (For a six-month policy, you charge one-sixth of the premium cost to each of the six months covered.) At the time the premium is paid, the entire amount is recorded as an increase in the prepaid expenses asset account. For each period of coverage, the appropriate fraction of the cost is recorded as a decrease in the asset account and as an increase in the insurance expense account.

In another example, a business pays cash to stock up on office supplies that it may not use up for several months. The cost is recorded in the prepaid expenses asset account at the time of purchase; when the supplies are used, the appropriate amount is subtracted from the prepaid expenses asset account and recorded in the office supplies expense account.

TIP

Using the prepaid expenses asset account is not so much for the purpose of reporting all the assets of a business, because the balance in the account compared with other assets and total assets is typically small. Rather, using this account is an example of allocating costs to expenses in the period benefited by the costs, which isn't always the same period in which the business pays those costs. The prepayment of these expenses lays the groundwork for continuing operations seamlessly into the next year.

Understanding fixed assets: Depreciation expense

Long-term operating assets that are not held for sale in the ordinary course of business are called generically *fixed assets*. These include buildings, machinery, office equipment, vehicles, computers and data-processing equipment, and so on. The term *fixed assets* is informal, or accounting slang. The more formal term used in financial reports is *property, plant, and equipment*. It's easier to say *fixed assets*, which we do in this section.

Depreciation refers to spreading out the cost of a fixed asset over the years of its useful life to a business, instead of charging the entire cost to expense in the year of purchase. That way, each year of use bears a share of the total cost. For example, autos and light trucks are typically depreciated over five years; the idea is to charge a fraction of the total cost to depreciation expense during each of the five years. (The actual fraction each year depends on the method of depreciation used, which we explain in Chapter 9.)

TIP

Depreciation applies only to fixed assets that a business owns, not those it rents or leases. If a company leases or rents fixed assets, which is quite common, the rent it pays each month is charged to *rent expense*. (We don't go into the current controversy regarding leases and rent expense at this point.) Depreciation is a real expense but not a cash outlay expense in the year it's recorded. The cash outlay occurred when the fixed asset was acquired. See the nearby sidebar "The special character of depreciation" for more information.

TECHNICAL
STUFF

Suppose a business records $100,000 depreciation for the period. You'd think that the depreciation expense account would be increased $100,000 and one or more fixed asset accounts would be decreased $100,000. Well, not so fast. Instead of directly decreasing the fixed asset account, the bookkeeper increases a contra asset account called *accumulated depreciation*. The balance in this negative account is deducted from the balance of the fixed asset account. In this manner, the original acquisition cost of the fixed asset is preserved, and the historical cost is reported in the balance sheet. We discuss this practice in Chapter 7.

TIP

Take a look at the technology company income statement example in Figure 6-1. From the information supplied in this income statement, you don't know the amount of depreciation expense the business recorded in 2020. However, the footnotes to the business's financial statements and its statement of cash flows reveal this amount. In 2020, the business recorded $1.239 million of depreciation expense. Basically, this expense decreases the book value (the recorded value) of its depreciable assets. *Book value* equals original cost minus the accumulated depreciation recorded so far. Book value may be different — indeed, quite a bit different — compared with the current replacement value of fixed assets.

Figuring unpaid expenses: Accounts payable, accrued expenses payable, and income tax payable

A typical business pays many expenses *after* the period in which the expenses are recorded. Following are common examples:

THE SPECIAL CHARACTER OF DEPRECIATION

To start with, let's agree that fixed assets wear out and lose their economic usefulness over time. Some fixed assets, such as office furniture and buildings, last many years. Other fixed assets, such as delivery trucks and computers, last just a few. Accountants argue, quite logically, that the cost of a fixed asset should be spread out or allocated over its predicted useful life to the business. Depreciation methods are rather arbitrary, but any reasonable method is much better than the alternative of charging off the entire cost of a fixed asset in the year it's acquired.

A business has to pass the cost of its fixed assets through to its customers and recover the cost of its fixed assets through sales revenue. For example, consider a taxicab driver who owns his cab. He sets his fares high enough to pay for his time; to pay for the insurance, license, gas, and oil; and to recover the cost of the cab. Included in each fare is a tiny fraction of the cost of the cab, which over the course of the year adds up to the depreciation expense that he passed on to his passengers and collected in fares. At the end of the year, he has collected a certain amount of money that pays him back for part of the cost of the cab.

In summary, fixed assets are gradually sold off and turned back into cash each year. Part of sales revenue recovers some of the cost of fixed assets, which is why the decrease in the fixed assets account to record depreciation expense has the effect of increasing cash (assuming your sales revenue is collected in cash during the year). What the company does with this cash recovery is another matter. Sooner or later, you need to replace fixed assets to continue in business.

>> A business hires a law firm that does lots of legal work during the year, but the company doesn't pay the bill until the following year.

>> A business matches retirement contributions made by its employees but doesn't pay its share of the latest payroll until the following year.

>> A business has unpaid bills for telephone service, gas, electricity, and water that it used during the year.

Accountants use three types of liability accounts to record a business's unpaid expenses:

>> **Accounts payable:** This account is used for items that the business buys on credit and for which it receives an invoice (a bill) either in hard copy or over the internet. For example, your business receives an invoice from its lawyers

for legal work done. As soon as you receive the invoice, you record in the accounts payable liability account the amount that you owe. Later, when you pay the invoice, you subtract that amount from the accounts payable account, and your cash goes down by the same amount.

>> **Accrued expenses payable:** A business has to make estimates for several unpaid costs at the end of the year because it hasn't received invoices or other types of bills for them. Examples of accrued expenses include the following:

- Unused vacation and sick days that employees carry over to the following year, which the business has to pay for in the coming year

- Unpaid bonuses or commissions to salespeople

- The cost of future repairs and part replacements (warranties) on products that customers have bought and haven't yet returned for repair

- The daily accumulation of interest on borrowed money that won't be paid until the end of the loan period

Without invoices to reference, you have to examine your business operations carefully to determine which liabilities of this sort to record.

>> **Income tax payable:** This account is used for income taxes that a business still owes to the IRS (Internal Revenue Service) at the end of the year. The income tax expense for the year is the total amount based on the taxable income for the entire year. Your business may not pay 100 percent of its income tax expense during the year; it may owe a small fraction to the IRS at year's end. You record the unpaid amount in the income tax payable account.

Note: A business may be organized legally as a *pass-through tax entity* for income tax purposes, which means that it doesn't pay income tax itself but instead passes its taxable income on to its owners. Chapter 5 explains these types of business entities. The business we refer to here is an ordinary corporation that pays income tax.

Reporting Unusual Gains and Losses

We have a small confession to make: The income statement examples in Figures 6-1, 6-2, and 6-3 are sanitized versions when compared with actual income statements in external financial reports. Suppose you took the trouble to read 100 income statements. You'd be surprised at the wide range of things you'd find in these statements. But we do know one thing for certain you'd discover.

Many businesses report *unusual gains and losses* in addition to their usual revenue and expenses (which we previously allude to as "other" expenses). Keep in mind that recording a gain increases an asset or decreases a liability. And recording a loss decreases an asset or increases a liability. The road to profit is anything but smooth and straight. Every business experiences an occasional gain or loss that's off the beaten path — a serious disruption that comes out of the blue, doesn't happen regularly, and impacts the bottom-line profit. Such unusual gains and losses are perturbations in the continuity of the business's regular flow of profit-making activities.

Here are some examples of unusual gains and losses:

» **Downsizing and restructuring the business:** Layoffs require severance pay or trigger early retirement costs. Major segments of the business may be disposed of, causing large losses.

» **Abandoning product lines:** When you decide to discontinue selling a line of products, you lose at least some of the money that you paid for obtaining or manufacturing the products, either because you sell the products for less than you paid or because you just dump the products you can't sell.

» **Settling lawsuits and other legal actions:** Damages and fines that you pay — as well as awards that you *receive* in a favorable ruling — are obviously nonrecurring losses or gains (unless you're in the habit of being taken to court every year).

» **Writing down (also called *writing off*) damaged and impaired assets:** If products become damaged and unsellable or if fixed assets need to be replaced unexpectedly, you need to remove these items from the assets accounts. Even when certain assets are in good physical condition, if they lose their ability to generate future sales or other benefits to the business, accounting rules say that the assets have to be taken off the books or at least written down to lower book values.

» **Changing accounting methods:** A business may decide to use a different method for recording revenue and expenses than it did in the past, in some cases because the accounting rules (set by the authoritative accounting governing bodies — see Chapter 2) have changed. Often, the new method requires a business to record a one-time cumulative effect caused by the switch in accounting method. These special items can be huge.

» **Correcting errors from previous financial reports:** If you or your accountant discovers that a past financial report had a serious accounting error, you make a catch-up correction entry, which means that you record a loss or gain that has nothing to do with your performance this year.

The basic tests for an unusual gain or loss are that it is unusual in nature or infrequently occurring. Deciding what qualifies as an unusual gain or loss is not a cut-and-dried process. Different accountants may have different interpretations of what fits the concept of an unusual gain or loss.

According to financial reporting standards, a business should disclose unusual gains and losses on a separate line in the income statement or, alternatively, explain them in a footnote to its financial statements. We explain the role of footnotes in Chapter 10. There seems to be a general preference to put an unusual gain or loss on a separate line in the income statement. Therefore, in addition to the usual lines for revenue and expenses, the income statement would disclose separate lines for these out-of-the-ordinary happenings.

WARNING

Every company that stays in business for more than a couple of years experiences an unusual gain or loss of one sort or another. But beware of a business that takes advantage of these discontinuities in the following ways:

>> **Discontinuities become continuities:** This business makes an extraordinary loss or gain a regular feature on its income statement. Every year or so, the business loses a major lawsuit, abandons product lines, or restructures itself. It reports certain "nonrecurring" gains or losses on a recurring basis.

>> **A discontinuity is used as an opportunity to record all sorts of write-downs and losses:** When recording an unusual loss (such as settling a lawsuit), the business opts to record other losses at the same time, and everything but the kitchen sink (and sometimes that, too) gets written off. This so-called *big-bath* strategy says that you may as well take a big bath now in order to avoid taking little showers in the future.

A business may just have bad (or good) luck regarding unusual events that its managers couldn't have predicted. If a business is facing a major, unavoidable expense this year, cleaning out all its expenses in the same year so it can start off fresh next year can be a clever, legitimate accounting tactic. But where do you draw the line between these accounting manipulations and fraud? All we can advise you to do is stay alert to these potential problems.

Watching for Misconceptions and Misleading Reports

One broad misconception about profit is that the numbers reported in the income statement are precise and accurate and can be relied on down to the last dollar. Call this the *exactitude* misconception. Virtually every dollar amount you see in an income statement probably would have been different if a different accountant had been in charge. We don't mean that some accountants are dishonest and deceitful. It's just that business transactions can get very complex and require forecasts and estimates. Different accountants would arrive at different interpretations of the "facts" and therefore record different amounts of revenue and expenses. Hopefully, the accountant is consistent over time so that year-to-year comparisons are valid.

Another serious misconception is that if profit is good, the financial condition of the business is good. As we write this sentence, the profit of Apple is very good. But we didn't automatically assume that its financial condition was equally good. We looked in Apple's balance sheet and found that its financial condition is very good indeed. (It has more cash and marketable investments on hand than the economy of many countries.) Our point is that its bottom line doesn't tell you anything about the financial condition of the business. You find this in the balance sheet, which we explain in Chapter 7.

REMEMBER

The income statement occupies center stage; the bright spotlight is on this financial statement because it reports profit or loss for the period. But a business reports *three* primary financial statements — the other two being the balance sheet and the statement of cash flows, which we discuss in the next two chapters. The three statements are like a three-ring circus. The income statement may draw the most attention, but you have to watch what's going on in all three places. As important as profit is to the financial success of a business, the income statement is not an island unto itself.

TIP

Keep in mind that financial statements are supplemented with footnotes and contain other commentary from the business's executives. If the financial statements have been audited, the CPA firm includes a short report stating whether the financial statements have been prepared in conformity with the appropriate accounting standards.

We don't like closing this chapter on a sour note, but we must point out that an income statement you read and rely on — as a business manager, an investor, or a lender — may not be true and accurate. In most cases (we'll even say in the large majority of cases), businesses prepare their financial statements in good faith, and their profit accounting is honest. They may bend the rules a little, but basically their accounting methods are within the boundaries of GAAP even though the business puts a favorable spin on its profit number.

WARNING

But some businesses resort to accounting fraud and deliberately distort their profit numbers. In this case, an income statement reports false and misleading sales revenue and/or expenses in order to make the bottom-line profit appear to be better than the facts would support. If the fraud is discovered at a later time, the business puts out revised financial statements. Basically, the business in this situation rewrites its profit history.

We wish we could say that financial reporting fraud doesn't happen very often, but the number of high-profile accounting fraud cases over the recent two decades (and longer in fact) has been truly alarming. The CPA auditors of these companies didn't catch the accounting fraud, even though this is one purpose of an audit. Investors who relied on the fraudulent income statements ended up suffering large losses.

Anytime we read a financial report, we keep in mind the risk that the financial statements may be "stage managed" to some extent — to make year-to-year reported profit look a little smoother and less erratic and to make the financial condition of the business appear a little better. Regrettably, financial statements don't always tell it as it is. Rather, the chief executive and chief accountant of the business fiddle with the financial statements to some extent. We say much more about this tweaking in later chapters.

Chapter **7**

Reporting Financial Condition in the Balance Sheet

This chapter explores one of the three primary financial statements reported by business and not-for-profit entities: the *balance sheet*, which is also called the *statement of financial condition* and the *statement of financial position*. This financial statement summarizes the assets of a business and its liabilities and owners' equity sources at a point in time, almost always at the end of the income statement reporting period. The balance sheet is a two-sided financial statement that lists assets on the left and liabilities and owners' equity on the right.

The balance sheet may seem to stand alone because it's presented on a separate page in a financial report, but keep in mind that the assets and liabilities reported in a balance sheet are the results of the activities, or transactions, of the business. *Transactions* are economic exchanges between the business and the parties it deals with: customers, employees, vendors, government agencies, creditors, and sources of capital. The other two financial statements — the income statement (see Chapter 6) and the statement of cash flows (see Chapter 8) — report transactions over a period of time (for example, 30 days), whereas the balance sheet reports values at an instant in time (for example, as of December 31, 2020). The balance sheet is almost always prepared as of the last day of the income statement period.

Unlike the income statement, the balance sheet doesn't have a natural bottom line, or one key figure that's the focus of attention. The balance sheet reports various assets, liabilities, and sources of owners' equity. Cash is a very important asset, but other assets are equally important as well, including trade account receivables; inventory; property, plant, and equipment; intangible assets; and company investments. The balance sheet, as we explain in this chapter, has to be read as a whole — you can't focus only on one or two items in this financial summary of the business. You shouldn't put on blinders in reading a balance sheet by looking only at two or three items. You might miss important information by not perusing the whole balance sheet.

Expanding the Accounting Equation

The *accounting equation*, which we discuss in previous chapters, is a very condensed version of a balance sheet. In its most concise form, the accounting equation is as follows:

Assets = Liabilities + Owners' Equity

Figure 7-1 expands the accounting equation to identify the basic accounts reported in a balance sheet.

Many of the balance sheet accounts you see in Figure 7-1 are introduced in Chapter 6, which explains the income statement and the profit-making activities of a business. In fact, most balance sheet accounts are driven by profit-making transactions.

Assets =	Liabilities +	Owners' Equity
Cash & Equivalents	Accounts Payable	Retained Earnings
		Invested Capital
Accounts Receivable	Accrued Liabilities	Accounts
Inventory	Income Taxes Payable	Other Equity
Prepaid Expenses	Other Current Liabilities	
Fixed Assets, Net	Short-Term Debt	
Intangible & Other, Net	Long-Term Debt	

FIGURE 7-1: Expanded accounting equation.

© John Wiley & Sons, Inc.

Certain balance sheet accounts are not involved in recording the profit-making transactions of a business. Short- and long-term debt accounts aren't used in recording revenue and expenses, and neither is the invested capital account, which records the investment of capital from the owners of the business. Transactions involving debt and owners' invested capital accounts have to do with *financing* the business — that is, securing the capital needed to run the business.

Presenting a Proper Balance Sheet

Figure 7-2 presents a two-year, comparative balance sheet for the business example that we introduce in Chapter 6. This technology business sells products and services and makes sales on credit to its customers. Its income statement for the year just ended is shown in Figure 6-1. The balance sheet is at the close of business, December 31, 2019 and 2020. In most cases, financial statements are not completed and released until a few weeks after the balance sheet date. Therefore, by the time you read this financial statement, it's already somewhat out of date, because the business has continued to engage in transactions since December 31, 2020.

When significant changes have occurred in the interim between the closing date of the balance sheet and the date of releasing its financial report, a business should disclose these subsequent developments in the footnotes to the financial statements.

The balance sheet in Figure 7-2 is in the vertical (portrait) layout, with assets on top and liabilities and owners' equity on the bottom. Alternatively, a balance sheet may be in the horizontal (landscape) mode, with liabilities and owners' equity on the right side and assets on the left.

The financial statement in Figure 7-2 is called a *classified* balance sheet because certain accounts are grouped into classes (groups). Although the accounts in the class are different, they have common characteristics. Two such classes are *current assets* and *current liabilities.* Notice that subtotals are provided for each class. We discuss the reasons for reporting these classes of accounts later in this chapter (see the section "Current assets and liabilities"). The total amount of assets and the total amount of liabilities plus owners' equity are given at the bottom of the columns for each year. We probably don't have to remind you that these two amounts should be equal; otherwise, the company's books aren't in balance.

If a business doesn't release its annual financial report within a month after the close of its fiscal year, you should be alarmed. There are reasons for such a delay, and the reasons are all bad. One reason might be that the business's accounting system isn't functioning well and the controller (chief accounting officer) has to do lots of work at year-end to get the accounts up to date and accurate for preparing its financial statements. Another reason is that the business is facing serious problems and can't decide on how to account for the problems. Perhaps a business is delaying the reporting of bad news. Or the business may have a serious dispute with its independent CPA auditor that hasn't been resolved.

REMEMBER

The balance sheet in Figure 7-2 includes a column for *changes* in the assets, liabilities, and owners' equity over the year (from year-end 2019 through year-end 2020). Including these changes is not required by financial reporting standards, and in fact most businesses do not include the changes. It's certainly acceptable to report balance sheet changes, but it's not mandated, and most companies don't. We include the changes for ease of reference in this chapter. Transactions generate changes in assets, liabilities, and owners' equity, which we summarize later in this chapter (see the section "Understanding That Transactions Drive the Balance Sheet").

Doing an initial reading of the balance sheet

Now suppose you own the business whose balance sheet is in Figure 7-2. (Most likely, you wouldn't own 100 percent of the ownership shares of the business; you'd own the majority of shares, giving you working control of the business.) You've already digested your most recent annual income statement (refer to Figure 6-1), which reports that you earned $4,482,000 net income on annual sales of $71,064,000. What more do you need to know? Well, you need to check your financial condition, which is reported in the balance sheet.

Is your financial condition viable and sustainable to continue your profit-making endeavor? The balance sheet helps answer this critical question. Perhaps you're on the edge of going bankrupt, even though you're making a profit. Your balance sheet is where to look for telltale information about possible financial troubles.

In reading through a balance sheet, you may notice that it doesn't have a punchline like the income statement does. The income statement's punchline is the net income line, which is rarely humorous to the business itself but can cause some snickers among analysts. (Earnings per share is also very important for public corporations.) You can't look at just one item on the balance sheet, murmur an appreciative "ah-ha," and rush home to watch the game. You have to read the whole thing (sigh) and make comparisons among the items. Chapters 11 and 12 offer information on interpreting financial statements.

QW Example Tech., Inc.			
Sales of Both Products & Software Services			
for the Fiscal Year Ending			
12/31/2020			

Statement of Financial Condition (aka Balance Sheet) Period Ending (All Numbers in Thousands)	FYE 12/31/2019	FYE 12/31/2020	Change
Assets			
Current Assets:			
Cash & Equivalents	$788	$11,281	$10,493
Accounts Receivable, Net	$6,718	$8,883	$2,165
Inventory, LCM	$4,061	$1,733	($2,328)
Prepaid Expenses	$300	$325	$25
Total Current Assets	$11,867	$22,222	$10,355
Long-Term Operating & Other Assets:			
Property, Plant, Equipment, & Machinery	$7,920	$8,670	$750
Accumulated Depreciation	($3,081)	($4,320)	($1,239)
Net Property, Plant, & Equipment	$4,839	$4,350	($489)
Other Assets:			
Intangible Assets & Goodwill, Net	$1,000	$500	($500)
Other Assets	$100	$100	$0
Total Long-Term Operating & Other Assets	$5,939	$4,950	($989)
Total Assets	$17,806	$27,172	$9,366
Liabilities			
Current Liabilities:			
Accounts Payable	$1,654	$1,929	$275
Accrued Liabilities & Other	$667	$830	$163
Current Portion of Debt	$1,000	$1,000	$0
Other Current Liabilities & Deferred Revenue	$408	$1,204	$796
Total Current Liabilities	$3,729	$4,963	$1,234
Long-Term Liabilities:			
Notes Payable & Other Long-Term Debt	$7,200	$6,250	($950)
Total Liabilities	$10,929	$11,213	$284
Stockholders' Equity			
Capital Stock — Common	$5,000	$5,000	$0
Capital Stock — Preferred	$0	$5,000	$5,000
Retained Earnings	$1,877	$5,959	$4,082
Total Stockholders' Equity	$6,877	$15,959	$9,082
Total Liabilities & Stockholders' Equity	$17,806	$27,172	$9,366

Confidential — Property of QW Example Tech., Inc.

FIGURE 7-2: Illustrative two-year comparative balance sheet for a technology business.

At first glance, you might be somewhat amazed that your cash balance increased by $10,493,000 during the year (refer to Figure 7-2) when your profit of $4,482,000 was less than half of this figure. Why would your cash balance increase so much? Well, think about it. Many other transactions affect your cash balance. For example, did you invest in new long-term operating assets (called *property, plant, and equipment* in the balance sheet)? Yes, you did, as a matter of fact. These fixed assets increased $750,000 during the year.

Overall, your total assets increased $9,366,000. All assets increased during the year except inventory and other long-term assets. One big reason is the $4,082,000 increase in your retained earnings owners' equity (which is derived from your net income of $4,482,000 less a dividend paid of $400,000). We explain in Chapter 6 that earning profit increases retained earnings. Profit was $4,482,000 for the year, but retained earnings increased only $4,082,000. Therefore, part of profit was distributed to the owners via issuing a $400,000 dividend, decreasing retained earnings. We discuss these things and other balance sheet interpretations as you move through this chapter. For now, the preliminary read of the balance sheet doesn't indicate any earth-shattering financial problems facing your business.

TIP

The balance sheet of a service business looks pretty much the same as our technology business (see Figure 7-2) — except a service business doesn't report an inventory of products held for sale. If it sells on credit, a service business has an accounts receivable asset, just like a product company that sells on credit. The size of its total assets relative to annual sales revenue for a service business varies greatly from industry to industry, depending on whether the service industry is *capital intensive* or not. Some service businesses, such as airlines, for-profit hospitals, and hotel chains, need to make heavy investments in long-term operating assets. Other service businesses do not.

REMEMBER

The balance sheet is unlike the income and cash flow statements, which report flows over a period of time (such as sales revenue that is the cumulative amount of all sales during the period). The balance sheet presents the *balances* (amounts) of a company's assets, liabilities, and owners' equity at an instant in time. Notice the two quite different meanings of the term *balance*. As used in *balance sheet*, the term refers to the equality of the two opposing sides of a business — total assets on the one side and total liabilities and owners' equity on the other side, like a scale. In contrast, the *balance* of an account (asset, liability, owners' equity, revenue, and expense) refers to the amount in the account after recording increases and decreases in the account — the net amount after all additions and subtractions have been entered. Usually, the meaning of the term is clear in context.

TIP

An accountant can prepare a balance sheet at any time that a manager wants to know how things stand financially. Some businesses — particularly financial institutions such as banks, mutual funds, and securities brokers — need balance sheets at the end of each day in order to track their day-to-day financial situation.

For most businesses, however, balance sheets are prepared only at the end of each month, quarter, or year. A balance sheet is always prepared at the close of business on the last day of the profit period. In other words, the balance sheet should be in sync with the income statement.

Kicking balance sheets out into the real world

The statement of financial condition, or balance sheet, in Figure 7-2 is about as lean and mean as you'll ever read. In the real world, many businesses are fat and complex. Also, we should make clear that Figure 7-2 shows the content and format for an *external* balance sheet, which means a balance sheet that's included in a financial report released outside a business to its owners and creditors. Balance sheets that stay within a business can be quite different.

Internal balance sheets

REMEMBER

For internal reporting of financial condition to managers, balance sheets include much more detail, either in the body of the financial statement itself or, more likely, in supporting schedules. For example, just one cash account is shown in Figure 7-2, but the chief financial officer of a business needs to know the balances on deposit in each of the business's checking accounts.

As another example, the balance sheet in Figure 7-2 includes just one total amount for accounts receivable, but managers need details on which customers owe money and whether any major amounts are past due. Greater detail allows for better control, analysis, and decision-making. Internal balance sheets and their supporting schedules should provide all the detail that managers need to make good business decisions. See Chapter 13 for details on how business managers use financial reports.

External balance sheets

Balance sheets presented in external financial reports (which go out to investors and lenders) don't include much more detail than the balance sheet in Figure 7-2. However, as we mention earlier, external balance sheets must *classify* (or group together) short-term assets and liabilities. These are called *current assets* and *current liabilities*, as you see in Figure 7-2. Internal balance sheets for management use only don't have to be classified if the managers don't want the information.

TIP

We need to make clear that the NSA doesn't vet balance sheets to prevent the disclosure of secrets that would harm national security. The term *classified,* when applied to a balance sheet, means that assets and liabilities are sorted into basic classes, or groups, for external reporting. Classifying certain assets and liabilities into *current* categories is done mainly to help readers of a balance sheet compare current assets with current liabilities for the purpose of judging the short-term solvency of a business.

Judging Liquidity and Solvency

REMEMBER

Solvency refers to the ability of a business to pay its liabilities on time. Delays in paying liabilities on time can cause serious problems for a business. In extreme cases, a business can be thrown into *involuntary bankruptcy*. Even the threat of bankruptcy can cause serious disruptions in the normal operations of a business, and profit performance is bound to suffer. The *liquidity* of a business isn't a well-defined term; it can take on different meanings. However, generally it refers to the ability of a business to keep its cash balance and its cash flows at adequate levels so that operations aren't disrupted by cash shortfalls. For more on this important topic, check out *Cash Flow For Dummies* (Wiley), which we coauthored.

If current liabilities become too high relative to current assets — which constitute the first line of defense for paying current liabilities — managers should move quickly to resolve the problem. A perceived shortage of current assets relative to current liabilities could ring alarm bells in the minds of the company's creditors and owners.

Therefore, notice the following points in Figure 7-2 (dollar amounts refer to year-end 2020):

>> **Current assets:** The first four asset accounts (cash, accounts receivable, inventory, and prepaid expenses) are added to give the $22.222 million subtotal for *current assets*.

>> **Current liabilities:** The first four liability accounts (accounts payable, accrued liabilities and other, current portion of debt, and other current liabilities and deferred revenue) are added to give the $4.963 million subtotal for *current liabilities*.

>> **Notes payable:** The total interest-bearing debt of the business is divided between $1 million in *short-term* notes payable (those due in one year or sooner) and $6.25 million in *long-term* notes payable and other long-term liabilities (those due after one year).

Read on for details on current assets and liabilities and on the current and quick ratios.

Current assets and liabilities

Short-term, or *current*, assets include the following:

>> Cash

>> Marketable securities that can be immediately converted into cash

>> Assets converted into cash within one operating cycle, the main components being accounts receivable and inventory

The *operating cycle* refers to the repetitive process of putting cash into inventory, holding products in inventory until they're sold, selling products on credit (which generates accounts receivable), and collecting the receivables in cash. In other words, the operating cycle is the "from cash, through inventory and accounts receivable, back to cash" sequence. The operating cycles of businesses vary from a few weeks to several months, depending on how long inventory is held before being sold and how long it takes to collect cash from sales made on credit.

Short-term, or *current*, liabilities include non-interest-bearing liabilities that arise from the operating (sales and expense) activities of the business. A typical business keeps many accounts for these liabilities — a separate account for each vendor, for example. In an external balance sheet, you usually find only three or four operating liabilities, and they aren't labeled as non-interest-bearing. It's assumed that the reader knows that these operating liabilities don't bear interest (unless the liability is seriously overdue and the creditor has started charging interest because of the delay in paying the liability).

TIP

The balance sheet example in Figure 7-2 discloses three operating liabilities: accounts payable, accrued liabilities and other, and other current liabilities and deferred revenue. Be warned that the terminology for these short-term operating liabilities varies from business to business.

In addition to operating liabilities, interest-bearing notes payable that have maturity dates one year or less from the balance sheet date are included in the current liabilities section. The current liabilities section may also include certain other liabilities that must be paid in the short run (which are too varied and technical to discuss here).

Current and quick ratios

The sources of cash for paying current liabilities are the company's current assets. That is, current assets are the first source of money to pay current liabilities when these liabilities come due. Remember that current assets consist of cash and assets that will be converted into cash in the short run.

The *current ratio* lets you size up current assets against total current liabilities. Using information from the balance sheet (refer to Figure 7-2), you compute the company's year-end 2020 current ratio as follows:

$22.222 million current assets ÷ $4.963 million current liabilities = 4.48 current ratio

Generally, businesses do not provide their current ratio on the face of their balance sheets or in the footnotes to their financial statements — they leave it to the reader to calculate this number. On the other hand, many businesses present a financial highlights section in their financial report, which often includes the current ratio.

The *quick ratio* is more restrictive. Only cash and assets that can be immediately converted into cash are included. The business in this example doesn't have any short-term marketable investments that could be sold on a moment's notice. You compute the quick ratio as follows (see Figure 7-2):

$20.164 million quick assets ÷ $4.963 million current liabilities = 4.06 quick ratio

Folklore has it that a company's current ratio should be at least 2.0, and its quick ratio, 1.0. However, business managers know that acceptable ratios depend a great deal on general practices in the industry for short-term borrowing. Some businesses do well with current ratios less than 2.0 and quick ratios less than 1.0, so take these benchmarks with a grain of salt. Lower ratios don't necessarily mean that the business won't be able to pay its short-term (current) liabilities on time. Chapters 11 and 12 explain solvency in more detail.

Understanding That Transactions Drive the Balance Sheet

A balance sheet is a snapshot of the financial condition of a business at an instant in time — the most important moment in time being at the end of the last day of the income statement period. The *fiscal*, or accounting, year of our business example ends on December 31. So its balance sheet is prepared at the close of business at midnight on December 31. (A company should end its fiscal year at the close of its natural business year or at the close of a calendar quarter — September 30, for example.)

This freeze-frame nature of a balance sheet may make it appear that a balance sheet is static. Nothing is further from the truth. A business doesn't shut down to prepare its balance sheet. The financial condition of a business is in constant motion because the activities of the business go on nonstop.

Transactions change the makeup of a company's balance sheet — that is, its assets, liabilities, and owners' equity. The transactions of a business fall into three fundamental types:

>> **Operating activities, which also can be called profit-making activities:** This category refers to making sales and incurring expenses, and it also includes accompanying transactions that lead or follow the recording of sales and expenses. For example, a business records sales revenue when sales are made on credit and then, later, records cash collections from customers. The transaction of collecting cash is the indispensable follow-up to making the sale on credit.

For another example, a business purchases products that are placed in its inventory (its stock of products awaiting sale), at which time it records an entry for the purchase. The expense (the cost of goods sold) is not recorded until the products are actually sold to customers. Keep in mind that the term *operating activities* includes the associated transactions that precede or are subsequent to the recording of sales and expense transactions.

>> **Investing activities:** This term refers to making investments in assets and (eventually) disposing of the assets when the business no longer needs them. The primary examples of investing activities for businesses that sell products and services are *capital expenditures,* which are the amounts spent to modernize, expand, and replace the long-term operating assets of a business. A business may also invest in *financial assets,* such as bonds and stocks or other types of debt and equity instruments. Purchases and sales of financial assets are also included in this category of transactions.

>> **Financing activities:** These activities include securing money from debt and equity sources of capital, returning capital to these sources, and making distributions from profit to owners. Note that distributing profit to owners is treated as a financing transaction. For example, when a business corporation pays cash dividends to its stockholders, the distribution is treated as a financing transaction. The decision of whether to distribute some of its profit depends on whether the business needs more capital from its owners to grow the business or to strengthen its solvency. Retaining part or all of the profit for the year is one way of increasing the owners' equity in the business. We discuss this topic later in "Financing a Business: Sources of Cash and Capital."

Figure 7-3 presents a summary of changes in assets, liabilities, and owners' equity during the year for the business example we introduce in Chapter 6 and continue in this chapter. Notice the middle three columns, which show each of the three basic types of transactions of a business. One column is for changes caused by its revenue and expenses and their connected transactions during the year, which collectively are called *operating activities* (although we prefer to call them *profit-making activities*). The second column is for changes caused by its *investing activities* during the year. The third column is for the changes caused by its *financing activities.*

Statement of Financial Condition (AKA Balance Sheet) Period Ending (All Numbers in Thousands) Assets	Beg. Balance 12/31/2019	Operating Activities	Investing Activities	Financing Activities	Change	End. Balance 12/31/2020
Current Assets:						
Cash & Equivalents	$788	$7,593	($750)	$3,650	$10,493	$11,281
Accounts Receivable, Net	$6,718	($2,165)	$0	$0	($2,165)	$8,883
Inventory, LCM	$4,061	$2,328	$0	$0	$2,328	$1,733
Prepaid Expenses	$300	($25)	$0	$0	($25)	$325
Total Current Assets	$11,867	$7,731	($750)	$3,650	$10,631	$22,222
Long-Term Operating & Other Assets:						
Property, Plant, Equipment, & Machinery	$7,920	$0	$750	$0	$750	$8,670
Accumulated Depreciation	($3,081)	$1,239	$0	$0	$1,239	($4,320)
Net Property, Plant, & Equipment	$4,839	$1,239	$750	$0	$1,989	$4,350
Other Assets:						
Intangible Assets & Goodwill, Net	$1,000	$500	$0	$0	$500	$500
Other Assets	$100	$0	$0	$0	$0	$100
Total Long-Term Operating & Other Assets	$5,939	$1,739	$750	$0	$2,489	$4,950
Total Assets	$17,806	$9,470	$0	$3,650	$13,120	$27,172
Liabilities						
Current Liabilities:						
Accounts Payable	$1,654	$275	$0	$0	$275	$1,929
Accrued Liabilities & Other	$667	$163	$0	$0	$163	$830
Current Portion of Debt	$1,000	$0	$0	$0	$0	$1,000
Other Current Liabilities & Deferred Revenue	$408	$796	$0	$0	$796	$1,204
Total Current Liabilities	$3,729	$1,234	$0	$0	$1,234	$4,963
Long-Term Liabilities:						
Notes Payable & Other Long-Term Debt	$7,200	$0	$0	($950)	($950)	$6,250
Total Liabilities	$10,929	$1,234	$0	($950)	$284	$11,213
Stockholders' Equity						
Capital Stock — Common	$5,000	$0	$0	$0	$0	$5,000
Capital Stock — Preferred	$0	$0	$0	$5,000	$5,000	$5,000
Retained Earnings	$1,877	$4,482	$0	($400)	$4,082	$5,959
Total Stockholders' Equity	$6,877	$4,482	$0	$4,600	$9,082	$15,959
Total Liabilities & Stockholders' Equity	$17,806	$5,716	$0	$3,650	$9,366	$27,172

QW Example Tech., Inc.
Sales of Both Products & Software Services
for the Fiscal Year Ending
12/31/2020

Confidential — Property of QW Example Tech., Inc.

© *John Wiley & Sons, Inc.*

FIGURE 7-3:
Summary of changes in assets, liabilities, and owners' equity during the year according to basic types of transactions.

Note: Figure 7-3 includes subtotals for current assets and liabilities; the formal balance sheet for this business is in Figure 7-2. Businesses don't report a summary of changes in their assets, liabilities, and owners' equity (though we think such a summary would be helpful to users of financial reports). The purpose of Figure 7-3 is to demonstrate how the three major types of transactions during the year change the assets, liabilities, and owners' equity accounts of the business during the year.

The 2020 income statement of the business is shown in Figure 6-1 in Chapter 6. You may want to flip back to this financial statement. On sales revenue of $71.064 million, the business earned $4.482 million bottom-line profit (net income) for the year. The sales and expense transactions of the business during the year plus the associated transactions connected with sales and expenses cause the changes shown in the operating-activities column in Figure 7-3. You can see that the $4.482 million net income has increased the business's owners' equity–retained earnings by the same amount. (The business paid $400,000 distributions from profit in the form of a dividend to its owners during the year, which decreases the balance in retained earnings.)

TIP

The operating-activities column in Figure 7-3 is worth lingering over for a few moments because the financial outcomes of making profit are seen in this column. In our experience, most people see a profit number, such as the $4.482 million in this example, and stop thinking any further about the financial outcomes of making the profit. This is like going to a movie because you like its title, without knowing anything about the plot and characters. You probably noticed that the $7.593 million increase in cash in this operating-activities column differs from the $4.482 million net income figure for the year. The cash effect of making profit (which includes the associated transactions connected with sales and expenses) is almost always different from the net income amount for the year. Chapter 8 explains this difference.

REMEMBER

The summary of changes in Figure 7-3 gives you a sense of the balance sheet in motion, or how the business got from the start of the year to the end of the year. Having a good sense of how transactions propel the balance sheet is important. This kind of summary of balance sheet changes can be helpful to business managers who plan and control changes in the assets and liabilities of the business. Managers need a solid understanding of how the three basic types of transactions change assets and liabilities. Figure 7-3 also provides a useful platform for the statement of cash flow in Chapter 8.

Sizing Up Assets and Liabilities

When you first read the balance sheet in Figure 7-2, did you wonder about the size of the company's assets, liabilities, and owners' equities? Did you ask, "Are the balance sheet accounts about the right size?" The balances in a company's balance sheet accounts should be compared with the sales revenue size of the business. The amounts of assets that are needed to carry on the profit-making transactions of a business depend mainly on the size of its annual revenue. And the sizes of its assets, in turn, largely determine the sizes of its liabilities — which, in turn, determines the size of its owners' equity accounts (although the ratio of liabilities and owners' equity depends on other factors as well).

Although the business example we use in this chapter is hypothetical, we didn't make up the numbers at random. We use a modest-sized technology business that has $71.064 million in annual sales revenue. The other numbers in its income statement and balance sheet are realistic relative to each other. We assume that the business earns 62 percent gross margin ($44.173 million gross margin ÷ $71.064 million sales revenue = 62 percent), which means its cost of goods sold expense is 38 percent of sales revenue. The sizes of particular assets and liabilities compared with their relevant income statement numbers vary from industry to industry and even from business to business in the same industry.

Based on the business's history and operating policies, the managers of a business can estimate what the size of each asset and liability should be; these estimates provide useful *control benchmarks* to which the actual balances of the assets and liabilities are compared. Assets (and liabilities, too) can be too high or too low relative to the sales revenue and expenses that drive them, and these deviations can cause problems that managers should try to remedy.

For example, based on the credit terms extended to its customers and the company's actual policies regarding how aggressively it acts in collecting past-due receivables, a manager determines the range for the proper, or within-the-boundaries, balance of accounts receivable. This figure is the control benchmark. If the actual balance is reasonably close to this control benchmark, accounts receivable is under control. If not, the manager should investigate why accounts receivable is smaller or larger than it should be.

This section discusses the relative sizes of the assets and liabilities in the balance sheet that result from sales and expenses (for the fiscal year 2020). The sales and expenses are the *drivers*, or causes, of the assets and liabilities. If a business earned profit simply by investing in stocks and bonds, it wouldn't need all the various assets and liabilities explained in this chapter. Such a business — a mutual fund, for example — would have just one income-producing asset: investments in securities. This chapter focuses on businesses that sell products on credit.

Sales revenue and accounts receivable

Annual sales revenue for the year 2020 is $71.064 million in our example (see Figure 6-1). The year-end accounts receivable is one-eighth of this, or $8.883 million (see Figure 7-2). So the average customer's credit period is roughly 45 days: 365 days in the year times the 12.5 percent ratio of ending accounts receivable balance to annual sales revenue. Of course, some customers' balances are past 45 days, and some are quite new; you want to focus on the average. The key question is whether a customer credit period averaging 45 days is reasonable.

Suppose that the business offers all customers a 30-day credit period, which is common in business-to-business selling (although not for a retailer selling to individual consumers). The small deviation of about 15 days (45 days average credit period versus 30 days normal credit terms) probably isn't a significant cause for concern; most businesses that actively sell on credit know larger customers will generally squeeze another two to four weeks from the business to remit payment. But suppose that, at the end of the period, the accounts receivable had been $12.900 million, which is 18 percent of annual sales, or about a 66-day average credit period. Such an abnormally high balance should raise a red flag; the responsible manager should look into the reasons for the abnormally high accounts receivable balance. Perhaps several customers are seriously late in paying and shouldn't be extended new credit until they pay up.

Cost of goods sold expense and inventory

In the example, the cost of goods sold expense for the year 2020 is $26.891 million, of which $10.395 million relates strictly to product sales and the balance of $16.496 million relates to software service sales. The year-end inventory is $1.733 million, or about 16.7 percent. In rough terms, the average product's inventory holding period is 61 days — 365 days in the year times the 16.7 percent ratio of ending inventory to annual cost of goods sold for products only. Of course, some products may remain in inventory longer than the 61-day average, and some products may sell in a much shorter period than 61 days. You need to focus on the overall average. Is an 61-day average inventory holding period reasonable?

One thing that should immediately jump out in our example is this: Why did the inventory balance decrease so drastically on a year-over-year basis (from $4.061 million to $1.733 million)? The answer lies in the fact that this technology company is pivoting its business from being "product focused" (that is, selling tangible computers and technology) to selling more software and services (which is labor intensive). This is a very common strategy and trend these days as companies expand their offerings of SaaS (software as a service) products.

REMEMBER

The "correct" average inventory holding period varies from industry to industry. In some industries, especially heavy equipment manufacturing, the inventory holding period is long — three months or more. The opposite is true for high-volume retailers, such as retail supermarkets, that depend on getting products off the shelves as quickly as possible. The 61-day average holding period in the example is reasonable for many businesses but would be too high for others.

The managers should know what the company's average inventory holding period should be — they should know what the control benchmark is for the inventory holding period. If inventory is much above this control benchmark, managers should take prompt action to get inventory back in line (which is easier said than done, of course). If inventory is at abnormally low levels, this should be investigated as well. Perhaps some products are out of stock and should be restocked to avoid lost sales.

Fixed assets and depreciation expense

Depreciation is like other expenses in that all expenses are deducted from sales revenue to determine profit. Other than this, however, depreciation is very different from most other expenses. (Amortization expense, which we get to later, is a kissing cousin of depreciation.) When a business buys or builds a long-term operating asset, the cost of the asset is recorded in a specific fixed asset account. *Fixed* is an overstatement; although the assets may last a long time, eventually they're retired from service. The main point is that the cost of a long-term operating or fixed asset is spread out, or allocated, over its expected useful life to the business. Each year of use bears some portion of the cost of the fixed asset.

The depreciation expense recorded in the period doesn't require any cash outlay during the period. (The cash outlay occurred when the fixed asset was acquired, or perhaps later when a loan was secured for part of the total cost.) Rather, *depreciation expense* for the period is that quota of the total cost of a business's fixed assets that is allocated to the period to record the cost of using the assets during the period. Depreciation depends on which method is used to allocate the cost of fixed assets over their estimated useful lives. We explain depreciation methods in Chapter 9.

The higher the total cost of a business's fixed assets (called *property, plant, and equipment* in a formal balance sheet), the higher its depreciation expense. However, there's no standard ratio of depreciation expense to the cost of fixed assets. Either the depreciation expense for the year is reported as a separate expense in the income statement, or the amount is disclosed in a footnote.

REMEMBER

Because depreciation is based on the gradual charging off or writing-down of the cost of a fixed asset, the balance sheet reports not one but two numbers: the original (historical) cost of its fixed assets and the *accumulated depreciation* amount (the total amount of depreciation that has been charged to expense from the time of acquiring the fixed assets to the current balance sheet date). The purpose isn't to confuse you by giving you even more numbers to deal with. Seeing both numbers gives you an idea of how old the fixed assets are and also tells you how much these fixed assets originally cost.

In the example in this chapter, the business has, over several years, invested $8.67 million in its fixed assets (that it still owns and uses), and it has recorded total depreciation of $4.32 million through the end of the most recent fiscal year, December 31, 2020. The business recorded $1.239 million of depreciation expense in its most recent year.

You can tell that the company's collection of fixed assets includes some old assets because the company has recorded $4.32 million total depreciation since assets were bought — a fairly sizable percent of original cost (roughly half). But many businesses use accelerated depreciation methods that pile up lots of the depreciation expense in the early years and less in the later years (see Chapter 9 for details), so it's hard to estimate the average age of the company's assets. A business could discuss the actual ages of its fixed assets in the footnotes to its financial statements, but hardly any businesses disclose this information — although they do identify which depreciation methods they're using.

Operating expenses and their balance sheet accounts

The sales, general, and administrative (SG&A) expenses of a business connect with three balance sheet accounts: the prepaid expenses asset account, the accounts payable liability account, and the accrued expenses payable liability account (see Figure 7-2). The broad SG&A expense category includes many types of expenses in making sales and operating the business. (Separate detailed expense accounts are maintained for specific expenses; depending on the size of the business and the needs of its various managers, hundreds or thousands of specific expense accounts are established.)

Many expenses are recorded when paid, such as wage and salary expenses that are recorded on payday. However, this record-as-you-pay method doesn't work for many expenses. For example, insurance and office supplies costs are prepaid and then released to expense gradually over time. The cost is initially put in the *prepaid expenses* asset account. (Yes, we know that "prepaid expenses" doesn't sound like an asset account, but it is.) Other expenses aren't paid until weeks after the expenses are recorded. The amounts owed for these unpaid expenses are recorded in an *accounts payable* or in an *accrued expenses payable* liability account.

REMEMBER

For details regarding the use of these accounts in recording expenses, see Chapter 6. Keep in mind that the accounting objective is to match expenses with sales revenue for the year, and only in this way can the amount of profit be measured for the year. So expenses recorded for the year should be the correct amounts, regardless of when they're paid.

Intangible assets and amortization expense

Our business example does include a small investment in intangible assets of approximately $500,000 at the end of 2020. *Intangible* means without physical existence, in contrast to tangible assets like buildings, vehicles, and computers. Here are some examples of intangible assets:

>> A business may purchase the customer list of another company that's going out of business.

>> A technology company may "capitalize" the cost of developing new software that it will sell in the future.

>> A business may buy patent rights from the inventor of a new product or process.

>> A business may buy another business lock, stock, and barrel and may pay more than the individual assets of the company being bought are worth — even after adjusting the particular assets to their current values. The extra amount is for *goodwill,* which may consist of a trained and efficient workforce, an established product with a reputation for high quality, or a very valuable location.

REMEMBER

Only intangible assets that are purchased or can be associated with directly incurred internal costs (for example, for the development of software) are recorded by a business. A business must expend cash, or take on debt, or issue owners' equity shares for an intangible asset in order to record the asset on its books. Building up a good reputation with customers or establishing a well-known brand is not recorded as an intangible asset. You can imagine the value of Coca-Cola's brand name, but this "asset" isn't recorded on the company's books. However, Coca-Cola protects its brand name with all the legal means at its disposal.

The cost of an intangible asset is recorded in an appropriate asset account, just like the cost of a tangible asset is recorded in a fixed asset account. Whether or when to allocate the cost of an intangible asset to expense has proven to be a difficult issue in practice, not easily amenable to accounting rules. At one time, the costs of most intangible assets were charged off according to some systematic method. The fraction of the total cost charged off in one period is called *amortization expense.*

Currently, however, the cost of an intangible asset isn't charged to expense unless its value has been impaired. A past study of 8,700 public companies found that they collectively recorded $26 billion of write-downs for goodwill impairment in 2014. Testing for impairment is a messy process. The practical difficulties of determining whether impairment has occurred and the amount of the loss in value of an intangible asset have proven to be a real challenge to accountants. For the latest developments, search for "impairment of intangible assets" on the internet, which will lead you to several sources. We don't go into the technical details here; because our business example doesn't include any intangible assets, there's no amortization expense.

KEEPING A CASH BALANCE

A business's cash account consists of the money it has in its checking accounts plus the money that it keeps on hand. Cash is the essential lubricant of business activity. Sooner or later, virtually all business transactions pass through the cash account. Every business needs to maintain a working cash balance as a buffer against fluctuations in day-to-day cash receipts and payments. You can't really get by with a zero cash balance, hoping that enough customers will provide enough cash to cover all the cash payments that you need to make that day.

At year-end 2020, the cash balance of the business whose balance sheet is presented in Figure 7-2 is $11.281 million, which equals a little more than eight weeks of annual sales revenue. How large of a cash balance should a business maintain? There's no simple answer. A business needs to determine how large of a cash safety reserve it's comfortable with to meet unexpected demands on cash while keeping the following points in mind:

- Excess cash balances are unproductive and don't earn any profit for the business.

- Insufficient cash balances can cause the business to miss taking advantage of opportunities that require quick action, such as snatching up a prized piece of real estate that just came on the market or buying out a competitor.

Debt and interest expense

Look back at the balance sheet shown in Figure 7-2. Notice that the sum of this business's short-term (current), long-term notes payable, and other long-term liabilities at year-end 2020 is $7.25 million. From the income statement in Figure 6-1, you see that the business's interest expense for the year is $350,000. Based on the year-end amount of debt, the annual interest rate is about 4.8 percent. (The business may have had more or less borrowed at certain times during the year, of course, and the actual interest rate depends on the debt levels from month to month.)

For most businesses, a small part of their total annual interest is unpaid at year-end; the unpaid part is recorded to bring interest expense up to the correct total amount for the year. In Figure 7-2, the accrued amount of interest is included in the *accrued expenses payable* liability account. In most balance sheets, you don't find accrued interest payable on a separate line; rather, it's included in the accrued expenses payable liability account. However, if unpaid interest at year-end happens to be a rather large amount, or if the business is seriously behind in paying interest on its debt, it should report the accrued interest payable as a separate liability.

Income tax expense and income tax payable

In its 2020 income statement, the business reports $6.895 million earnings before income tax — after deducting interest and all other expenses from sales revenue. The actual taxable income of the business for the year probably is different from this amount because of the many complexities in the income tax law. In the example, we use a realistic 35 percent tax rate (combined federal and state income tax rate), so the income tax expense is $2.413 million of the pretax income of $6.895 million.

A large part of the federal and state income tax amounts for the year must be paid before the end of the year. But a small part is usually still owed at the end of the year. The unpaid part is recorded in the *income tax payable* liability account, which has been consolidated in the other current liability account balance of $1.204 million in Figure 7-2. In the example, the unpaid part is $804,000 of the total $2.413 million income tax for the year, but we don't mean to suggest that this ratio is typical. Generally, the unpaid income tax at the end of the year is fairly small, but just how small depends on several technical factors.

Net income and cash dividends (if any)

The business in our example earned $4.482 million net income for the year (see Figure 6-1). Earning profit increases the owners' equity account *retained earnings* by the same amount. Either the $4.482 million profit (here we go again using *profit* instead of *net income*) stays in the business, or some of it is paid out and divided among the owners of the business.

During the year, the business paid out $400,000 total cash distributions from its annual profit. This is included in Figure 7-3's summary of transactions — look in the financing-activities column on the retained earnings line. If you own 10 percent of the shares, you'd receive one-tenth, or $40,000 cash, as your share of the total distributions. Distributions and dividends from profit to owners (shareholders) are not expenses. In other words, bottom-line net income is before any distributions to owners. Despite the importance of distributions from profit, you can't tell from the income statement or the balance sheet the amount of cash dividends. You have to look in the statement of cash flows for this information (which we explain in Chapter 8). You can also find distributions from profit (if any) in the *statement of changes in stockholders' equity*. See Chapter 9 for more on this supplementary schedule, which is usually included in financial reports of businesses.

Financing a Business: Sources of Cash and Capital

REMEMBER

To run a business, you need financial backing, otherwise known as *capital*. In Chapter 18, we explore how businesses are capitalized in much more depth, but at a macro level, businesses secure capital from one of two primary sources: debt and equity. Borrowed money is known as *debt* and usually comes in one of two forms — secured or formally structured debt such as a bank providing loan, or unsecured or more informal such as a vendor providing a company 30-day payment terms. Capital invested in the business by its owners or investors and retained profits are the two primary sources of *owners' equity.*

How did the business whose balance sheet is shown in Figure 7-2 finance its assets? Its total assets are $27.172 million at fiscal year-end 2020. The company's profit-making activities generated three liabilities — accounts payable, accrued expenses payable, and other current liabilities (including income tax payable as previously noted) — and in total these three liabilities provided $3.963 million of the total assets of the business. Debt provided $7.250 million, and the three sources of owners' equity provided the other $15.959 million. All three sources add up to $27.172 million, which equals total assets, of course. Otherwise, its books would be out of balance, which is a definite no-no.

Accounts payable, accrued expenses payable, and income tax payable are short-term, non-interest-bearing liabilities that are sometimes called *spontaneous liabilities* because they arise directly from a business's expense activities — they aren't the result of borrowing money but rather are the result of buying things on credit or delaying payment of certain expenses.

It's hard to avoid these three liabilities in running a business; they're generated naturally in the process of carrying on operations. In contrast, the mix of debt (interest-bearing liabilities) and equity (invested owners' capital and retained earnings) requires careful thought and high-level decisions by a business. There's no natural or automatic answer to the debt-versus-equity question. The business in the example has a large amount of debt relative to its owners' equity, which would make many business owners uncomfortable.

Debt is both good and bad, and in extreme situations, it can get very ugly. The advantages of debt are as follows:

>> Most businesses can't raise all the capital they need from owners' equity sources, and debt offers another source of capital (though, of course, many lenders are willing to provide only part of the capital that a business needs).

>> Interest rates charged by lenders are lower than rates of return expected by owners. Owners expect a higher rate of return because they're taking a greater risk with their money — the business isn't required to pay them back the same way that it's required to pay back a lender. For example, a business may pay 6 percent annual interest on its debt and be expected to earn a 12 percent annual rate of return on its owners' equity. (See Chapter 11 for more on earning profit for owners.)

WARNING

Here are the disadvantages of debt:

>> A business must pay the fixed rate of interest for the period even if it suffers a loss for the period or earns a lower rate of return on its assets.

>> A business must be ready to pay back the debt on the specified due date, which can cause some pressure on the business to come up with the money on time. (Of course, a business may be able to *roll over* or renew its debt, meaning that it replaces its old debt with an equivalent amount of new debt, but the lender has the right to demand that the old debt be paid and not rolled over.)

WARNING

If a business defaults on its debt contract — it doesn't pay the interest on time or doesn't pay back the debt on the due date — it faces some major unpleasantness. In extreme cases, a lender can force it to shut down and liquidate its assets (that is, sell off everything it owns for cash) to pay off the debt and unpaid interest. Just as you can lose your home if you don't pay your home mortgage, a business can be forced into involuntary bankruptcy if it doesn't pay its debts. A lender may allow the business to try to work out its financial crisis through bankruptcy procedures, but bankruptcy is a nasty affair that invariably causes many problems and can really cripple a business.

Recognizing the Hodgepodge of Values Reported in a Balance Sheet

In our experience, the values reported for assets in a balance sheet can be a source of confusion for business managers and investors, who tend to put all dollar amounts on the same value basis. In their minds, a dollar is a dollar, whether it's in accounts receivable; inventory; property, plant, and equipment; accounts payable; or retained earnings. But some dollars are much older than other dollars.

The dollar amounts reported in a balance sheet are the result of the transactions recorded in the assets, liabilities, and owners' equity accounts. (Hmm, where have you heard this before?) Some transactions from years ago may still have life in the present balances of certain assets. For example, the land owned by the business that is reported in the balance sheet goes back to the transaction for the purchase of the land, which could be 20 or 30 years ago. The balance in the land asset is standing in the same asset column, for example, as the balance in the accounts receivable asset, which likely is only one or two months old.

REMEMBER

Book values are the amounts recorded in the accounting process and reported in financial statements. Don't assume that the book values reported in a balance sheet equal the current *market values.* Generally speaking, the amounts reported for cash, accounts receivable, and liabilities are equal to or are very close to their current market or settlement values. For example, accounts receivable will be turned into cash for the amount recorded on the balance sheet, and liabilities will be paid off at the amounts reported in the balance sheet. It's the book values of fixed assets, as well as any other assets in which the business invested some time ago, that are likely lower than their current replacement values.

Also, keep in mind that a business may have "unrecorded" assets. These off-balance-sheet assets include such things as a well-known reputation for quality products and excellent service, secret formulas (think Coca-Cola here), patents that are the result of its research and development over the years, and a better trained workforce than its competitors. These are intangible assets that the business did not purchase from outside sources but rather accumulated over the years through its own efforts. These assets, though not reported in the balance sheet, should show up in better-than-average profit performance in the business's income statement.

WARNING

The current replacement values of a company's fixed assets may be quite a bit higher than the recorded costs of these assets, in particular for buildings, land, heavy machinery, and equipment. For example, the aircraft fleet of United Airlines, as reported in its balance sheet, is hundreds of millions of dollars less than the current cost it would have to pay to replace the planes. Complicating matters is the fact that many of its older planes aren't being produced anymore, and United would replace the older planes with newer models.

Businesses are not permitted to write up the book values of their assets to current market or replacement values. (Well, investments in marketable securities held for sale or available for sale have to be written up or down, but this is an exception to the general rule.) Although recording current market values may have intuitive appeal, a market-to-market valuation model isn't practical or appropriate for businesses that sell products and services. These businesses do not stand ready to sell their assets (other than inventory); they need their assets for operating the business into the future. At the end of their useful lives, assets are sold for their disposable values (or traded in for new assets).

TIP

Don't think that the market value of a business is simply equal to its owners' equity reported in its most recent balance sheet. Putting a value on a business depends on several factors in addition to the latest balance sheet of the business. We discuss business valuation in our books *Small Business Financial Management Kit For Dummies* (Wiley) and *Business Financial Information Secrets* (Wiley).

IN THIS CHAPTER

» **Clarifying why the statement of cash flows is reported**

» **Presenting the statement of cash flows in two flavors**

» **Earning profit versus generating cash flow from profit**

» **Reading lines and between the lines in the statement of cash flows**

» **Offering advice and observations on cash flow**

Chapter **8**

Reporting Cash Sources and Uses in the Statement of Cash Flows

You could argue that the income statement (see Chapter 6) and balance sheet (see Chapter 7) are enough. These two financial statements answer the most important questions about the financial affairs of a business. The income statement discloses revenue and how much profit the business squeezed from its revenue, and the balance sheet discloses the amounts of assets being used to make sales and profit, as well as its capital sources. What more do you need to know? Well, it's also helpful to know about the cash flows of the business.

This chapter explains the third primary financial statement reported by businesses: the *statement of cash flows.* This financial statement has two purposes: It explains why cash flow from profit differs from bottom-line profit, and it summarizes the investing and financing activities of the business during the period. This may seem an odd mix to put into one financial statement, but it actually makes sense. Earning profit (net income) generates net cash inflow (at least, it should normally). Making profit is a primary source of cash to a business. The investing and financing transactions of a business hinge on its cash flow from profit. All sources and uses of cash hang together and should be managed in an integrated manner.

REMEMBER

To further emphasize the importance of the statement of cash flows, we offer this bit of important advice: When reading the financial statements, you should always make sure you *understand* the income statement, *trust* the balance sheet, but most importantly, *rely* on the statement of cash flows. While the statement of cash flows is generally the most difficult of the financial statements to understand and analyze, it also provides invaluable information as it relates to how a business *generates* (comes up with) and *consumes* (uses) its all-important lifeline: cash! It's one thing for the management team of a business to explain why sales revenue came in below forecasts or an anticipated profit turned into an actual loss. These discussions are painful enough but do not even compare to having to explain why a business actually ran out of cash. Trust us when we say that this is one conversation that a business owner absolutely does not want to have with investors or creditors. The statement of cash flows represents critical financial information to assist businesses with always ensuring they have enough cash to support ongoing operations. In short, the importance of cash flow in showing the financial health of a business is often misunderstood but can't be overestimated.

Meeting the Statement of Cash Flows

The income statement (see Chapter 6) has a natural structure:

Revenue – Expenses = Profit (Net Income)

So does the balance sheet (see Chapter 7):

Assets = Liabilities + Owners' Equity

The statement of cash flows doesn't have an obvious natural structure, so the accounting rule-making body had to decide on the basic format for the statement. They settled on the following structure:

± Cash Flow from Operating Activities

± Cash Flow from Investing Activities

± Cash Flow from Financing Activities

= Cash Increase or Decrease during Period

+ Beginning Cash Balance

= Ending Cash Balance

The plus-minus signs mean that the cash flow could be positive or negative. Generally, the cash flow from investing activities of technology businesses is negative, which means that the business spent more on new investments in long-term assets, including intangible assets, than cash received from disposals of previous investments. And generally, the cash flow from operating activities (profit-making activities) should be positive, unless the business suffered a big loss for the period that drained cash out of the business.

The threefold classification of activities (transactions) reported in the statement of cash flows — operating, investing, and financing — are the same ones we introduce in Chapter 7, in which we explain the balance sheet. Figure 7-3 summarizes these transactions for the technology company example that we continue in this chapter.

In the example, the business's cash balance increases by $10.493 million during the year ending 2020. You see this increase in the company's balance sheets for the years ended December 31, 2019 and 2020 (see Figure 7-2). The business started the year with $788,000 cash and ended the year with $11.281 million. What does the balance sheet, by itself, tell you about the reasons for the cash increase? The two-year comparative balance sheet provides some clues about the reasons for the cash increase. However, answering such a question isn't the purpose of a balance sheet.

Presenting the direct method

The statement of cash flows begins with the cash from making profit, or *cash flow from operating activities,* as accountants call it. *Operating activities* is the term accountants adopted for sales and expenses, which are the "operations" that a business carries out to earn profit. Furthermore, the term *operating activities* also includes the transactions that are coupled with sales and expenses. For example, making a sale on credit is an operating activity, and so is collecting the cash from the customer at a later time. Recording sales and expenses can be thought of as primary operating activities because they affect profit. Their associated transactions are secondary operating activities because they don't affect profit. However, they do affect cash flow, which we explain in this chapter.

Figure 8-1 presents the statement of cash flows for the technology business example we introduce in Chapters 6 and 7. What you see in the first section of the statement of cash flows is called the *direct method* for reporting cash flow from operating activities. The dollar amounts are the cash flows connected with sales and expenses. For example, the business collected $68.949 million from customers during the year, which is the direct result of making sales. The company paid $24.288 million for the products and services it sells, some of which went toward increasing the inventory of products awaiting sale next period.

Statement of Cash Flows For the Twelve-Month Period Ending (All Numbers in Thousands)	FYE 12/31/2019	FYE 12/31/2020
QW Example Tech., Inc. **Sales of Both Products & Software Services** **for the Fiscal Year Ending** **12/31/2020**		
Cash Inflows, Collections from Sales	$53,051	$68,949
Cash Outflows:		
Payments for Products & Other Costs of Goods Sold	($23,053)	($24,288)
Payments for General, Selling, & Admin. Expenses	($27,646)	($34,801)
Payments for Other Expenses	($250)	($250)
Payments for Interest Expense	($400)	($350)
Payments for Income Tax Expense	($211)	($1,667)
Net Cash Flow from Operating Activities	$1,491	$7,593
Investing Activities, Cash Provided (Used):		
Capital Expenditures	($720)	($750)
Net Cash Flow from Investing Activities	($720)	($750)
Financing Activities, Cash Provided (Used):		
Dividends or Distributions Paid	$0	($400)
Sale (Repurchase) of Capital Stock	$0	$5,000
Proceeds from Issuance of Debt	$0	$0
Repayments of Long-Term Debt	($1,000)	($1,000)
Other Financing Activities	$50	$0
Net Cash Flow from Financing Activities	($950)	$3,600
Other Cash Flow Adjustments — Asset Impairment	$0	$50
Net Increase (Decrease) in Cash & Equivalents	($179)	$10,493
Beginning Cash & Equivalents Balance	$967	$788
Ending Cash & Equivalents Balance	$788	$11,281

Confidential — Property of QW Example Tech., Inc.

FIGURE 8-1:
The statement of cash flows, illustrating the direct method for cash flow from operating activities.

Note: Because we use the same business example in this chapter that we use in Chapters 6 and 7, you may want to take a moment to review the 2020 income statement in Figure 6-1. And you may want to review Figure 7-3, which summarizes how the three types of activities changed the business's assets, liabilities, and owners' equity accounts during the year 2020. (Go ahead, we'll wait.)

TIP

The basic idea of the direct method is to present the sales revenue and expenses of the business on a cash basis, in contrast to the amounts reported in the income statement, which are on the accrual basis for recording revenue and expenses. *Accrual-basis* accounting is real-time accounting that records transactions when economic events happen: Accountants record sales on credit when the sales take place, even though cash isn't collected from customers until some time later. Cash payments for expenses occur before or after the expenses are recorded. *Cash basis* accounting is just what it says: Transactions aren't recorded until there's actual cash flow (in or out).

The revenue and expense cash flows you see in Figure 8-1 differ from the amounts you see in the accrual accounting basis income statement (see Figure 6-1). Herein lies a problem with the direct method. If you, a conscientious reader of the financial statements of a business, compare the revenues and expenses reported in the income statement with the cash flow amounts reported in the statement of cash flows, you may get confused. Which set of numbers is the correct one? Well, both are. The numbers in the income statement are the "true" numbers for measuring profit for the period. The numbers in the statement of cash flows are additional information for you to ponder.

Notice in Figure 8-1 that cash flow from operating activities for the year is $7.593 million, which is greater than the company's $4.482 million net income for the year (refer to Figure 6-1). The accounting rule-making board thought that financial report readers would want some sort of explanation for the difference between these two important financial numbers. Therefore, the board decreed that a statement of cash flows that uses the direct method of reporting cash flow from operating liabilities should include a reconciliation schedule that explains the difference between cash flow from operating activities and net income.

Opting for the indirect method

Having to read both the operating activities section of the cash flow statement and a supplemental schedule gets to be rather demanding for financial statement readers. Accordingly, the accounting rule-making body decided to permit an alternative method for reporting cash flow from operating activities. The alternative method starts with net income and then makes adjustments in order to reconcile cash flow from operating activities with net income. This alternative method is called the *indirect method*, which we show in Figure 8-2. The rest of the cash flow statement is the same, no matter which option is selected for reporting cash flow from operating activities. Compare the investing and financing activities in Figures 8-1 and 8-2; they're the same.

QW Example Tech., Inc.		
Sales of Both Products & Software Services		
for the Fiscal Year Ending		
12/31/2020		

Statement of Cash Flows For the Twelve-Month Period Ending (All Numbers in Thousands)	FYE 12/31/2019	FYE 12/31/2020
Net Profit (Loss)	$323	$4,482
Operating Activities, Cash Provided (Used):		
Depreciation & Amortization	$1,631	$1,739
Decrease (Increase) in Trade Receivables	($746)	($2,165)
Decrease (Increase) in Inventory	$150	$2,328
Decrease (Increase) in Other Current Assets	($50)	($25)
Increase (Decrease) in Trade Payables	$111	$275
Increase (Decrease) in Accrued Liabilities	$59	$163
Increase (Decrease) in Other Liabilities	$13	$796
Net Cash Flow from Operating Activities	$1,491	$7,593
Investing Activities, Cash Provided (Used):		
Capital Expenditures	($720)	($750)
Investments in Other Assets	$0	$0
Net Cash Flow from Investing Activities	($720)	($750)
Financing Activities, Cash Provided (Used):		
Dividends or Distributions Paid	$0	($400)
Sale (Repurchase) of Capital Stock	$0	$5,000
Proceeds from Issuance of Debt	$0	$0
Repayments of Long-Term Debt	($1,000)	($1,000)
Other Financing Activities	$50	$0
Net Cash Flow from Financing Activities	($950)	$3,600
Other Cash Flow Adjustments — Asset Impairment	$0	$50
Net Increase (Decrease) in Cash & Equivalents	($179)	$10,493
Beginning Cash & Equivalents Balance	$967	$788
Ending Cash & Equivalents Balance	$788	$11,281

Confidential — Property of QW Example Tech., Inc.

FIGURE 8-2:
The statement of cash flows, illustrating the indirect method for presenting cash flow from operating activities.

TIP

By the way, the adjustments to net income in the indirect method for reporting cash flow from operating activities (see Figure 8-2) constitute the supplemental schedule of changes in assets and liabilities that has to be included under the direct method. So the indirect method kills two birds with one stone: Net income is adjusted to the cash flow basis, and the changes in assets and liabilities affecting cash flow are included in the statement. It's no surprise that the vast majority of businesses use the indirect method.

The indirect method for reporting cash flow from operating activities focuses on the *changes* during the year in the assets and liabilities that are directly associated with sales and expenses. We explain these connections between revenue and expenses and their corresponding assets and liabilities in Chapter 7. (You can trace the amounts of these changes back to Figure 7-2.)

REMEMBER

Both the direct method and the indirect method report the same cash flow from operating activities for the period. Almost always, this important financial metric for a business differs from the amount of its bottom-line profit, or net income, for the same period. Why? Read on.

Explaining the Variance between Cash Flow and Net Income

The amount of cash flow from profit, in the large majority of cases, is a different amount from profit. Both revenue and expenses are to blame. Cash collected from customers during the period is usually higher or lower than the sales revenue booked for the period. And cash actually paid out for operating costs is usually higher or lower than the amounts of expenses booked for the period. You can see this by comparing cash flows from operating activities in Figure 8-1 with sales revenue and expenses in the company's income statement (Figure 6-1). The accrual-based amounts (Figure 6-1) are different from the cash-based amounts (Figure 8-1).

Now, how to report the divergence of cash flow and profit? A business could, we suppose, present only one line for cash flow from operating activities (which in our example is $7.593 million). Next, the financial report reader would move on to the investing and financing sections of the cash flow statement. But this approach won't do, according to financial reporting standards.

REMEMBER

The premise of financial reporting is that financial statement readers want more information than just a one-line disclosure of cash flow from operating activities. The standard practice is to disclose the major factors that cause cash flow to be higher or lower than net income. Smaller factors are often collapsed on one line called "other factors" or something like that. The business example we use in Chapters 6, 7, and 8 is traceable. You can trace all the specific reasons that cause the variance between cash flow and net income.

The business in our example experienced a strong growth year, and it decided to pivot more aggressively from selling just technology products to products, software, and related support services. Its accounts receivable increased by a relatively large amount while the inventory decreased as a result of shifting the business. In fact, most of its assets and liabilities intimately connected with sales and expenses increased (with the exception of inventory); their ending balances are larger than their beginning balances (which are the amounts carried forward from the end of the preceding year). Of course, this may not always be the case in a growth situation; one or more assets and liabilities could decrease during the year. For flat, no-growth situations, it's likely that there will be a mix of modest-sized increases and decreases.

In this section, we explain how asset and liability changes affect cash flow from operating activities. As a business manager, you should keep a close watch on the changes in each of your assets and liabilities and understand the cash flow effects of these changes. Investors and lenders should focus on the business's ability to generate a healthy cash flow from operating activities, so they should be equally concerned about these changes. In some situations, these changes indicate serious problems!

TIP

We realize that you may not be too interested in the details of these changes, so at the start of each section, we present the synopsis. If you want, you can just read this short explanation and move on (though the details are fascinating — well, at least to accountants).

Note: Instead of using the full phrase "cash flow from operating activities" every time, we use the shorter term "cash flow." All data for assets and liabilities are found in the two-year comparative balance sheet of the business (see Figure 7-2).

Accounts receivable change

Synopsis: An increase in accounts receivable consumes cash flow; a decrease generates cash flow.

REMEMBER

The accounts receivable asset shows how much money customers who bought products on credit still owe the business; this asset is a promise of cash that the business will receive. Basically, accounts receivable is the amount of uncollected sales revenue at the end of the period. Cash doesn't increase until the business collects money from its customers.

The business started the year with $6.718 million and ended the year with $8.883 million in accounts receivable. The beginning balance was collected during the year, but the ending balance hadn't been collected at the end of the year. Thus, the *net* effect is a shortfall in cash inflow of $2.165 million. The key point is that you need to keep an eye on the increase or decrease in accounts receivable from the beginning of the period to the end of the period. Here's what to look for:

>> **Increase in accounts receivable:** If the amount of credit sales you made during the period is greater than what you collected from customers during the period, your accounts receivable increased over the period, and you need to *subtract* from net income that difference between start-of-period accounts receivable and end-of-period accounts receivable. In short, an increase in accounts receivable consumes cash flow by the amount of the increase.

>> **Decrease in accounts receivable:** If the amount you collected from customers during the period is greater than the credit sales you made during the period, your accounts receivable decreased over the period, and you need to *add* to net income that difference between start-of-period accounts receivable and end-of-period accounts receivable. In short, a decrease in accounts receivable generates cash flow by the amount of the decrease.

In our business example, accounts receivable increased $2.165 million. Cash collections from sales were $2.165 million less than sales revenue. Ouch! The business increased its sales substantially over the last period, so its accounts receivable increased. When credit sales increase, a company's accounts receivable generally increases about the same percent, as it did in this example. (If the business takes longer to collect its credit sales, then its accounts receivable would increase even more than can be attributed to the sales increase.) In this example, the higher sales revenue was good for profit but bad for cash flow.

REMEMBER

The "lagging behind" effect of cash flow is the price of growth — business managers, lenders, and investors need to understand this point. Increasing sales without increasing accounts receivable is a happy situation for cash flow, but in the real world, you usually can't have one increase without the other.

Inventory change

Synopsis: An increase in inventory consumes cash flow; a decrease generates cash flow.

Inventory is usually the largest short-term, or *current*, asset of businesses that sell products. If the inventory account is greater at the end of the period than at the start of the period — because unit costs increased or because the quantity of products increased — the amount the business actually paid out in cash for inventory purchases (or for manufacturing products) is more than what the business recorded in the cost of goods sold expense for the period. To refresh your memory here: The cost of inventory is not charged to cost of goods sold expense until products are sold and sales revenue is recorded.

In our business example, inventory decreased $2.328 million from start-of-year to end-of-year as a result of the company pivoting from selling just products to focus on selling software and related services. In our business example, the company was actually able to reduce the amount of inventory it owned as it was able to successfully liquidate a number of product lines that were not replaced. So the company was able to turn $2.328 million into cash by not having to replace these items. Thus, this was a very nice "bump" to cash flow as the money spent in previous years to invest in inventory was instead turned into cash via aggressively selling or liquidating older or discontinued product lines.

Prepaid expenses change

Synopsis: An increase in prepaid expenses (an asset account) consumes cash flow; a decrease generates cash flow.

A change in the prepaid expenses asset account works the same way as a change in inventory and accounts receivable, although changes in prepaid expenses are usually much smaller than changes in the other two asset accounts.

The beginning balance of prepaid expenses is charged to expense this year, but the cash of this amount was actually paid out last year. This period (the year 2020 in our example), the business paid cash for next period's prepaid expenses, which affects this period's cash flow but doesn't affect net income until next period. In short, the $25,000 increase in prepaid expenses in this business example has a negative effect on cash flow.

REMEMBER

As a business grows, it needs to increase its prepaid expenses for such things as insurance (premiums have to be paid in advance of the insurance coverage), property taxes, software subscriptions that are purchased in advance, and other like items. Increases in accounts receivable, inventory, and prepaid expenses are the cash-flow price a business has to pay for growth. Rarely do you find a business that can increase its sales revenue without increasing these assets.

Depreciation: Real but noncash expense

Synopsis: No cash outlay is made in recording depreciation. In recording depreciation, a business simply decreases the book (recorded) value of the asset being depreciated. Cash isn't affected by the recording of depreciation (keeping in mind that depreciation is deductible for income tax).

Recording depreciation expense decreases the value of long-term, fixed operating assets that are reported in the balance sheet. The original costs of fixed assets are recorded in a *property, plant, and equipment* type account. Depreciation is recorded in an *accumulated depreciation* account, which is a so-called *contra* account because its balance is deducted from the balance in the fixed asset account (see Figure 7-2). Recording depreciation increases the accumulated depreciation account, which decreases the book value of the fixed asset.

TIP

There's no cash outlay when recording depreciation expense. Sales prices should be set high enough so that the cash inflow from revenue "reimburses" the business for the use of its long-term operating assets as they gradually wear out over time. The amount of depreciation expense recorded in the period is a portion of the original cost of the business's fixed assets, most of which were bought and paid for years ago. (Chapters 6 and 7 explain more about depreciation.) Because the depreciation expense isn't a cash outlay this period, the amount is added to net income to determine cash flow from operating activities (see Figure 8-2). Depreciation is just one adjustment factor to get from net income reported in the income statement to cash flow from operating activities reported in the statement of cash flows.

For measuring profit, depreciation is definitely an expense — no doubt about it. Buildings, machinery, equipment, tools, vehicles, computers, and office furniture are all on an irreversible journey to the junk heap (although buildings usually take a long time to get there). Fixed assets (except for land) have a finite life of usefulness to a business; depreciation is the accounting method that allocates the total cost of fixed assets to each year of their use in helping the business generate sales revenue. In our example, the business recorded $1.239 million of depreciation expense for the year. Notice that the total amount recorded in the statement of cash flows is $1.739 million, or $500,000 higher. The reason for this difference is that the company also recorded $500,000 of amortization expense during the year (to reduce the value of certain intangible assets). The combination of these two items amounts to the $1.739 million figure in the statement of cash flows.

TIP

Instead of looking at depreciation only as an expense, consider the investment-recovery cycle of fixed assets. A business invests money in fixed assets that are then used for several or many years. Over the life of a fixed asset, a business has to recover through sales revenue the cost invested in the fixed asset (ignoring any salvage value at the end of its useful life). In a real sense, a business "sells" some of its fixed assets each period to its customers — it factors the cost of fixed assets into the sales prices that it charges its customers.

For example, when you go to a supermarket, a very small slice of the price you pay for that quart of milk goes toward the cost of the building, the shelves, the refrigeration equipment, and so on. (No wonder they charge so much!) Each period, a business recoups part of the cost invested in its fixed assets. In the example, $1.739 million of sales revenue went toward reimbursing the business for the use of its fixed and intangible assets during the year.

COMPARING DEPRECIATION AND AMORTIZATION

The business in our example owns a small amount of intangible assets and thus recorded $500,000 of amortization expense. (See Chapter 7 for an explanation of intangible assets and amortization.) When a business does own intangible assets, the amortization expense on these assets for the year is treated the same as depreciation is treated in the statement of cash flows. In other words, the recording of amortization expense doesn't require cash outlay in the year being charged with the expense. The cash outlay occurred in prior periods when the business invested in intangible assets. But in contrast to tangible depreciable assets, amortization expense is recorded as a decrease in the intangible asset account; the accountant doesn't use a contra account. There's no accumulated amortization account, but if you look closely enough at Figure 7-3, you will notice a decrease in intangible assets of $500,000 (our amortization expense). That's just one of the quirks of accounting.

Changes in operating liabilities

Synopsis: An increase in a short-term operating liability generates cash flow; a decrease consumes cash flow.

The business in our example, like almost all businesses, has three basic liabilities inextricably intertwined with its expenses:

>> Accounts payable

>> Accrued expenses payable

>> Income tax payable

When the beginning balance of one of these liability accounts is the same as its ending balance (not too likely, of course), the business breaks even on cash flow for that liability. When the end-of-period balance is higher than the start-of-period balance, the business didn't pay out as much money as was recorded as an expense in the year. You want to refer back to the company's comparative balance sheet of the business in Figure 7-2 to compare the beginning and ending balances of these three liability accounts.

In our business example, the business disbursed $1.654 million to pay off last year's accounts payable balance. (This $1.654, million was the accounts payable balance on December 31, 2019, the end of the previous fiscal year.) Its cash this year decreased $1.654 million because of these payments. But this year's ending balance sheet (on December 31, 2020) shows accounts payable of $1.929 million that the business won't pay until the following year. This $1.929 million amount was recorded to expense in the year 2020. So the amount of expense was $275,000 more than the cash outlay for the year, or, in reverse, the cash outlay was $275,000 less than the expense — an increase in accounts payable benefits cash flow for the year. In other words, an increase in accounts payable has a positive cash flow effect (until the liability is paid). An increase in accrued expenses payable or income tax payable works the same way.

REMEMBER

In short, liability increases are favorable to cash flow — in a sense, the business ran up more on credit than it paid off. Such an increase means that the business delayed paying cash for certain things until next year. So you need to add the increases in the three liabilities to net income to determine cash flow, as you see in the statement of cash flows (refer to Figure 8-2). The business avoided cash outlays to the extent of the increases in these three liabilities. In some cases, of course, the ending balance of an operating liability may be lower than its beginning balance, which means that the business paid out more cash than the corresponding expenses for the period. In that case, the decrease is a negative cash flow factor.

Putting the cash flow pieces together

Taking into account all the adjustments to net income, the company's cash balance increased $7.593 million from its operating activities during the course of the year, getting a big help from depreciation and amortization expense as well as the reduction in inventory. The operating activities section in the statement of cash flows (refer to Figure 8-2) shows the stepping stones from net income to the amount of cash flow from operating activities.

Recall that the business experienced sales growth during this period. The downside of sales growth is that assets and liabilities also grow — the business needs higher sales level and also has higher accounts receivable. The business's prepaid expenses and liabilities also increased, although not nearly as much as accounts receivable and inventory. Still, the business had $7.593 million cash at its disposal. What did the business do with this $7.593 million in available cash? You have to look to the remainder of the cash flow statement to answer this very important question.

Sailing through the Rest of the Statement of Cash Flows

After you get past the first section of the statement of cash flows, the remainder is a breeze. Well, to be fair, you *could* encounter some rough seas in the remaining two sections. But generally speaking, the information in these sections isn't too difficult to understand. The last two sections of the statement report on the other sources of cash to the business and the uses the business made of its cash during the year.

Understanding investing activities

The second section of the statement of cash flows (see Figure 8-1 or 8-2) reports the investment actions that a business's managers took during the year. Investments are like tea leaves indicating what the future may hold for the company. Major new investments are sure signs of expanding or modernizing the production and distribution facilities and capacity of the business. Major disposals of long-term assets and shedding off a major part of the business could be good news or bad news for the business, depending on many factors. Different investors may interpret this information differently, but all would agree that the information in this section of the cash flow statement is very important.

Certain long-lived operating assets are required for doing business. For example, Federal Express and UPS wouldn't be terribly successful if they didn't have airplanes and trucks for delivering packages and computers for tracking deliveries. When these assets wear out, the business needs to replace them. Also, to remain competitive, a business may need to upgrade its equipment to take advantage of the latest technology or to provide for growth. These investments in long-lived, tangible, productive assets, which are called *fixed assets*, are critical to the future of the business. In fact, these cash outlays are called *capital expenditures* to stress that capital is being invested for the long haul.

One of the first claims on the $7.593 million cash flow from operating activities is for capital expenditures. Notice that the business spent $750,000 on fixed assets, which are referred to more formally as *property, plant,* and *equipment* in the cash flow statement (to keep the terminology consistent with account titles used in the balance sheet; the term *fixed assets* is rather informal).

A typical statement of cash flows doesn't go into much detail regarding what specific types of fixed assets the business purchased (or constructed): how many additional square feet of space the business acquired, how many new drill presses it bought, and so on. Some businesses do leave a clearer trail of their investments, though. For example, in the footnotes or elsewhere in their financial reports, airlines generally describe how many new aircraft of each kind were purchased to replace old equipment or to expand their fleets.

Usually, a business disposes of some of its fixed assets every year because they reached the end of their useful lives and will no longer be used. These fixed assets are sent to the junkyard, traded in on new fixed assets, or sold for relatively small amounts of money. The value of a fixed asset at the end of its useful life is called its *salvage value*. The disposal proceeds from selling fixed assets are reported as a source of cash in the investing activities section of the statement of cash flows. Usually, these amounts are fairly small. Also, a business may sell off fixed assets because it's downsizing or abandoning a major segment of its business; these cash proceeds can be fairly large.

Looking at financing activities

Note that in the annual statement of cash flows for the business example, cash flow from operating activities is a positive $7.593 million, and the negative cash flow from investing activities is $750,000 (refer to Figure 8-1 or 8-2). The result to this point, therefore, is a net cash increase of $6.843 million, which would have increased the company's cash balance this much if the business had no financing activities during the year. However, the business decreased its long-term debt during the year (by paying the required annual loan installments), its owners invested additional money in the business, and it distributed some of its profit to stockholders. The third section of the cash flow statement summarizes these *financing activities* of the business over the period.

The managers didn't have to go outside the business for the $7.593 million cash increase generated from its operating activities for the year. Cash flow from operating activities is an *internal* source of money generated by the business itself, in contrast to *external* money that the business raises from lenders and owners. A business doesn't have to go hat in hand for external money when its internal cash flow is sufficient to provide for its growth. Making profit is the cash flow spigot that should always be turned on.

REMEMBER

We should mention that a business that earns a profit could, nevertheless, have a *negative* cash flow from operating activities — meaning that despite posting a net income for the period, the changes in the company's assets and liabilities cause its cash balance to decrease. In contrast, a business could report a bottom-line *loss* for the year yet have a *positive* cash flow from its operating activities. The cash recovery from depreciation plus the cash benefits from decreases in accounts receivable and inventory could be more than the amount of loss. However, a loss usually leads to negative cash flow or very little positive cash flow.

The term *financing* refers to a business raising capital from debt and equity sources — by borrowing money from banks and other sources willing to loan money to the business and by its owners putting additional money in the business. The term also includes the flip side — that is, making payments on debt and returning capital to owners. The term *financing* also includes cash distributions by the business from profit to its owners. (Keep in mind that interest on debt is an expense reported in the income statement.)

Most businesses borrow money for the short term (generally defined as less than one year) as well as for longer terms (generally defined as more than one year). In other words, a typical business has both short-term and long-term debt. (Chapter 7 explains that short-term debt is presented in the current liabilities section of the balance sheet.)

The business in our example has both short-term and long-term debt. Although this isn't a hard-and-fast rule, most cash flow statements report just the *net* increase or decrease in short-term debt, not the total amounts borrowed and total payments on short-term debt during the period. In contrast, both the total amounts of borrowing from and repayments on long-term debt during the year are generally reported in the statement of cash flows — the numbers are reported gross, instead of net.

In our example, $1 million of long-term debt was paid down during the year, but short-term debt was paid off during the year and replaced with new short-term notes payable. However, no net increase is reported in the cash flow statement (as the amount didn't change).

The financing section of the cash flow statement also reports the flow of cash between the business and its owners (stockholders of a corporation). Owners can be both a *source* of a business's cash (capital invested by owners) and a *use* of a business's cash (profit distributed to owners). The financing activities section of the cash flow statement reports additional capital raised from its owners, if any, as well as any capital returned to the owners. In the cash flow statement, note that the business issued additional stock shares for $5 million during the year, and it paid a total of $400,000 cash dividends from profit to its owners.

At this point you may stop and ask: Why in the world did the company raise an additional $5 million of cash through the sale of stock on top of generating $7.593 million of operating cash flow? These two figures combine for roughly $12.593 million of available cash, of which $1 million was used to repay debt, $750,000 for capital equipment purchases, and $400,000 in the form of a dividend payment to the shareholders. So the company's cash increased by approximately $10.493 million during the year. And the answer is simple: The company is going to be making a large business acquisition in the coming 12 to 24 months, which will require large amounts of cash to complete. You wouldn't know about this acquisition if we didn't tell you or unless you had access to confidential information, but when you see a company that is building large cash balances without returning it to the owners, it usually indicates the company will be looking to "deploy" or use the cash to generate a strong, positive economic return. This is one of the inherent problems with company-issued financial statements. That is, they only report historical operating results and almost never include future projections or forecasts on where they believe the company is headed.

Reading actively

REMEMBER

As a business lender or investor, your job is to ask questions (at least in your own mind) when reading an external financial statement. You should be an active reader, not a ho-hum passive reader, when reading the statement of cash flows. You should mull over certain questions to get full value out of the financial statement.

The statement of cash flows reveals what financial decisions the business's managers made during the period. Of course, management decisions are always subject to second-guessing and criticism, and passing judgment based on reading a financial statement isn't totally fair because it doesn't capture the pressures the managers faced during the period. Maybe they made the best possible decisions in the circumstances. Then again, maybe not.

One issue, in our minds, comes to the forefront when reading the company's statement of cash flows. The business in our example (see Figure 8-1 or 8-2) distributed $400,000 cash from profit to its owners — a 9 percent *payout ratio* (which equals the $400,000 distribution divided by its $4.482 million net income). In analyzing whether the payout ratio is too high, too low, or just about right, you need to look at the broader context of the business's sources of and needs for cash.

The company's $7.593 million cash flow from operating activities is enough to cover the business's $750,000 capital expenditures during the year as well as the $1 million of debt repayments, leaving a very healthy $5.843 million available. The owners also kicked in another $5 million during the year, for a grand total of $10,843,000. Its cash balance didn't increase by this amount because the business paid out $400,000 in dividends from profit to its stockholders as well as realized a small $50,000 additional adjustment to cash flow, so the net increase to cash was approximately $10.493 million.

If we were shareholders of this company, we certainly would ask the chief executive and board of directors why cash dividends to shareowners were limited to $400,000, given the significant increase in cash. And as previously disclosed, the answer is simple. The company is going to make a significant investment over the next two years and needs to build cash to complete it.

Additionally, you should remember the following basic logic as it relates to issuing dividends. For younger, rapidly growing businesses, dividends are generally not issued as the business needs to retain as much cash to finance — that is, support — its growth (as assets tend to grow rapidly, consuming cash). For older, more mature and stable or predictable businesses, paying dividends is more common (assuming profits are generated) because the management team generally has a good line of sight on its annual operating performance.

Some small and privately owned businesses don't report a statement of cash flows — though according to current financial reporting standards that apply to all businesses, they should. We've seen several small, privately owned businesses that don't go to the trouble of preparing this financial statement. Perhaps someday accounting standards for private and smaller businesses will waive the requirement for the cash flow statement. (We discuss developments of accounting standards for larger public versus smaller private companies in Chapter 2.) Without a cash flow statement, the reader of the financial report could add back depreciation and amortization expense to net income to get a starting point. From there on, it gets more challenging to determine cash flow from profit. Adding depreciation and amortization expense to net income is no more than a first step in determining cash flow from profit — but we have to admit it's better than nothing.

Pinning Down "Free Cash Flow"

The term *free cash flow* has emerged in the lexicon of finance and investing. This piece of language is not — we repeat, *not* — officially defined by the rule-making body of any authoritative accounting or financial institution. Furthermore, the term does not appear in cash flow statements reported by businesses.

Rather, *free cash flow* is street language, and the term appears in *The Wall Street Journal* as well as countless other business publications. Securities brokers and investment analysts use the term freely (pun intended). Unfortunately, the term *free cash flow* hasn't settled down into one universal meaning, although most usages have something to do with cash flow from operating activities.

The term *free cash flow* can refer to the following:

>> Net income plus depreciation expense, plus any other expense recorded during the period that doesn't involve the outlay of cash — such as amortization of costs of the intangible assets of a business and other asset write-downs that don't require cash outlay

>> Cash flow from operating activities as reported in the statement of cash flows, although the very use of a different term *(free cash flow)* suggests that a different meaning is intended

>> Cash flow from operating activities minus the amount spent on capital expenditures during the year (purchases or construction of property, plant, and equipment)

>> Earnings before interest, tax, depreciation, and amortization (EBITDA) — although this definition ignores the cash flow effects of changes in the short-term assets and liabilities directly involved in sales and expenses, and it obviously ignores that interest and income tax expenses in large part are paid in cash during the period

REMEMBER

In the strongest possible terms, we advise you to be very clear on which definition of *free cash flow* a speaker or writer is using. Unfortunately, you can't always determine what the term means even in context, so you need to be careful out there.

One definition of free cash flow, in our view, is quite useful: cash flow from operating activities minus capital expenditures for the year. The idea is that a business needs to make capital expenditures in order to stay in business and thrive. And to make capital expenditures, the business needs cash. Only after providing for its capital expenditures does a business have "free" cash flow that it can use as it likes. For the example in this chapter, the free cash flow according to us is

$7.593 million cash flow from operating activities – $750,000 capital expenditures = $6.843 million free cash flow

But you need to be very careful with completing this type of analysis. For our technology company, one year of operating results may not represent the best measurement of free cash flow. As previously noted, the company is going to pursue an acquisition to help support continued sales growth. This acquisition did not occur in the current year 2020 but will most likely show up in 2021 or 2022. A key question that should be raised with the 2020 operating results would be centered in whether our sample company "milked" the current operating results to drive as much sales as possible from old products and technology that need to be replaced in the coming two years. Hence, free cash flow as defined for 2020 may in fact be distorted, as a company such as this may have to invest anywhere from $3 million to $5 million annually to support its business plan, including acquiring new technology. So again, proceed with caution when calculating these types of figures and ratios; understanding projected financial statements is just as important as historical financial statements.

In many cases, cash flow from operating activities falls short of the money needed for capital expenditures. To close the gap, a business has to borrow more money, persuade its owners to invest more money in the business, or dip into its cash reserve. Should a business in this situation distribute any of its profit to owners? After all, it has a cash *deficit* after paying for capital expenditures. But, in fact, many businesses make cash distributions from profit to their owners even when they don't have any free cash flow.

Limitations of the Statement of Cash Flows

Being elder statesmen in accounting (at least, that's how we like to imagine ourselves), we remember the days before the cash flow statement was required in the externally reported financial statements of businesses. In 1987, the cash flow statement was made mandatory. Most financial report users, in our view, thought that this new financial statement would be quite useful and should open the door for deeper insights into the business. However, over the years, we've seen serious problems develop in the actual reporting of cash flows.

Focusing on cash flows is understandable. If a business runs out of money, it will likely come to an abrupt halt and may not be able to start up again. Even running low on cash (as opposed to running out of cash) makes a business vulnerable to all sorts of risks that could be avoided if it had enough sustainable cash flow. Managing cash flow is as important as making sales and controlling expenses. You'd think that the statement of cash flows would be carefully designed to make it as useful as possible and reasonably easy to read so that the financial report reader could get to the heart of the matter.

Would you like to hazard a guess on the average number of lines in the cash flow statements of publicly owned corporations? Typically, their cash flow statements have 30 to 40 or more lines of information by our reckoning. So it takes quite a while to read the cash flow statement — more time than the average reader probably has available. Each line in a financial statement should be a truly useful piece of information. Too many lines baffle the reader rather than clarify the overall cash flows of the business. We have to question why companies overload this financial statement with so much technical information. One could even suspect that many businesses deliberately obscure their statements of cash flows.

The main problem in understanding the statement of cash flows is the first section for cash flow from operating activities. What a terrible way to start the statement of cash flows! As it is now, the financial report reader has to work down numerous adjustments that are added or deducted from net income to determine the amount of cash flow from operating activities (see Figure 8-2). You could read quickly through the whole balance sheet or income statement in the time it takes to do this. In short, the first section of the cash flow statement isn't designed for an easy read. Something needs to be done to improve this opening section of the cash flow statement.

We must say that you don't hear much feedback on the cash flow statement from principal external users of financial reports, such as business lenders and investors. Whether this is due to neglect, lack of education, or simple shortsightedness, we're not sure. However, we do wonder how financial report users would react if the cash flow statement were accidently omitted from a company's annual financial report. How many would notice the missing financial statement and complain? The SEC and other regulators would take action, of course. But in our view, few readers would even notice the omission. In contrast, if a business failed to include an income statement or balance sheet, the business would hear from its lenders and owners, that's for sure.

Instead of the statement of cash flows, we favor presenting a summary of operating, investing, and financial transactions such as the one in Figure 7-3. You might compare this summary with the statement of cash flows shown in Figure 8-2. Which is better for the average financial report reader? You be the judge.

» Disclosing changes in owners' equity

» Realizing that accounting is as much an art form as a science

» Grasping the impacts of alternative accounting methods in recording profit

» Taking a closer look at cost of goods sold and depreciation expenses

» Monitoring current hot topics with sales revenue and expense

» Using the statement of cash flows as a sanity check

Chapter **9**

Financial Accounting Issues

As you dive into this chapter, it's important to remember that accounting is a constantly evolving profession that is almost always in a perpetual state of playing catch-up with the dizzying rate of change occurring throughout the global economic, tax, and financial landscape. You need look no further than the impact Covid-19 has had on businesses spanning the globe. In short order, entire businesses were left worthless overnight, assets such as inventory that once had value needed to be written off, potential unforeseen and extremely large contingent liabilities were now on the radar (for example, if a business opened and exposed customers to Covid-19, is the business liable?), and advancements in technology rendered the old way of doing business obsolete. For accountants, all types of new questions needed to be asked related to properly valuing assets and representing liabilities that evolved in less than 24 months.

All this is quite a change but also indicative of the fact that accounting is a constantly changing profession that strives to adhere to a simple mandate of providing complete, accurate, reliable, and timely financial information on which to base business and economic decisions. The importance of this concept is how we begin this chapter because understanding just how dynamic accounting environments have become and the associated disclosures that should come along with all the "numbers" should be kept in mind at all times.

To start, we broach the topic of providing adequate disclosures in external financial reports that are provided to the creditors and investors of a business. Actually, accountants prefer to use the term *adequate disclosure* compared to alternative descriptions. Accountants certainly don't like the term *full disclosure,* which could involve a very high legal standard that might require providing highly sensitive information. Businesses don't have to reveal everything in their external financial reports. Businesses are justified in protecting their competitive advantages by withholding disclosure about some matters. At the same time, business financial reports should reveal all the information that the creditors and investors are entitled to know about the business. Thus the term *adequate disclosure.*

The three primary financial statements — income statement, balance sheet, and statement of cash flows (see Chapters 6, 7, and 8) — constitute the bedrock disclosure by a business. Public companies are subject to many rules regarding the disclosure of information in addition to their three basic financial statements. Private companies should carefully consider what information they should disclose beyond their three primary financial statements in accordance with financial reporting standards. Virtually all businesses include (or should include) footnotes with their financial statements, which we discuss in Chapter 10.

One thing businesses do not have to disclose is how different their profit and financial condition would have been had they used alternative accounting methods. In recording revenue, expenses, and other transactions of a business, the accountant must choose among different methods for recording the economic reality of the transactions. You may think that accountants are in agreement on the exact ways of recording business transactions, but this isn't the case. An old joke is that when two economists get together, there are three economic opinions; it's no different in accounting.

REMEMBER

Accounting for the economic activity of a business can be compared to selecting the best new book of the year. Judges may agree that the books on the short list for the prize are good, but the best book is sure to vary from judge to judge. The best accounting method is in the eye of the accountant.

Reporting Changes in Owners' Equity

The three primary financial statements (income statement, balance sheet, and cash flow statement) — as important as they are — can't convey all the information that the lenders and investors of a business want to know and are entitled to know, so a business should include additional information. One prime example is the *statement of changes in owners' equity*. This statement supplements the information disclosed in the owners' equity section of the balance sheet. The term *statement* is overkill, if you ask us. It's more of a schedule or summary of the activities during the year that changed the company's owners' equity accounts.

Figure 9-1 presents the statement of changes in stockholders' equity for the technology company example we use in Chapters 6, 7, and 8. The company in the example had various transactions occur during the year involving its owners' equity accounts, including rolling $4.482 million of net income into retained earnings, raising $5 million of new equity in the form of preferred stock, and issuing a dividend on the preferred stock of $400,000. You could argue that the statement is not really needed because the reader could pick up the same information from the company's primary financial statements. However, presenting the statement of changes in stockholders' equity is very convenient for the financial report reader.

QW Example Tech., Inc. **Unaudited Financial Statements** **Statement of Changes in Stockholders' Equity** **for the Fiscal Year Ending** **12/31/2020**						
Description	Common Stock Shares	Common Stock Amount	Preferred Stock Shares	Preferred Stock Amount	Retained Earnings	Total
Balance, January 1, 2020	1,000,000	$5,000,000	0	$0	$1,877,000	$6,877,000
Sale of Preferred Stock			500,000	$5,000,000		$5,000,000
Net Income					$4,482,000	$4,482,000
Dividends					($400,000)	($400,000)
Other Accumulated Income (Expenses)					$0	$0
Balance, December 31, 2020	1,000,000	$5,000,000	500,000	$5,000,000	$5,959,000	$15,959,000

Fully Diluted Shares:

Common	1,000,000
Preferred	500,000
Stock Option Grants	125,000
Total	1,625,000

Note: The company has issued and outstanding 125,000 employee stock option grants as of 12/31/20.

Confidential — Property of QW Example Tech., Inc.

FIGURE 9-1: Example of a statement of changes in stockholders' equity.

Larger businesses generally have more complicated ownership structures than smaller and medium-sized companies. Larger businesses are most often organized as corporations. (We discuss the legal organization of business in Chapter 5.) Corporations can issue more than one class of stock shares, and many do, which is the case in our sample technology company. One class may have preferences over the other class and thus is called *preferred stock.* A corporation may have both voting and nonvoting stock shares. Also, business corporations, believe it or not, can engage in cannibalization: They buy their own stock shares. A corporation may not cancel the shares it has purchased. Shares of itself that are held by the business are called *treasury stock.*

Well, we could go on and on, but the main point is that many businesses, especially larger public companies, engage in a broad range of activities during the year involving changes in their owners' equity components. These owners' equity activities tend to get lost from view in a comparative balance sheet and in the statement of cash flows. Yet the activities can be very important. Therefore, the business prepares a separate statement of changes in stockholders' equity covering the same periods as its income statements. Some of these are monsters and have upwards of ten columns for the elements of stockholders' equity.

WARNING

The statement of changes in stockholders' equity is where you find certain technical gains and losses that increase or decrease owners' equity but that are *not* reported in the income statement. You have to read this summary of changes in the owners' equity accounts to find out whether the business had any such gains or losses. Look in a column headed *comprehensive income* for these gains and losses, which are very technical.

TIP

The general format of the statement of changes in stockholders' equity includes columns for each class of stock, treasury stock, retained earnings, and the comprehensive income element of owners' equity. Professional stock analysts have to pore over these statements. Average financial report readers probably quickly turn the page when they see this statement, but it's worth a quick glance if nothing else.

Recognizing Reasons for Accounting Differences

The financial statements reported by a business are just one version of its financial history and performance. A different accountant for the business undoubtedly would have recorded a different version, at least to some extent. The income statement and balance sheet of a business depend on which particular accounting methods the accountant chooses. Moreover, on orders from management, the financial statements could be tweaked to make them look better. We discuss how businesses can (and do!) put spin on their financial statements in Chapters 10 and 14.

The dollar amounts reported in the financial statements of a business aren't simply "facts" that depend only on good bookkeeping. Here's why different accountants record transactions differently. The accountant

>> Must make choices among different accounting methods for recording the amounts of revenue and expenses

>> Can select between pessimistic and optimistic estimates and forecasts when recording certain revenue and expenses

>> Has some wiggle room in implementing accounting methods, especially regarding the precise timing of when to record sales and expenses

>> Can carry out certain tactics at year-end to put a more favorable spin on the financial statements, usually under the orders or tacit approval of top management (we discuss these manipulations in Chapter 10)

REMEMBER

A popular notion is that accounting is an exact science and that the amounts reported in the financial statements are true and accurate down to the last dollar. When people see an amount reported to the last digit in a financial statement, they naturally get the impression of exactitude and precision. However, in the real world of business, the accountant has to make many arbitrary choices between ways of recording revenue and expenses and of recording changes in their corresponding assets and liabilities. (In Chapter 6, we explain that revenue and expenses are coupled with assets and liabilities.) To this point, it's sometimes helpful to remember that accounting is often just as much of an art form as an exact science.

We don't discuss accounting errors in this chapter. It's always possible that the accountant doesn't fully understand the transaction being recorded or relies on misleading information, with the result that the entry for the transaction is wrong. And bookkeeping processing slip-ups happen. The term *error* generally refers to honest mistakes; there's no intention of manipulating the financial statements. Unfortunately, a business may not detect accounting mistakes, and therefore its financial statements end up being misleading to one degree or another. (We point out in Chapter 3 that a business should institute effective internal controls to prevent accounting errors.)

Looking at a More Conservative Version of the Company's Income Statement

TIP

Everyone who has a financial stake in a business should understand and keep in mind the bias or tilt of the financial statements they're reading. Using a baseball analogy, the version of financial statements in your hands may be in left field, right field, or center field. All versions are in the ballpark of general financial accounting standards, which define the playing field but don't dictate that every business has to play straight down the middle. In their financial reports, businesses don't comment on whether their financial statements as a whole are liberal, conservative, or somewhere in between. However, a business does have to disclose in the footnotes to its statements its major accounting methods. (Chapter 10 discusses getting a financial report ready for release.)

Presenting an alternative income statement

REMEMBER

Only one set of financial statements is included in a business's financial report: one income statement, one balance sheet, and one statement of cash flows (and one statement of changes in owners' equity). A business doesn't provide a second, alternative set of financial statements that would have been generated if the business had used different accounting methods and if the business hadn't tweaked its financial statements. The financial statements would have been different if alternative accounting methods had been used to record sales revenue and expenses and if the business hadn't engaged in certain end-of-period maneuvers to make its financial statements look better. (Sometimes these tricks of the trade are referred to as "fluffing the pillows.")

Figure 9-2 presents a comparison that you never see in real-life financial reporting. The *Actual* column presents the income statement reported by the business. The *Alternative* column reveals an income statement for the year that the business could have reported (but didn't) if it had used alternative but acceptable accounting methods. The *Difference* column shows the impact on profit between the two methods. For example, sales revenue is less in the Alternative scenario in addition to costs of goods sold increasing, and thus operating income is less, so you see a negative $1 million difference. In the Alternative scenario, income tax expense is lower as a result of the decrease in gross profit and thus profit has been reduced by $650,000, which you see as a negative number.

REMEMBER

If you've read Chapter 6, the Actual account balances in the income statement should be familiar — these are the same numbers from the financial statements we use in that chapter. The dollar amounts in the Alternative column are the amounts that would have been recorded using different accounting methods.

You don't need the statement of cash flows here, because cash flow from profit (operating activities) is the same amount under both accounting scenarios and because the cash flows from investing and financing activities are the same. Keep in mind these important points.

QW Example Tech., Inc. Sales of Both Products & Software Services for the Fiscal Year Ending 12/31/2020			
Income Statement For the Twelve-Month Periods Ending (All Numbers in Thousands)	ACTUAL FYE 12/31/2020	ALTERNATIVE FYE 12/31/2020	DIFFERENCE FYE 12/31/2020
Sales Revenue, Net	$71,064	$70,314	($750)
Costs of Goods Sold	$26,891	$27,041	$150
Gross Profit	$44,173	$43,273	($900)
Selling, General, & Administrative Expenses	$36,678	$36,778	$100
Operating Income (Loss)	$7,495	$6,495	($1,000)
Other Expenses (Income):			
Other Expenses & (Income)	$250	$250	$0
Interest Expense	$350	$350	$0
Total Other Expenses (Income)	$600	$600	$0
Net Profit (Loss) Before Income Taxes	$6,895	$5,895	($1,000)
Income Tax Expense (Benefit)	$2,413	$2,063	($350)
Net Income (Loss)	$4,482	$3,832	($650)
Earnings Per Share (Fully Diluted)	$2.76	$2.36	($0.40)
Confidential — Property of QW Example Tech., Inc.			

FIGURE 9-2: Actual versus alternative income statements for a company.

© John Wiley & Sons, Inc.

The business in our example adopted accounting methods that were more aggressive and resulted in strong profits. But keep in mind that some businesses go the opposite direction. They adopt conservative accounting methods for recording profit performance, and they wouldn't think of tinkering with their financial statements at the end of the year, even when their profit performance falls short of expectations and their financial condition has some trouble spots. The Alternative column in Figure 9-2 reports the results of using more conservative accounting methods. As you see, using alternative accounting methods results in a lower bottom line. Net income would have been $650,000 smaller, resulting in a decrease in earnings per share of $0.40 or approximately 15 percent lower.

Now, you may very well ask, "Where in the devil did you get the numbers for the alternative financial statements?" The dollar amounts are our best estimates of what conservative numbers would be for this business — a company that has been in business for several years, has made a profit most years, and has not gone through bankruptcy. Both the Actual and the Alternative income statements are hypothetical but realistic and are not dishonest or deceitful.

Spotting significant differences

It's a little jarring to see a second set of numbers for the income statement. You're bound to raise your eyebrows when we say that both sets of accounting numbers are true and correct yet different. Financial report users have been conditioned to accept one version for financial statements without thinking about what alternative financial statements would look like. Seeing an alternative scenario takes a little time to get used to, like learning how to drive on the left side of the road in Great Britain. There's always an alternative set of numbers lurking in the shadows, even though you don't get to see them.

The differences in revenue and expenses don't look that big, until you get to the bottom line. Net income is $650,000 lower in the alternative scenario, which is 14.5 percent smaller. Suppose that in putting a market value on the business, you use the earnings multiple method. (For information on the valuation of a small business, see our books *Small Business Financial Management Kit For Dummies* and *Business Financial Information Secrets,* both published by Wiley.) Suppose you're willing to pay six times the most recent annual profit of the business. Using the actual financial statements, you would offer $26.892 million for the business ($4.482 million net income × 6 = $26.892 million). If the alternative accounting methods were used, you'd offer $22.992 million ($3.832 million net income × 6 = $22.992 million). If the business had used the more conservative accounting methods, you would offer $3.90 million less for the business!

Explaining Differences

REMEMBER

Keep in mind the following points about revenue and expenses (from Chapter 6):

>> Recording sales revenue increases an asset (or decreases a liability in some cases).

>> Recording an expense decreases an asset or increases a liability.

Therefore, assets are lower and/or liabilities are higher having used conservative accounting methods, and collectively these differences should equal the difference in retained earnings.

This section briefly explains each of the differences in Figure 9-2. We keep the explanations brief and to the point. The idea is to give you a taste of some of the reasons for the differences.

Accounts receivable and sales revenue

Here are some common reasons sales revenue and accounts receivable are lower when conservative accounting methods are adopted:

>> A business waits a little longer to record sales made on credit, to be more certain that all aspects of delivering products and the acceptance by customers are finalized and that there's little chance the customers will return the products. This delay in recording sales causes its accounts receivable balance to be lower, because at December, some credit sales weren't yet recorded because they were still in the process of final acceptance by the customers. (Of course, the cost of goods sold for these sales wouldn't have been recorded.)

If products are returnable and the deal between the seller and buyer doesn't satisfy normal conditions for a completed sale, the recording of sales revenue should be postponed until the return privilege no longer exists. For example, some products are sold *on approval,* which means the customer takes the product and tries it out for a few days or longer to see whether the customer really wants it.

WARNING

Businesses should be consistent from year to year regarding when they record sales. For some businesses, the timing of recording sales revenue is a major problem — especially when the final acceptance by the customer depends on performance tests or other conditions that must be satisfied. Some businesses engage in *channel stuffing* by forcing their dealers or customers to take delivery of more products than they wanted to buy. A good rule to follow is to read the company's footnote in its financial statements that explains its revenue recognition method, to see whether there's anything unusual. If the footnote is vague, be careful — be very careful!

>> A business may be quicker in writing off a customer's past-due balance as uncollectible. After it's made a reasonable effort to collect the debt but a customer still hasn't sent a check, a more conservative business writes off the balance as a *bad debts* expense. It decreases the past-due accounts receivable balance to zero and records an expense of the same amount. In contrast, a business could wait much longer to write off a customer's past-due amount. Both accounting methods end up writing off a customer's debt if it has been outstanding too long — but a company could wait until the last minute to make the write-off entry.

Inventory and cost of goods sold expense

The business in the example sells products mainly to other businesses. A business either manufactures the products it sells or purchases products for resale to customers. (Chapter 16 explains the determination of product costs for manufacturing businesses.) For this discussion, it isn't too important whether the business manufactures or purchases the products it sells. The costs of its products have drifted upward over time because of inflation and other factors. The business increased its sales prices to keep up with the product cost increases. When product costs change, a business must choose which accounting method to use for recording cost of goods sold expense.

One accounting method takes product costs out of the inventory asset account and records the costs to the cost of goods sold expense in the sequence in which the costs were entered in the asset account. This scheme is called the *first-in, first-out* (FIFO) method. A business may instead choose to use the reverse method, in which the latest product costs entered in the inventory asset account are selected for recording the cost of goods sold expense, which leaves the oldest product costs in the asset account. This method is called the *last-in, first-out* (LIFO) method. We explain these opposing methods in more detail in the later section "Calculating Cost of Goods Sold Expense and Inventory Cost." In Figure 9-2, FIFO is being used in the Actual scenario, and LIFO is what you see in the Alternative scenario.

When product costs drift upward over time, the FIFO method yields a lower cost of goods sold expense and a higher inventory asset balance compared with LIFO. In Figure 9-2, you see that cost of goods sold expense is $150,000 higher. The inventory balance would be lower, which makes total current assets in the balance sheet lower. The lower balance sheet value due to LIFO is the cumulative effect, which includes the carry-forward effects from previous years.

TIP

Some of the $150,000 cost of goods expense difference for 2020 is due to differences in how rigorously the business applies the *lower of cost or market* (LCM) rule. Before being sold, products may suffer loss in value due to deterioration, damage, theft, lower replacement costs, and diminished sales demand. A business tests regularly for such product losses and records the losses by decreasing its inventory balance and charging cost of goods sold expense. The LCM test can be applied loosely or tightly. It's applied more strictly in the Alternative accounting scenario than in the Actual scenario, resulting in a larger amount of write-down of inventory (and higher expense).

Fixed assets and depreciation expense

Most accountants agree that the costs of long-term operating assets that have limited useful lives to a business should be spread out over those predicted useful lives instead of being charged off entirely to expense in the year of acquisition. These long-lived operating assets are labeled *property, plant, and equipment* and, less formally, are called *fixed assets.* (The cost of land owned by a business isn't depreciated because land is a property right that has perpetual life.) The allocation of the cost of a fixed asset over its estimated useful economic life to a business is called *depreciation.* The principle of depreciation is beyond criticism, but the devil is in the detail.

The original costs of fixed assets should theoretically include certain costs in addition to their purchase or construction costs. However, in practice, these fringe costs aren't always included in the original cost of fixed assets. For example, it's theoretically correct to include the installation and connection costs of the power sources for heavy machinery and equipment. It's correct to include the cost of painting logos on the sides of delivery trucks. The cost of an older building just bought by a business should include the preparatory cleanup costs and the safety inspection cost. But in practice, a business may not include such additional costs in the original costs of its fixed assets. The business should be careful concerning IRS rules in this area of accounting. The IRS recently cracked down on the abusive expensing of such costs (and also asset improvement costs that were being charged to repair and maintenance expense).

In the Actual accounting scenario, the business does include these additional costs in the original costs of its fixed assets, which means that the cost balances of its fixed assets are higher compared with the Alternative, conservative scenario. These additional costs aren't expensed immediately but are included in the total amount to be depreciated over future years. Also, in the Actual scenario, the company uses straight-line depreciation (discussed later in this chapter), which spreads out the cost of a fixed asset evenly over the years of its useful life.

In the conservative scenario, the business doesn't include any costs other than purchase or construction costs in its fixed asset accounts, which means the additional costs are charged to expense immediately. Also, and most importantly, the business uses accelerated depreciation (discussed later) for allocating the cost of its fixed assets to expense. Higher amounts are allocated to early years, and smaller amounts, to later years. The result is that the accumulated depreciation amount in the Alternative scenario is higher, which signals that more depreciation expense has been recorded over the years.

Accrued expenses payable, income tax payable, and expenses

REMEMBER

A typical business at the end of the year has liabilities for certain costs that have accumulated but that won't be paid until sometime after the end of the year — costs that are an outgrowth of the current year's operating activities. The amounts of these delayed-payment expenses should be recorded and matched against the sales revenue for the year. For example, a business should *accrue* (calculate and record) the amount it owes to its employees for unused vacation or paid time off. A business may not have received its property tax bill yet, but it should estimate the amount of tax to be assessed and record the proper portion of the annual property tax to the current year. The accumulated interest on notes payable that hasn't been paid yet at the end of the year should be recorded.

Here's another example: Most products are sold with expressed or implied warranties and guarantees. Even when good quality controls are in place, some products sold by a business don't perform up to promises, and the customers want the problems fixed. A business should estimate the cost of these future obligations and record this amount as an expense in the same period that the goods are sold (along with the cost of goods sold expense, of course). It shouldn't wait until customers actually return products for repair or replacement, because if it waits to record the cost, then some of the expense for the guarantee work won't be recorded until the following year. After being in business a few years, a company can forecast with reasonable accuracy the percent of products sold that will be returned for repair or replacement under the guarantees and warranties offered to its customers. On the other hand, brand-new products that have no track record may be a serious problem in this regard.

In the Actual scenario, the business doesn't make the effort to estimate future product warranty and guarantee costs and certain other costs that should be accrued. It records these costs on a when-paid basis. It waits until it actually incurs these costs to record an expense. The company has decided that although its liabilities are understated, the amount is not material. In the Alternative scenario, on the other hand, the business takes the high road and goes to the trouble of estimating future costs that should be matched against sales revenue for the year. Therefore, its accrued expenses payable liability account is higher.

In the Alternative, conservative scenario (see Figure 9-2), we assume that the business uses the same accounting methods for income tax, which gives a lower taxable income and income tax for the year. Accordingly, the income tax expense for the year is $350,000 lower, and the year-end balance of income tax payable is lower. A business makes installment payments during the year on its estimated income tax for the year, so only a fraction of the annual income tax is still unpaid at the end of the year. (A business may use different accounting methods for income tax than it does for recording its transactions, which leads to complexities we don't follow here.)

Wrapping things up

REMEMBER

To be frank, our numbers for the Alternative, conservative scenario are no more than educated guesses. Businesses keep only one set of books. Even a business itself doesn't know how different its financial statements would be if it had used different accounting methods. Financial report readers can read the footnotes to determine whether liberal or conservative accounting methods are being used. Footnotes aren't easy to read. It's very difficult, if not impossible, to determine exactly how much profit would have been and how much different balance sheet amounts would be if a business had used other accounting methods.

TIP

If you own or manage a business, get involved in deciding which accounting methods to use for measuring your profit and how these methods are actually implemented. As Chapter 19 explains, a manager has to answer questions about their financial reports on many occasions. However, "get involved" shouldn't mean manipulating the amounts of sales revenue and expenses recorded in the year — to make profit look higher, to smooth fluctuations in profit from year to year, or to improve the amounts of assets and liabilities reported in your ending balance sheet. You shouldn't even consider doing these things. (Of course, these manipulations go on in the real world. Some people also drive under the influence, but that doesn't mean you should.)

Calculating Cost of Goods Sold Expense and Inventory Cost

Companies that sell products must select which method to use for recording cost of goods sold expense, which is the sum of the costs of the products sold to customers during the period. You deduct cost of goods sold from sales revenue to determine *gross profit* — the first profit line on the income statement (see Figure 9-2). Cost of goods sold is a very important figure; if gross profit is wrong, bottom-line profit (net income) is wrong.

A business can choose between two opposite methods for recording its cost of goods sold and the cost balance that remains in its inventory asset account:

>> The first-in, first-out (FIFO) cost sequence

>> The last-in, first-out (LIFO) cost sequence

Other methods are acceptable, but these two are the primary options.

Product costs are entered in the inventory asset account in the order in which the products are acquired, but they aren't necessarily taken out of the inventory asset account in this order. The FIFO and LIFO terms refer to the order in which product costs are *taken out* of the inventory asset account. You may think that only one method is appropriate; however, American accounting standards permit these two alternatives.

REMEMBER

The choice between the FIFO and LIFO accounting methods does *not* depend on the actual physical flow of products. Generally speaking, products are delivered to customers in the order the business bought or manufactured the products — one reason being that a business doesn't want to keep products in inventory too long because the products may deteriorate or show their age. So products generally move out of inventory in a first-in, first-out sequence. Nevertheless, a business may choose the last-in, first-out accounting method.

REMEMBER

One note: FIFO and LIFO aren't the only games in town. Businesses use other methods for cost of goods sold and inventory, including average cost methods, retail price–based methods, and so on. However, FIFO and LIFO tend to dominate product-centric businesses.

FIFO (first-in, first-out)

With the FIFO method, you charge out product costs to cost of goods sold expense in the chronological order in which you acquired the goods. The procedure is that simple. It's like how the first people in line to see a movie get in the theater first. The ticket-taker collects the tickets in the order in which they were bought.

Suppose that you acquire four units of a product during a period, one unit at a time, with unit costs as follows (in the order in which you acquire the items): $100, $102, $104, and $106, for a total of $412. By the end of the period, you have sold three of these units. Using FIFO, you calculate the cost of goods sold expense as follows:

$$\$100 + \$102 + \$104 = \$306$$

In short, you use the first three units to calculate cost of goods sold expense.

The cost of the ending inventory asset, then, is $106, which is the cost of the most recent acquisition. The $412 total cost of the four units is divided between the $306 cost of goods sold expense for the three units sold and the $106 cost of the one unit in ending inventory. The total cost has been accounted for; nothing has fallen between the cracks.

FIFO has two things going for it:

>> **Products generally move out of inventory in a first-in, first-out sequence.** The earlier-acquired products are delivered to customers before later-acquired products are delivered, so the most recently purchased products are the ones still in ending inventory to be delivered in the future. Using FIFO, the inventory asset reported in the balance sheet at the end of the period reflects recent purchase (or manufacturing) costs, which means the balance in the asset is close to the current *replacement costs* of the products.

>> **When product costs are steadily increasing, many (but not all) businesses follow a first-in, first-out sales price strategy and hold off raising sales prices as long as possible.** They delay raising sales prices until they have sold their lower-cost products. Only when they start selling from the next batch of products, acquired at a higher cost, do they raise sales prices. We favor the FIFO cost of goods sold expense method when a business follows this basic sales pricing policy, because both the expense and the sales revenue are better matched for determining gross margin. We realize that sales pricing is complex and may not follow such a simple process, but the main point is that many businesses use a FIFO-based sales pricing approach. If your business is one of them, we urge you to use the FIFO expense method to be consistent with your sales pricing.

LIFO (last-in, first-out)

Imagine a movie ticket-taker goes to the back of a line of people waiting to get into the next showing and lets them in first. The later you bought your ticket, the sooner you get into the theater. This is what happens in the LIFO method, which stands for *last-in, first-out.* The people in the front of a movie line wouldn't stand for it, of course, but for U.S. businesses, the LIFO method is acceptable for determining the cost of goods sold expense for products sold during the period.

The main feature of the LIFO method is that it selects the *last* item you purchased and then works backward until you have the total cost for the total number of units sold during the period. What about the ending inventory — the products you haven't sold by the end of the year? Using the LIFO method, the earliest cost remains in the inventory asset account (unless all products are sold and the business has nothing in inventory).

Using the same example from the preceding section, assume that the business uses the LIFO method. The four units, in order of acquisition, had costs of $100, $102, $104, and $106. If you sell three units during the period, the LIFO method calculates the cost of goods sold expense as follows:

$$\$106 + \$104 + \$102 = \$312$$

The ending inventory cost of the one unit not sold is $100, which is the oldest cost. The $412 total cost of the four units acquired less the $312 cost of goods sold expense leaves $100 in the inventory asset account. Determining which units you actually delivered to customers is irrelevant; when you use the LIFO method, you always count backward from the most recent unit you acquired.

The two main arguments in favor of the LIFO method are these:

>> **Assigning the most recent costs of products purchased to the cost of goods sold expense makes sense because you have to replace your products to stay in business, and the most recent costs are closest to the amount you'll have to pay to replace your products.** Ideally, you should base your sales prices not on original cost but on the cost of replacing the units sold.

>> **During times of rising costs, the most recent purchase cost maximizes the cost of goods sold expense deduction for determining taxable income and thus minimizes income tax.** In fact, LIFO was invented for income tax purposes. True, the cost of inventory on the ending balance sheet is lower than recent acquisition costs, but the taxable income effect is more important than the balance sheet effect.

WARNING

Here are the reasons LIFO is problematic:

>> Unless you're able to base sales prices on the most recent purchase costs or you raise sales prices as soon as replacement costs increase — and most businesses would have trouble doing this — using LIFO depresses your gross margin and therefore your bottom-line net income.

>> The LIFO method can result in an ending inventory cost value that's seriously out of date, especially if the business sells products that have very long lives. For instance, for several years, Caterpillar's LIFO-based inventory has been billions less than what it would have been under the FIFO method.

>> Unscrupulous managers can use the LIFO method to manipulate their profit figures if business isn't going well. They deliberately let their inventory drop to abnormally low levels, with the result that old, lower product costs are taken

out of inventory to record the cost of goods sold expense. This gives a one-time boost to gross margin. These "LIFO liquidation gains" — if sizable in amount compared with the normal gross profit margin that would have been recorded using current costs — have to be disclosed in the footnotes to the company's financial statements. (Dipping into old layers of LIFO-based inventory cost is necessary when a business phases out obsolete products; the business has no choice but to reach back into the earliest cost layers for these products. The sales prices of products being phased out usually are set low, to move the products out of inventory, so gross margin isn't abnormally high for these products.)

If you sell products that have long lives and for which your product costs rise steadily over the years, using the LIFO method has a serious impact on the ending inventory cost value reported on the balance sheet and can cause the balance sheet to look misleading. Over time, the current cost of replacing products becomes further and further removed from the LIFO-based inventory costs. In our business example (Figure 9-2), the 2020 balance sheet may very well include products with 2010, 2003, or 1990 costs. The product costs reported for inventory could go back even further.

Note: A business must disclose in a footnote with its financial statements the difference between its LIFO-based inventory cost value and its inventory cost value according to FIFO. However, not many people outside of stock analysts and professional investment managers read footnotes very closely. Business managers get involved in reviewing footnotes in the final steps of getting annual financial reports ready for release (see Chapter 10). If your business uses FIFO, ending inventory is stated at recent acquisition costs, and you don't have to determine what the LIFO value would have been.

TIP

Many products and raw materials have very short lives; they're regularly replaced by new models (you know, with those "New and Improved!" labels) because of the latest technology or marketing wisdom. These products aren't around long enough to develop a wide gap between LIFO and FIFO, so the accounting choice between the two methods doesn't make as much difference as with long-lived products.

WARNING

LIFO may become obsolete if international accounting standards are adopted in the United States. As we discuss in Chapter 2, for several years, there have been serious efforts toward developing a unified set of global accounting and financial reporting standards. The international-standards group doesn't approve LIFO, and this position doesn't seem open to negotiation.

Recording Depreciation Expense

In theory, depreciation expense accounting is straightforward enough: You divide the cost of a fixed asset (except land) among the number of years that the business expects to use the asset. In other words, instead of having a huge lump-sum expense in the year in which you make the purchase, you charge a fraction of the cost to expense for each year of the asset's lifetime. Using this method is much easier on your bottom line in the year of purchase, of course.

WARNING

Theories are rarely as simple in real life as they are on paper, and depreciation expense is no exception. Do you divide the cost evenly across the asset's lifetime, or do you charge more to certain years than others? Furthermore, when it eventually comes time to dispose of fixed assets, the assets may have some salvage value. In theory, only cost minus the salvage value should be depreciated. But in practice, most companies ignore salvage value, and the total cost of a fixed asset is depreciated. Moreover, how do you estimate how long an asset will last in the first place? Do you consult an accountant psychic hotline?

As it turns out, the IRS runs its own little psychic business on the side, with a crystal ball known as the Internal Revenue Code. Okay, so the IRS can't tell you that your truck is going to conk out in five years, seven months, and two days. The Internal Revenue Code doesn't predict how long your fixed assets will *last*; it only tells you what kind of timeline to use for income tax purposes as well as how to divide the cost along that timeline.

REMEMBER

Hundreds of books have been written on depreciation, but the book that really counts is the Internal Revenue Code. Most businesses adopt the useful lives allowed by the income tax law for their financial statement accounting; they don't go to the trouble of keeping a second depreciation schedule for financial reporting. Why complicate things if you don't have to? Why keep one depreciation schedule for income tax and a second for preparing your financial statements?

The IRS rules offer two depreciation methods that can be used for particular classes of assets. Buildings must be depreciated just one way, but for other fixed assets, you can take your pick:

>> **Straight-line depreciation:** With this method, you divide the cost evenly among the years of the asset's estimated lifetime. Buildings have to be depreciated this way. Suppose that a building purchased by a business costs $390,000, and its useful life — according to the tax law — is 39 years. The depreciation expense is $10,000 (1/39 of the cost) for each of the 39 years.

You may choose to use the straight-line method for other types of assets, too. After you start using this method for a particular asset, you can't change your mind and switch to another depreciation method later.

>> **Accelerated depreciation:** This term is a generic catchall for several methods. What they all have in common is that they're *front-loading* methods, meaning that you charge a larger amount of depreciation expense in the early years and a smaller amount in the later years. The term *accelerated* also refers to adopting useful lives that are shorter than realistic estimates. (Very few automobiles are useless after five years, for example, but they can be fully depreciated over five years for income tax purposes.)

The *salvage value* of fixed assets (the estimated disposal values when the assets are taken to the junkyard or sold off at the end of their useful lives) is ignored in the calculation of depreciation for income tax. Put another way, if a fixed asset is held to the end of its entire depreciation life, then its original cost will be fully depreciated, and the fixed asset from that time forward will have a zero book value. (Recall that *book value* is equal to original cost minus the balance in the accumulated depreciation account.)

Fully depreciated fixed assets are grouped with all other fixed assets in external balance sheets. All these long-term resources of a business are reported in one asset account called *property, plant, and equipment* (instead of *fixed assets*). If all its fixed assets were fully depreciated, the balance sheet of a company would look rather peculiar — the cost of its fixed assets would be offset by its accumulated depreciation. Keep in mind that the cost of land (as opposed to the structures on the land) is not depreciated. The original cost of land stays on the books as long as the business owns the property.

The straight-line depreciation method has strong advantages: It's easy to understand, and it stabilizes the depreciation expense from year to year. Nevertheless, many business managers and accountants favor an accelerated depreciation method in order to minimize the size of the checks they have to write to the IRS in the early years of using fixed assets. This lets the business keep the cash, for the time being, instead of paying more income tax. Keep in mind, however, that the depreciation expense in the annual income statement is higher in the early years when you use an accelerated depreciation method, and so bottom-line profit is lower. Many accountants and businesses like accelerated depreciation because it paints a more conservative picture of profit performance in the early years. Fixed assets may lose their economic usefulness to a business sooner than expected. If this happens, using the accelerated depreciation method would look very wise in hindsight.

REMEMBER

Except for brand-new enterprises, a business typically has a mix of fixed assets — some in their early years of depreciation, some in their middle years, and some in their later years. There's a balancing-out effect among the vintages of fixed assets being depreciated. Therefore, the overall depreciation expense for the year using accelerated depreciation may not be too different from what the straight-line depreciation amount would be. A business does *not* have to disclose in its external financial report what its depreciation expense would have been if it had been using an alternative method. Readers of the financial statements can't tell how much difference the choice of accounting methods would have made in depreciation expense that year.

Scanning the Revenue and Expense Radar Screen

Recording sales revenue and other income can present some hairy accounting problems. As a matter of fact, the accounting rule-making authorities rank revenue recognition as a major problem area and have focused a great deal of attention on this subject over the past decade. If you are a glutton for punishment or really just want to become an expert on sales revenue recognition, refer to ASC 606, which represents a newly released accounting standard pertaining to sales revenue recognition. (ASC stands for Accounting Standards Codification, a go-to source for accounting principles as established by the Financial Accounting Standards Board.)

WARNING

A good part of the reason for putting revenue recognition high on the list of accounting problems is that many high-profile financial accounting frauds have involved recording bogus sales revenue that had no economic reality or attempting to "front load" sales revenue and realize it as fully earned when in actuality, the sales revenue should be deferred. In either case, sales revenue is being overstated, which, needless to say, is extremely misleading to investors and creditors alike.

But in our view, the accounting for many key expenses is equally important. Frankly, it's damn difficult to account for and measure expenses on a consistent year-by-year basis, especially in light of just how fast economic conditions change in today's global economy.

We could write a book on expense accounting, which would have at least 20 or 30 major chapters and still cover only a fraction of the potential topic. All we can do here is to call your attention to a few major expense accounting issues:

>> **Asset impairment write-downs:** Inventory shrinkage, bad debts, and depreciation by their very nature are asset write-downs. Other asset write-downs are required when an asset becomes *impaired,* which means that it has lost some or all of its economic utility to the business and has little or no disposable value. An asset write-down reduces the book (recorded) value of an asset (and at the same time records an expense or loss of the same amount).

>> **Employee-defined benefits pension plans and other post-retirement benefits:** The U.S. accounting rule on this expense is complex. Several key estimates must be made by the business, including the expected rate of return on the investment portfolio set aside for these future obligations. This and other estimates affect the amount of expense recorded. In some cases, a business uses an unrealistically high rate of return in order to minimize the amount of this expense. Using unrealistically optimistic rates of investment return continues to be a pernicious problem.

>> **Certain discretionary operating expenses:** Many operating expenses involve timing problems and/or serious estimation problems. Furthermore, some expenses are discretionary in nature, which means how much to spend during the year depends almost entirely on the discretion of managers. Managers can defer or accelerate these expenses in order to manipulate the amount of expense recorded in the period. For this reason, businesses filing financial reports with the SEC are required to disclose certain expenses, such as repairs and maintenance expense and advertising expense. (To find examples, go to the Securities and Exchange Commission website at www. sec.gov.)

>> **Income tax expense:** A business can use different accounting methods for some of the expenses reported in its income statement than it uses for calculating its taxable income. Oh, boy! The hypothetical amount of taxable income is calculated as if the accounting methods used in the income statement were used in the tax return; then the income tax based on this hypothetical taxable income is figured. This is the income tax expense reported in the income statement. This amount is reconciled with the actual amount of income tax owed based on the accounting methods used for income tax purposes. A reconciliation of the two different income tax amounts is provided in a technical footnote schedule to the financial statements.

>> **Equity incentive plans:** Equity incentive plans are used by a number of companies to provide additional "incentives" to employees, board members, key parties, and so on to enhance their base compensation. For corporations, stock option plans are created, and they can issue a *stock option grant* to the recipient, which is a contract between an employee and the business that grants the stock option to purchase a certain number of the corporation's

capital stock shares at a fixed price (called the *exercise* or *strike* price) after certain conditions are satisfied. Usually a stock option doesn't vest until the employee has been with the business for a certain number of years.

The question is whether the granting of stock options should be recorded as an expense. This issue had been simmering for some time. The U.S. rule-making body finally issued a pronouncement that requires that a value measure be put on stock options when they're issued and that this amount be recorded as an expense.

You could argue that management stock options are simply an arrangement between the stockholders and the privileged few employees of the business, by which the stockholders allow the employees to buy shares at bargain prices. The granting of stock options doesn't reduce the assets or increase the liabilities of the business, so you could argue that stock options aren't a direct expense of the business; instead, the cost falls on the stockholders. Allowing employees to buy stock shares at below-market prices increases the number of shares over which profit has to be spread, thus decreasing earnings per share. Stockholders have to decide whether they're willing to do this; the granting of management stock options must be put to a vote by the stockholders.

Please don't think that the short list here does justice to all the expense accounting problems of businesses. U.S. businesses — large and small, public and private — operate in a highly developed and very sophisticated economy. One result is that expense accounting has become very complicated and confusing.

WARNING

As if accountants didn't already have enough problems in measuring profit, there's a growing trend among public corporations to undercut their own income statements. In press releases and meetings with stock analysts, it seems an increasing number of public companies promote a version of "adjusted earnings," on the grounds that these alternative concepts of profit are better guides to the future of the business. It's difficult to tell whether private businesses are following this trend. Private companies with few exceptions do not issue press releases or meet with stock analysts. Their communications and dealings with their sources of capital are private, of course.

REMEMBER

In particular, many public companies use the metric of earnings before interest, tax, depreciation, and amortization (EBITDA) as a useful measure of their profit. You don't have to read very far between the lines to see that these companies want to draw attention away from their income statements in order to put their profit performance in a more favorable light. In our view, these companies are trying to pull a fast one on investors. We admit that EBITDA has use in the management analysis of profit performance, but it's not the final, all-things-considered measure of profit that investors should focus on. Net income, not EBITDA, is the bottom line.

Using the Statement of Cash Flows as an Audit/Sanity Test

Chapter 8 covers the statement of cash flows in depth and highlights its importance and value to external parties. Looking at the statement of cash flows from a different perspective, we like to think of in terms of the Disney movie *Cinderella*. If you recall, the two attention-starved stepsisters (in other words, the balance sheet and income statement) demand all the attention and relegate Cinderella to performing demeaning tasks. However, as the story moves forward, Cinderella blossoms into the most beautiful sister of all, as her true, deep, and rich value comes to light. You might think of the statement of cash flows in this same light because, after you truly understand its importance and meaning, you will find that it shines an amazing light on the operating performance of a business.

Okay, so this might be a bit of an overreach, but this analogy drives home a critical concept associated with the big three financial statements covered in Chapters 6, 7, and 8. That is, the income statement and, to a lesser extent, the balance sheet tend to get most of the attention from financial experts, as in today's "time is of the essence" business mindset, these questions generally first come to mind:

>> What are top-line sales (and how much did they grow)?

>> What's the company's bottom-line profit?

>> How financially strong is the company?

REMEMBER

All good questions, but none of these addresses the most important question of all: Can the business generate enough cash to support ongoing operations? This, in a nutshell, represents the essence of the statement of cash flows and why it can be such a useful tool to potentially help ferret out potential reporting problems in the income statement or balance sheet.

For example, if a company is growing rapidly, you would expect sales revenue and associated trade accounts receivables and inventory to grow in a proportional manner because the company needs more inventory to support higher sales revenue and would anticipate extending additional credit to customers. This would be a normal relationship, but in a situation where sales revenue is growing at, say, 25 percent per year yet inventory and trade accounts receivables have ballooned higher by 45 percent, this may indicate that the company has potential valuation problems associated with inventory (such as slow-moving inventory that should be written down) or potential customer bad debts that have not been addressed. The statement of cash flows can help identify these potential issues by asking one simple question: Why is the company in the black (generating a profit) but not generating any green (positive cash flow)?

In the end, cash flows should, over a period of time, mirror a company's ability to generate profit or incur losses, so this in effect is one of the values of the statement of cash flows. If a company seems to be able to always generate solid profits but cannot seem to produce real positive internal cash flows, then questions should be raised as to the actual, fair, or real value of the assets it is reporting (and if the company needs to write down or reduce the value of the assets). Here, the statement of cash flows can act in the capacity of a simple man's audit tool or sanity check to help validate the accuracy and reliability of the income statement and balance sheet.

3

Understanding Financial Reports, Financial Statements, and Financial Information

IN THIS PART . . .

Develop a basis for the inside story of how business financial reports are produced. (It's not as bad as making sausage, but there are several messy details.)

Discover how to dig deeper into a financial report, decipher operating performance summaries provided by management, and identify "devil in the detail" issues of importance.

Find out how both internal and external parties use financial statement analysis techniques and ratio calculations to interpret and better understand the financial performance of a company.

Get the lowdown on the more detailed and highly confidential accounting information that company executives, managers, and owners (in other words, the insiders) of the business need for identifying problems and opportunities — in short, for running the business.

Find out the latest games being played by Wall Street with an entire chapter dedicated to helping you understand current trends in financial reporting and how companies utilize "financial engineering" to help tell their stories.

Chapter **10**

Producing Financial Reports

F inancial statements are the core content of a financial report, to be sure. But the term *financial report* connotes more content than the basic set of financial statements. To start this chapter, we briefly review the three primary business financial statements. Then we move on to a broader view of what's in a financial report.

Lest you think that accountants prepare the whole of a financial report, we explain the role of top management in preparing the financial report of a business. Accountants are the main actors in whipping together the financial statements of the business. That's their job. Then the top-level managers of the business take over. The managers are the primary actors in deciding the additional content to put in the financial report, from the letter to the shareholders to a historical summary of the key financial data of the business.

We also call your attention to the seamy side of financial reporting. The company's managers may put a spin on the financial statement numbers generated by the accountant. Managers may override the accountant's numbers to make profit look better (or at least smoother year to year) or to improve the appearance of the company's financial condition. In this chapter, we also compare the financial reports of the typical public corporation with those of private and smaller businesses.

Quickly Reviewing the Theory of Financial Reporting

Business managers, creditors, and investors rely on financial reports because these reports provide information regarding how the business is doing and where it stands financially. Like newspapers, financial reports deliver financial "news" about the business. One big difference between newspapers and business external financial reports is that businesses themselves, not independent reporters, decide what goes into their financial reports. If you read financial information on websites such as Yahoo! Finance, for instance, keep in mind that the information comes from the financial reports prepared and issued by the business.

Starting with the financial statements

In Chapters 6, 7, and 8, we explain the fundamentals of the three primary financial statements of a business. To review briefly:

>> **Income statement:** The income statement summarizes sales revenue and other income (if any) and expenses and losses (if any) for the period. It ends with the bottom-line profit for the period, which most commonly is called *net income* or *net earnings.* (Inside a business, a profit performance statement is commonly called the *profit and loss,* or *P&L,* report.)

>> **Balance sheet:** The balance sheet summarizes the financial condition, consisting of amounts of assets, liabilities, and owners' equity at the closing date of the income statement period (and at other times as needed by managers). Its formal name is the *statement of financial condition* or *statement of financial position.*

>> **Statement of cash flows:** The statement of cash flows reports the net cash increase or decrease during the period from the profit-making activities reported in the income statement and the reasons this key figure is different from bottom-line net income for the period. It also summarizes sources and uses of cash during the period from investing and financing activities.

REMEMBER

This troika of financial statements constitutes the bedrock of a financial report. At a minimum, every financial report should include these three financial statements and their footnotes. (Smaller private businesses are notoriously skimpy on their footnotes.)

The three primary statements, plus footnotes to the financials and other content, are packaged in an annual financial report that is distributed to the company's investors and lenders so they can keep tabs on the business's financial health and performance. Abbreviated versions of their annual reports are distributed quarterly by public companies, as required by federal securities laws. Private companies do not have to provide interim financial reports, though many do. In this chapter, we shine a light on the process of preparing the annual financial report so you can recognize key decisions that must be made before a financial report hits the streets.

Keeping in mind the reasons for financial reports

A financial report is designed to answer certain basic financial questions:

>> Is the business making a profit or suffering a loss, and how much?

>> Is the business's sales revenue increasing or decreasing?

>> How do assets stack up against liabilities?

>> Where did the business get its capital, and is it making good use of the money?

>> What is the cash flow from the profit or loss for the period?

>> Did the business reinvest all its profit or distribute some of the profit to owners?

>> Does the business have enough capital for future growth?

>> Does the business have enough liquidity to pay its bills, and is it solvent?

TIP

People should read a financial report like a road map: to point the way and check how the trip is going. Managing and putting money into a business is a financial journey. A manager is like the driver and must pay attention to all the road signs; investors and lenders are like the passengers who watch the same road signs. Some of the most important road signs are the ratios between sales revenue and expenses and their related assets and liabilities in the balance sheet.

In short, the purpose of financial reporting is to deliver important information that the lenders and owners of the business need and are entitled to receive. Financial reporting is part of the essential contract between a business and its lenders and investors. Although lawyers may not like this, the contract can be stated in a few words:

Give us your money, and we'll give you the information you need to know regarding how we're doing with your money.

Financial reporting is governed by statutory and common law, and it should abide by ethical standards. Unfortunately, financial reporting sometimes falls short of both legal and ethical standards.

WARNING

Businesses assume the readers of the financial statements and other information in their financial reports are knowledgeable about business and finance in general and understand basic accounting terminology and measurement methods. Financial reporting practices, in other words, take a lot for granted about readers of financial reports. Don't expect to find friendly hand-holding and helpful explanations in financial reports. Reading financial reports is not for the faint of heart. You need to sit down with a cup of coffee (or something stronger) and be ready for serious concentration.

Recognizing Top Management's Role

The annual financial report of a business consists of the three primary financial statements with their associated footnotes and a variety of additional content, such as photographs of executives, vision statements, highlights of key financial performance measures, letters to stockholders from top management, MDORs or MD&As (that is, management discussion of operating results or management discussion and analysis), and more. Public companies provide considerably more content than private companies. Much of the additional content falls outside the realm of financial accounting and to a large extent is at the discretion of the business.

The business's top managers assisted by their top lieutenants play an essential role in the preparation of the financial reports of the company — which they (and outside investors and lenders) should understand. The managers should perform certain critical steps before the financial report of the company is released to the outside world:

1. **Confer with the company's chief financial officer and controller (chief accountant) to make sure that the latest accounting and financial reporting standards and requirements have been applied in its financial report. (A smaller business may consult with an independent CPA on these matters.)**

    In recent years, we've seen a high degree of flux in accounting and financial reporting standards and requirements. The U.S. and international rule-making bodies, as well as the U.S. federal regulatory agency, the Securities and Exchange Commission (SEC), have been very busy. International financial accounting and reporting standards haven't taken root in the United States, although in late 2015, the SEC indicated its inclination to allow U.S. companies to include international standards–compliant information as an "add-on" in their U.S.-based financial statements.

    Looking in the other direction, small and medium-sized businesses are urged by the AICPA (American Institute of Certified Public Accountants) to adopt a separate financial reporting framework. And private companies can adopt certain alternative accounting methods. A business needs to know how it fits into the general classification of business entities (public or private, large or small to medium-sized).

REMEMBER

    A business and its independent CPA auditors can't simply assume that the accounting methods and financial reporting practices that have been used for many years are still correct and adequate. A business must check carefully whether it's in full compliance with current accounting standards and financial reporting requirements.

2. **Carefully review the disclosures to be made in the financial report.**

    The top managers and financial officers of the business should make sure that the *disclosures* — all information other than the financial statements — are adequate according to financial reporting standards and that all the disclosure elements are truthful but not unnecessarily damaging to the business. Ideally, the disclosures should be written in clear language. We mention this because many disclosures seem purposely difficult to read (excuse us for getting on the soapbox here).

TIP

    This disclosure review can be compared with the concept of *due diligence,* which is done to make certain that all relevant information is collected, that the information is accurate and reliable, and that all relevant requirements and regulations are being complied with. This step is especially important for public corporations whose securities (stock shares and debt instruments) are traded on securities exchanges. Public businesses fall under the jurisdiction of federal securities laws, which require technical and detailed filings with the SEC.

3. **Consider whether the financial statement numbers need touching up.**

We know, this sounds a little suspicious, doesn't it? It's not as bad as putting lipstick on a pig. The idea is to smooth the jagged edges of the company's year-to-year profit gyrations or to improve the business's short-term solvency picture. Although this can be described as putting your thumb on the scale, you can argue that sometimes the scale is a little out of balance to begin with, and the manager should approve adjusting the numbers in the financial statements in order to make them jibe better with the normal circumstances of the business.

WARNING

When we discuss touching up the financial statement numbers, we're venturing into a gray area that accountants don't much like to talk about. These topics are rather delicate. Nevertheless, in the real world of business, top-level managers have to strike a balance between the interests of the business on the one hand and the interests of its owners (investors) and creditors on the other. For a rough comparison, think of the advertising done by a business. Advertising should be truthful, but businesses have lots of leeway regarding how to advertise their products, and much advertising uses lots of hyperbole. Managers exercise the same freedoms in putting together their financial reports. Financial reports may have some hype, and managers may put as much positive spin on bad news as possible without making deceitful and deliberately misleading comments. See the later section "Putting a Spin on the Numbers (Short of Cooking the Books)" for details.

Keeping Current with Financial Accounting and Reporting Standards

Standards and regulatory requirements for accounting and financial reporting don't stand still. For many years, accounting and financial reporting standards moved like glaciers — slowly and not too far. But just like the climate, the activity of the accounting and financial reporting authorities has warmed up. In fact, it's hard to keep up with the changes.

Without a doubt, the rash of accounting and financial reporting scandals over the period of 1980–2000 (and continuing today) was one reason for the step-up in activity by the standard-setters. The infamous Enron accounting fraud scandal brought down a major international CPA firm (Arthur Andersen) and led to the passage of federal legislation that requires public companies to report on their internal controls to prevent financial reporting fraud. Furthermore, CPA auditors have come under increasing pressure to do better audits, especially by the Public Company Accounting Oversight Board, which is an arm of the SEC.

The other reason for the heightened pace of activity by the standard-setters is the increasing complexity of doing business. When you look at how business is conducted these days, you find more and more complexity — for example, the use of financial derivative contracts and instruments. It's difficult to put definite gain and loss values on these financial devices before the day of reckoning (when the contracts terminate). The legal exposure of businesses has expanded, especially in respect to environmental laws and regulations.

REMEMBER

In our view, the standard-setters should be given lots of credit for their attempts to deal with the problems that have emerged in recent decades and for trying to prevent repetition of the accounting scandals of the past. But the price of doing so has been a rather steep increase in the range and rapidity of changes in accounting and financial reporting standards and requirements. Top-level managers of businesses have to make sure that the financial and accounting officers of the business are keeping up with these changes and make sure that their financial reports follow all current rules and regulations. Managers lean heavily on their chief financial officers and controllers for keeping in full compliance with accounting and financial reporting standards.

Making Sure Disclosure Is Adequate

The financial statements are the backbone of a financial report. In fact, a financial report isn't deserving of the name if financial statements aren't included. But a financial report is much more than just the financial statements; a financial report needs *disclosures.* Of course, the financial statements themselves provide disclosure of important financial information about the business. The term *disclosures,* however, usually refers to additional information provided in a financial report.

The CEO of a public corporation, the president of a private corporation, or the managing partner of a partnership has the primary responsibility to make sure that the financial statements have been prepared according to applicable accounting and reporting standards and that the financial report provides adequate disclosure. They work with the chief financial officer and controller of the business to make sure that the financial report meets the standard of adequate disclosure. (Many smaller businesses hire an independent CPA to advise them on their financial reports.)

REMEMBER

For a quick survey of disclosures in financial reports, the following distinctions are helpful:

>> **Footnotes** provide additional information about the figures included in the financial statements. Virtually all financial statements need footnotes to

provide additional information for several of the items included in the three financial statements. (Even so, many small companies include only the bare bones of footnotes or no footnotes at all.)

>> **Supplementary financial schedules and tables** to the financial statements provide more details than can be included in the body of financial statements.

>> A wide variety of **other information** is presented, some of which is required if the business is a public corporation subject to federal regulations regarding financial reporting to its stockholders. Other information is voluntary and not strictly required legally or by financial reporting standards that apply to the business.

Footnotes: Nettlesome but needed

Footnotes are attached to the three primary financial statements and are usually placed at the end of the financial statements. Within the financial statements, you see references to particular footnotes. And at the bottom of each financial statement, you find the following sentence (or words to this effect): "The footnotes are integral to the financial statements."

You should read all footnotes for a full understanding of the financial statements, although we should mention that some footnotes are dense and technical. For one exercise, try reading a footnote that explains how a public corporation puts the value on its management stock options in order to record the expense for this component of management compensation. Then take two aspirin to get rid of your headache.

Footnotes come in two types:

>> **One or more footnotes identify the major accounting policies and methods that the business uses.** The business must reveal the principal accounting methods it uses for booking its revenue and expenses. In particular, the business must identify its cost of goods sold and depreciation expense methods. Some businesses have unusual problems regarding the timing for recording sales revenue, and a footnote should clarify their revenue recognition method. Other accounting methods that have a material impact on the financial statements are disclosed in footnotes as well. (Chapter 9 explains that a business must choose among alternative accounting methods for recording revenue and expenses and for their corresponding assets and liabilities.)

>> **Other footnotes provide additional information and details for many assets and liabilities.** For example, a business may owe money on many short-term and longer-term debt issues; a footnote presents a schedule of maturity dates and interest rates of the debt issues. Details about stock option plans for executives are the main type of footnote for the capital stock account in the stockholders' equity section of the balance sheet of corporations.

Some footnotes are always required; a financial report would be naked without them. Deciding whether a footnote is needed (after you get beyond the obvious ones disclosing the business's accounting methods) and how to write the footnote is largely a matter of judgment and opinion. The general benchmark is whether footnote information is relevant to the investors and creditors of the business. But how relevant? This is the key question. For public companies, keep in mind that the SEC lays down specific requirements regarding disclosures in the quarterly and annual filings with the SEC.

Look at the following footnote from Caterpillar's annual report. For your reading pleasure, here's footnote D in its 2014 annual 10–K report filed with the SEC (page A–13):

> **D. Inventories:** *Inventories are stated at the lower of cost or market. Cost is principally determined using the last-in, first-out (LIFO) method. The value of inventories on the LIFO basis represented about 60% of total inventories at December 31, 2014, 2013, and 2012.*
>
> *If the FIFO (first-in, first-out) method had been in use, inventories would have been $2,430 million, $2,504 million, and $2,750 million higher than reported at December 31, 2014, 2013, and 2012 respectively.*

Yes, these dollar amounts are in *millions* of dollars. Caterpillar's inventory cost value for its inventories at the end of 2014 would have been $2,430 million (or $2.43 billion) higher if the FIFO accounting method had been used. Of course, it helps to have a basic understanding of the difference between the two accounting methods — LIFO and FIFO — to make sense of this note (see Chapter 9).

You may wonder how different Caterpillar's annual profits would have been if the FIFO cost of goods sold expense accounting method had been in use. A business's managers can ask its accounting department to do this analysis, but as an outside investor, you would have to compute these amounts yourself (assuming you had all the necessary information). Businesses disclose their accounting methods, but they don't disclose how different annual profits would have been if alternative methods had been used.

Other disclosures in financial reports

The following discussion includes a fairly comprehensive list of the various types of disclosures (in addition to footnotes) found in annual financial reports of publicly owned businesses. A few caveats are in order:

» Not every public corporation includes every one of the following items, although the disclosures are fairly common.

» The level of disclosure by private businesses — after you get beyond the financial statements and footnotes — is generally much less than in public corporations. A private business may include one or more of the following disclosures, but by and large, it isn't required to do so — and in our experience, only a minority do.

» Tracking the actual disclosure practices of private businesses is difficult because their annual financial reports are circulated only to their owners and lenders. In other words, a private business keeps its financial report as private as possible.

In addition to the three financial statements and footnotes to the financials, public corporations typically include the following disclosures in their annual financial reports to their stockholders:

» **Cover (or transmittal) letter:** A letter from the chief executive of the business to the stockholders, which usually takes credit for good news and blames bad news on big government, unfavorable world political developments, a poor economy, or something else beyond management's control

» **Management's report on internal control over financial reporting:** An assertion by the chief executive officer and chief financial officer regarding their satisfaction with the effectiveness of the internal controls of the business, which are designed to ensure the reliability of its financial reports and to prevent financial and accounting fraud

» **Highlights table:** A table presenting key figures from the financial statements, such as sales revenue, total assets, profit, total debt, owners' equity, number of employees, and number of units sold (such as the number of vehicles sold by an automobile manufacturer or the number of "revenue seat miles" flown by an airline, meaning one airplane seat occupied by a paying customer for 1 mile); the idea is to give the stockholder a financial thumbnail sketch of the business

» **Management discussion and analysis (MD&A):** A discussion of the major developments and changes during the year that affected the financial performance and situation of the business (by the way, the SEC requires this disclosure to be included in the annual financial reports of publicly owned corporations)

>> **Segment information:** A report of the sales revenue and operating profits (before interest and income tax and perhaps before certain costs that cannot be allocated among different segments) for the major divisions of the organization or for its different markets (international versus domestic, for example)

>> **Historical summaries:** A financial history that extends back three years or longer that includes information from past financial statements

>> **Graphics:** Bar charts, trend charts, and pie charts representing financial conditions; photos of key people and products

>> **Promotional material:** Information about the company, its products, its employees, and its managers, often stressing an overarching theme for the year

Most companies use their annual financial report as an advertising or public relations opportunity.

>> **Profiles:** Information about members of top management and the board of directors

Of course, everyone appears to be well qualified for their position. Negative information (such as prior brushes with the law) is not reported. One interesting development in recent years is that several high-level executives have lied about their academic degrees.

>> **Quarterly summaries of profit performance and stock share prices:** Summaries that show financial performance for all four quarters in the year and stock price ranges for each quarter (required by the SEC for public companies)

>> **Management's responsibility statement:** A short statement indicating that management has primary responsibility for the accounting methods used to prepare the financial statements, for writing the footnotes to the statements, and for providing the other disclosures in the financial report

Usually, this statement appears near the independent CPA auditor's report.

>> **Independent auditor's report:** The report from the CPA firm that performed the audit, expressing an opinion on the fairness of the financial statements and accompanying disclosures

Public corporations are required to have audits; private businesses may or may not have their annual financial reports audited. Unfortunately, the wording of audit reports has become more and more difficult to understand. The standards that govern CPA audit reports have mimicked the trend of accounting and financial reporting standards. Audit reports used to be three paragraphs that you could understand with careful reading. Even we can't be sure about some audit reports we read these days.

>> **Company contact information:** Information on how to contact the company, the web address of the company, how to get copies of the reports filed with the SEC, the stock transfer agent and registrar of the company, and other information

We should mention that annual financial reports have virtually no humor — no cartoons, no one-liners, no jokes. (Well, the CEO's letter to shareowners may have some humorous comments, even when the CEO doesn't mean to be funny.) Financial reports are written in a somber and serious vein. The tone of most annual financial reports is that the fate of the Western world depends on the financial performance of the company. Give us a break!

Managers of public corporations rely on lawyers, CPA auditors, and their financial and accounting officers to make sure that everything that should be disclosed in the business's annual financial reports is included and that the exact wording of the disclosures is not misleading, inaccurate, or incomplete. This is a tall order.

WARNING

Both federal and state laws, as well as authoritative accounting standards, must be observed in financial report disclosures. Inadequate disclosure is just as serious as using wrong accounting methods for measuring profit and for determining values for assets, liabilities, and owners' equity. A financial report can be misleading because of improper accounting methods or because of inadequate or misleading disclosure. Both types of deficiencies can lead to nasty lawsuits against the business and its managers.

Putting a Spin on the Numbers (Short of Cooking the Books)

This section discusses two accounting tricks that involve manipulating, or "massaging," the accounting numbers. We don't endorse either technique, but you should be aware of both.

In some situations, the financial statement numbers don't come out exactly the way the business prefers. With the connivance of top management, accountants can use certain tricks of the trade — some would say sleight of hand, or shenanigans — to move the numbers closer to what the business prefers. One trick improves the appearance of the *short-term solvency* of the business and the cash balance reported in its balance sheet at the end of the year. The other device shifts some profit from one year to the next to report a smoother trend of net income from year to year.

WARNING

We don't mean to suggest that all businesses engage in these accounting machinations — but many do. The extent of use of these unholy schemes is hard to pin down because no business would openly admit to using them. The evidence is convincing, however, that many businesses massage their numbers to some degree. We're sure you've heard the term *loopholes* applied to income tax. Well, some loopholes exist in financial statement accounting as well.

Window dressing: Pumping up the ending cash balance and cash flow

Suppose you manage a business and your controller has just submitted for your review the *preliminary*, or first draft, of the year-end balance sheet. (Chapter 7 explains the balance sheet, and Figure 7-2 shows a balance sheet for a business.) Figure 10-1 shows the current assets and current liabilities sections of the balance sheet draft, which is all we need here.

FIGURE 10-1:
Current assets and current liabilities of a business, before window dressing.

Statement of Financial Condition (AKA Balance Sheet) Period Ending	FYE 12/31/2020		FYE 12/31/2020
Current Assets:		Current Liabilities:	
Cash & Equivalents	$30,000	Accounts Payable	$235,000
Accounts Receivable, Net	$486,000	Accrued Expenses	$187,000
Inventory, LCM	$844,000	Income Taxes Payable	$58,000
Prepaid Expenses	$72,000	Short-Term Debt	$200,000
Total Current Assets	$1,432,000		$680,000

© John Wiley & Sons, Inc.

Wait a minute: a $30,000 cash balance? How can that be? Maybe your business has been having some cash flow problems and you've intended to increase your short-term borrowing and speed up collection of accounts receivable to help the cash balance. No one likes to see a near-zero cash balance — it makes them kind of nervous, to put it mildly, no matter how you try to cushion it. So what do you do to avoid setting off alarm bells?

Your controller is probably aware of a technique called *window dressing*, a very simple method for making the cash balance look better. Suppose your fiscal year-end is October 31. Your controller takes the cash collections from customers paying their accounts receivable that are actually received on November 1, 2, 3, and 4 and records these four days of cash receipts as if these cash collections had been received on October 31. After all, the argument can be made that the customers' checks were in the mail — that money is yours, as far as the customers are concerned.

Window dressing reduces the amount in accounts receivable and increases the amount in cash the same amount — it has no effect on your profit figure for the period. It makes your cash balance look a touch better. Window dressing can also be used to improve other accounts' balances, which we don't go into here. All these techniques involve holding the books open to record certain events that take place after the end of the fiscal year (the ending balance sheet date) to make things look better than they actually were at the close of business on the last day of the year.

Sounds like everybody wins, doesn't it? You look like you've done a better job as manager, and your lenders and investors don't panic. Right? Wrong! Window dressing is deceptive to your creditors and investors, who have every right to expect that the end of your fiscal year as stated on your financial reports is truly the end of your fiscal year. We should mention, however, that when we were in auditing, we encountered situations in which a major lender of the business was fully aware that it had engaged in window dressing. The lender did not object because it wanted the business to fluff the pillows to make its balance sheet look better. The loan officer wanted to make the loan to make the business look better. Essentially, the lender was complicit in the accounting manipulation.

Window dressing can be the first step on a slippery slope. A little window dressing today, and tomorrow, who knows? Maybe giving the numbers a nudge now will lead to more serious accounting deceptions or even out-and-out accounting fraud. Moreover, when a business commits some accounting hanky-panky, should the chief executive of the business brief its directors on the accounting manipulation? Things get messy, to say the least!

Be aware that window dressing improves cash flow from operating activities, which is an important number in the statement of cash flows that creditors and investors closely watch. (We discuss the statement of cash flows and cash flow from operating activities in Chapter 8.) Suppose, for example, that a business holds open its cash receipts journal for several days after the close of its fiscal year. The result is that its ending cash balance is reported $3.25 million higher than the business actually had in its checking accounts on the balance sheet date. Also, its accounts receivable balance is reported $3.25 million lower than was true at the end of its fiscal year. This makes cash flow from profit (operating activities) $3.25 million higher, which could be the main reason in the decision to do some window dressing.

Smoothing the rough edges off year-to-year profit fluctuations

You shouldn't be surprised when we tell you that business managers are under tremendous pressure to make profit and keep profit on the up escalator year after year. Managers strive to make their numbers and to hit the milestone markers set for the business. Reporting a loss for the year, or even a dip below the profit trend line, is a red flag that stock analysts and investors view with alarm. Everyone likes to see a steady upward trend line for profit; no one likes to see a profit curve that looks like a roller coaster. Most investors want a smooth journey and don't like putting on their investment life preservers.

Managers can do certain things to deflate or inflate profit (net income) recorded in the year, which are referred to as *profit-smoothing* techniques. Other names for these techniques are *income smoothing* and *earnings management.* Profit smoothing is like a white lie told for the good of the business and perhaps for the good of managers as well. Managers know that there's always some noise in the accounting system. Profit smoothing muffles the noise.

WARNING

The general view in the financial community is that profit smoothing is not nearly as serious as *cooking the books,* or *juggling the books.* These terms refer to deliberate, fraudulent accounting practices such as recording sales revenue that hasn't happened or not recording expenses that have happened. Nevertheless, profit smoothing is still serious and, if carried too far, could be interpreted as accounting fraud. Managers have gone to jail for fraudulent financial statements.

WARNING

Theoretically, having an audit by a CPA firm should root out any significant accounting fraud when the business is knowingly perpetrating the fraud or when it's an innocent victim of fraud against the business. But in fact, there continue to be many embarrassing cases in which the CPA auditor failed to discover major fraud by or against the business. We could write a whole book on accounting fraud and not worry about running out of material. Several books have been published on this topic, which you can find by using the search words "accounting fraud" or "cooking the books" in your search engine. We recommend *Forensic Accounting For Dummies* by Frimette Kass-Shraibman and Vijay Sampath (Wiley).

The pressure on public companies

Managers of publicly owned corporations whose stock shares are actively traded are under intense pressure to keep profits steadily rising. Security analysts who follow a particular company make profit forecasts for the business, and their buy/hold/sell recommendations are based largely on these earnings forecasts. If a business fails to meet its own profit forecast or falls short of stock analysts' forecasts, the market price of its stock shares usually takes a hit. Stock option and bonus incentive compensation plans are also strong motivations for achieving the profit goals set for the business.

WARNING

The evidence is fairly strong that publicly owned businesses engage in some degree of profit smoothing. Frankly, it's much harder to know whether private businesses do so. Private businesses don't face the public scrutiny and expectations that public corporations do. On the other hand, key managers in a private business may have bonus arrangements that depend on recorded profit. In any case, business investors and managers should know about profit smoothing and how it's done.

Compensatory effects

Most profit smoothing involves pushing some amount of revenue and/or expenses into years other than those in which they would normally be recorded. For example, if the president of a business wants to report more profit for the year, he or she can instruct the chief accountant to accelerate the recording of some sales revenue that normally wouldn't be recorded until next year or to delay the recording of some expenses until next year that normally would be recorded this year.

Chapter 9 explains that managers choose among alternative accounting methods for several important expenses (and for revenue as well). After making these choices, the managers should let the accountants do their jobs and let the chips fall where they may. If bottom-line profit for the year turns out to be a little short of the forecast or target for the period, so be it. This hands-off approach to profit accounting is the ideal way. However, managers often use a hands-on approach — they intercede (one could say interfere) and override the normal methods for recording sales revenue or expenses.

REMEMBER

Both managers who do profit smoothing and investors who rely on financial statements in which profit smoothing has been done must understand one thing: These techniques have *compensatory effects.* The effects next year offset and cancel out the effects this year. Less expense this year is counterbalanced by more expense next year. Sales revenue recorded this year means less sales revenue recorded next year. Of course, the compensatory effects work the other way as well: If a business depresses its current year's recorded profit, its profit next year benefits. In short, a certain amount of profit can be brought forward into the current year or delayed until the following year.

WARNING

A business can go only so far in smoothing profit. If a business has a particularly bad year, all the profit-smoothing tricks in the world won't close the gap. And if managers are used to profit smoothing, they may be tempted in this situation to resort to accounting fraud, or cooking the books.

Management discretion in the timing of revenue and expenses

Several smoothing techniques are available for filling the potholes and straightening the curves on the profit highway. Most profit-smoothing techniques require one essential ingredient: management discretion in deciding *when* to record expenses or *when* to record sales.

A common technique for profit smoothing is to delay normal maintenance and repairs, which is referred to as *deferred maintenance.* Many routine and recurring maintenance costs required for autos, trucks, machines, equipment, and buildings can be put off, or deferred, until later. These costs are not recorded to expense until the actual maintenance is done, so putting off the work means recording the expense is delayed.

Here are a few other techniques used:

>> A business that spends a fair amount of money for employee training and development may delay these programs until next year so the expense this year is lower.

>> A company can cut back on its current year's outlays for market research and product development (though this could have serious long-term effects).

>> A business can ease up on its rules regarding when slow-paying customers are written off to expense as *bad debts* (uncollectible accounts receivable). The business can, therefore, put off recording some of its bad debts expense until next year.

>> A fixed asset out of active use may have very little or no future value to a business. But instead of writing off the undepreciated cost of the *impaired asset* as a loss this year, the business may delay the write-off until next year.

Keep in mind that most of these costs will be recorded next year, so the effect is to rob Peter (make next year absorb the cost) to pay Paul (let this year escape the cost).

WARNING

Clearly, managers have a fair amount of discretion over the timing of some expenses, so certain expenses can be accelerated into this year or deferred to next year in order to make for a smoother year-to-year profit trend. But a business doesn't divulge in its external financial report the extent to which it has engaged in profit smoothing. Nor does the independent auditor comment on the use of profit-smoothing techniques by the business — unless the auditor thinks that the company has gone too far in massaging the numbers and that its financial statements are downright misleading.

Comparing Public and Private Companies

Suppose you had the inclination (and the time!) to compare 100 annual financial reports of publicly owned corporations with 100 annual reports of privately owned businesses (assuming you could assemble 100 private company financial reports). You'd see many differences. Public companies are generally much larger (in terms of annual sales and total assets) than private companies, as you would expect. Furthermore, public companies generally are more complex — concerning employee compensation, financing instruments, multinational operations, federal laws that impact big business, legal exposure, and so on.

TIP

At the time of revising this book, private and public businesses are more or less bound by the same accounting rules for measuring profit; for valuing assets, liabilities, and owners' equity; and for making disclosures in their financial reports. We say "more or less" because private companies have the option to modify certain technical financial accounting rulings laid down by the Financial Accounting Standards Board (FASB). We discuss this in more detail in Chapter 2. In any case, for all practical purposes, financial report readers have to accept the numbers and other information presented in a financial report. In other words, readers cannot "order up" additional information not included in the financial report. (But investors in private companies may be able to ask the managers about the financial report.)

Reports from publicly owned companies

Around 7,000 corporations in the United States are publicly owned, and their stock shares are traded on the New York Stock Exchange, Nasdaq, or other electronic stock markets. Publicly owned companies must file annual financial reports with the SEC — the federal agency that makes and enforces the rules for trading in securities (stocks and bonds). These filings are available to the public on the SEC's huge database (see the nearby sidebar "Financial reporting on the internet").

The annual financial reports of publicly owned corporations include most of the disclosure items we list earlier in the chapter (see the section "Making Sure Disclosure Is Adequate"). As a result, annual reports published by large publicly owned corporations run 30, 40, or 50 pages (or more). As we've mentioned before, the large majority of public companies make their annual reports available on their websites. Many public companies also present condensed versions of their financial reports — see the later section "Recognizing condensed versions."

Annual reports from public companies generally are very well done — the quality of the editorial work and graphics is excellent; the color scheme, layout, and design have good eye appeal. But be warned that the volume of detail in their financial reports is overwhelming. (See the next section for advice on dealing with the information overload in annual financial reports.)

Publicly owned businesses live in a fish bowl. When a company goes public with an *IPO* (initial public offering of stock shares), it gives up much of the privacy that a closely held business enjoys. A public company is required to have its annual financial report audited by an independent CPA firm. In doing an audit, the CPA passes judgment on the company's accounting methods and adequacy of disclosure. The CPA auditor has a heavy responsibility to evaluate the client's internal controls to prevent financial reporting fraud.

Reports from private businesses

Compared with their public brothers and sisters, private businesses generally issue less impressive annual financial reports. Their primary financial statements with accompanying footnotes are pretty much it for most small private businesses. Often, their financial reports may be printed on plain paper and stapled together. A privately held company may have few stockholders, and typically one or more of the stockholders are active managers of the business, who already know a great deal about the business. We suppose that a private company could email its annual financial report to its lenders and shareowners, although we haven't seen this.

TIP

Investors in private businesses have one potential advantage compared with public companies. They can request confidential information from managers at the annual stockholders' meetings (which isn't practical for a stockholder in a large public corporation). The annual stockholders' meeting of a private business is not open to the public, so information can be kept private. Also, major lenders to a private business can demand that certain items of information be disclosed to them on a confidential basis as a condition of the loan.

Up to the present, we have had one set of accounting and financial reporting standards for all businesses, large and small, public and private. However, the blunt truth of the matter is that smaller private companies do not comply fully with all the disclosure requirements that public companies have to comply with. The business and financial communities at large have accepted the "subpar" financial reporting practices of smaller private businesses. Perhaps the Private Company Council (see Chapter 2) will recommend adopting less-demanding disclosure rules by private companies. Or they might leave well enough alone.

A private business may have its financial statements audited by a CPA firm but generally is not required by law to do so. Frankly, CPA auditors cut private businesses lots of slack regarding disclosure. We don't entirely disagree with enforcing a lower standard of disclosure for private companies. The stock share market prices of public corporations are extremely important, and full disclosure of information should be made publicly available so that market prices are fairly determined. On the other hand, you could argue that the ownership shares of privately owned businesses are not traded, so there's no urgent need for a complete package of information.

Dealing with Information Overload

As a general rule, the larger a business, the longer its annual financial report. We've seen annual financial reports of small, privately owned businesses that you could read in 30 minutes to an hour. In contrast, the annual reports of large, publicly owned business corporations are typically 30, 40, or 50 pages (or more). You would need two hours to do a quick read of the entire annual financial report, without trying to digest its details. Our comments in this section refer to the typical annual financial report of a large public company.

WARNING

If you did try to digest all the details of an annual financial report of a public company, which is a long, dense document not unlike a lengthy legal contract, you would need many hours (perhaps the whole day) to do so. (Also, to get the complete picture, you should read the company's filings with the SEC in conjunction with its annual financial report. Tack on a few more hours for that!) For one thing, there are many, many numbers in an annual financial report. We've never taken the time to count the number of distinct numbers in an average annual financial report, but we can guarantee there are hundreds, and reports for large, diversified, global, conglomerate businesses must have over a thousand.

Browsing based on your interests

How do investors in a business deal with the information overload of annual financial reports? Very few persons take the time to plow through every sentence, every word, every detail, and every number on every page — except for those professional accountants, lawyers, and auditors directly involved in the preparation and review of the financial report. It's hard to say how most managers, investors, creditors, and others interested in annual financial reports go about dealing with the massive amount of information — very little research has been done on this subject. But we have some observations to share with you.

An annual financial report is like the Sunday edition of a large city newspaper, such as *The New York Times* or the *Los Angeles Times*. Hardly anyone reads every sentence on every page of these Sunday papers, much less every word in the advertisements — most people pick and choose what they want to read. They browse their way through the paper, stopping to read only the particular articles or topics they're interested in. Some people just skim through the paper. Some glance at the headlines. We think most investors read annual financial reports like they read Sunday newspapers. The complete information is there if you really want to read it, but most readers pick and choose which information they have time to read in depth.

TIP

Annual financial reports are designed for *archival purposes,* not for a quick read. Instead of addressing the needs of investors and others who want to know about the profit performance and financial condition of the business but have only a limited amount of time, accountants produce an annual financial report that is a voluminous financial history of the business. Accountants leave it to the users of annual reports to extract the main points. Financial statement readers use certain key ratios and other tests to get a feel for the financial performance and position of the business. (See Chapters 12 and 20.)

Recognizing condensed versions

TIP

Here's a well-kept secret: Many public businesses and nonprofit organizations don't send a complete annual financial report to their stockholders or members. They know that few persons have the time or the technical background to read thoroughly the full-scale financial statements, footnotes, and other disclosures in their comprehensive financial reports. So they present relatively brief summaries that are boiled-down versions of their complete financial reports. For example, my (coauthor John) retirement fund manager, TIAA-CREF, puts out only financial summaries to its participants and retirees. Also, AARP issues condensed financial reports to its members.

Typically, these summaries — called *condensed financial statements* — do not provide footnotes or the other disclosures that are included in the complete and comprehensive annual financial reports. If you want to see the official financial report of the organization, you can ask its headquarters to send you a copy (or, for public corporations, you can go to the SEC database — see the earlier sidebar "Financial reporting on the internet").

Using other sources of business information

Annual financial reports are only one of several sources of information to owners, creditors, and others who have a financial interest in the business. Annual financial reports, of course, come out only once a year — usually two months or so after the end of the company's fiscal (accounting) year. You should keep abreast of developments during the year by reading the quarterly reports of the business. Also, we'd advise you to follow the businesses you invest in by reading the financial press and watching TV programs. And it's a good idea to keep up with blogs about the companies on the internet, subscribe to newsletters, and so on. Financial reports present the sanitized version of events; they don't divulge scandals about the business. You have to find out the negative news about a business by the means we just mentioned.

REMEMBER

Not everything you may like to know as an investor is included in the annual financial report. For example, information about salaries and incentive compensation arrangements with the top-level managers of the business are disclosed in the proxy statement, not in the annual financial report. A *proxy statement* is the means by which the corporation solicits the vote of stockholders on issues that require stockholder approval — one of which is compensation packages of top-level managers. Proxy statements are filed with the SEC and are available on its database.

Chapter **11**

Deciphering a Financial Report

This chapter focuses on the *external* financial report that a business sends to its lenders and shareowners. Many topics explained in the chapter apply to not-for-profit (NFP) entities as well. But the main focus is reading the financial reports of profit-motivated business entities. External financial reports are designed for the *non-manager* stakeholders in the business. The business's managers should understand how to read and analyze its external financial statements, and managers should do additional financial analysis, discussed in Chapter 13. This additional financial analysis by managers uses confidential accounting information that is not circulated outside the business.

You could argue that this chapter goes beyond the domain of accounting. Yes, this chapter ventures into the field of financial statement analysis. Some argue that this is in the realm of finance and investments, not accounting. Well, our answer is this: We assume one of your reasons for reading this book is to understand and learn how to read financial statements. From this perspective, this chapter definitely should be included, whether or not the topics fit into a strict definition of accounting.

Some years ago, a private business needed additional capital to continue its growth. Its stockholders could not come up with all the additional capital the business needed. So they decided to solicit several people to invest money in the company, including us. We studied the business's most recent financial report. We had an advantage that you can have, too, if you read this chapter: We know how to read a financial report and what to look for.

After studying the financial report, we concluded that the profit prospects of this business looked promising and that we probably would receive reasonable cash dividends on our investment. We also thought the business might be bought out by a bigger business someday, and we would make a capital gain. That proved to be correct: The business was bought out a few years later, and we doubled our money (and earned dividends along the way).

Not all investment stories have a happy ending, of course. As you know, stock share market prices go up *and* down. A business may go bankrupt, causing its lenders and shareowners large losses. This chapter isn't about guiding you toward or away from making specific types of investments. Our purpose is to explain basic tools that lenders and investors use for getting the most information value out of a business's financial reports — to help you become a more intelligent lender and investor.

Knowing the Rules of the Game

When you invest money in a business venture or lend money to a business, you should receive regular financial reports from the business. We use the term "should" because for publicly traded companies, there is no question that financial reports are available — they are required by law. However, for privately owned companies, "should" does not guarantee that all investors or lenders actually receive financial reports. Unless the investor or lender specifically requires the private company to provide financial reports on a periodic basis (for example, quarterly or annually) as part of their committing capital to the company (in the form of equity or debt), then the private company may not be legally bound to provide critical financial reports and statements to these parties.

REMEMBER

A word to the wise: To protect your investment in privately held companies, demand that financial reporting provisions are included in your investment documents to ensure you receive complete, accurate, reliable, and timely financial reports on which to base sound business decisions.

The primary premise of external financial reporting is *accountability* — to inform the sources of a business's ownership and debt capital about the financial performance and condition of the business. Generally speaking, abbreviated financial reports are sent to owners and lenders every three months with any supporting analyses or supplemental reporting requirements (for example, a bank may request a borrowing base certificate be provided). Annually, a full and comprehensive financial report should be forwarded.

REMEMBER

There are written rules for financial reports, and there are unwritten rules:

>> The written rules in the United States are called *generally accepted accounting principles* (GAAP). The movement toward adopting international accounting standards isn't dead, but it is on life support, so in this chapter, we assume that U.S. GAAP are used to prepare the financial statements.

>> The unwritten rules don't have a name. For example, there's no explicit rule prohibiting the use of swear words and vulgar expressions in financial reports. Yet, quite clearly, there is a strict unwritten rule against improper language in financial reports. There's one unwritten rule in particular that you should understand: A financial report isn't a confessional. A business doesn't have to lay bare all its problems in its financial reports. A business doesn't comment on all its difficulties in reporting its financial affairs to the outside world.

Making Investment Choices

An investment opportunity in a private business won't show up on your doorstep every day. However, if you make it known that you have money to invest as an equity shareholder, you may be surprised at how many offers come your way. It's safe to say that the vast majority of private investment opportunities we've seen come across our plates over the years represent relatively high-risk ventures that, to be frank, fail at a much higher rate than succeed. But then again, certain private investment opportunities may result in massive returns; remember, companies such as Facebook and Uber were small, private companies in their early days. Of course, whether you're able to actually participate in the early-stage investment opportunity for these companies is another question; generally speaking, the large VC (venture capitalist) firms tend to crowd out smaller investors.

Alternatively, you can invest in publicly traded *securities*, those stocks and bonds traded every day in major securities markets. Your stockbroker would be delighted to execute a buy order for 1,000 shares of, say, Apple for you. Keep in mind that your money doesn't go to Apple; the company isn't raising additional money. Your money goes to the seller of the 1,000 shares. You're investing in the *secondary capital market* — the trading in stocks by buyers and sellers after the shares were originally issued some time ago.

In contrast, we invested in the *primary capital market*, which means that our money went directly to the business. These days, a wide range of capital-raising techniques and strategies are being utilized (some legitimate and others a bit shady), including the growth in leveraging the internet to secure capital, such as undertaking *crowdfunding*. On a website, a new or early-stage business invites anyone with money to join in the venture and become an equity owner by issuing stock, member units (from an LLC), and so on. Usually, you can invest a relatively small amount of money in a crowdfunding venture. The business seeking the money is counting on a large number of people or legal entities to invest money in the opportunity.

WARNING

A word of caution when investing in private companies: The responsibility of managing the investment almost always falls directly on you, the investor, as large, third-party professional investment groups (for example, an investment bank such as Morgan Stanley) generally can't and don't want to be responsible for providing investment advice on private companies that they know little or nothing about. And for good reason: Too many unknowns equate to too much risk for little or no return in the form of fees.

Managing investments alone or using a third party

REMEMBER

When investing in public companies, you may choose to manage your securities investments directly using any number of online trading platforms such as E*TRADE, TD Ameritrade, and more recently Robinhood. An explosion of online investment security trading platforms has occurred over the past decade, so before you decide which platform to use, do your homework. We also want to point out that when managing your investments directly, for lack of a better term, "the buck stops with you." That is, when you make decisions to buy, sell, or trade any type of investment security, the decision is yours (and is not being supported by a professional advisor).

Conversely, you can put your money in any of the thousands of mutual funds available today, in an exchange-traded fund (ETF), in closed-end investment companies, in unit investment trusts, and so on, all of which are managed by third-party professionals. Using this tactic, you're relying on third-party professional that hopefully have extensive experience and knowledge to assist you with managing your investments. You'll have to read other books to understand the choices you have for investing your money and managing your investments. Be very careful about books that promise spectacular investment results with no risk and little effort. One book that is practical, well-written, and levelheaded is *Investing For Dummies* by Eric Tyson (Wiley).

Finding and understanding information sources

TIP

Investors in a private business have just one main pipeline of financial information about the business they've put their hard-earned money in: its financial reports. Of course, investors should carefully read these reports. By "carefully," we mean they should look for the vital signs of progress and problems. The financial statement ratios that we explain in Chapter 12 point the way — like signposts on the financial information highway.

Investors in securities of public businesses have many sources of information at their disposal. Of course, they can read the financial reports of the businesses they have invested in and those they're thinking of investing in. Instead of thoroughly reading these financial reports, they may rely on stockbrokers, the financial press, internet blogs, social media sites, and countless other sources of information. Many investors turn to their stockbrokers for investment advice. Brokerage firms put out all sorts of analyses and publications, and they participate in the placement of new stock and bond securities issued by public businesses. A broker will be glad to provide you with information from companies' latest financial reports. So why should you bother reading this chapter if you can rely on other sources of investment information?

REMEMBER

The more you know about interpreting a financial report, the better prepared you are to evaluate the commentary and advice of stock analysts and other investment experts. If you can at least nod intelligently while your stockbroker talks about a business's P/E and EPS, you'll look like a savvy investor — and you may get more favorable treatment. (P/E and EPS, by the way, are two of the key ratios explained in Chapter 12.) You may regularly watch financial news on television, listen to one of today's popular radio financial talk shows, or follow online influencers or blogs. The ratios explained in Chapter 12 are frequently mentioned in the media. As a matter of fact, a business may include one or more of the ratios in its financial report (public companies have to disclose earnings per share, or EPS).

Chapter 12 covers financial statement ratios that you should understand, as well as signs to look for in audit reports. (Part 2 of this book explains the three primary financial statements that are the core of every financial report: the income statement, the balance sheet, and the statement of cash flows.) We also suggest how to sort through the footnotes that are an integral part of every financial report to identify those that have the most importance to you.

Contrasting Reading Financial Reports of Private Versus Public Businesses

REMEMBER

Public companies make their financial reports available to the public at large; they don't limit distribution only to their present shareowners and lenders. We don't happen to own any stock shares of Apple. So how did we get its annual financial report? We simply went to Apple's website. In contrast, private companies generally keep their financial reports private — they distribute their financial reports only to their shareowners and lenders. Even if you were a close friend of the president of a private business, we doubt that the president would let you see a copy of its latest financial report. You may as well ask to see the president's latest individual income tax return. (You're probably not going to see it, either, but given recent trends in the Trump and Biden Administrations, a president's individual income tax returns are in more demand than ever before.)

WARNING

Although accountants are loath to talk about it, the blunt fact is that many private companies simply ignore, don't understand, or aren't aware of various authoritative standards in preparing their financial reports. This doesn't mean that their financial reports are misleading — perhaps substandard, but not seriously misleading. In any case, a private business's annual financial report is generally bare bones. It includes the three primary financial statements (balance sheet, income statement, and statement of cash flows; see Part 2) plus some footnotes — and that's about it. We've seen private company financial reports that don't even have a letter from the board of directors or CEO. In fact, we've seen financial reports of private businesses (mostly very small companies) that don't include a statement of cash flows, even though this financial statement is required according to U.S. GAAP.

Public businesses are saddled with the additional layer of requirements issued by the Securities and Exchange Commission. (This federal agency has no jurisdiction over private businesses.) The financial reports and other forms filed with the SEC are available to the public at www.sec.gov. The anchor of these forms is the annual 10-K, which includes the business's financial statements in prescribed formats, with many supporting schedules and detailed disclosures that the SEC requires.

TIP

Most publicly owned businesses present very different annual financial reports to their stockholders compared with their filings with the SEC. A number of public companies include only *condensed* financial information in their annual stockholder reports (not their full-blown and complete financial statements). They refer the reader to their more detailed SEC financial report for specifics. The financial information in the two documents can't differ in any material way. In essence, a stock investor can choose from two levels of information — one quite condensed and the other very technical.

A typical annual financial report by a public company to its stockholders is a glossy booklet with excellent art and graphic design, including high-quality photographs. The company's products are promoted, and its people are featured in glowing terms that describe teamwork, creativity, and innovation — you get the picture. In contrast, the reports to the SEC look like legal briefs — there's nothing fancy in these filings. The SEC filings contain information about certain expenses and require disclosure about the history of the business, its main markets and competitors, its principal officers, any major changes on the horizon, the major risks facing the business, and so on. Professional investors and investment managers definitely should read the SEC filings. By the way, if you want information on the compensation of the top-level officers of the business, you have to go to its *proxy statement* (see the nearby sidebar "Studying the proxy statement").

Explaining the Role of MDORs and MD&As

Almost every public company produces and includes what's commonly referred to as a *management discussion of operating results* or MDOR, generally located at the beginning of its annual financial report. The MDOR, sometimes referred to as the MD&A (management discussion and analysis), is a section of a business's financial report that is generally reserved for management to provide an assessment or overview of key operating results, market trends, industry data, strategies, and so on, that management believes would be beneficial to external parties to help them more fully understand the operating results of a business. The MDOR is usually located at the front of the periodically prepared externally distributed financial report and quite often starts with a shareholder or investor letter prepared by the company's chairman of the board or CEO, for example.

No doubt, the MDOR can provide useful information to external parties, but it should be noted that generally speaking, the information provided in the MDOR has not been audited by the independent CPA firm (but rather represents information being presented by a company's management team). Translation: The MDOR tends to include a broader range of business information that has been internally prepared by the company and incorporates more "opinions" and "perspectives" than audited financial statements (which tend to stay factual in nature). We're not saying that the information provided in the MDOR is not valuable, because usually some very interesting topics are covered along with supporting data (and we encourage you to thoroughly read the information presented). However, it's important to understand the role of the MDOR, the source of the information presented, and the fact that it can be "skewed" somewhat to direct a reader to topics that only tell a portion of the financial performance story.

Frolicking through the Footnotes

In contrast to MDOR disclosures (see the previous section), financial statement footnotes are part of the audited financial statements, prepared by an independent CPA firm (with support from company financial executives and legal counsel), and are most often located toward the back of the externally prepared financial report, just after the financial statements. Reading the footnotes in annual financial reports is no walk in the park. The investment pros read them because, in providing service and consultation to their clients, they're required to comply with due-diligence standards — or because of their legal duties and responsibilities of managing other people's money. When I (coauthor John) was an accounting professor, I had to stay on top of financial reporting; every year, I read a sample of annual financial reports to keep up with current practices. But beyond the group of people who get paid to read financial reports, does anyone read footnotes?

For a company you've invested in (or are considering investing in), we suggest that you do a quick read-through of the footnotes and identify the ones that seem to have the most significance. Generally, the most important footnotes are those dealing with the following:

>> **Stock options or other equity incentives awarded by the business to its executives:** The additional stock shares issued under stock options dilute (thin out) the earnings per share of the business, which in turn puts downside pressure on the market value of its stock shares, assuming everything else remains the same. Further, GAAP requires companies to report stock incentive compensation in financial statements to reflect the fact that an expense should be recorded for these types of transactions similar to paying

employees in cash. (We would ask "What's the difference?" because both represent compensation to employees.)

>> **Pending lawsuits, litigation, and investigations by government agencies:** These intrusions into the normal affairs of the business can have enormous consequences and always should be clearly understood.

>> **Revenue recognition policies, procedures, and guidelines:** Companies have come under increased scrutiny about how they report "earned sales revenue" in the income statement because using overly aggressive reporting techniques has become a focal point of potential fraud. Translation: Companies are "pulling forward" earned sales revenue to help enhance the operating results.

WARNING

>> **Employee retirement and other post-retirement benefit plans:** Your concerns here should be whether these future obligations of the business are seriously underfunded. We have to warn you that this particular footnote is one of the most complex pieces of communication you'll ever encounter. Good luck.

>> **Accounting for intangible assets:** The economy has shifted dramatically over the past 30-plus years into the new "information and digital age." Data, intellectual property, computer software code, goodwill, trade secrets, original content (think movies), and the like are now just as valuable of an asset as a manufacturing building, machine and equipment, and good old-fashioned hard or tangible assets. The accounting for intangible assets is evolving and relatively subjective, so you may want to pay extra attention to footnotes that focus specifically on how these assets are valued and amortized.

>> **Debt problems:** It's not unusual for companies to get into problems with their debt. Debt contracts with lenders can be very complex and are financial straitjackets in some ways. A business may fall behind in making interest and principal payments on one or more of its debts, which triggers provisions in the debt contracts that give its lenders various options to protect their rights. Some debt problems are normal, but in certain cases, lenders can threaten drastic action against a business, which should be discussed in its footnotes.

>> **Segment information for the business:** Public businesses have to report information for the major segments of the organization — sales and operating profit by territories or product lines. This gives a better glimpse of the parts making up the whole business. (Segment information may be reported elsewhere in an annual financial report than in the footnotes, or you may have to go to the SEC filings of the business to find this information.)

TIP

Stay alert for other critical matters that a business may disclose in its footnotes. We suggest scanning every footnote for potentially important information. Finding a footnote that discusses a major lawsuit against the business, for example, may make the stock too risky for your stock portfolio.

Checking Out the Auditor's Report

REMEMBER

All public companies are required by federal securities laws to have annual audits. Private companies aren't covered by these laws and generally don't have regular audits, but they may receive what's referred to as "reviewed financial statements" from an external CPA firm.

Reviewed financial statements are frequently prepared and utilized for external reporting purposes by smaller to medium-sized private companies because they are much lower in cost, easier to produce, and often satisfy external capital source reporting requirements. Reviewed financial statements are usually prepared by an independent CPA firm and involve the CPA's completing a more thorough evaluation of a company's financial performance using various analytical and financial analysis procedures.

The CPA firm attempts to present the financial statements in accordance with GAAP and generally attaches and includes financial statement footnotes. It should be noted that the CPA firm issues a review report that clearly states that they have not audited the company's financial information and, as such, do not guarantee compliance with GAAP (or other similar accounting frameworks). However, the review report often makes a statement that provides limited assurance that the company's financial statements are in compliance with GAAP without knowledge of any material modifications.

For larger private companies that have raised large amounts of capital, are envisioning going public, or need to establish a higher level of credibility, audits are completed because they know that an audit report adds credibility to their financial report, even though the audit is expensive.

TIP

If a private business's financial report doesn't include an audit report, you have to trust that the business has prepared accurate financial statements according to applicable accounting and financial reporting standards and that the footnotes to the financial statements cover all important points and issues. One thing you could do is to find out the qualifications of the company's chief accountant. Is the accountant a CPA? Does the accountant have a college degree with a major in accounting? Does the financial report omit a statement of cash flows or have any other obvious deficiencies?

In the following sections, we focus on why audits are so important and the general mechanics of an audit.

Why audits?

The top managers, along with their finance and accounting officers, oversee the preparation of the company's financial statements and footnotes (see Chapter 10 for details). These executives have a vested interest in the profit performance and financial condition of the business; their yearly bonuses usually depend on recorded profit, for example. This situation is somewhat like the batter in a baseball game calling the strikes and balls. Where's the umpire? Independent CPA auditors are like umpires in the financial reporting game. The CPA comes in, does an audit of the business's accounting system and methods, critically examines the financial statements, and gives a report that's attached to the company's financial statements.

We hope we're not the first people to point this out to you, but the business world is not like Sunday school. Not everything is honest and straight. A financial report can be wrong and misleading because of innocent, unintentional *errors* or because of deliberate, cold-blooded *fraud.* Errors can happen because of incompetence and carelessness. Audits are one means of keeping misleading financial reporting to a minimum. The CPA auditor should definitely catch all major errors. The auditor's responsibility for discovering fraud isn't as clear-cut. You may think catching fraud is the purpose of an audit, but we're sorry to tell you it's not as simple as that.

WARNING

Sometimes the auditor fails to discover major accounting fraud. Furthermore, the implementation of accounting methods is fairly flexible, leaving room for interpretation and creativity that's just short of *cooking the books* (deliberately defrauding and misleading readers of the financial report). Some massaging of the numbers is tolerated by auditors, which may mean that what you see on the financial report isn't exactly an untarnished picture of the business. We explain *window dressing* and *profit smoothing* — two common examples of massaging the numbers — in Chapter 10.

What's in an auditor's report?

REMEMBER

The large majority of financial statement audit reports give the business a clean bill of health, or what's called a *clean opinion.* (The technical term for this opinion is an *unmodified opinion,* which means that the auditor doesn't qualify or restrict his opinion regarding any significant matter.) At the other end of the spectrum, the auditor may state that the financial statements are misleading and shouldn't be relied upon. This negative, disapproving audit report is called an *adverse opinion.* That's the big stick that auditors carry: They have the power to give a company's financial statements a thumbs-down opinion, and no business wants that.

The threat of an adverse opinion almost always motivates a business to give way to the auditor and change its accounting or disclosure in order to avoid getting the kiss of death of an adverse opinion. An adverse audit opinion says that the financial statements of the business are misleading. The SEC doesn't tolerate adverse opinions by auditors of public businesses; it would suspend trading in a company's securities if the company received an adverse opinion from its CPA auditor.

If the auditor finds no serious problems, the CPA firm gives the business's financial report an *unmodified* or *clean* opinion. The key phrase auditors love to use is that the financial statements *present fairly* the financial position and performance of the business. However, the standard audit report has enough defensive, legalistic language to make even a seasoned accountant blush. If you have any doubts, go to the website of any public corporation and look at its most recent financial statements, particularly the auditor's report.

TIP

The following summary cuts through the jargon and explains what the clean audit report really says:

> » **First paragraph:** We did an audit of the financial report of the business at the date and for the periods covered by the financial statements (which are specifically named).

> » **Second paragraph:** Here's a description of management's primary responsibility for the financial statements, including enforcing internal controls for the preparation of the financial statements.

> » **Third paragraph:** We carried out audit procedures that provide us a reasonable basis for expressing our opinion, but we didn't necessarily catch everything.

> » **Fourth paragraph:** The company's financial statements conform to accounting and financial reporting standards and are not misleading in any significant respect.

WARNING

Unfortunately, auditors' reports have become increasingly difficult to read. Even seasoned stock analysts have trouble figuring out the nuances of wording in an audit opinion. Much of this creeping obfuscation of audit report language has been caused by the legal responsibilities imposed on CPA auditors. In any case, be prepared to struggle through the language in reading an audit report. Sorry, but that's how it is in our litigation-prone society.

An audit report that does *not* give a clean opinion may look similar to a clean-opinion audit report to the untrained eye. Some investors see the name of a CPA firm next to the financial statements and assume that everything is okay — after all, if the auditor had seen a problem, the feds would have pounced on the business and put everyone in jail, right? Well, not exactly. For example, the auditor's report may point out a flaw in the company's financial statements but not a fatal flaw that would require an adverse opinion. In this situation, the CPA issues a *modified opinion.* The auditor includes a short explanation of the reasons for the modification. You don't see this type of audit opinion that often, but you should read the auditor's report to be sure.

One type of an auditor's report is very serious — when the CPA expresses substantial doubts about the capability of the business to continue as a going concern. A *going concern* is a business that has sufficient financial wherewithal and momentum to continue its normal operations into the foreseeable future and that would be able to absorb a bad turn of events without having to default on its liabilities. A business could be under some financial distress but overall still be judged a going concern. Unless there is evidence to the contrary, the CPA auditor assumes the business is a going concern.

Discovering fraud, or not

Auditors have trouble discovering fraud for several reasons. The most important reason, in our view, is that those managers who are willing to commit fraud understand that they must do a good job of concealing it. Managers bent on fraud are clever in devising schemes that look legitimate, and they're good at generating false evidence to hide the fraud. These managers think nothing of lying to their auditors. Also, they're aware of the standard audit procedures used by CPAs and design their fraud schemes to avoid audit scrutiny as much as possible.

Over the years, the auditing profession has taken somewhat of a wishy-washy position on the issue of whether auditors are responsible for discovering accounting and financial reporting fraud. The general public is confused because CPAs seem to want to have it both ways. CPAs don't mind giving the impression to the general public that they catch fraud, or at least catch fraud in most situations. However, when a CPA firm is sued because it didn't catch fraud, the CPA pleads that an audit conducted according to generally accepted auditing standards doesn't necessarily discover fraud in all cases.

In the court of public opinion, it's clear that people think that auditors should discover material accounting fraud — and, for that matter, auditors should discover any other fraud against the business by its managers, employees, vendors, or customers. CPAs refer to the difference between their responsibility for fraud detection (as they define it) and the responsibility of auditors perceived by the general public as the *expectations gap.* CPAs want to close the gap — not by taking on more responsibility for fraud detection but by lowering the expectations of the public regarding their responsibility.

You'd have to be a lawyer to understand in detail the case law on auditors' legal liability for fraud detection, and we're not lawyers. But quite clearly, CPAs are liable for gross negligence in the conduct of an audit. If the judge or jury concludes that gross negligence was the reason the CPA failed to discover fraud, the CPA is held liable. (CPA firms have paid millions and millions of dollars in malpractice lawsuit damages.)

REMEMBER

In a nutshell, standard audit procedures don't always uncover fraud, except when the perpetrators of the fraud are particularly inept at covering their tracks. Using tough-minded forensic audit procedures would put auditors in adversarial relationships with their clients, and CPA auditors want to maintain working relationships with clients that are cooperative and friendly. A friendly auditor, some would argue, is an oxymoron. Also, there's the cost factor. Audits are already expensive. The CPA audit team spends many hours carrying out many audit procedures.

An audit would cost much more if extensive fraud detection procedures were used in addition to normal audit procedures. To minimize their audit costs, businesses assume the risk of not discovering fraud. They adopt internal controls (see Chapter 3) that are designed to minimize the incidence of fraud. But they know that clever fraudsters can circumvent the controls. They view fraud as a cost of doing business (as long as it doesn't get out of hand).

One last point: In many accounting fraud cases that have been reported in the financial press, the auditor knew about the accounting methods of the client but didn't object to the misleading accounting — you may call this an *audit judgment failure.* In these cases, the auditor was overly tolerant of questionable accounting methods used by the client. Perhaps the auditor had serious objections to the accounting methods, but the client persuaded the CPA to go along with the methods.

In many respects, the failure to object to bad accounting is more serious than the failure to discover accounting fraud, because it strikes at the integrity and backbone of the auditor. CPA ethical standards demand that a CPA resign from an audit if the CPA judges that the accounting or financial reporting by the client is seriously misleading. The CPA may have a tough time collecting a fee from the client for the hours worked up to the point of resigning.

Chapter **12**

Analyzing Financial Information with Ratios

Whether from an internal or external perspective, financial ratio analysis represents an invaluable tool to help assess how a company is performing financially.

External parties rely heavily on completing detailed financial ratio analyses to evaluate the financial performance of a company but deal with two limiting factors:

» First, external parties generally can complete their analyses only on an annual or quarterly basis (when financial reports are issued).

» Second, and more importantly, external parties don't have access to the same amount of confidential or detailed financial information as internal management (which enables internal management to complete a more thorough and informative analysis).

Internal management can dig deeper and complete financial ratio analyses more frequently, but make no mistake — these tools are essential for both internal and external parties!

Understanding the Importance of Using Ratios to Digest Financial Statements

Financial statements have lots of numbers in them. (Duh!) All these numbers can seem overwhelming when you're trying to see the big picture and make general conclusions about the financial performance and condition of the business. Instead of actually reading your way through the financial statements — that is, carefully reading every line reported in all the financial statements — one alternative is to compute certain ratios to extract the main messages from the financial statements. Many financial report readers go directly to ratios and don't bother reading everything in the financial statements. In fact, five to ten ratios can tell you so much about a business.

REMEMBER

Financial statement ratios enable you to compare a business's current performance with its past performance or with another business's performance, regardless of whether sales revenue or net income was bigger or smaller for the other years or the other business. In other words, using ratios cancels out size differences. (We bet you knew that, didn't you?)

As a rule, you don't find too many ratios in financial reports. Publicly owned businesses are required to report just one ratio (earnings per share, or EPS, covered later in this chapter), and privately owned businesses generally don't report any ratios. Generally accepted accounting principles (GAAP) don't demand that any ratios be reported (except EPS for publicly owned companies). However, you still see and hear about ratios all the time, especially from stockbrokers and other financial professionals, so you should know what the ratios mean, even if you never go to the trouble of computing them yourself.

Improving Your Knowledge of Financial Language and Lingo

Before we provide a listing of what are considered the standard or basic financial ratio analyses in the rest of this chapter, it will be helpful to walk through a list of commonly used financial and accounting terminology (to ensure that you're well versed with financial lingo):

>> **Top Line:** A company's net sales revenue generated over a period of time (for example, for a 12-month period). This is found at the top of the income statement.

>> **COGS and COS:** Acronyms for costs of goods sold (for a product-based business) and costs of sales (for a service-based business). COGS or COS tend to vary directly (or in a linear fashion) with the top-line sales revenue.

>> **Gross Profit and Margin:** Sometimes used interchangeably, gross profit equals your top line less your COGS or COS. The gross margin (a percentage calculation) is determined by dividing your gross profit by the top line.

>> **Op Ex:** A rather broad term short for operating expenses, which may include selling, general, administrative, corporate overhead, and other related expenses. Unlike COGS or COS, Op Ex tends to be fixed in nature and does not vary directly with the top-line sales revenue.

>> **SG&A:** Selling, general, and administrative expenses. Companies may distinguish between Op Ex and SG&A to assist parties with understanding the expense structure of its operations in more detail.

>> **Bottom Line:** A company's net profit or loss after all expenses have been deducted from net sales revenue. Being in the "black" indicates that a net profit is present, and being in the "red" indicates that a net loss was generated. This information can usually be found at the end of the income statement.

>> **Breakeven:** The operating level where a company generates zero in profit or loss as it "broke even." Or, conversely, it's the amount of sales revenue that needs to be generated to cover all COGS/COS and Op Ex.

>> **Contribution Margin:** The profit generated by a specific operating unit or division of a company (but not for the company as a whole). Most larger companies have multiple operating units or divisions, so the profit (or loss) of each operating unit or division is calculated to determine how much that specific unit or division "contributed" to the overall performance of the entire company.

>> **Cap Ex:** Stands for capital expenditures and is a calculation of how much a company invested in tangible or intangible assets during a given period (for equipment, machinery, new buildings, investments in intangible assets, and so on).

>> **YTD, QTD, MTD:** Acronyms for year to date, quarter to date, and month to date. For example, a flash report may present QTD sales for the period of 10/1/20 through 11/15/20 (so management can evaluate sales levels through the middle of a quarter).

>> **FYE and QE:** Acronyms for fiscal year-end and quarter-end. Most companies utilize a fiscal year-end that is consistent with a calendar year-end of 12/31/xx

(which would make their quarter-ends 3/31/xx, 6/30/xx, 9/30/xx, and 12/31/xx).

Please note that several companies utilize FYEs that are different than a calendar year-end to match their business cycle with that of a specific industry. For example, companies that cater to the education industry may use a FYE of 6/30/xx to coincide with the typical operating year for schools or colleges (which tend to run from 7/1/xx through 6/30/xx).

One thing that you find when completing ratio analysis is that financial professionals often use a variety of rather unique terms and "lingo" (for lack of a better term) associated with the financial and accounting profession so the better versed you are from the start, the more effective your ratio analysis will be.

Starting with Sample Company Financial Statements

Figures 12-1, 12-2, and 12-3 present an income statement, a balance sheet, and a statement of cash flows for a business that serves as the example for the rest of the chapter. We don't present the footnotes to the company's financial statements, but we discuss reading footnotes in Chapter 11. In short, the following discussion focuses on ratios from the income statement, balance sheet, and statement of cash flows.

We want to point out that this chapter does not pretend to cover the field of *securities analysis* (that is, the analysis of stocks and debt instruments issued by corporations), but this is a topic touched on in Chapters 10 and 11. The broad field of securities analysis includes the analysis of competitive advantages and disadvantages of a business, domestic and international economic developments, business combination possibilities, general economic conditions, and much more. The key ratios explained in this chapter are basic building blocks in securities analysis.

Also, this chapter does not discuss *trend analysis,* which involves comparing a company's latest financial statements with its previous years' statements to identify important year-to-year changes. For example, investors and lenders are extremely interested in the sales growth or decline of a business, and the resulting impact on profit performance, cash flow, and financial condition. The concept of trend analysis is touched on in Chapters 13 and 17.

This chapter has a more modest objective: to explain basic ratios used in financial statement analysis and what those ratios indicate about a business. Only a handful of ratios are discussed in the chapter, but they are fundamentally important and represent the most widely used by industry professionals.

```
┌─────────────────────────────────────────────────────────────┐
│                    QW Example Tech., Inc.                     │
│            Sales of Both Products & Software Services         │
│                   for the Fiscal Year Ending                  │
│                         12/31/2020                            │
├─────────────────────────────────────────────────────────────┤
│                                                               │
│            Income Statement                         FYE       │
│       For the Twelve-Month Period Ending        12/31/2020    │
│          (All Numbers in Thousands)                           │
│   Sales Revenue, Net                              $71,064     │
│   Costs of Goods Sold                             $26,891     │
│   Gross Profit                                    $44,173     │
│                                                               │
│   Selling, General, & Administrative Expenses     $36,678     │
│                                                               │
│   Operating Income (Loss) — EBIT                   $7,495     │
│                                                               │
│   Other Expenses (Income):                                    │
│   Other Expenses & (Income)                          $250     │
│   Interest Expense                                   $350     │
│   Total Other Expenses (Income)                      $600     │
│                                                               │
│   Net Profit (Loss) Before Income Taxes            $6,895     │
│   Income Tax Expense (Benefit)                     $2,413     │
│                                                               │
│   Net Income (Loss)                                $4,482     │
│                                                               │
│   Earnings Per Share (Basic)                        $4.08     │
│   Earnings Per Share (Fully Diluted)                $2.76     │
│                                                               │
│   Confidential — Property of QW Example Tech., Inc.           │
└─────────────────────────────────────────────────────────────┘
```

FIGURE 12-1:
Base income
statement for
sample company.

On opening a company's financial report, probably one of the first things most investors do is to give the financial statements a once-over; they do a quick scan of the financial statements. What do most financial report readers first look for? In our experience, they look first at the bottom line of the income statement, to see whether the business made a profit or suffered a loss for the year. As one sports celebrity put it when explaining how he keeps tabs on his various business investments, he looks first to see if the bottom line has "parentheses around it." The business in our example does not; it made a profit. Its income statement reports that the business earned $4.482 million (rounded; see Figure 12-2) net income, or bottom-line profit for the year. Is this profit performance good, mediocre, or poor? Ratios help answer this question.

QW Example Tech., Inc. Sales of Both Products & Software Services For the Fiscal Year Ending 12/31/2020	
Statement of Financial Condition (AKA Balance Sheet) Period Ending (All Numbers in Thousands)	**FYE 12/31/2020**
Assets	
Current Assets:	
Cash & Equivalents	$11,281
Accounts Receivable, Net	$8,883
Inventory, LCM	$1,733
Prepaid Expenses	$325
Total Current Assets	$22,222
Long-Term Operating & Other Assets:	
Property, Plant, Equipment, & Machinery	$8,670
Accumulated Depreciation	($4,320)
Net Property, Plant, & Equipment	$4,350
Other Assets:	
Intangible Assets & Goodwill, Net	$500
Other Assets	$100
Total Long-Term Operating & Other Assets	$4,950
Total Assets	$27,172
Liabilities	
Current Liabilities:	
Accounts Payable	$1,929
Accrued Liabilities & Other	$830
Current Portion of Debt	$1,000
Other Current Liabilities & Deferred Revenue	$1,204
Total Current Liabilities	$4,963
Long-Term Liabilities:	
Notes Payable & Other Long-Term Debt	$6,250
Total Liabilities	$11,213
Stockholders' Equity	
Capital Stock — Common	$5,000
Capital Stock — Preferred	$5,000
Retained Earnings	$5,959
Total Stockholders' Equity	$15,959
Total Liabilities & Stockholders' Equity	$27,172

Confidential — Property of QW Example Tech., Inc.

FIGURE 12-2:
Base balance sheet for sample company.

QW Example Tech., Inc.	
Sales of Both Products & Software Services	
for the Fiscal Year Ending	
12/31/2020	

Statement of Cash Flows For the Twelve-Month Period Ending (All Numbers in Thousands)	FYE 12/31/2020
Net Profit (Loss)	$4,482
Operating Activities, Cash Provided (Used):	
Depreciation & Amortization	$1,739
Decrease (Increase) in Trade Receivables	($2,165)
Decrease (Increase) in Inventory	$2,328
Decrease (Increase) in Other Current Assets	($25)
Increase (Decrease) in Trade Payables	$275
Increase (Decrease) in Accrued Liabilities	$163
Increase (Decrease) in Other Liabilities	$796
Net Cash Flow from Operating Activities	$7,593
Investing Activities, Cash Provided (Used):	
Capital Expenditures	($750)
Investments in Other Assets	$0
Net Cash Flow from Investing Activities	($750)
Financing Activities, Cash Provided (Used):	
Dividends or Distributions Paid	($400)
Sale (Repurchase) of Capital Stock	$5,000
Proceeds from Issuance of Debt	$0
Repayments of Long-Term Debt	($1,000)
Other Financing Activities	$0
Net Cash Flow from Financing Activities	$3,600
Other Cash Flow Adjustments — Asset Impairment	$50
Net Increase (Decrease) in Cash & Equivalents	$10,493
Beginning Cash & Equivalents Balance	$788
Ending Cash & Equivalents Balance	$11,281

Confidential — Property of QW Example Tech., Inc.

FIGURE 12-3:
Base sample statement of cash flows for sample company.

After reading the income statement, most financial statement readers probably then take a quick look at the company's assets and compare them with the liabilities of the business. Are the assets adequate to the demands of the company's liabilities? Again, ratios help answer this question.

Benchmark Financial Ratios: Financial Strength and Solvency

Stock analysts, investment managers, individual investors, investment bankers, economists, company directors and executive management teams, and many others are interested in the fundamental financial aspects of a business. Ratios are a big help in analyzing the financial situation and performance of a business. To start our discussion on financial ratio analysis, you might anticipate that we'll begin with profit analysis. No, we start with something more important — solvency and liquidity.

REMEMBER

Solvency and liquidity refer to the ability of a business to pay its liabilities when they come due. If a business is insolvent and cannot pay its liabilities on time, its very continuance is at stake. In many respects, solvency comes first and profit second (as the first rule in business is to never run out of cash to operate). The ability to earn a profit rests on the ability of the business to continue on course and avoid being shut down or interfered with by its lenders. In short, earning a profit demands that a business remain solvent. Maintaining solvency (its debt-paying ability) is essential for every business. If a business defaults on its debt obligations, it becomes vulnerable to legal proceedings that could stop the company in its tracks, or at least could interfere with its normal operations.

Bankers and other lenders, when deciding whether to make and renew loans to a business, direct their attention to certain key financial statement ratios to help them evaluate the solvency situation and prospects of the business. These ratios provide a useful financial profile of the business in assessing its creditworthiness and for judging the ability of the business to pay interest and to repay the principal of its loans on time and in full.

REMEMBER

One additional concept that is important to understand is the difference between solvency and liquidity. In certain cases, you may evaluate a business that appears solvent (that is, assets are greater than liabilities with ample stockholders' equity) yet is not liquid. This situation can occur when a business mismanages its cash resources, which come under stress (it may have over invested in fixed assets and is running short on cash to pay current bills). The financial ratio analyses provided address both solvency and liquidity issues for our fictitious company.

See Figure 12-4 for an analysis of all the ratios in the following sections.

QW Example Tech., Inc. Financial Ratio Analysis: Strength and Solvency for the Fiscal Year Ending 12/31/2020	
Current Ratio — FYE:	31-Dec-2020
Total Current Assets	$22,222
Total Current Liabilities	$4,963
Current Ratio	4.48
Net Working Capital — FYE:	31-Dec-2020
Total Current Assets	$22,222
Total Current Liabilities	$4,963
Net Working Capital	$17,259
Quick or Acid Test Ratio — FYE:	31-Dec-2020
Total Current Assets	$22,222
Less: Inventory & Other Current Assets	($1,408)
Net Current Assets	$20,814
Current Liabilities	$4,963
Quick or Acid Test Ratio	4.19
Debt-to-Equity Ratio — FYE:	31-Dec-2020
Total Debt (i.e., Liabilities)	$11,213
Total Owners' Equity	$15,959
Debt-to-Equity Ratio	0.70
Debt-to-Tangible Net Equity Ratio — FYE:	31-Dec-2020
Total Liabilities	$11,213
Total Owners' Equity	$15,959
Less: Intangible Assets	($500)
Tangible Net Equity	$15,459
Debt-to-Tangible Net Equity Ratio	0.73

© John Wiley & Sons, Inc.

FIGURE 12-4: Solvency ratios for sample company.

Current ratio

The *current ratio* tests the short-term liability-paying ability of a business. It is calculated by dividing total current assets by total current liabilities in a company's most recent balance sheet. The current ratio for the company is computed as follows:

Current assets ÷ Current liabilities = Current ratio

The current ratio is hardly ever expressed as a percent (which would be 348 percent for our example company for the FYE 12/31/20). The current ratio for the business example is stated as 4.48 to 1.00, or more simply just as 4.48.

The common opinion is that the current ratio for a business should be 2 to 1 or higher (although this depends on the type of industry the company operates within as in some instances, current ratios closer to 1.25 to 1.00 are acceptable). Most businesses find that their creditors expect this minimum current ratio. In other words, short-term creditors generally like to see a business limit its current liabilities to one-half or less of its current assets.

Why do short-term creditors put this limit on a business? The main reason is to provide a safety cushion of protection for the payment of the company's short-term liabilities. A current ratio of 2 to 1 means there is $2 of cash and current assets that should be converted into cash during the near future that will be available to pay each $1 of current liabilities that come due in roughly the same time period. Each dollar of short-term liabilities is backed up with $2 of cash on hand or near-term cash inflows. The extra dollar of current assets provides a margin of safety for the creditors.

A company may be able to pay its liabilities on time with a current ratio of less than 2 to 1, or perhaps even if its current ratio were as low as 1 to 1. In our business example, the company has borrowed $1 million using short-term notes payable, which equals 4.5 percent of its total current assets (see Figure 12-2). In this situation, the company's lenders would probably be willing to provide additional short-term loans to the business given its solid current ratio, relatively low short-term borrowing ratio to current assets (of 4.5 percent), and its solid profitability (in 2020).

Net working capital

We also want to note that the company's net working capital (defined as total current assets less total current liabilities) amounts to approximately $17.259 million as of the FYE 12/31/20. The reason we present net working capital right after the current ratio is that lenders often incorporate loan covenants that state a business must maintain net working capital of X millions of dollars (to ensure ample internal liquidity is maintained). Here's the ratio:

Current assets – Current liabilities = Net working capital

REMEMBER

In summary, short-term sources of credit generally like to see a company's current assets be double its current liabilities (again, depending on the industry) along with maintaining strong levels of net working capital. After all, creditors are not owners — they do not share in the profit earned by the business. The income on their loans is limited to the interest they charge (and collect). As creditors, they quite properly minimize their loan risks; as limited-income (fixed-income) investors, they are not compensated to take on much risk.

Acid test ratio (aka quick ratio)

REMEMBER

Inventory is many weeks or months away from conversion into cash. Products are typically held two, three, or four months before being sold. If sales are made on credit, which is normal when one business sells to another business (that is, a B-to-B business model), there is a second waiting period before the receivables are collected. In short, inventory is not nearly as liquid as accounts receivable; it takes much longer to convert inventory first into sales and then into cash. Furthermore, there is no guarantee that all the products in inventory will be sold, because inventory can become obsolete, spoiled, lost/stolen, and so on.

A more severe measure of the short-term liability-paying ability of a business is the *acid test ratio* (also known as *quick ratio*), which excludes inventory (and prepaid expenses). Only cash, short-term marketable securities investments (if any), and accounts receivable are counted as sources to pay the current liabilities of the business.

This ratio is also called the quick ratio because only cash and assets quickly convertible into cash are included in the amount available for paying current liabilities; it is more in the nature of a liquidity ratio that focuses on how much cash and near-cash assets a business possesses to pay its short-term liabilities.

In this example, the company's acid test ratio is calculated as follows (the business has no investments in marketable securities):

Liquid assets ÷ Current liabilities = Acid test ratio

The general rule is that a company's acid test ratio should be 1 to 1 or better, although there are many exceptions. In our sample company, its quick ratio amounts to 4.19 to 1.00 — again a very healthy ratio and one that indicates financial strength.

Debt-to-equity ratio

Some debt is generally good, but too much debt is dangerous. The *debt-to-equity ratio* is an indicator of whether a company is using debt prudently, or perhaps has gone too far and is overburdened with debt that may cause problems. For this example, the company's debt-to-equity ratio calculation is as follows:

Total debt ÷ Total owners' equity = Debt-to-equity ratio

This ratio tells us that the company is using $0.70 of liabilities in addition to each $1 of stockholders' equity in the business. Notice that all liabilities (non-interest-bearing as well as interest-bearing, and both short-term and long-term) are included in this ratio, and that all owners' equity (invested capital stock and retained earnings) is included.

This business, with its 0.70 debt-to-equity ratio, would be viewed as moderately leveraged. *Leverage* refers to using the equity capital base to raise additional capital from nonowner sources. In other words, the business is using $.070 of total capital for every $1 of equity capital.

Historically, most businesses have tended to stay below a 1-to-1 debt-to-equity ratio. They don't want to take on too much debt, or they cannot convince lenders to put up more than one-half of their assets. However, some capital-intensive (asset-heavy) businesses such as public utilities and financial institutions operate with debt-to-equity ratios much higher than 1 to 1. In other words, they are highly leveraged.

But a word of caution in today's world (which we address more fully in Chapter 14). Over the decade since the Great Recession of 2007–2009, the world was flooded with massive cash infusions from global central banks by undertaking highly accommodative monetary policies and driving interest rates down. By some estimates, over $20 trillion of cash/currency has been injected into the global economy by the world's leading central banks, which was amplified by the global Covid-19 pandemic starting in 2020. This has resulted in a drastic decline in interest rates that, unbelievable as it may sound, has resulted in over $15 trillion of global debt generating negative interest rates (yes, you heard us right).

WARNING

These policy changes have encouraged businesses to secure new and unbelievably cheap debt to be used for business purposes ranging from investing in capital equipment to repurchasing its issued shares, helping drive up earnings per share (EPS, covered later in this chapter). This so-called "easy" monetary environment has unfortunately also produced two unwanted side effects:

>> First, debt-to-equity ratio historical "norms" (for lack of a better term) of, let's say, less than 1-to-1 (as previously noted) have been sacrificed in the name of debt that is cheap (low interest rates), abundant (large amounts of fresh/new capital), and easy (limited financial performance covenant requirements). So not only are companies becoming more and more leveraged, the quality of the debt, via establishing performance covenants to ensure that a company's performance is acceptable, is being reduced or in some cases eliminated. It doesn't take a genius to quickly conclude that a more leveraged company with lower-quality debt is generally a recipe for disaster.

>> Second, when companies use debt to repurchase their own shares (a very common practice over the past few years), the number of shares outstanding when calculating its EPS decreases (for example, Company XYZ had 1 million shares outstanding and elected to repurchase 100,000, leaving 900,000 shares remaining as outstanding). With fewer outstanding shares and a relatively constant net profit, the company provides the appearance, or some may say illusion, that its EPS is increasing even though its net profit did not change. This concept is a perfect example of what is commonly referred to as *financial engineering* — a topic that we dig into in Chapter 14 and that is something extremely important to understand in today's world economy.

Debt-to-tangible net equity

This financial ratio analysis takes the debt-to-net worth (or debt-to-equity) analysis one step further by extracting intangible assets from the calculation. Intangible assets represent a broad range of assets including software development costs, capitalized intellectual property (such as patents), content creation, acquisition goodwill, and similar types of assets that are not tangible in nature.

REMEMBER

The reason this calculation is important to lenders is that in today's rapidly moving economy, especially for technology-based companies, what may be of value today could be completely worthless in two years. Thus, by stripping out the intangible assets from the debt-to-equity ratio, a lender has a better view of a company's real financial leverage.

The debt-to-tangible net equity for our sample company tells an interesting story as follows:

Total debt ÷ (Total owners' equity less intangible assets) = Debt-to-tangible net equity ratio

For our sample company, the debt-to-tangible net equity ratio of 0.73 to 1.00 is approximately the same as the debt-to-equity ratio of 0.70, which indicates that the company's financial strength is not being significantly influenced by intangible assets. However, and a word of caution, this ratio is very important to monitor as companies that aggressively expand operations via buying or investing in "soft" or intangible assets (including goodwill) may be viewed as being higher risk due to the fickle nature of valuing intangible assets.

Benchmark Financial Ratios: Financial Performance

Shifting gears somewhat, we now turn our attention to presenting ratio analysis that is centered on analyzing financial information that is derived from both the income statement and balance sheet. The general idea with these ratios is to evaluate how a company is performing in relation to its total investment in assets and capital required to operate the business (debt and equity). See Figure 12-5 for an analysis of all the ratios in the following sections.

Return on sales (ROS)

Generating sales while controlling expenses is how a business makes profit. The profit residual slice of a company's total sales revenue pie is expressed by the *return on sales ratio*, which is profit divided by sales revenue for the period. The company's return on sales ratio for its latest two years is as follows:

Profit ÷ Sales revenue = Return on sales (ROS)

There is another way of explaining the return on sales ratio. For the FYE 12/31/20, each $100 of sales revenue the business earned generated $6.31 of net income and expenses of $93.69. Return on sales varies quite markedly from one industry to another. Some businesses do well with only a 2–4 percent return on sales; others need more than 20 percent to justify the large amount of capital invested in their assets. For a company operating in the technology market, especially with a focus on software, return on sales far north of 10 percent is now the norm (so this company appears to be underperforming compared to its peers).

```
                        QW Example Tech., Inc.
               Financial Ratio Analysis: Financial Performance
                          for the Fiscal Year Ending
                                12/31/2020


Return on Sales — FYE:                                       31-Dec-2020
  Net Income (Loss)                                             $4,482
  Revenue, Net                                                 $71,064
  Return on Sales                                                6.31%

Return on Owners' Equity — FYE:                              31-Dec-2020
  End-of-Year Total Owners' Equity                             $15,959
  Net Income (Loss)                                             $4,482
  Return on Average Owners' Equity                              28.08%

Return on Assets — FYE:                                      31-Dec-2020
  End-of-Year Total Assets                                     $27,172
  Net Income (Loss) Before Interest & Income Taxes              $7,245
  Return on Average Assets                                      26.67%

Earnings Per Share, Fully Diluted — FYE:                     31-Dec-2020
  Net Profit (Loss)                                             $4,482
  Shares Outstanding, Fully Diluted (#)                          1,625
  Earnings Per Share, Fully Diluted                              $2.76

Earnings Per Share, Basic — FYE:                             31-Dec-2020
  Net Profit (Loss)                                             $4,482
  Less: Preferred Dividends                                     ($400)
  Earnings Available for Common                                 $4,082
  Shares Outstanding, Basic                                      1,000
  Earnings Per Share, Basic                                      $4.08

Price/Earnings Ratio — FYE:                                  31-Dec-2020
  Market Value Per Share (*)                                    $70.00
  Earnings Per Share, Fully Diluted                              $2.76
  Price-Earnings Ratio                                           25.36

Debt Service Coverage Ratio — FYE:                           31-Dec-2020
  Net Income (Loss)                                             $4,482
  Interest Expense                                                $350
  Depreciation & Amortization Expense                           $1,739
  Adjusted Debt Service Cash Flow                               $6,571
  Interest Expense                                                $350
  Loan Principal Payments Due, 1 Year                           $1,000
  Total Debt Service Payments, 1 Year                           $1,350
  Debt Service Coverage Ratio                                     4.87
```

© John Wiley & Sons, Inc.

FIGURE 12-5: Financial performance ratios for sample company.

Return on equity (ROE)

Owners take the risk of whether their business can earn a profit and sustain its profit performance over the years. How much would you pay for a business that consistently suffers a loss? The value of the owners' investment depends first and foremost on the past and potential future profit performance of the business — or not just profit, we should say, but profit relative to the capital invested to earn that profit.

For instance, suppose a business earns $100,000 annual net income for its stockholders. If its stockholders' equity is $250,000, then its profit performance relative to the stockholders' capital used to make that profit is 40 percent, which is very good indeed. If, however, stockholders' equity is $2,500,000, then the company's profit performance equals only 4 percent of owners' equity, which is weak relative to the owners' capital used to earn that profit.

REMEMBER

In short, profit should be compared with the amount of capital invested to earn that profit. Profit for a period divided by the amount of capital invested to earn that profit is generally called *return on investment* (ROI). ROI is a broad concept that applies to almost any sort of investment of capital.

The owners' historical investment in a business is the total of the owners' equity accounts in the company's balance sheet. Their profit is bottom-line net income for the period — well, maybe not all net income. A business corporation may issue *preferred stock,* on which a fixed amount of dividends must be paid each year. The preferred stock shares have the first claim on dividends from net income. Therefore, preferred stock dividends are subtracted from net income to determine the *net income available for the common stockholders.* Our company has issued preferred stock, so not all net income "belongs" to its common stockholders. However, for simplicity in displaying this calculation, we assume that all the net income earned by the company is available to all the equity owners (both common and preferred).

Dividing annual net income by stockholders' equity gives the *return on equity* (ROE) ratio. The calculation for the company's ROE in this example is as follows:

Net income ÷ Owners' equity = Return on equity (ROE)

TIP

We use the ending balance of stockholders' equity to simplify the calculation. Alternatively, the weighted average during the year could be used, and should be if there have been significant changes during the year.

By most standards, this company's 28.08 percent annual ROE for the FYE 12/31/20 would be considered very strong, but then again, technology companies often generate these types of returns. However, everything is relative. ROE should be compared with industrywide averages and with investment alternatives. Also, the risk factor is important: Just how risky is the stockholders' capital investment in the business?

We need to know much more about the history and prospects of the business to reach a conclusion regarding whether it's 28.08 percent ROE is good, mediocre, or poor. Also, we should consider the *opportunity cost of capital* — that is, the ROI the stockholders could have earned on the next-best use of their capital. Furthermore, we have not considered the personal income tax on dividends paid to its individual stockholders. In summary, judging ROE is not a simple matter!

Return on assets (ROA)

Here is another useful profit performance ratio:

EBIT ÷ Total assets = Return on assets (ROA)

The *return on assets* (ROA) ratio reveals that the business earned $26.67 before interest and income tax expenses on each $100 of assets. The ROA is compared with the annual interest rate on the company's borrowed money. In this example, the company's annual interest rate on its short-term and long-term debt is approximately 5.0 percent. The business earned 26.67 percent on the money borrowed, as measured by the ROA. The difference or spread between the two rates is a favorable spread equal to 21.67 percentage points, which increases the earnings after interest for stockholders. This source of profit enhancement is called *financial leverage gain.* In contrast, if a company's ROA is less than its interest rate, it suffers a financial leverage loss.

REMEMBER

Ratios do not provide final answers — they're helpful indicators, and that's it. For example, if you're in the market for a house, you may consider cost per square foot (the total cost divided by total square feet) as a way of comparing the prices of the houses you're looking at. But you have to put that ratio in context: Maybe one neighborhood is closer to public transportation than another, and maybe one house needs more repairs than another. In short, the ratio isn't the only factor in your decision.

Earnings per share (EPS), basic and fully diluted

Publicly owned businesses, according to GAAP, must report earnings per share (EPS) below the net income line in their income statements — giving EPS a certain distinction among ratios. Why is EPS considered so important? Because it gives investors a means of determining the amount the business earned on their stock share investments: EPS tells you how much net income the business earned for each stock share you own. The essential equation for EPS is as follows:

Net income ÷ Total number of capital stock shares = Earnings per share (EPS)

For the example in Figures 12-1 and 12-2, the company's $4.482 million net income is divided by the 1.625 million shares of stock the business has issued to compute its fully diluted $2.76 EPS. If its basic EPS is calculated, the resulting figure would be $4.08. (Refer to Figure 12-5 for the math.)

REMEMBER

The computation based on the higher number of stock shares is called the *diluted* earnings per share. (*Diluted* means thinned out or spread over a larger number of shares.) The computation based on the number of stock shares issued and outstanding is called *basic* earnings per share. Both are reported at the bottom of the income statement (see Figure 12-1).

REMEMBER

EPS is extraordinarily important to the stockholders of businesses whose stock shares are publicly traded. These stockholders pay close attention to market price per share. They want the net income of the business to be communicated to them on a per-share basis so they can easily compare it with the market price of their stock shares. The stock shares of privately owned corporations aren't actively traded, so there's no readily available market value for the stock shares. Private businesses don't have to report EPS. The thinking behind this exemption is that their stockholders don't focus on per-share values and are more interested in the business's total net income.

WARNING

Publicly owned businesses report two EPS figures — unless they have a *simple capital structure* that doesn't require the business to issue additional stock shares in the future. Generally, publicly owned corporations have *complex capital structures* and must report two EPS figures, as you see in Figure 12-1. Sometimes it's not clear which of the two EPS figures is being used in press releases and in articles in the financial press. You must be careful to determine which EPS ratio is being used — and which is being used in the calculation of the P/E ratio (explained in the next section). The more conservative approach is to use diluted EPS, although this calculation includes a hypothetical number of shares that may or may not actually be issued in the future.

TECHNICAL
STUFF

Calculating basic and diluted EPS isn't always as simple as our example may suggest. Here are just two examples of complicating factors that require the accountant to adjust the EPS formula. During the year, a company may do the following:

> » **Issue additional stock shares and buy back some of its stock shares:** (Shares of its stock owned by the business itself that aren't formally cancelled

are called *treasury stock*.) The weighted average number of outstanding stock shares is used in these situations.

 » **Issue more than one class of stock, causing net income to be divided into two or more pools — one pool for each class of stock:** EPS refers to the *common* stock, or the most junior of the classes of stock issued by a business. (Let's not get into *tracking stocks* here, in which a business divides itself into two or more sub-businesses and you have an EPS for each sub-part of the business; few public companies do this.)

Price/earnings (P/E) ratio

The price/earnings (P/E) ratio is another ratio that's of particular interest to investors in public businesses. The P/E ratio gives you an idea of how much you're paying in the current price for stock shares for each dollar of earnings (the net income being earned by the business). Remember that earnings prop up the market value of stock shares.

TIP

The P/E ratio is, in one sense, a reality check on just how high the current market price is in relation to the underlying profit that the business is earning. Extraordinarily high P/E ratios are justified when investors think that the company's EPS has lots of upside potential in the future.

The P/E ratio is calculated as follows:

> Current market price of stock ÷ Most recent trailing 12 months diluted EPS* = P/E ratio

Note: If the business has a simple capital structure and doesn't report a diluted EPS, its basic EPS is used for calculating its P/E ratio (see the preceding section).

Suppose the capital stock shares of the business in our example are trading at $70, and its fully diluted EPS for the latest year is $2.76. *Note:* For the remainder of this section, we use the term EPS; we assume you understand that it refers to fully diluted EPS for businesses with complex capital structures or to basic EPS for businesses with simple capital structures.

Stock share prices of public companies bounce around day to day and are subject to big changes on short notice. To illustrate the P/E ratio, we use the $70 price, which is the closing price on the latest trading day in the stock market. This market price means that investors trading in the stock think that the shares are worth about 25.4 times EPS ($70 market price ÷ $2.76 EPS = 25.36, rounded up to 25.4). This P/E ratio should be compared with the average stock market P/E to gauge whether the business is selling above or below the market average.

TECHNICAL STUFF

Over the last century, average P/E ratios have fluctuated more than you may think. We remember when the average P/E ratio was less than 10 and a time when it was more than 20. Also, P/E ratios vary from business to business, industry to industry, and year to year. One dollar of EPS may command only a $12 market value for a mature business in a no-growth industry, whereas a dollar of EPS for dynamic businesses in high-growth industries may be rewarded with a $35 market value per dollar of earnings (net income).

Debt service coverage ratio

Thus far, the ratios provided and associated analyses have tended to focus on the income statement and balance sheet (ignoring the cash flow statement). This is traditionally where most parties focus their attention, because the information gleaned from the calculations is especially useful. But cash flow ratios and analyses are just as informative and in today's world have become mainstays when evaluating a company's operating performance and financial viability. Here, we present a basic cash flow ratio and analysis tool that is widely used in the market: the debt service coverage ratio.

The goal with the debt service coverage ratio (DSCR) is to ensure that the company can not only cover its interest expense but in addition make all necessary debt principal payments as well. For our sample company, here is the calculation:

Net income + Interest expense + Depreciation and amortization expense ÷ Interest expense + Loan principal payments due in one year = Debt service coverage ratio

For our sample company, here is how the math would work (all figures expressed in thousands of dollars):

$4,482 + $350 + $1,739 = $6,571

$6,571 ÷ ($350 + $1,000) = 4.87

It goes without saying that this ratio needs to be north of 1.00 to 1.00 with most lenders demanding a minimum ratio of at least 1.50 to 1.00 (and often higher) to ensure there is a cushion available to cover any potential cash flow problems or hiccups. So, the good news for our example company for the FYE 12/31/20 is that their 4.87 DSCR is well above the target of 1.50 — but it does highlight the importance of managing available cash flow in relation to both total interest expense and debt principal payments due.

You should also note that no adjustment has been made for the $400,000 of annual preferred stock dividends or income taxes of $2.413 million. The reason is that the company's lenders sit in a senior position to the preferred stockholders and are most interested in the company being able to cover the total debt service prior to any preferred stock dividends. In fact, experienced lenders often incorporate a covenant in the loan agreement that states that preferred dividends cannot be paid unless the DSCR is above 2.00. As for income taxes, this represents a firm expense commitment of the company so it is not added back to the calculation.

Making Time for Additional Ratios (If Needed)

The list of ratios earlier in this chapter is bare bones; it covers the hardcore, everyday tools for interpreting financial statements. You could certainly calculate many more ratios from the financial statements, such as the inventory turnover ratio. (Chapter 13 explains additional ratios that managers of a business use based on internal information that's not revealed in its external financial statements.) How many ratios to calculate is a matter of judgment and is limited by the time you have for reading a financial report.

Computer-based databases are at our disposal, and it's relatively easy to find many other financial statement ratios. Which of these additional ratios provide valuable insight?

REMEMBER

Be careful about wasting time on ratios that don't really add anything to the picture you get from the basic ratios explained in this chapter. Almost any financial statement ratio is interesting, we suppose. For instance, you could calculate the ratio of inventory divided by retained earnings to see what percent of retained earnings is tied up in the inventory asset. (This ratio isn't generally computed in financial statement analysis.) But we'd advise you to limit your attention to the handful of ratios that play a central role in looking after your investments.

> » **Understanding the primary differences between internal and external financial information**
>
> » **Examining the additional information needed for managing assets and liabilities**
>
> » **Identifying the in-depth information needed for managing profit**
>
> » **Providing additional information for managing cash flow**
>
> » **Steering clear of rookie mistakes with internal financial information**

Chapter **13**

Generating Internal Financial Information for Management Use

f you're a business manager, we strongly suggest that you read the preceding two chapters before continuing with this one:

>» Chapter 11 discusses how a business's external, nonmanagerial lenders and investors read an external financial report. These stakeholders are entitled to regular financial reports so they can determine whether the business is making good use of their money.

>> Chapter 12 explains key ratios that the external stakeholders use for interpreting the financial condition, profit performance, and cash flows of a business — which are equally relevant for the managers of the business.

TIP

Business managers should understand the financial statement ratios in Chapter 12. Every ratio does double duty; it's useful to the outside lenders and investors of the business and equally useful to its internal managers. For example, the profit ratio and return on assets ratio are extraordinarily important to both the external stakeholders and the managers of a business — the first measures the profit yield from sales revenue, and the second measures profit on the assets employed by the business.

As important as they are, external financial statements don't provide all the accounting information that managers need to plan and control the financial affairs of a business. Managers who look no further than these statements really don't have all the information they need to do their jobs. This additional information, which is largely confidential, is available from the accounting system of the business (or should be).

The accounts reported in external financial statements are like the table of contents of a book; each account is like a chapter title. Managers need to do more than skim chapter titles. They need to read the chapters. This chapter looks behind the accounts reported in the external financial statements. We explain the types of additional accounting information that managers need in order to control financial condition, profit performance, and cash flows and to plan the financial future of their business.

Building on the Foundation of the External Financial Statements

Managers are problem solvers. Every business has problems, perhaps even some serious ones. However, external financial statements aren't designed to highlight such problems. Except in extreme cases — in which the business is obviously in dire financial straits — you'd never learn about its problems just from reading its external financial statements. To borrow lyrics from an old Bing Crosby song, external financial statements are designed to "accentuate the positive, eliminate the negative . . . [and] don't mess with Mister In-Between."

Seeking out problems and opportunities

REMEMBER

Business managers need more accounting information than what's disclosed in external financial statements for two basic purposes:

>> **To alert them to problems** that exist or may be emerging that threaten the profit performance, cash flow, and financial condition of the business

>> **To suggest opportunities** for improving the financial performance and health of the business

A popular expression these days is "mining the data." The accounting system of a business is the mother lode of management information, but you have to dig that information out of the accounting database. Working with the controller (chief accountant), a manager should decide what information they need beyond what's reported in the external financial statements.

Avoiding information overload

Business managers are very busy people. Nothing is more frustrating than getting reams of information that you have no use for. For that reason, the controller should guard carefully against information overload. While some types of accounting information should stream to business managers on a regular basis, other types should be provided only as needed.

Ideally, the controller reads the mind of every manager and provides exactly the accounting information that each manager needs. In practice, that can't always happen, of course. A manager may not be certain about which information they need and which they don't. The flow of information has to be worked out over time.

Furthermore, *how* to communicate the information is open to debate and individual preferences. Some of the additional management information can be put in the main body of an accounting report, but most is communicated in supplemental schedules, graphs, and commentary. The information may be delivered to the manager's computer, or the manager may be given the option to call up selected information from the accounting database of the business.

REMEMBER

Our point is simply this: Managers and controllers must communicate — early and often — to make sure managers get the information nuggets they need without being swamped with unnecessary data. No one wants to waste precious time compiling reports that are never read. So before a controller begins the process of compiling accounting information for managers' eyes only, be sure there's ample communication about what each manager needs.

Distinguishing Internal and External Financial Statements

To start this section, we want to pass along a spoiler alert, which should be both obvious and logical. The results of a financial statement, be it a balance sheet, an income statement, or a statement of cash flows, are the exact same between the internal and external financial statements; that is, total assets reported in the balance sheet are the same, the net profit or loss reported in the income statement is the same, and the ending cash balance reported in the statement of cash flows is the same. What is different basically boils down to understanding five key items — format, detail, confidentiality, timeliness, and completeness.

REMEMBER

In a nutshell, internally produced financial information must be presented in a manner that assists your target audience with efficiently and effectively interpreting critical financial data and results. We can't emphasize enough the importance of this function — the ability for accountants and financial types to effectively communicate complex information to other professionals and management team members is often the Achilles heel of the so-called numbers people. Do the numbers people know debits, credits, generally accepted accounting principles (GAAP), the Financial Accounting Standards Board (FASB) rules, and how to communicate to external numbers people? Yes. But what really separates the best-in-class companies from the pack is having their numbers people be extremely strong communicators and educators as well.

Format

The format should be much more user- and management-friendly (to drive home key points) as dictated by the company and not driven by external guidelines, such as those of the Internal Revenue Service (IRS) or Securities and Exchange Commission (SEC). We want to strike a proper balance between providing too much information (pushing the user toward "getting lost in the forest") versus not enough; the idea is to give the reviewing party what they ask for and need (based on their level of responsibility).

REMEMBER

Further, we do not want to divulge data that a party does not need or understand, that confuses them, and/or that is confidential (translation: above their security clearance, so to speak). Most readers are not sophisticated accounting and financial professionals, but they do understand basic math, so the goal with the format is to provide financial information in the easiest-to-understand and reliable manner.

Detail

Obviously, the level of detail presented is far greater. For example, when internal financial statements are prepared, marketing, selling, advertising, and promotional expenses are often presented in a split format between direct operating expenses and corporate costs. The difference between these two expense groups is that direct operating advertising and selling expenses capture what are commonly referred to as "call to action" expenses that are designed to turn a prospect into an actual customer (by placing an order). Corporate marketing and branding expenses, on the other hand, represent a broader range of costs designed to help build awareness of the business and enhance its brand. For most businesses, understanding the difference between these two expense groups is especially important.

Confidentiality

REMEMBER

The information presented in internally prepared financial statements is highly confidential and must be controlled and safeguarded from external parties and prying eyes (for example, a competitor) and from internal parties who may not understand the financial information and accidently disclose it to an unwanted party. Companies must manage the delicate balance between disclosing confidential, valuable, and sensitive information to external parties (who can help them accurately assess the operating results) and not providing too much detail.

Timeliness

With internal financial information, quick is not an option; however, company management team members need access to financial statements that are prepared, distributed, and analyzed well in advance of issuing external financial statements and reports. This is done for two reasons:

>> Key management team members have an opportunity to evaluate the results and identify any potential errors, mistakes, or omissions.

>> If either good or bad news needs to be delivered to external parties, the management team has an opportunity to prepare for the inevitable "grilling" that is forthcoming.

Speed in reporting goes well beyond the financial statements; different types of flash reports are produced daily, hourly, and even by the minute as heavily data-dependent businesses (such as retailers) can now, thanks to digital information and technology, literally monitor the effectiveness of a new advertising campaign within minutes of its being launched.

Finally, we also want to emphasize that strength in accuracy is critical; speed in reporting is dependent on highly accurate information.

Completeness

The concept of completeness lies in the eye of beholder, or rather is based on the specific needs of the target audience. For example, a general manager of a manufacturing plant needs a complete income statement for that plant, but not necessarily for the entire company. Further, the income statement should include all relevant financial information, including prior-year comparisons, a budget-to-actual-variance analysis, key performance indicators (KPIs), and so on.

Another example is a sales team manager who is focused on top-line sales for a region through the gross profit or margin generated, which may be compared against the budget or even other regions' performances. If that person does not have bottom-line responsibility, then there is no need to provide a complete income statement.

Gathering Financial Condition Information

The balance sheet — one of three primary financial statements included in an external financial report — summarizes the financial condition of the business. (See Chapter 7 for details.) Figure 13-1 presents an example of an externally reported balance sheet. A business may report more than the accounts included in the example. For example, a business may invest in marketable securities or have receivables from loans made to officers of the business. A business corporation may issue more than one class of capital stock and would report a separate account for each class. And so on.

The idea of the figure is to focus on the *core* assets and liabilities of a typical business. Notice two assets in the balance sheet: accounts receivable and inventory. These two accounts in the balance sheet tell you that the business sells products and makes sales on credit to its customers. Businesses that sell services don't have an inventory asset account, and businesses that sell only for cash and cash equivalents (credit/debit cards) don't report accounts receivable. A balance sheet reflects the nature and practices of the business entity, of course.

QW Example Tech., Inc. Sales of Both Products & Software Services for the Fiscal Year Ending 12/31/2020			

Statement of Financial Condition (aka Balance Sheet) Period Ending (All Numbers in Thousands) Assets	FYE 12/31/2019	FYE 12/31/2020	Change
Current Assets:			
Cash and Equivalents	$788	$11,281	$10,493
Accounts Receivable, Net	$6,718	$8,883	$2,165
Inventory, LCM	$4,061	$1,733	($2,328)
Prepaid Expenses	$300	$325	$25
Total Current Assets	$11,867	$22,222	$10,355
Long-Term Operating and Other Assets:			
Property, Plant, Equipment, and Machinery	$7,920	$8,670	$750
Accumulated Depreciation	($3,081)	($4,320)	($1,239)
Net Property, Plant, and Equipment	$4,839	$4,350	($489)
Other Assets:			
Intangible Assets and Goodwill, Net	$1,000	$500	($500)
Other Assets	$100	$100	$0
Total Long-Term Operating & Other Assets	$5,939	$4,950	($989)
Total Assets	$17,806	$27,172	$9,366
Liabilities			
Current Liabilities:			
Accounts Payable	$1,654	$1,929	$275
Accrued Liabilities and Other	$667	$830	$163
Current Portion of Debt	$1,000	$1,000	$0
Other Current Liabilities and Deferred Revenue	$408	$1,204	$796
Total Current Liabilities	$3,729	$4,963	$1,234
Long-Term Liabilities:			
Notes Payable and Other Long-Term Debt	$7,200	$6,250	($950)
Total Liabilities	$10,929	$11,213	$284
Stockholders' Equity			
Capital Stock — Common	$5,000	$5,000	$0
Capital Stock — Preferred	$0	$5,000	$5,000
Retained Earnings	$1,877	$5,959	$4,082
Total Stockholders' Equity	$6,877	$15,959	$9,082
Total Liabilities and Stockholders' Equity	$17,806	$27,172	$9,366

Confidential — Property of QW Example Tech., Inc.

FIGURE 13-1:
Balance sheet
example.

Notice that in Figure 13-1 the balance sheet is for last year and this year (the fiscal year just ended). And the balance sheet includes a column for changes in each account during the year. For example, you may notice that the company's cash balance actually increased $10.493 million during the year. Don't hit the overjoyed button just yet. An increase in cash of this magnitude doesn't mean that the business produced a record profit for the year. Indeed, Figure 13-2 shows that the business made a nice profit for the year, but the cash increase was far greater.

QW Example Tech., Inc. Sales of Both Products & Software Services for the Fiscal Year Ending 12/31/2020	
Income Statement For the Twelve-Month Periods Ending (All Numbers in Thousands)	FYE 12/31/2020
Sales Revenue, Net	$71,064
Costs of Goods Sold	($26,891)
Gross Profit	$44,173
Selling, General, and Administrative Expenses	($34,939)
Depreciation and Amortization Expense	($1,739)
Operating Income (Loss) Before Income Taxes and Interest	$7,495
Other Expenses (Income):	
Other Expenses and (Income)	($250)
Interest Expense	($350)
Total Other Expenses (Income)	($600)
Net Profit (Loss) Before Income Taxes	$6,895
Income Tax Expense (Benefit)	($2,413)
Net Income (Loss)	$4,482
Cash Flow from Operating Activity	$7,593
Confidential — Property of QW Example Tech., Inc.	

FIGURE 13-2: Income statement example.

© John Wiley & Sons, Inc.

The following sections walk down the balance sheet — assets first, then liabilities, and last, owners' equity accounts — stressing what sorts of inside financial information managers need to carry out their job.

Cash

The external balance sheet (see Figure 13-1) reports just one cash account. But many businesses keep several bank checking and deposit accounts, and some (such as casinos and supermarkets) keep a fair amount of currency on hand. A business may have foreign bank deposits in euros, British pounds, or other currencies. Most businesses set up separate checking accounts for payroll; only payroll checks are written against these accounts.

REMEMBER

Managers should monitor the balances in every cash account in order to control and optimize the deployment of their cash resources. Therefore, information about each bank account should be reported to the manager.

Managers should ask these questions regarding cash:

>> Is the ending balance of cash the actual amount at the balance sheet date, or did the business engage in window dressing in order to inflate its ending cash balance? *Window dressing* refers to holding the books open after the ending balance sheet date in order to record additional cash inflow, as if the cash were received on the last day of the period. Window dressing is not uncommon. (For details, see Chapter 10.) If window dressing has gone on, the manager should know the true, actual ending cash balance of the business.

>> Were there any *cash zero days* during the year? In other words, did the company's cash balance actually fall to zero (or near zero) during the year? How often did this happen? Is there a seasonal fluctuation in cash flow that causes "low tide" for cash, or are the cash-out days due to running the business with too little cash?

>> Are there any limitations on the uses of cash imposed by loan covenants by the company's lenders? Do any of the loans require compensatory balances that require that the business keep a minimum balance relative to the loan balance? In this situation, the cash balance isn't fully available for general operating purposes.

>> Are there any out-of-the-ordinary demands on cash? For example, a business may have entered into buyout agreements with a key shareholder or with a vendor to escape the terms of an unfavorable contract. Any looming demands on cash should be reported to managers.

Accounts receivable

A business that makes sales on credit has the accounts receivable asset — unless it has collected all its customers' receivables by the end of the period, which isn't very likely. To be more correct, the business has hundreds or thousands of individual accounts receivable from its credit customers. In its external balance sheet, a business reports just one summary amount for all its accounts receivable. However, this total amount isn't nearly enough information for the business manager.

Here are some key questions a manager should ask about accounts receivable:

>> Of the total amount of accounts receivable, how much is current (within the normal credit terms offered to customers), slightly past due, and seriously past due? A past-due receivable causes a delay in cash flow and increases the risk of its becoming a *bad debt* (a receivable that ends up being partially or wholly uncollectible).

>> Has an adequate amount been recorded for bad debts? Is the company's method for determining its bad debts expense consistent year to year? Was the estimate of bad debts this period tweaked in order to boost or dampen profit for the period? Has the IRS raised any questions about the company's method for writing off bad debts? (Chapter 9 discusses bad debts expense.)

>> Who owes the most money to the business? (The manager should receive a schedule of customers that shows this information.) Which customers are the slowest payers? Do the sales prices to these customers take into account that they typically don't pay on time?

TIP

It's also useful to know which customers pay quickly to take advantage of prompt payment discounts. In short, the payment profiles of credit customers are important information for managers.

>> Are there "stray" receivables buried in the accounts receivable total? A business may loan money to its managers and employees or to other businesses. There may be good business reasons for such loans. In any case, these receivables shouldn't be included with accounts receivable, which should be reserved for receivables from credit sales to customers. Other receivables should be listed in a separate schedule.

Inventory

For businesses that sell products, inventory is typically a major asset. It's also typically the most problematic asset from both the management and accounting points of view. First off, the manager should understand the accounting method being used to determine the cost of inventory and the cost of goods sold expense.

(You may want to quickly review the section in Chapter 9 that covers this topic.) In particular, the manager should have a good feel regarding whether the accounting method results in conservative or liberal profit measures.

Managers should ask these questions regarding inventory:

>> How long, on average, do products remain in storage before they're sold? The manager should receive a *turnover analysis* of inventory that clearly exposes the holding periods of products. Slow-moving products cause nothing but problems. The manager should ferret out products that have been held in inventory too long. The cost of these sluggish products may have to be written down or written off, and the manager has to authorize these accounting entries. The manager should review the sales demand for slow-moving products, of course.

>> If the business uses the LIFO method (last-in, first-out), was there a *LIFO liquidation gain* during the period that caused an artificial and one-time boost in profit for the year? (We explain this aspect of the LIFO method in Chapter 9.)

TIP

The manager should also request these reports:

>> **Inventory reports that include a side-by-side comparison of the costs and the sales prices of products (or at least the major products sold by the business):** It's helpful to include the mark-up percent for each product, which allows the manager to compare mark-up percent differences from product to product.

>> **Regular reports summarizing major product cost changes during the period and forecasts of near-term changes:** It may be useful to report the current replacement cost of inventory, assuming it's feasible to determine this amount.

Fixed assets less accumulated depreciation

REMEMBER

Fixed assets is the all-inclusive term for the wide range of long-term operating assets used by a business — from buildings and heavy machinery to office furniture. Except for the cost of land, the cost of a fixed asset is spread over its estimated useful life to the business; the amount allocated to each period is called *depreciation expense.* The manager should know the company's accounting policy regarding which fixed assets are *capitalized* (the cost is recorded in a fixed asset account) and which are *expensed* immediately (the cost is recorded entirely to expense at the time of purchase).

Under the current Internal Revenue Code, up to $500,000 of costs each year that theoretically should be capitalized and depreciated can be charged immediately to depreciation expense. The manager should know whether the business took an abnormally large hit against earnings this year due to the immediate expensing of such costs.

Most businesses adopt a cost limit below which minor fixed assets (a screwdriver, stapler, or wastebasket, for example) are recorded to expense instead of being depreciated over some number of years. The controller should alert the manager if an unusually high amount of these small-cost fixed assets was charged off to expense during the year, which could have a significant impact on the bottom line.

The manager should be aware of the general accounting policies of the business regarding estimating useful lives of fixed assets and whether the straight-line or accelerated methods of allocation are used. Indeed, the manager should have a major voice in deciding these policies and not simply defer to the controller. In Chapter 9, we explain these accounting issues.

Using accelerated depreciation methods may result in certain fixed assets that are fully depreciated but are still in active use. These assets should be reported to the manager — even though they have a zero book value — so the manager is aware that these fixed assets are still being used but no depreciation expense is being recorded for their use.

TIP

Generally, the manager doesn't need to know the current replacement costs of *all* fixed assets — just those that will be replaced in the near future. At the same time, it's useful for the manager to get a status report on the company's fixed assets, which takes more of an engineering approach than an accounting approach. The status report includes information on the capacity, operating efficiency, and projected remaining life of each major fixed asset. The status report should include leased assets that aren't owned by the business and therefore aren't included in the fixed asset account.

The manager needs an *insurance summary report* for all fixed assets that are (or should be) insured for fire and other casualty losses; this report lists the types of coverage on each major fixed asset, deductibles, claims during the year, and so on. Also, the manager needs a list of the various liability risks of owning and using the fixed assets. The manager has to decide whether the risks should be insured.

Intangible assets

The balance sheet in Figure 13-1 reveals that the company had $1 million invested in intangible assets as of the fiscal year ending (FYE) December 31, 2019, which decreased to $500,000 as of the FYE December 31, 2020. Intangible assets can include a wide variety of things. The cost of acquiring the legal rights for using a patent or trademark could be in this asset account. Perhaps the business bought out another business and paid more than the current market values of identifiable assets being acquired — the extra amount being for the *goodwill* of the business acquired. The cost of the goodwill is recorded in the intangible assets account.

Accounting for these types of assets is tricky, if you don't mind our saying so. In any case, the costs that are recorded in the intangible assets account should be justified on the grounds that the costs will provide profit one way or another. The business should be better off owning the intangible asset versus not owning it.

After acquiring intangible assets, the business should regularly take a hard look at the items making up the balance in its intangible assets account to test whether the items continue to have value to the business or perhaps have deteriorated in terms of their profit payoff. The accountants refer to this as testing for the possible *impairment* of value of intangible assets. The appropriate managers — most likely including marketing managers — should receive reports about each component of the balance of the intangible assets account. Managers, in most cases, are the ones to initiate a hard look at whether there's been impairment of one or more of the intangible assets of the business.

Instead of the impairment testing approach, a private business has the option to adopt a period of years over which the cost of intangibles is charged to *amortization expense.* Clearly, managers should know which method the business is using.

Last, we should mention that the IRS rules can get very complicated in the matter of intangible costs. It's best to stay on the right side of the IRS.

Accounts payable

As you know, individuals have credit scores that affect their ability to borrow money and the interest rates they have to pay. Likewise, businesses have credit scores. If a business has a really bad credit rating or reputation, it may not be able to buy on credit and may have to pay steep interest rates. We don't have space here to go into the details of how credit ratings are developed for businesses. Suffice it to say that a business should pay its bills on time. If a business consistently pays its accounts payable late, this behavior gets reported to a credit rating agency (such as Dun & Bradstreet).

The manager needs a schedule of accounts payable that are *past due* (beyond the credit terms given by the vendors and suppliers). Of course, the manager should know why the accounts have become overdue. The manager may have to personally contact these creditors and convince them to continue offering credit to the business.

Frankly, some businesses operate on the principle of paying late. Their standard operating procedure is to pay their accounts payable two, three, or more weeks after the due dates. This could be due to not having adequate cash balances or wanting to hang onto their cash as long as possible. In the past, IBM was notorious for paying late, but because its credit rating was unimpeachable, it got away with this policy.

Accrued expenses payable

The controller should prepare a schedule for the manager that lists the major items making up the balance of the accrued expenses payable liability account. Many operating liabilities accumulate or, as accountants prefer to say, *accrue* over the course of the year; they aren't paid until sometime later. One main example is employee vacation and sick pay; an employee may work for almost a year before being entitled to take two weeks' vacation with pay. The accountant records an expense each payroll period for this employee benefit, and it accumulates in the liability account until the liability is paid (the employee takes his vacation). Another payroll-based expense that accrues is the cost of federal and state unemployment taxes on the employer.

WARNING

Accrued expenses payable can be a tricky liability from the accounting point of view. There's plenty of room for management discretion (or manipulation, depending on how you look at it) regarding which particular operating liabilities to record as expense during the year and which not to record as expense until they're paid. The basic choice is whether to expense as you go or expense later. If you decide to record the expense as you go through the year, the accountant must make estimates and assumptions, which are subject to error. Then there's the question of expediency. Employee vacation and sick pay may seem to be obvious expenses to accrue, but in fact many businesses don't accrue the expense on the grounds that it's simply too time-consuming and that some employees quit and forfeit the rights to their vacations.

Many businesses guarantee the products they sell for a certain period of time, such as 90 days or one year. The customer has the right to return the product for repair (or replacement) during the guarantee period. For example, when someone returns an iPhone for repair, Apple should have already recorded in a liability account the estimated cost of repairing iPhones that are returned after the point of sale. Businesses have more "creeping" liabilities than you might imagine. With a little work, we could list 20 or 30 of them, but we'll spare you the details. Our point is that the manager should know what's in the accrued expenses payable liability account and what isn't. Also, the manager should have a good fix on when these liabilities will be paid.

Income tax payable

It takes an income tax professional to comply with federal and state income tax laws on a business. The manager should make certain that the accountant responsible for its tax returns is qualified and up to date.

The controller should explain to the manager the reasons for a relatively large balance in this liability account at the end of the year. In a normal situation, a business should have paid 90 percent or more of its annual income tax by the end of the year. However, there are legitimate reasons that the ending balance of the income tax liability could be relatively large compared with the annual income tax expense — say, 20 or 30 percent of the annual expense. It behooves the manager to know the reasons for a large ending balance in the income tax liability. The controller should report these reasons to the chief financial officer and perhaps the treasurer of the business.

The manager should also know how the business stands with the IRS and whether the IRS has raised objections to the business's tax returns. The business may be in the middle of legal proceedings with the IRS, which the manager should be briefed on, of course. The CEO (and perhaps other top-level managers) should be given a frank appraisal of how things may turn out and whether the business is facing any additional tax payments and penalties. Needless to say, this is very sensitive information, and the controller may prefer that none of it be documented in a written report.

Finally, the chief executive officer working closely with the controller should decide how aggressive to be on income tax issues and alternatives. Keep in mind that tax *avoidance* is legal, but tax *evasion* is illegal. As you probably know, the income tax law is exceedingly complex, but ignorance of the law is no excuse. The controller should make abundantly clear to the manager whether the business is walking on thin ice in its income tax returns.

Interest-bearing debt

In Figure 13-1, the balance sheet reports two interest-bearing liabilities: one for short-term debts (those due in one year or less) and one for long-term debt. The reason is that financial reporting standards require that external balance sheets report the amount of *current liabilities* so the reader can compare this amount of short-term liabilities to the total of *current assets* (cash and assets that will be converted into cash in the short term). Interest-bearing debt that is due in one year or less is included in the current liabilities section of the balance sheet. (See Chapter 7 for details.)

TIP

The ending balances of short-term and long-term debt that are reported in the external balance sheet aren't nearly enough information for the manager. The best practice is to lay out in one comprehensive schedule for the manager *all* the interest-bearing obligations of the business. The obligations should be organized according to their due (maturity) dates, and the schedule should include other relevant information, such as the lender, the interest rate on each debt, the plans to roll over the debt (or not), the collateral, and the main covenants and restrictions on the business imposed by the lender.

Recall that debt is one of the two sources of capital to a business (the other being owners' equity, which we get to next). The sustainability of a business depends on the sustainability of its sources of capital. The more a business depends on debt capital, the more important it is to manage its debt well and maintain excellent relations with its lenders.

Raising and using debt and equity capital, referred to as *financial management* or *corporate finance*, is a broad subject that we cover in Chapter 18 at some length.

Owners' equity

REMEMBER

External balance sheets report two kinds of ownership accounts: one for *capital invested* by the owners in the business and one for *retained earnings* (profit that hasn't been distributed to shareowners). In Figure 13-1, two invested capital accounts are shown in the owners' equity section, one for common equity and the other for preferred equity. Most business corporations, limited liability companies, partnerships, and other types of business legal entities can have complex ownership structures. The owners' equity sections in their balance sheets may report several invested capital accounts — one for each class of ownership interest in the business.

Broadly speaking, the manager faces four basic issues regarding the owners' equity of the business:

>> Is more capital needed from the owners or other investors?

>> If more capital is needed, what terms should be provided to the parties providing capital, including any preferences or other beneficial terms?

>> Should some capital be returned to the owners?

>> Can and should the business make a cash distribution from profit to the owners and, if so, how much?

These questions belong in the field of financial management and extend beyond the scope of this book. However, we should mention that the external financial statements are very useful in deciding these key financial management issues. For example, the manager needs to know how much total capital is needed to support the sales level of the business. For every $100 of sales revenue, how much in total assets does the business need? The *asset turnover ratio* equals annual sales revenue divided by total assets. This ratio provides a good touchstone for the amount of capital being used for sales.

The external financial report of a business doesn't divulge the individual share-owners of the business and the number of shares each person or institution owns. The manager may want to know this information. Any major change in the ownership of the business usually is important information to the manager.

Culling Profit Information

The sales revenue (and other income, if any) and expenses (and losses, if any) of a business over a period of time are summarized in its *income statement.* Profit (sales revenue minus expenses) is the bottom line of the external income statement. Chapter 6 explains the externally reported income statement as well as how sales revenue and expenses are interconnected with the operating assets and liabilities of the business. The income statement fits hand in glove with the balance sheet.

Presenting an income statement for managers

Figure 13-2 presents the most recent annual income statement of the business whose balance sheet is shown in Figure 13-1. The two financial statements go together, of course. *Note:* The income statement in Figure 13-2 is prepared according to generally accepted accounting principles (GAAP) that have been established for external financial reporting. No EPS (earnings per share) is reported because the business is a private company.

In Figure 13-2, we made one significant modification to the standard external income statement. We added a line for cash flow from operating activities, or cash flow from profit, as we prefer to call it. So you see two "bottom lines":

>> Net income based on the accrual-basis accounting methods for recording revenue and expenses during the period, according to GAAP

>> Cash flow from the profit-making (operating) activities for the period

Why two bottom lines? Not only do business managers have to make profit, but they also have to convert that profit into cash flow as soon as possible.

TIP

Managers should track cash flow as well as their profit performance. It's dangerous to simply assume that if profit is okay, then cash flow is okay. As Chapter 8 explains, cash flow deviates from profit, possibly by quite a bit. In reporting profit performance to managers, we think it's a good idea to keep accrual-basis profit and the cash flow from profit side by side in the income statement to managers, as in Figure 13-2.

Calculating cash flow on the back of an envelope

In the income statement (see Figure 13-2), notice that cash flow from profit (operating activities) is higher than profit for the year: $7.593 million cash flow − $4.482 million net income = $3.111 million higher cash flow. This difference, which is fairly significant, deserves an explanation.

When it comes to explaining the difference between profit (net income) and cash flow, we think accountants do a lousy job, as we argue in Chapter 8. For one thing, cash flow from profit (operating activities) is reported in a separate financial statement — the statement of cash flows — instead of being placed next to net income in the income statement. Furthermore, accountants present a complicated schedule that shows how they determined cash flow instead of explaining the difference in a brief summary.

We suggest that managers get in the habit of doing a quick calculation of cash flow, one they could do on the back of an envelope. Doing such a calculation would reinforce the manager's understanding of and comfort level with cash flow.

Why is cash flow $3.111 million higher than profit for the year? The nearby sidebar "Cash flow characteristics of sales and expenses" offers a short review of the differences between accrual-basis profit accounting and cash flow from revenue and for expenses. The numbers in the following calculation come from the balance sheet (Figure 13-1) and income statement (Figure 13-2).

In our business example, the difference between net income and cash flow can be summarized as follows:

$1.739 million depreciation and amortization expense for the year

$138,000 decrease in short-term operating assets, primarily from a large decrease in inventory offset by a large increase in trade accounts receivables

$1.234 million increase in short-term operating liabilities

= $3.111 million excess of cash flow over net income

The $1.739 million of depreciation and amortization expense recorded for the year is not a cash outlay; indeed, it's just the opposite. The amount of depreciation and amortization has been recovered through sales revenue cash flow and thus is a positive cash flow factor. Accounts receivable and prepaid expenses both increased during the year, but inventory decreased. The net of these asset decreases have the effect of increasing cash flow from profit by $138,000 during the year. Accounts payable, accrued expenses payable, and income tax payable all increase during the year; the total of these three positive factors is $1.234 million. Adding the three lines gives you the $3.111 million cash overflow.

You may automatically think that it's good that cash flow is more than profit. Well, not so fast. There are many aspects to cash flow, and in some situations, a cash flow lower than profit is just what the doctor ordered.

CASH FLOW CHARACTERISTICS OF SALES AND EXPENSES

When reading internal income statements (also called *profit and loss,* or P&L, reports), keep in mind that the accountant records sales revenue when sales are made — instead of when cash is received from customers. Also, the accountant records expenses to match expenses with sales revenue and to put expenses in the period where they belong — instead of when cash is paid for the expenses. A manager shouldn't assume that sales revenue equals cash inflow and that expenses equal cash outflow.

The cash flow characteristics of sales and expenses are as follows:

- Cash sales generate immediate cash inflow. Keep in mind that sales returns and sales price adjustments after the point of sale reduce cash flow from sales.

- Credit sales do not generate immediate cash inflow. There's no cash flow until the customers' receivables are actually collected. There's a cash-flow lag from credit sales.

- Many operating costs aren't paid until several weeks (or months) after they're recorded as expense, and a few operating costs are paid before the costs are charged to expense.

- Depreciation expense is recorded by reducing the book value of an asset and doesn't involve cash outlay in the period in which it's recorded. The business paid out cash when the asset was acquired. Amortization expense on intangible assets is the same.

Managing operating cash flows

REMEMBER

In a small, one-owner/one-manager business, one person has to manage both profit and cash flow from profit. In larger businesses, managers who have profit responsibility may or may not have cash flow responsibility. The profit manager may ignore the cash flow aspects of their sales and expense activities. The responsibility for controlling cash flow falls on some other manager. Of course, someone should manage the cash flows of sales and expenses.

As the calculation in the preceding section shows, the net cash flow during the period from carrying on profit-making operations depends on the changes in the operating assets and liabilities directly connected with sales revenue and expenses. Changes in these accounts during the year determine the cash flow from operating activities. In other words, changes in these accounts boost or crimp cash flow. One or more managers should closely monitor the changes in operating assets and liabilities. Controlling cash flow from profit (operating activities) means controlling changes in the operating assets and liabilities of making sales and incurring expenses — there's no getting around this fact of business life.

TIP

A good general rule is that each operating asset and liability should change about the same percent as the percent change in the sales activity of the business. If sales revenue increases by 10 percent, then operating assets and liabilities should increase *about* 10 percent. The percents of increase in the operating assets and liabilities (in particular, accounts receivable, inventory, accounts payable, and accrued expenses payable) should be emphasized in the cash flow report to the manager.

Scrutinizing sales revenue and expenses

In this section, we offer examples of sales revenue and expense information that managers need but that isn't reported in the external income statement of a business. Given the broad range of different businesses and different circumstances, we can't offer extensive details — just common examples.

Here's a sampling of the kinds of accounting information that business managers need either in their internal income statements (P&L reports) or in supplementary schedules and analyses:

>> **Sales volumes** (quantities sold) for all sources of sales revenue

>> **List sales prices** and **discounts, allowances, and rebates** against list sales prices; for many businesses, sales pricing is a two-sided affair that starts with list prices (such as the manufacturer's suggested retail price) and includes deductions of all sorts from the list prices

>> **Sales returns** — products that were bought but later returned by customers

>> **Special incentives** offered by suppliers that effectively reduce the purchase cost of products

>> **Cost per acquisition or customer acquisition cost (CPA or CAC)** — how much a company spends on digital and social media advertising campaigns

>> Significant **variations in discretionary expenses** from year to year, such as repair and maintenance, employee training costs, and advertising

>> **Illegal payments** to secure business, including bribes, kickbacks, and other under-the-table payments (Keep in mind that businesses do not admit to making such payments, much less report them in internal communications. Therefore, the manager should know how these payments are disguised in the accounts of the business.)

>> Sales revenue and margin for **new products**

>> Significant **changes in fixed costs** and reasons for the changes

>> **Expenses that surged** much more than increases in sales volume or sales revenue

>> **New expenses** that show up for the first time

>> **Accounting changes** (if any) regarding when sales revenue and expenses are recorded

REMEMBER

This list isn't exhaustive, but it covers many important types of information that managers need in order to interpret their P&L reports and to plan profit improvements in the future. Analyzing profit is a very open-ended process. There are many ways to slice and dice sales and expense data. Managers have only so much time at their disposal, but they should take the time to understand and analyze the main factors that drive profit.

Avoiding Rookie Mistakes

REMEMBER

For those of you who are aspiring accountants, whether currently employed in an accounting role, looking to join the profession, or simply attempting to expand your knowledge of accounting and financial reporting, we leave you with these four pearls of wisdom when it comes to understanding and managing internal financial statements, reports, and information:

>> Do not ever confuse internal financial information with external financial reporting. If it is not clear by now, these two have vastly different uses, purposes, and audiences.

>> Never just hit the Send button. Although tempting, any financial information distributed to external parties should always be reviewed and approved by all appropriate personnel and management.

>> A word of caution to aspiring entrepreneurs: Assumption is the mother of all mistakes. If financial statements are requested, by internal or external parties (especially external), your policy should be loud and clear. The financial information is always reviewed and scrubbed by the appropriate company personnel before it is distributed. Do not assume that you can push a couple of buttons and print a report from accounting systems such as QuickBooks, Sage 50, or Net Suite, and then distribute this information. This can be a fatal mistake and almost always leads to far more questions and problems than it solves.

>> All financial information distributed, whether to external parties or for internal use, should clearly note two key items: that the financial information is either audited or unaudited, and that the financial information is confidential and the property of the company. Even for companies that have the best safe-guards installed to protect their internal financial information, at some point this information is going to end up outside the organization, so it is always helpful (from a legal perspective) to have clear disclosures as to the confiden-tial nature of the information.

Chapter **14**

Applying Wall Street's Tricks and Treats to Engineer Financial Results

The title of this chapter makes a gesture to Halloween; we all know that this is the yearly event when you go house to house with your kids and hopefully receive free treats. To a certain extent, the same logic applies with Wall Street because recently it seems that they can hand out all types of free "treats" when companies report financial results. While on the surface, the financial treat may appear to be very appealing, the tricks should be closely watched and understood to ensure you're not getting a rotten apple in your bag.

With this edition of *Accounting For Dummies,* we felt it was important to include a chapter that specifically addresses how businesses can massage, manipulate, tweak, and/or package financial results to achieve specific or desired results (when presenting operating results to external parties). In a nutshell, we refer to this strategy simply as *financial engineering.*

REMEMBER

We should note that financial engineering is not to be confused with what is commonly referred to as "cooking the books" or the intentional and willful attempt to present fraudulent financial information to deceive external parties. This represents a completely different subject matter, which we touch on throughout this book. Rather, financial engineering is a broader concept that, whether utilized by Wall Street or Main Street (that is, private businesses), offers a lesson on how businesses can massage, tweak, adjust, and, for lack of a better term, manipulate financial information and results to present a financial story that helps achieve a specific goal or objective (which usually involves increasing a company's valuation).

Knowing What Financial Engineering Is Not

Before we dive into the concept of financial engineering and what it entails later in this chapter, it is helpful to identify what financial engineering is *not.* We want to put out of your mind any preconceived notions about the topics of fraudulent financial reporting or heavy-handed manipulation of accounting and other deliberately misleading information put into financial reports.

REMEMBER

There are two specific points that are important to understand:

>> First, financial engineering does *not* refer to the intentional misreporting and misleading presentation of accounting transactions and financial operating results. It does not refer to cooking the books. While we would love to recall some of the great accounting frauds of the past (for example, Enron), this subject would warrant a whole book to itself. We just point out here that almost all "great" accounting frauds were supported by executive-level management collusion. Multiple members of the executive management team worked in complicity to report financial information with the willful intent to deceive and mislead.

We offer here only a few advisory points to remember when it comes to fraudulent financial information. Be on the lookout for any signs of executive-level collusion, such as boards of directors that are not truly independent. Be careful if the CPA auditor of the financial report is relatively unknown. Finally, be extra careful of tightly controlled insider-operated businesses, which are more conducive to accounting and financial reporting abuse.

» Second, financial engineering usually does *not* refer to companies adopting aggressive accounting methods and highly favorable estimates for recording transactions and reporting financial operating results. Using aggressive accounting methods by itself does not represent a fraudulent activity as long as the accounting methods fall within the guidelines of generally accepted accounting principles (GAAP). The use of one accounting method over another is a decision best left for the company's management team, board of directors, and independent auditors to resolve and agree upon.

With this said, we would offer a tip as it relates to sniffing out companies that may be utilizing more aggressive accounting methods than are justified: Aggressive accounting methods can be used to accelerate sales revenue and defer expenses, thereby inflating earnings. While this makes the income statement look good and gives the appearance of strong profits, do not forget that the income statement (see Chapter 6) is generally the easiest of the three fundamental financial statements to manipulate. This is one reason we emphasize the importance of understanding how cash is generated and consumed in a business, which can readily be found in the cash flows statement (see Chapter 8).

Defining What Financial Engineering Is

When you know what financial engineering is not (see the preceding section), you can explore what financial engineering refers to. However, we encounter a problem right off the bat. The term has more than one meaning. Broadly speaking, it refers to the use of highly sophisticated mathematical methods and computer-based algorithms for analyzing financial reports data.

REMEMBER

Here we use the term *financial engineering* in an important but much more limited sense. In the rest of this chapter, we use the term to refer to going a step beyond simple ratios to use other techniques for analyzing and reconfiguring financial report information. This additional layer of analysis may very well sway or shift the reader's sentiment about a company's operating performance and financial position. The primary goal of financial engineering, as we use the term in this chapter, is to assist external parties with gaining a better understanding of a business's reported operating results and financial position.

One example of how businesses utilize financial engineering strategies directly in their financial reports concerns the issue of *extraordinary gains and losses*. Companies have been able to produce financial statements that present core operating results and carve out extreme or unique, one-time events that negatively impacted net profits (called extraordinary events) during a specific reporting period. For example, a manufacturing company based in the South might have experienced a massive, once-in-a-generation loss from a devastating weather event such as a hurricane. With the loss being so significant and the event so unusual, it would not be expected recur for quite a while, so it could be captured as a one-time loss reported as *other expenses* in the income statement (below the operating income level). By carving out this rather unusual expense, an external reader of the financial statements could clearly and efficiently understand why the company incurred such a large loss, allowing them to focus on the remaining base operations to evaluate the company's financial performance.

Up to this point, we agree that presenting more complete, accurate, and revealing financial operating results in the financial statements is warranted and beneficial to outside parties. But it is also at this point where the concept of modern-day financial engineering needs to be appreciated and that accounting as an "art" form versus a science needs to be clearly understood by defining financial engineering in the simplest form.

REMEMBER

Financial engineering is based in the idea of taking GAAP financial statements and accounting information (as presented) and then engineering, or rearranging the information into a different format, structure, comparison, and so on. The *engineered* data should offer invaluable additional information and perspectives for the purpose of allowing users to make better-informed business decisions. Without the engineered information, external parties may depend solely on a financial report, which can manipulate or distort information that could lead external parties to different conclusions on a company's financial performance and position.

TIP

When undertaking financial engineering, you take GAAP financial information and reconfigure it into a different financial framework. In doing this, you'll start to notice a series of rather commonly used terms and expressions frequently associated with companies that present financially engineered information. These terms, usually abbreviated with acronyms, include non-GAAP, adjusted GAAP, EBITDA, adjusted EBITDA, proforma results, sales bookings, and free cash flow. The list goes on and on. Your antennae should definitely be raised, and you should plan to apply additional scrutiny to the information when this type of terminology appears.

WARNING

The risk of the information not being in compliance with GAAP increases because consistency and comparability may be lacking when it comes to how companies define, interpret, and present this information. Furthermore, companies may be much more selective in the type of information they present (to influence/direct a reader toward a specific conclusion). In short, financially engineered information, by itself, is not fraudulent in nature but rather a somewhat subjective method of reporting financial results that warrants additional scrutiny from external parties.

Ultimately, it is up to the financial report reader to decide how important the financially engineered information is, how credible it is, and whether it should be relied upon. There is no real school for this other than knowledge and experience, which we hope to help you build, at least a little bit, with our book and specifically this chapter.

Identifying Commonly Used "Tricks of the Trade"

In the previous section, we help provide a little more clarity on what constitutes financial engineering, so here we consider a handful of financial engineering examples that have been used (or abused) over the past two or more decades. The lists in the following sections are by no means all-inclusive but rather are designed to provide a smattering of the breadth of tools and strategies used by companies to highlight (and we use this term with an abundance of caution) certain operating results.

Using tricks that fit within GAAP but need more digging

In this section, we offer three examples of financial engineering that are fully blessed by GAAP but need deeper dives to properly understand a company's financial performance.

Discontinued operations and/or extraordinary events

We touch on this topic earlier in this chapter as it relates to properly disclosing an extraordinary, one-time event that is material and unusual in nature. We agree with this concept, as these types of events are best reported in a clear, concise, and separate manner.

WARNING

Where companies begin to push the limit on this concept and enter somewhat of a gray zone can be found in two primary areas:

>> First, are we truly dealing with a one-off event or does the company have a habit of reporting these types of losses year after year? You would be amazed

at how many companies convince themselves that a bad business decision warrants a separate disclosure in the financial statements as an extraordinary event (assuming that the loss was beyond the control of management). When a pattern of continued losses from these types of events emerges period after period, you must ask whether it is really a one-off event or just a means to deflect external parties from bad business decisions being made by the company's management team.

» Second, the definition of what constitutes an extraordinary event is often very subjective. GAAP and other accounting pronouncements attempt to provide guidance on this subject, but ultimately, the disclosure decision is generally made by the company's executive management team and external auditors. Furthermore, definitions may change over time when operating in different business environments, when new management teams are brought on board, and so on. This leads to consistency concerns over different reporting periods, which makes it difficult to compare performance over time.

Stock buybacks

Stock buybacks have been around for decades but have really kicked in since 2012 as a result of ultra-cheap debt being available and from the benefits received from the 2017 Tax Cuts and Jobs Act, making stock buybacks one of the hottest topics in the financial community. When a company buys back its own stock, the results often look great on the surface. This is because when EPS (earnings per share) is calculated as profit and divided over fewer outstanding shares, it increases. From a GAAP perspective, this is technically correct because the remaining shareholders have the right to increased earnings moving forward (so EPS would be higher).

But digging deeper, you must ask whether this type of transaction or event represents real internal growth that is sustainable year over year or whether it has weakened the company's financial position by increasing debt levels (thus increasing financial leverage) or reducing cash holdings (and liquidity).

Tax rates and jurisdictions

In 2017, the Trump Administration spearheaded a meaningful change to the tax code, which included, among other things, a significant decrease to corporate marginal tax rates. Of course, this was hailed by the corporate world as a significant win. By lowering income tax rates, corporate profits would automatically increase, which was generally the case. But again, and similar to the concept of stock buybacks in the preceding section, the question of sustainability needs to be addressed, as when external parties compared a company's 2017 net profit (assuming a 35 percent tax rate) against its 2018 net profit (assuming a 21 percent tax rate), the resulting appearance of significant growth in EPS was artificially bumped higher for a one-year period (such as whether the company really realized a 22 percent increase in earnings).

However, when 2018 and 2019 operating results are compared, the impact of the lower tax rate will have passed, and a more stable picture of real earnings growth emerges. This concept can also be expanded to companies utilizing or leveraging low-tax-rate jurisdictions to massage net income (for example, sheltering earnings in foreign countries that have exceptionally low corporate tax rates). Again, the question must be asked whether this is a real benefit or simply a company being more interested in playing a shell game with taxable income.

REMEMBER

The lesson here is simple: It's important to not rely on changing tax laws or profit-shifting strategies (to manage earnings so they appear higher) as a cure-all for what ails a business. (In the end, if a company is losing money, income taxes are really a moot point.) It goes without saying that proper comparisons at equivalent tax rates should be completed.

Understanding commonly used tricks outside the realm of GAAP

In this section, we provide three examples of what we will call the *real* or *pure* financial engineering strategies that are outside the scope of GAAP but are frequently utilized by companies.

EBITDA and addbacks

First, we need to ask the question as to why EBITDA (earnings before interest, taxes, depreciation, and amortization) is important. Simply put, EBITDA is a measurement of internal cash flow (a) used to evaluate a company's ability to service debt or support distributions/dividends and (b) relied upon as a basis for valuing a business (for example, when one company is looking to buy another business). It should make sense that a higher EBITDA generally translates into the ability for a company to support higher debt levels. It also indicates that the company's value is higher.

We need to emphasize that the concept of EBITDA is subjective and for the most part beyond the scope of GAAP (so it needs to be taken with a grain of salt). But where the real fun begins with EBITDA is when companies start to discuss or disclose *adjusted* EBITDA with operating performance addbacks. "What are addbacks?" you may ask. Addbacks as such are really nothing more than management's assessment of either increased revenue (that should have been earned but for some reason was not) or decreased expenses (that will be nonrecurring) that should be included or added back in calculating adjusted EBITDA to support a valuation analysis, debt service calculation, and so on.

WARNING

At this point, it should be abundantly clear just how badly not only EBITDA but addbacks can be abused to inflate earnings and company valuations to achieve a financial objective. Countless examples of the aggressive use of addbacks to inflate EBITDA could be provided, but the general concept we are driving home is that adjusting EBITDA is a very common strategy and a negotiating point when negotiating a financial transaction that can be manipulated beyond belief.

Sales revenue recognition

One of the hottest and most important topics in GAAP relates to recognizing sales and determining when the earnings process is complete. More than a few accountants and authoritative groups have weighed in on this subject as, with so many types of sales transactions utilized in the global economy today, there is no shortage of opinions and fact patterns available to help guide a company with recognizing sales revenue. Furthermore, several subjective elements must be taken into consideration when recognizing sales revenue, ranging from the validity of the sale to begin with (at the initial point of sales) through to the ultimate collectability of the sale (can the customer even pay).

REMEMBER

What companies have begun to do on a more frequent basis is to present a non-GAAP sales revenue to reflect, for example, just how many bookings they have (but have not yet delivered to the market or have not satisfied the tests to fully realize the sales revenue in the current period). Is this useful information? Absolutely. But does it mean the company has earned the revenue/sales? Absolutely not! So take care to understand the difference between GAAP-recognized sales revenue and the countless other forms of non-GAAP sales revenue that a company may disclose.

Pro forma operating results

Another quite common non-GAAP financial disclosure and analysis companies like to provide relates to presenting *pro forma* operating results. For example, a company may undertake a major acquisition toward the end of the year. Suppose the acquisition holds the promise of significant expense reductions being realized over the next two to three years with the combined operations because economies of scale are realized with large personnel expense reductions anticipated. So a company may take actual, audited GAAP-based financial results for both companies and then present a hypothetical combination of the two entities as if they were operating together and just how many costs/expenses could be eliminated.

WARNING

Again, this information may be interesting, but is it 100 percent factual and supported by an audit? Generally no, and it may not be in 100 percent compliance with GAAP. One thing is for certain: The information is highly dependent on management assessments and estimates that are based on forward-looking statements that may or may not come to fruition.

Manufacturing Imaginary Profits (and, Yes, Losses)

We start our discussion on how companies can manufacture profits by referring you back to the beginning of this chapter, where the concept of financial engineering is first discussed, as to what it is and what it is not, and we take this opportunity to expand our presentation on how profits can be "manufactured" by using accounting strategies. In effect, this represents a form or type of financial engineering that is more technical in nature as it closely relates to applying GAAP.

REMEMBER

Again, we would also like to be perfectly clear that the content provided in this section should not be confused with accounting or financial fraud. Rather, the concepts highlighted here originate from companies adjusting or changing specific accounting policies, procedures, use of estimates, and so on over several years as business conditions or operating circumstances change. These are legitimate (per GAAP) but warrant a closer look by both internal and external parties when companies move down this path.

Reviewing examples of "manufacturing" profits

We provide four examples for you to chew (or maybe the more appropriate word would be gag) on:

>> **Change in estimate:** Companies generally need to make periodic investments in various assets, tangible and intangible, to support their ongoing operations. When making investments in assets, the company must select appropriate depreciation, amortization, or depletion estimates (to appropriately expense the consumption of an asset over a period of time). Companies may elect to revise these estimates based on changes to their operating environment.

For example, if an asset was originally anticipated to be fully consumed and depreciated over a five-year period but, based on revised management estimates that indicate the asset has a longer life, the life was extended to seven years, then the period depreciation expense would naturally decrease, because the asset would be depreciated over a longer period. The same logic could be used when amortizing intellectual property (for example, the value assigned to a customer list that was purchased), but the point is that a simple change in an estimate from, say, five years to seven years could impact operating performance significantly. Other examples would be a company changing an estimate for potential sales returns or future warranty-related costs as they "scrub" operating results to be more accurate. We will let you decide whether a company scrubbing operating results is being done so legitimately or to achieve a specific performance target, but calculating accounting estimates is always an area that should demand attention.

>> **Change in policy:** A change in accounting estimate should not be confused with a change in accounting policy. For example, a company may change its policy related to capitalizing assets on the balance sheet versus expensing costs in the income statement. Research and development costs that were expensed historically may now be capitalized as an intangible asset and amortized over an appropriate period (because management has determined that the R&D costs are a valuable long-term asset). In either case, cash still flows out the door, but companies may want to "park" the capitalized asset on the balance sheet and then depreciate or amortize the asset over a period of time, helping improve the income statement.

>> **Interest rates:** Interest rates are currently at historical lows (and some would say they are artificially low, manipulated by the Fed). Interest rates represent a critical component in valuing businesses as low interest rates (either market driven or artificially suppressed) generally have the effect of propping up business valuations. The same logic holds for bonds because an inverse relationship is present between interest rates and bond values (that is, the lower the interest rate, the higher the bond value). Further, the same logic applies to specific assets such as intellectual property or proprietary content that will generate future cash flows.

In effect, low interest rates prop up asset values by discounting the future cash flow at a low rate (which increases the future value of the asset). Companies may attempt to justify using lower interest rates to support a higher asset value and avoid writing off the asset or having to expense the asset over a shorter period.

>> **Cleaning house:** The three previous examples focused on how a company may inflate operating profits and earnings. The concept of cleaning house does the exact opposite; a common strategy companies use when bad news needs to be delivered (to the market or investors) is to deliver all the bad news at once. Or, simply put, let us clean house with all potential write-offs, adjustments, losses, and so on in one time period to sacrifice the current year to build a clean basis to drive profits in future years.

Mind you, no cash changes hands with these types of events; rather, the balance sheet is simply adjusted to eliminate the garbage (for lack of a better term) that has accumulated on the balance sheet over a period of time (for example, worthless inventory, unsupportable assets, quickly fading IP/content, and so on). Further, management may conclude that these types of adjustments represent one-time expenses from a discontinued product line, an extraordinary type of event (for example, the impact of Covid-19), and so on, that will be nonrecurring (thus the reason it is captured below the operating income or EBITDA line).

Keeping critical points in mind

REMEMBER

We would like to emphasize two important points as related to manufacturing profits:

>> First, in the four examples provided in the preceding section, no cash changes hands. None, zero, zip! This is to say that the losses are not real, as somewhere in the past cash was impacted by either investing in a long-term asset or buying inventory (to provide two examples). Yes, the losses are very much real and the company's management team needs to be held accountable for any performance issues. But the adjustments noted earlier represent somewhat of a sleight of accounting hand to move expenses or costs between the balance sheet and income statement in a manner that is, for lack of a better term, desirable (to achieve certain goals or confirm a story).

>> Second, there is nothing inherently wrong with these strategies, especially when a company's external CPA auditor has agreed to the changes and confirms that the changes comply with GAAP. But you should always watch for these items in relation to the size of adjustments, the frequency, and the reasoning/validity, because they may indicate either a management effort to "massage" the financial results or, worse yet, weaknesses in the company's internal accounting system and financial information reporting.

Looking Out for Particular Trends and Terminology

We conclude our discussion on financial engineering by emphasizing once again that there is nothing inherently illegal or dishonest about providing supplemental information, which is often especially useful to external parties. But in the same breath, it's important to note that this type of information tends to be much more subjective in nature and is provided to sway or influence external-party analysis of a company, often not in conformity with GAAP and generally not audited by an external CPA firm.

WARNING

Red flags should be raised when you see terms like *EBITDA*, *adjusted GAAP*, *pro forma*, *non-GAAP*, *booked revenue* (not yet earned), and the like, especially when you notice a trend developing over a period of time (that is, year over year, a company is focusing on non-GAAP results as opposed to GAAP results).

WARNING

Further, when you see a company implementing changes to accounting policies, revisions to accounting estimates, and similar types of accounting events, make sure you pay close attention to the pertinent reasons; again, any trends that start to appear and repeat year after year should raise an eyebrow or two. If nothing else, it may indicate that the company's internal accounting and financial professional staff and team are struggling with getting a handle on critical financial transactions and information to report complete, accurate, reliable, and timely financial operating results (in its financial statements).

4

Leveraging Accounting in Managing a Business

Understand how accounting helps managers achieve the financial objectives of the business.

Find out how to take advantage of time-tested accounting tools and techniques to help you achieve your business's financial goals.

Determine how to insightfully analyze profit with a well-thought-out P&L report.

Become familiar with the costs that managers work with day in and day out and the problems associated with measuring costs.

Develop and utilize best-in-class forecasts and projections to improve the financial performance of a business.

Discover the basics of securing different types of debt and equity capital and how businesses are valued in today's economy.

Chapter **15**

Analyzing Profit

As a business manager, executive, or owner (collectively referred to as "manager" through the remainder of this chapter), you get paid to make profit happen. That's one thing that separates you from the employees at your business. Of course, you should be a motivator, innovator, consensus builder, lobbyist, and maybe sometimes a babysitter, but the hardcore purpose of your job is to make and improve profit. No matter how much your staff loves you (or do they love those doughnuts you bring in every Monday?), if you don't meet your profit goals, you're facing the unemployment line.

Competition in most industries is fierce, and you can never take profit performance for granted. Changes take place all the time — changes initiated by the business and changes from outside forces. Maybe a new superstore down the street is causing your profit to fall off, and you figure that you'll have a huge sale to draw customers, complete with splashy ads on TV and Dimbo the Clown in the store. Whoa, not so fast! First, make sure that you can afford to cut prices and spend money on advertising and still turn a profit. Maybe price cuts and Dimbo's balloon creations would keep your cash register singing, but making sales does not guarantee that you make a profit. Profit is a two-sided challenge: Profit comes from making sales *and* controlling expenses.

This chapter focuses on the fundamental factors that drive profit — the *levers of profit*. Business managers need a sure-handed grip on these profit handles. One of the purposes of accounting is to provide this critical information to the managers — and to present the information in the most useful format for managers. Chapter 13 explains that externally reported income statements don't provide all the information that business managers need for sustainable profit performance. Managers need to thoroughly understand their external income statements, and they also need to look deeper into the bowels of the business.

Helping Managers: The Fourth Pillar of Accounting

As previous chapters explain, accounting serves critical functions in a business:

>> **Recordkeeping:** A business needs a dependable recordkeeping and bookkeeping system for operating in a smooth and efficient manner. Strong internal accounting controls are needed to minimize errors and fraud.

>> **Tax compliance:** A business must comply with a myriad of tax laws, and it depends on its chief accountant (controller) to make sure that all its tax returns are prepared on time and correctly.

>> **Financial reporting:** A business prepares financial statements that should conform to established accounting and financial reporting standards, which are reported on a regular basis to its creditors and external shareowners.

>> **Internal reporting and analysis:** Accounting should help managers in their decision-making, controlling, and planning by providing the information they need in the most helpful format. This branch of accounting is generally called *managerial* or *management accounting*.

So the accountant has to wear four different hats. And don't forget that the accounting system of a business has to serve all four of these demands on it.

Branching out in the field of management accounting

This is the first of four chapters devoted to managerial accounting. In this chapter, we pay particular attention to the internal reporting of profit to managers and providing essential information needed for plotting profit strategy and controlling profit performance. Chapter 16 examines the methods and problems of determining product costs (generally called *cost accounting*). Chapter 17 concentrates on financial planning, forecasting, projections, and budgeting. And finally, Chapter 18 provides a brief introduction on how companies raise capital, debt, and equity, and the hows and whys of business valuations.

Designing and monitoring the accounting recordkeeping system, complying with complex federal and state tax laws, and preparing external financial reports put heavy demands on the time and attention of the accounting department of a business. Even so, managers' special needs for additional accounting information should not be given second-level priority or be done by default. The chief accountant (controller) has the responsibility of ensuring that the accounting information needs of managers are served with maximum usefulness. Managers should demand this from their accountants.

Following the organizational structure

In a small business, there's often only one manager (or in a number of cases, one owner) in charge of profit. As businesses get larger, two or more managers have profit responsibility. The overarching rule of managerial accounting is to follow the organizational structure: to report relevant information for which each individual manager is responsible. (This principle is logically referred to as *responsibility accounting*.) If a manager is in charge of a product line, for instance, the accounting department should report the sales and expenses for that product line to the manager in charge. If a manager is in charge of building maintenance, all relevant costs should be reported to that manager.

Generally speaking, a manager is responsible for one of two types of basic organizational segments:

>> **Profit centers:** These are separate, identifiable sources of sales revenue and connected expenses so that a measure of profit can be determined for each. A profit center can be a particular product or a product line, a particular location or territory in which a wide range of products is sold, or a channel of distribution. Rarely is an entire business managed as one conglomerate profit center, with no differentiation of its various sources of sales and profit.

>> **Cost centers:** Certain departments and other organizational units do not generate sales, but they have costs that can be identified to their operations. Examples are the accounting department, the headquarters staff of a business, the legal department, and the security department. The managers responsible for these organizational units need accounting reports that keep them informed about the costs of running their departments. The managers should keep their costs under control, of course, and they need informative accounting reports to do this.

The term *center* is simply a convenient word that includes a variety of types of organizational segments, such as departments, divisions, branches, territories, and other monikers.

Centering on profit centers

In this chapter, we concentrate on profit centers. We don't mean to shun cost centers, but frankly, the type of accounting information needed by the managers of cost centers is relatively straightforward. They need lots of detailed information, including comparisons with the last period and with the budgeted targets for the current period. And we don't mean to suggest that the design of cost center reports is a trivial matter. Sorting out significant cost variances and highlighting these cost problems for management attention is very important. But the spotlight of this chapter is on profit analysis techniques using accounting information for managers with profit responsibility.

We should mention that large businesses commonly create relatively autonomous units within the organization that, in addition to having responsibility for their profit and cost centers, also have broad authority and control over investing in assets and raising capital for their assets. These organization units are called, quite logically, *investment centers.* Basically, an investment center is a mini business within the larger conglomerate, company-wide setting. Discussing investment centers is beyond the scope of this chapter.

From a one-person sole proprietorship to a mammoth business organization like Disney or Apple, one of the most important tasks of managerial accounting is to identify each source of profit within the business and to accumulate the sales revenue and the direct expenses for each of these sources of profit. Can you imagine an auto dealership, for example, not separating revenue and expenses between its new car sales and its service and parts departments? For that matter, an auto dealer may earn more profit from its financing operations (originating loans) than from selling new and used cars.

Even small businesses may have a relatively large number of different sources of profit. In contrast, even a relatively large business may have just a few mainstream sources of profit. There are no sweeping rules for classifying sales revenue and costs for the purpose of segregating sources of profit — in other words, for defining the profit centers of a business. Every business has to sort this out on its own. The controller (chief accountant) can advise top management regarding how to organize the business into profit centers. But the main job of the controller is to identify the profit centers that have been (or should be) established by management and to make sure that the managers of these profit centers get the accounting information they need. Of course, managers should know how to use the information.

Internal Profit Reporting

External financial statements, including the profit report (income statement; see Chapter 6), comply with well-established rules and conventions, which we discuss in several places. In contrast, the format and content of internal accounting reports to managers is a wide-open field. If you could sneak a peek at the internal financial reports of several businesses (discussed in Chapter 13), we think you would be surprised at the diversity among the businesses. All businesses include sales revenue and expenses in their internal P&L (profit and loss) reports. Beyond this broad comment, it's very difficult to generalize about the specific format and level of detail included in P&L reports, particularly regarding how operating expenses are reported.

Designing internal profit (P&L) reports

Profit performance reports prepared for a business's managers typically are called *P&L* (profit and loss) reports. These reports should be prepared as frequently as managers need them, usually monthly or quarterly — perhaps even weekly or daily in some businesses. A P&L report is prepared for the manager in charge of each profit center; these confidential profit reports do not circulate outside the business. The P&L contains sensitive information that competitors would love to get hold of.

TIP

Accountants are not in the habit of preparing brief, summary-level profit reports. Accountants tend to err on the side of providing too much detailed data and information. Their mantra is to give managers more information, even if the information is not asked for. Our attitude is just the reverse. We're sure it's not news to you that managers are very busy people, and they don't have spare time to waste, whether on reading long, rambling emails or on deciphering multipage profit reports with too much detail. Our preference is that profit reports be compact for a quick read. If managers want more detail, they can request it as time permits. Ideally, the accountant should prepare a profit *main page* that would fit on one computer screen, although this may be a smidgeon too small as a practical matter. In any case, keep it brief.

REMEMBER

Businesses that sell products deduct the cost of goods sold expense from sales revenue and then report *gross profit* (alternatively called *gross margin*) both in their externally reported income statements and in their internal P&L reports to managers. However, internal P&L reports have much more detail about sources of sales and the components of cost of goods sold expense. In this chapter, we use the example of a business that sells products. Businesses that sell products manufactured by other businesses generally fall into one of two types: *retailers* that sell products to final consumers and *wholesalers* (distributors) that sell to retailers. The following discussion applies to both.

One thing we've learned over the years is that there's a need for short-to-the-point or quick-and-dirty profit models that managers can use for decision-making analysis and plotting profit strategy. By "short," we mean on one page or even smaller than one full page — like on one computer screen that the manager can interact with in order to test the critical factors that drive profit. For example, if sales prices were decreased 5 percent to gain 10 percent more sales volume, what would happen to profit? Managers of profit centers need a tool to quickly answer such questions. Later in this chapter, we introduce just such a profit analysis template for managers (see the section "Presenting a profit analysis template").

Reporting operating expenses

Below the gross margin line in an internal P&L statement, reporting practices vary from company to company. There is no standard pattern. One question looms large: How should the *operating expenses* of a profit center be presented in its P&L report? There's no authoritative answer to this question. One basic choice for reporting operating expenses is between the *object of expenditure basis* and the *cost behavior basis.*

Reporting operating expenses on the object of expenditure basis

By far the most common way to present operating expenses in a profit center's P&L report is to list them according to the *object of expenditure basis.* This means that expenses are classified according to what is purchased (the object of the expenditure) — such as salaries and wages, commissions paid to salespersons, rent, depreciation, shipping costs, real estate taxes, advertising, insurance, utilities, office supplies, telephone costs, and so on. To do this, the operating expenses of the business have to be recorded in such a way that these costs can be traced to each of its various profit centers. For example, employee salaries of persons working in a particular profit center are recorded as belonging to that profit center.

The object of expenditure basis for reporting operating costs to managers of profit centers is practical. And this information is useful for management control because, generally speaking, controlling costs focuses on the particular items being bought by the business. For example, a profit center manager analyzes wages and salary expense to decide whether additional or fewer personnel are needed relative to current and forecast sales levels. A manager can examine the property insurance expense relative to the types of assets being insured and their risks of losses.

For cost control purposes, the object of expenditure basis works well. But there is a downside. This method for reporting operating costs to profit center managers obscures the all-important factor in making profit: *margin.* Yes, internal P&L reports include gross margin, which is sales revenue minus the cost of goods sold.

But gross margin isn't the final amount of operating margin that managers need to know. This leads to the important distinction between the two types of operating expenses.

Separating operating expenses further on their behavior basis

The first and usually largest *variable* expense of making sales is the cost of goods sold expense (for companies that sell products). In addition to cost of goods sold, an obvious variable expense, businesses have other expenses that depend either on the volume of sales (quantities sold) or the dollar amount of sales (sales revenue). And virtually all businesses have *fixed* expenses that are not sensitive to sales activity — at least, not in the short run. Therefore, it makes sense to take operating expenses classified according to object of expenditure and further classify each expense into either variable or fixed. There would be a variable or fixed tag on each expense.

TIP

The principal advantage of separating operating expenses between variable and fixed is that margin can be reported. *Margin* is the residual amount after all variable expenses of making sales are deducted from sales revenue. In other words, margin equals profit after all variable costs are deducted from sales revenue but before fixed costs are deducted from sales revenue. Margin is compared with total fixed costs for the period. This head-to-head comparison of margin against fixed costs is critical. We come back to this important point in the next section.

Although it's hard to know for sure — because internal profit reporting practices of businesses are not publicized or generally available — our experience is that the large majority of companies do not attempt to classify operating expenses as variable or fixed. If you gave us a dollar for every company you found that classifies its operating expenses on the object of expenditure basis and we gave you a dollar for every business that further separates between variable and fixed behavior, we guarantee you that we would end up with many more dollars than you. Yet for making profit decisions, managers need to know the variable versus fixed nature of their operating expenses.

Looking at Strategic Profit Analysis

First, a word or two on expense analysis and control versus strategic analysis and planning. The well-worn expression in real estate is "location, location, location." In expense management, an equivalent expression is "detail, detail, detail." Controlling expenses is done at a very detailed level. Another expression comes to mind here: "The devil is in the detail." In short, managers need lots of detailed information to analyze expenses and to make decisions regarding these expenses — no surprise there.

We could go on and on about expense analysis and control. But instead, we shift attention here to the higher-level topic of making strategic decisions for profit maintenance and improvement. In particular, what can the accountant do to help the manager clearly understand and correctly analyze the factors that drive profit, which also helps the manager understand the interactions and tradeoffs among these factors? In our view, this key function of the accountant starts with a profit analysis template that the manager can use to think through and do the math.

Presenting a profit analysis template

Figure 15-1 presents a profit analysis template that has broad applicability for our sample technology business that sells both products and services.

The example is for the same business introduced in Chapter 13. Figure 13-2 presents its income statement for the most recent year. The company's $34.939 million of total selling, general, and administrative (SG&A) expenses reported in Figure 13-1 are reclassified into three distinct types in Figure 15-1: revenue-driven, volume-driven, and fixed.

In Figure 15-1, we divide SG&A expenses according to how they behave relative to sales activity. There are four lines for expenses above the profit line EBITDA, namely cost of goods sold (a variable expense), two variable operating expenses, and fixed operating expenses. The profit template stops at the operating earnings line, or earnings before interest and income tax (EBIT). Also, EBITDA is shown on a separate line. The business is treated as one conglomerate profit center. Of course, the business could have its accounting staff prepare separate profit templates for each different profit center of the business.

REMEMBER

The purpose of a strategic profit analysis template is to provide the manager with a different look at profit — one that's useful for thinking about how the business makes profit, for reaching profit decisions, and for planning based on forecasts of changes in the basic factors that drive the company's profit outcome. The template demands that SG&A expenses be separated into variable and fixed types. This is the one key difference between the standard income statement (Figure 13-2) and the strategic profit template (Figure 15-1). In our view, redesigning the profit report based on expense behavior has high value to managers, but frankly, many businesses don't take the time to classify their expenses this way.

QW Example Tech., Inc.
Unaudited Financial Statements
for the Fiscal Year Ending
12/31/2020

Income Statement For the Twelve-Month Period Ending (All Numbers in Thousands)	FYE 12/31/2020	% of Sales
Sales Revenue, Net	$71,064	100.0%
Costs of Goods Sold	$26,891	37.8%
Gross Profit (or Gross Margin)	$44,173	62.2%
Selling, General, & Administrative Expenses:		
Revenue-Driven Expenses	$10,660	15.0%
Volume-Driven Expenses	$8,528	12.0%
Operating Margin (aka Contribution Margin)	$24,986	35.2%
Fixed SG&A Expenses	$15,752	22.2%
Earnings Before Interest, Taxes, Depreciation, & Amortization Expense (EBITDA)	$9,234	13.0%
Depreciation & Amortization Expense	$1,739	2.4%
Operating Earnings (Loss) Before Income Taxes & Interest	$7,495	10.5%

Confidential — Property of QW Example Tech., Inc.

FIGURE 15-1:
Strategic profit
analysis template.

© *John Wiley & Sons, Inc.*

Separating variable and fixed expenses

For managers to analyze a business's profit behavior thoroughly, they need to know which expenses are *variable* and which are *fixed* — in other words, which expenses change according to the level of sales activity in a given period and which don't. The title of each expense account often gives a pretty good clue. For example, the cost of goods sold expense is variable because it depends on the number of units of product sold, and sales commissions are variable expenses as well. On the other hand, real estate property taxes and property and general liability insurance premiums are fixed for a period of time. Managers should always have a good feel for how their operating expenses behave relative to sales activity.

Variable expenses

Virtually every business has *variable expenses*, which move up and down in tight proportion with changes in sales volume or sales revenue, like soldiers obeying orders barked out by their drill sergeant. Here are examples of common variable expenses:

>> The cost of goods sold expense, which is the cost of products sold to customers

>> Commissions paid to salespeople based on their sales

>> Franchise fees based on total sales for the period, which are paid to the franchisor

>> Digital advertising costs spent on social media (think Instagram ads), which have a direct correlation to customer sales

>> Transportation costs of delivering products to customers via FedEx, UPS, and freight haulers (railroads and trucking companies)

>> Fees that a retailer pays when a customer uses a credit or debit card (in other words, merchant account fees)

REMEMBER

Cost of goods sold is usually (but not always) the largest variable expense of a business that sells products, as you'd suspect. Other variable expenses are the costs of making sales and running the business. The sizes of variable operating expenses, relative to sales revenue, vary from industry to industry. Delivery costs of Walmart and Costco, for instance, are minimal because their customers take the products they buy with them. (Walmart and Costco employees generally don't even help carry purchases to their customers' vehicles.) Other businesses deliver products to their customers' doorsteps, so that expense is obviously much higher (and dependent on which delivery service the company uses — FedEx or UPS versus the U.S. Postal Service, for example).

Fixed expenses

Fixed operating expenses include many costs that a business is obligated to pay and cannot decrease over the short run without major surgery on the human resources and physical facilities of the business.

As an example of fixed expenses, consider the typical self-service car wash business — you know, the kind where you drive in, put some coins in a box, and use the water spray to clean your car. Most of the operating costs of this business are fixed; rent on the land, depreciation of the structure and the equipment, and the annual insurance premium don't depend on the number of cars passing through the car wash. The main variable expenses are the water and the soap and perhaps the cost of electricity.

Fixed expenses are the costs of doing business that, for all practical purposes, are stuck at a certain amount over the short term. Fixed expenses do not react to changes in the sales level. Here are some more examples of fixed operating expenses:

>> Gas and electricity costs to heat, cool, and light the premises (although these will be influenced by seasonality factors)

>> Facility rent expense or lease payments made on equipment

>> Employees' salaries and benefits

>> Dues, subscriptions, and software licenses

>> Property taxes for any owned real estate or tangible personal property

>> Depreciation expense (which, of course, as previously explained is not a cash expense but is fixed in nature)

>> Annual audit fee (if the business has its financial reports audited)

>> General liability, E&O (errors and omissions), employment practices, and officers' and directors' insurance premiums

WARNING

If you want to decrease fixed expenses significantly, you need to downsize the business (lay off workers, sell off property, and so on). When looking at the various ways for improving profit, significantly cutting down on fixed expenses is generally the last-resort option. Refer to the later section "Know your options for improving profit." A business should be careful not to overreact to a temporary downturn in sales by making drastic reductions in its fixed costs, which it may regret later if sales pick up again.

Stopping at operating earnings

In Figure 15-1, the profit template terminates at the *operating earnings* line; the template doesn't include interest expense, income tax expense, other miscellaneous income, or other expenses. Interest expense and income tax expense are business-wide types of expenses, which are the responsibility of the financial executive(s) of the business. Generally, interest and income tax expenses aren't assigned to profit centers unless a profit center is a rather large and autonomous organizational division of the business that has responsibility for its own assets, finances, and income tax. Other miscellaneous income and expenses are often driven at the company-wide level and tend to be excluded for the operating earnings line of a specific P&L center.

REMEMBER

The measure of profit before interest and income tax is commonly called *operating earnings* or *operating profit*. It also goes by the name *earnings before interest and tax*, or EBIT. It is not and should not be called *net income*, because this term is reserved for the final bottom-line profit number of a business, after all expenses (including interest and income tax) are deducted from sales revenue.

Focusing on margin — the catalyst of profit

Figure 15-1 includes a very important line of information: operating margin (sometimes referred to as *contribution margin*). *Operating margin* is operating profit before fixed expenses are deducted. Don't confuse this number with *gross margin*, which is profit after the cost of goods sold expense is subtracted from sales revenue but before any other expenses are deducted.

DIFFERENT USES OF THE TERM *MARGIN*

Gross profit, also called *gross margin,* equals sales revenue minus the cost of goods sold expense. Gross profit doesn't reflect other variable operating expenses that are deducted from sales revenue. In contrast, the term *operating margin* refers to sales revenue less *all* variable expenses. Some people use the term *contribution margin* instead of just *margin* to stress that margin contributes toward the recovery of fixed expenses (and to profit after fixed expenses are covered); however, the word *contribution* isn't necessary.

As a general rule, businesses that sell products report gross profit in their external income statements (although some don't). However, they don't disclose their variable and fixed operating expenses. They report expenses according to an object of expenditure basis, such as "selling, general, and administrative expenses." The broad expense categories reported in external income statements include both variable and fixed cost components. Therefore, the operating margin of a business (sales revenue after all variable expenses but before fixed expenses) isn't reported in its external income statement. Managers carefully guard information about margins. They don't want competitors to know the margins of their business.

Further complicating the issue, unfortunately, is that journalists frequently use the term *margin* when referring to operating earnings. Inside the world of accounting, however, *margin* means profit after all variable expenses are deducted from sales revenue but before fixed expenses are deducted. So be careful when you see the term *margin:* It may refer to gross margin, to what accountants mean by *margin,* or to operating earnings (used in the press).

TIP

As a manager, your attention should be riveted on margin, and you should understand the reasons for changes in this key profit driver from period to period. A small change in unit margin can have a big impact on operating earnings. (See the later section "Don't underestimate the impact of small changes in sales price.")

Using the template to explain profit

Suppose you're the CEO of the business whose profit template is shown in Figure 15-1. You should know how your business made its profit — beyond the obvious explanation that sales revenue is more than expenses. Your explanation should be expressed in terms of the dynamics of the business. As the CEO, you should be able to articulate the company's business model. In like manner, you should have at your fingertips an analytical model that explains how the company's profit factors blend together to yield profit.

So how did the business make profit? To be frank, there's no one universal way to answer the profit question. GAAP (generally accepted accounting principles) are no help here. Ask ten accountants, and we're sure you'll get ten different answers.

Our answer to the profit question pivots on the company's *breakeven point*. In Figure 15-1, notice that the company's fixed operating expenses (excluding depreciation) were $15.752 million for the year. Also, notice that the company's operating margin was approximately 35.2 percent of sales revenue. In other words, variable expenses required 64.8 percent of sales revenue; only 35.2 percent was "left over" after deducting variable costs.

In Figure 15-1, depreciation expense is presented on the line below EBITDA. The amount of depreciation is a fixed expense for the year. To calculate the breakeven point, the total of all fixed costs is needed. Therefore, fixed operating expenses above the EBITDA line and depreciation expense below the line are added to get total fixed expenses for the year. With this information, the company's breakeven point is calculated as follows (refer to Figure 15-1 for data; all numbers are in thousands):

$15.752 million fixed operating expenses + $1.739 million fixed depreciation and amortization expense = $17.491 million total fixed expenses (excluding interest expense)

$17.491 million total fixed expenses ÷ 35.2% margin on sales revenue = $49.690 million sales revenue breakeven point

The company's sales revenue was $21.374 million higher than its breakeven point for the year, which is good news, of course. Even more important, in just one more step you can determine operating profit for the year:

$21.374 million excess sales revenue over breakeven × 35.2% margin ratio = approximately $7.495 million EBIT for year (slight rounding difference)

After the breakeven sales level is achieved, each additional dollar of sales revenue yields 35.2 cents of "pure" profit because fixed expenses have been covered by the first $49.690 million of sales revenue. As soon as the company hurdles its breakeven point, it's in its profit zone.

An irksome detail: The preceding breakeven point calculation includes depreciation expense as a fixed expense for the period. The accountant records a fixed amount of depreciation expense for the period, so depreciation is logically included as a fixed expense. On the other hand, whether to include interest expense as a fixed expense is an open question. Most breakeven calculations exclude it; only *operating* fixed expenses are included. Interest is a financial cost that depends on how much debt capital the business uses. In short, breakeven analysis is usually based on the EBIT measure of profit — but not always.

TIP

Beyond explaining how the business made its profit for the year, the profit template is especially useful in asking what-if questions for exploring the profit impacts of changes in sales prices, sales volume, product costs, and operating costs. See the later section "Using the Profit Template for Decision-Making Analysis."

Taking a Closer Look at the Lines in the Profit Template

Profit center managers depend heavily on the information in their P&L reports. Managers need to thoroughly understand these profit reports, so we want to spend some time going through each element of the profit template. Go back to Figure 15-1 as needed.

Sales revenue

Sales revenue is the net amount of money earned by the business from the sales of products, software, and services during the period. Notice the word *net* here. The business in our example, like most, offers its customers many incentives to buy its products and to pay quickly for their purchases. The sales revenue amount takes into account deductions for rebates, allowances, sales promotions, prompt payment discounts, and any other incentives offered to customers that reduce the amount of revenue received by the business. (The manager can ask that these revenue offsets be included in the supplementary layer of schedules to the main page of the P&L report.)

As we're sure you know, the amount of sales revenue equals the number of units sold times the final, net sales prices. The number of units sold is called the *sales volume*. Sales volume should include only units that actually brought in revenue to the business. In general, businesses do a good job of keeping track of the sales volumes of their products (and services). These are closely monitored figures in, for example, the automobile and personal computer industries.

But here's a nagging problem: Some businesses sell a huge variety of products. No single product or product line brings in more than a small fraction of the total sales revenue. For instance, McGuckin Hardware, a popular hardware store in Boulder, Colorado, carries more than 100,000 products according to its advertising. The business may keep count of customer traffic or the number of individual sales made over the year, but it probably doesn't track the quantities sold for each and every product it sells.

Cost of goods sold

Cost of goods sold is the cost of the products and services during the period. This expense should be net of discounts, rebates, and allowances the business receives from its vendors and suppliers. The cost of goods sold means different things for different types of businesses:

» To determine product costs, manufacturers add together three costs:

- The costs of raw materials

- Labor and direct burden costs

- Production overhead costs

Accounting for the cost of manufactured products is a major function of *cost accounting,* which we discuss in Chapter 16.

» For retailers and distributors, product cost basically is purchase cost. However, refer to Chapter 9, where we explain the differences between the FIFO and LIFO methods for releasing inventory costs to the cost of goods sold expense. The profit center manager should have no doubts about which cost of goods sold expense accounting method is being used. For that matter, the manager should be aware of any other costs that are included in total product cost (such as inbound freight and handling costs in some cases).

DEALING WITH INVENTORY SHRINKAGE

One common problem is how to report to managers the loss from *inventory shrinkage*, which refers to losses from shoplifting by customers, physical deterioration of products as they sit in inventory, employee theft of products, damage caused in the handling and storage of products, and so on. The amount of inventory shrinkage can be included in the cost of goods sold expense, or it may be included in volume-driven operating expenses. A manager definitely should know which other costs have been placed in the cost of goods sold expense, in addition to the product cost of units sold during the period.

Variable operating expenses

In the profit analysis template (see Figure 15–1), variable operating expenses are divided into two types:

>> *Revenue-driven expenses* depend on the dollar amount of sales revenue. This group of variable operating expenses includes commissions paid to salespersons based on the dollar amount of their sales, credit and debit card fees paid by retailers, franchise fees based on sales revenue, and any other cost that depends directly on the amount of sales revenue. In Figure 15-1, the company's revenue-driven variable expenses are 15.0 percent of sales revenue. If sales revenue increases $1 million, these expenses would increase $150,000.

>> *Volume-driven expenses* are driven by and depend primarily on the number of units sold or the total quantity of products sold during the period (as opposed to the dollar value of the sales). These expenses include delivery and transportation costs paid by the business, packaging costs, and any costs that depend primarily on the size and weight of the products sold. If sales volume increases 5 percent, these expenses would increase 5 percent.

Most businesses have both types of variable operating expenses. However, one or the other may be so minor that reporting it as a separate item wouldn't be useful. Only the dominant type of variable operating expense would be presented in the profit analysis template; the one expense would absorb the other type — which is good enough for government work, as they say.

Fixed operating expenses

REMEMBER

Managers may view fixed operating expenses as an albatross around the neck of the business. But in fact, these costs provide the infrastructure and support for making sales. The main characteristic of fixed operating costs is that they do not decline when sales during the period fall short of expectations. A business commits to many fixed operating costs for the coming period. For all practical purposes, these costs can't be decreased much over the short run. Examples of fixed costs are wages and burden of employees on fixed salaries (from managers to company executives), property taxes, depreciation, certain forms of insurance, rent on the buildings and equipment used in making sales, utility bills, professional fees for accountants and lawyers, and so on.

Certain fixed costs can be matched with a particular profit center. For example, a business may advertise a specific product, and the fixed cost of the advertisement can be matched against revenue from sales of that product. A major product line may have its own employees on fixed salaries or its own delivery trucks on which depreciation is recorded. A business may purchase specific liability insurance covering a particular product it sells.

In contrast, you can't directly couple company-wide fixed operating expenses to particular products, product lines, or other types of profit units in the organizational structure of a business. General administrative expenses (such as the CEO's annual salary and corporate legal expenses) are incurred on an entity-as-a-whole basis and can't be connected directly with any particular profit center. A business may therefore allocate these fixed costs among its different profit centers. In our profit template example (see Figure 15-1), the entire business is treated as one profit center, so the allocation of total fixed operating expenses is not an issue.

DEALING WITH A SHORTCOMING

The profit template in Figure 15-1 hinges on the separation of variable and fixed operating costs. The classification between variable and fixed operating expenses isn't needed for external financial statements and income tax returns. Operating expenses are reported on the object of expenditure basis in external financial reports and tax returns, so the accounting systems of many businesses don't tag operating expense accounts as fixed or variable. As a result, variable versus fixed information for operating expenses isn't readily available from the accounting system. What's a manager to do?

Well, here's a practical solution: As the profit center manager, you can tell your accountant whether an operating expense is variable or fixed. Give your classification of the operating expenses in your profit center to the accountant, and stress that you want this classification in the profit template for your profit center. This may be extra work for your accountant, but the variable versus fixed classification of operating expense is of great value for your management decision-making, control, and planning.

Using the Profit Template for Decision-Making Analysis

The profit template (see Figure 15-1) is useful for decision-making analysis. To demonstrate, suppose that you're under intense competitive pressure to lower the sales price of one product you sell. This product is one "slice" of the total activity reported in Figure 15-1. During the year, you sold 10,000 units of the product at $100 sales price, bringing in $1 million total sales revenue. (As you go along in this section, you may want to double-check our math.) The sales revenue from this product is a relatively significant part of your total sales revenue for the year. More importantly, how much margin does this product generate?

Suppose that the product's cost structure mimics the one shown in Figure 15-1 for the company as a whole. The product's cost of goods sold is 37.8 percent of sales revenue, its revenue-driven expenses equal 15 percent of sales revenue, and its volume-driven expenses equal 12 percent of sales revenue. Thus, the product's expenses equal 64.8 percent of sales revenue, and its margin equals 35.2 percent of sales revenue. (See Figure 15-1 again.) On a per-unit basis, the margin is

$100 sales price – $37.80 cost of goods sold expense – $15 revenue-driven expenses – $12 volume-driven expenses = $35.20 margin per unit

Therefore, total margin from sales of the product is

$35.20 margin per unit × 10,000 units sales volume = $352,000 margin

Now suppose your competitors are undercutting your sales price, so you're thinking of cutting the sales price 10 percent next year, or $10 per unit. You predict that the price reduction will boost sales volume 25 percent and increase your market share. Seems like a good idea — or does it? You should run some numbers before making a final decision, just to be sure. Let's plug the new numbers into the formulas and see what happens if the sales price is dropped $10 and the business sells 12,500 units (an increase of 25 percent):

$90 sales price – $37.8 cost of goods sold expense – $13.50 revenue-driven expenses – $12 volume-driven expenses = $26.70 margin per unit

Therefore, total margin from sales of the product would be

$26.70 margin per unit × 12,500 units sales volume = $333,750 margin

The revenue-driven operating expense would drop $1.50 per unit with the $10 sales price decrease. Therefore, the new margin per unit would be $26.70 per unit. That's a 24 percent drop in margin per unit. A 25 percent gain in sales volume cannot make up for the 24 percent plunge in margin per unit. You'd need a larger sales volume increase just to keep margin the same and even more sales to increase margin next year. You'd better think twice about dropping the sales price.

You may gain a larger market share, but your margin would drop from $352,000 to $333,750 on this product if you go ahead with the sales price cut. Is the larger market share worth this much sacrifice of margin? That's why you get paid the big bucks: to make decisions like this. As your controller, we can only help you do the analysis and calculate the impact on profit before you make a final decision.

REMEMBER

Another factor to consider is this: Fixed expenses (people, warehouse space, distribution channels, and so on) provide the *capacity* to make sales and carry on operations. A small increase in sales volume, such as selling 250 more units of the product in question, shouldn't push up the total fixed expenses of your profit center (unless you're already bursting at the seams). On the other hand, a major sales volume increase across the board would require additional capacity, and your fixed expenses would have to be increased.

This sales price reduction decision is just one example of the many decisions business managers have to deal with day in and day out. The profit analysis template is a useful — indeed, invaluable — analysis framework for many decisions facing business managers.

Tucking Away Some Valuable Lessons

The profit analysis template shown in Figure 15-1 offers managers several important lessons. As with most tools, the more you use it, the more you learn. In this section, we summarize some important lessons from the template.

Recognize the leverage effect caused by fixed operating expenses

Suppose sales volume had been 10 percent higher or lower in the year, holding other profit factors the same. Would profit have been correspondingly 10 percent higher or lower? The intuitive answer is yes, profit would have been 10 percent higher or lower. Wouldn't it? Not necessarily. *Margin* would have been 10 percent higher or lower because sales revenue would have been 10 percent higher or lower (assuming variable expenses remain at the same percent on sales revenue). A 10 percent change in margin in our example would be $2.499 million ($24.986 million margin from Figure 15-1 × 10 percent = $2.499 million change in margin, rounded). This is an awkward number, so let's round it off to an even $2.5 million. (Accountants actually round off some numbers.)

The $2.5 million change in margin would carry down to operating earnings *unless* fixed expenses would have been higher or lower at the different sales volume. The very nature of fixed expenses is that these costs do not change with relatively small changes in sales volume. In all likelihood, fixed expenses would have been pretty much the same at a 10 percent higher or lower sales level. Let's assume so.

Therefore, operating earnings would have been $2.5 million higher or lower. On the base profit of $7.495 million (see the operating earnings in Figure 15-1), the $2.5 million swing in margin equals a 33 percent shift in profit. Thus, a 10 percent swing in sales volume causes a 33 percent swing in profit. This wider swing in profit is called the *operating leverage* effect. The idea is that a business makes better use of its fixed expenses when sales go up; its fixed expenses don't increase with the sales volume increase. Of course, the downside is that fixed expenses don't decrease when sales volume drops.

Don't underestimate the impact of small changes in sales price

What might seem to be a relatively small change in sales price can have a big impact on margin and the bottom line. The savvy manager knows to pay close attention to margin, which is the primary driver of profit. As an earlier example shows, cutting the product's sales price 10 percent would have caused a 24 percent plunge in margin per unit on sales of the product.

Most businesses don't take the time or effort to classify their operating expenses into fixed versus variable. The result is that their managers don't know margin — that is, they don't have a measure of profit after all variable costs are deducted from sales revenue but before fixed costs are deducted. Margin is a very useful metric for managers, but if they don't get this information in their internal P&L reports, what can they do? Well, they can at least keep an eye on *gross margin*, which is sales revenue after cost of goods sold expense is deducted.

Using the same example as earlier, if the manager were to drop the sales price $10, or 10 percent (from $100 to $90), gross margin would also drop $10 (from $62.2 to $52.2 per unit). So the gross margin per unit would decrease 16 percent, which is much more than the 10 percent sales price decrease. The 16 percent drop in gross margin gives the manager some idea of how much sales volume would have to increase to offset the sales price decrease. In fact, sales volume would have to increase to 11,916 units, which would be a roughly 20 percent increase over the 10,000 units sales volume to begin with:

$622,000 present gross margin ÷ $52.2 gross margin per unit after sales price reduction = 11,916 units sales volume just to hold even

A 20 percent jump in sales volume may not be feasible, of course.

REMEMBER

The moral of the story is to protect margin per unit above all else. Every dollar of margin per unit that's lost — due to decreased sales prices, increased product cost, or increases in other variable costs — has a tremendously negative impact on profit. Conversely, if you can increase the margin per unit without hurting sales volume, you reap very large profit benefits.

Know your options for improving profit

TIP

Improving profit boils down to three critical factors, listed in order from the most effective to the least effective:

» Increasing margin per unit

» Increasing sales volume

» Reducing fixed expenses

Say you want to improve your operating earnings (EBIT) 10 percent next year. See Figure 15-1 again for the most recent year. So how are you going to increase profit 10 percent? Here are your basic options:

» Increase your operating margin 10 percent, from 35.2 percent of sales revenue to 38.72 percent. This would require some combination of improvements in sales prices, product costs, and variable expenses.

» Sell 10 percent additional units at the present margin per unit.

» Use a combination of these two strategies: Increase both the margin per unit and sales volume such that the combined effect is to improve total margin 10 percent.

» Reduce fixed expenses substantially, enough to provide all the needed increase in total margin.

The last alternative may not be very realistic. Reducing direct fixed expenses by a large amount would probably reduce the company's capacity to make sales and carry out its operations. Perhaps the managers could do a little belt-tightening in the fixed expenses area, but in all likelihood, they would have to turn to the other alternatives for increasing profit.

The second approach is obvious — you just need to set a sales goal of increasing the number of products sold by 10 percent. (How you motivate the already over-worked sales staff to accomplish that sales volume goal is up to the CEO.) But how do you go about the first approach, increasing the margin from 35.2 percent to 38.72 percent? As we've said before, answering this question is why managers get paid the big bucks.

IN THIS CHAPTER

» **Measuring costs: the second most important thing accountants do**

» **Recognizing the different needs for cost information**

» **Determining the right costs for different purposes**

» **Assembling the product cost of manufacturers**

» **Padding profit by producing too many products**

Chapter **16**

Accounting for Costs

You could argue that measuring costs is the second most important thing accountants do, right after measuring profit. In fact, you need to measure costs in order to measure profit. But really, can measuring a cost be very complicated? You just take numbers off a purchase invoice and call it a day, right? Not if your business manufactures the products you sell, that's for sure! In this chapter, we demonstrate that a cost, any cost, is not as obvious and clear-cut as you may think. Yet obviously, costs are extremely important to businesses and other organizations.

Consider an example close to home: Suppose you just returned from the grocery store with several items in the bag. What's the cost of the loaf of bread you bought? Should you include the sales tax? Should you include the cost of gas you used driving to the store? Should you include some amount of depreciation expense on your car? Suppose you returned some aluminum cans for recycling while you were at the grocery store, and you were paid a small amount for the cans. Should you subtract this amount against the total cost of your purchases? Or should you subtract the amount directly against the cost of only the sodas in aluminum cans that you bought? And is cost the *before-tax* cost? In other words, is your cost equal to the amount of income you had to earn before income tax so that you had enough after-tax income to buy the items? And what about the time you spent shopping?

Your time could have been used for other endeavors. We could raise many other such questions, but you get the point.

These questions about the cost of your groceries are interesting (well, to us at least). But you don't really have to come up with definite answers for such questions in managing your personal financial affairs. Individuals don't have to keep cost records of their personal expenditures, other than what's needed for their annual income tax returns. In contrast, businesses must carefully record all their costs correctly so profit can be determined each period and so managers have the information they need to make decisions and to make a profit.

Looking Down the Road to the Destination of Costs

All businesses that sell products must know their *product costs* — in other words, the costs of each and every item they sell. Companies that manufacture the products they sell — as opposed to distributors and retailers of products — have many problems in figuring out their product costs. Two examples of manufactured products are a new iPhone just rolling off the assembly line at Apple and a copy of our book *Accounting For Dummies*, 7th Edition, hot off the printing presses.

Most production (manufacturing) processes are fairly complex, so product cost accounting for manufacturers is fairly complex; every step in the production process has to be tracked carefully from start to finish. Many manufacturing costs cannot be directly matched with particular products; these are called *indirect costs*. To arrive at the *full cost* of each product manufactured, accountants devise methods for allocating indirect production costs to specific products. Surprisingly, accounting standards in the United States, called *generally accepted accounting principles* (GAAP), provide little authoritative guidance for measuring the manufacturing costs of products. Therefore, manufacturing businesses have more than a little leeway regarding how to determine their product costs. Even businesses in the same industry — Samsung versus Apple, for example — may use different product cost accounting methods.

Accountants determine many other costs, in addition to product costs:

>> The costs of departments, regional distribution centers, and virtually any identifiable organizational unit of the business

>> The cost of the retirement plan for the company's employees (with the help of actuaries)

>> The cost of marketing programs and advertising campaigns

>> The cost of restructuring the business or the cost of a major recall of products sold by the business, when necessary

A common refrain among accountants is "different costs for different purposes." True enough, but at its core, cost accounting serves two broad purposes: measuring profit and providing relevant information to managers for planning, control, and decision-making.

WARNING

In our experience, people are inclined to take cost numbers for granted, as if they were handed down on stone tablets. The phrase *actual cost* often gets tossed around without a clear definition or with only a vague understanding. An actual cost depends entirely on the particular methods used to measure the cost. We can assure you that these cost measurement methods have more in common with the scores from judges in an ice skating competition than the times clocked in a Formula One auto race. Many arbitrary choices are behind every cost number you see. There's no one-size-fits-all definition of *cost*, and there's no one correct and best-in-all-circumstances method of measuring cost.

The conundrum is that, in spite of the inherent ambiguity in determining costs, we need exact amounts for costs. Managers should understand the choices an accountant has to make in measuring costs. Some cost accounting methods result in conservative profit numbers; other methods boost profit, at least in the short run. Chapter 9 discusses the choices among different accounting methods that produce financial statements with a conservative or liberal hue.

This chapter covers cost concepts and cost measurement methods that apply to all businesses, as well as basic product cost accounting of manufacturers. We discuss how a manufacturer could be fooling around with its production output to manipulate product cost for the purpose of artificially boosting its profit figure. (Service businesses encounter their own problems in allocating their operating costs for assessing the profitability of their separate sales revenue sources.)

Are Costs Really That Important?

Without good cost information, a business operates in the dark. Cost data is needed for the following purposes:

>> **Setting sales prices:** The common method for setting sales prices (known as *cost-plus* or *markup on cost*) starts with cost and then adds a certain percentage. If you don't know exactly how much a product costs, you can't be as shrewd and competitive in your pricing as you need to be. Even if sales prices

are dictated by other forces and not set by managers, managers need to compare sales prices against product costs and other costs that should be matched against each sales revenue source.

» **Formulating a legal defense against charges of predatory pricing practices:** Many states have laws prohibiting businesses from selling below cost except in certain circumstances. And a business can be sued under federal law for charging artificially low prices intended to drive its competitors out of business. Be prepared to prove that your lower pricing is based on lower costs and not on some illegitimate purpose.

» **Measuring gross profit:** Investors and managers judge business performance by the bottom-line profit figure. This profit figure depends on the *gross profit* figure you get when you subtract your cost of goods sold expense from your sales revenue. Gross profit (also called *gross margin*) is the first profit line in the income statement (for examples, refer to Figure 6-1 as well as Figure 16-1 later in this chapter). If gross profit is wrong, bottom-line net income is wrong — no two ways about it. The cost of goods sold expense depends on having correct product costs (see the later section "Assembling the Product Cost of Manufacturers").

» **Valuing assets:** The balance sheet reports cost values for many (though not all) assets. To understand the balance sheet, you should understand the cost basis of its inventory and certain other assets. See Chapter 7 for more about assets and how asset values are reported in the balance sheet (also called the *statement of financial condition*).

» **Making optimal choices:** You often must choose one alternative over others in making business decisions. The best alternative depends heavily on cost factors, and you have to be careful to distinguish *relevant* costs from *irrelevant* costs, as we describe in the later section "Relevant versus irrelevant costs."

TIP

In most situations, the historic book value recorded for a fixed asset is an *irrelevant* cost. Say book value is $35,000 for a machine used in the manufacturing operations of the business. This is the amount of original cost that has not yet been charged to depreciation expense since it was acquired, and it may seem quite relevant. However, in deciding between keeping the old machine or replacing it with a newer, more efficient machine, the *disposable value* of the old machine is the relevant amount, not the undepreciated cost balance of the asset.

Suppose the old machine has an estimated $20,000 salvage value at this time; this is the relevant cost for the alternative of keeping it for use in the future — not the $35,000 book value that hasn't been depreciated yet. To keep using it, the business forgoes the $20,000 it could get by selling the asset, and this $20,000 is the relevant cost in this decision situation. Making decisions involves looking forward at the future cash flows of each alternative — not looking backward at historical-based cost values.

ACCOUNTING VERSUS ECONOMIC COSTS

Accountants focus mainly on *actual costs* (though they disagree regarding how exactly to measure these costs). Actual costs are rooted in the actual, or historical, transactions and operations of a business. Accountants also determine *projected costs* for businesses that prepare forecasts (see Chapter 17), and they develop *standard costs* that serve as yardsticks to compare with the actual costs of a business.

Other concepts of cost are found in economic theory. You encounter a variety of economic cost terms when reading *The Wall Street Journal* as well as in many business discussions and deliberations. Don't reveal your ignorance of the following cost terms:

- **Opportunity cost** is the amount of income (or other measurable benefit) given up when you follow a better course of action. For example, say that you quit your $50,000 job, invest $200,000 you saved up, and start a new business. You earn $80,000 profit in your new business for the year. Suppose also that you would have earned 5 percent on the $200,000 (a total of $10,000) if you'd kept the money in whatever investment you took it from. So you gave up a $50,000 salary and $10,000 in investment income with your course of action; your opportunity cost is $60,000. Subtract that figure from what your actual course of action netted you — $80,000 — and you end up with a "real" economic profit of $20,000. Your income is $20,000 better by starting your new business, according to economic theory.

- **Marginal cost** is the *incremental,* out-of-pocket outlay required for taking a particular course of action. Generally speaking, it's the same thing as a *variable* cost (see the later section "Fixed versus variable costs"). Marginal costs are important, but in actual practice, managers must recover fixed (committed) costs as well as marginal costs through sales revenue in order to remain in business. Marginal costs are most relevant for analyzing one-time ventures, which don't last over the long term.

- **Replacement cost** is the estimated amount it would take today to purchase an asset that the business already owns. The longer ago an asset was acquired, the more likely that its current replacement cost is higher than its original cost. Economists are of the opinion that current replacement costs are relevant in making rational economic decisions. For insuring assets against fire, theft, and natural catastrophes, the current replacement costs of the assets are clearly relevant. Other than for insurance, however, replacement costs are not on the front burners of decision-making — except in situations in which one alternative being seriously considered actually involves replacing assets.

- **Imputed cost** is an ideal, or hypothetical, cost number that is used as a benchmark against which actual costs are compared. Two examples are *standard costs* and the *cost of capital.* Standard costs are set in advance for the manufacture of products during the coming period, and then actual costs are compared against standard

(continued)

(continued)

costs to identify significant variances. The cost of capital is the weighted average of the interest rate on debt capital and a target rate of return that should be earned on equity capital. The *economic value added* (EVA) method compares a business's cost of capital against its actual return on capital, to determine whether the business did better or worse than the benchmark.

For the most part, these types of cost aren't reflected in financial reports. We've included them here to familiarize you with terms you're likely to see in the financial press and hear on financial talk shows. Business managers toss these terms around often.

Becoming More Familiar with Costs

This section explains important cost distinctions that managers should understand in making decisions and exercising control. Also, these cost distinctions help managers better appreciate the cost figures that accountants attach to products that are manufactured or purchased by the business.

Retailers (such as Walmart, Amazon, and Costco) purchase products in a condition ready for sale to their customers — although some products have to be removed from shipping containers, and a retailer does a little work making the products presentable for sale and putting the products on display. Manufacturers don't have it so easy; their product costs have to be "manufactured" in the sense that the accountants have to accumulate various production costs and compute the cost per unit for every product manufactured. We focus on the special cost concerns of manufacturers in the upcoming section "Assembling the Product Cost of Manufacturers."

REMEMBER

We cannot exaggerate the importance of correct product costs (for businesses that sell products, of course). The total cost of goods (products) sold is the first, and usually the largest, expense deducted from sales revenue in measuring profit. The bottom-line profit amount reported in a business's income statement depends heavily on whether its product costs have been measured properly during that period. Also, keep in mind that product cost is the value for the inventory asset reported in the balance sheet of a business. (For a balance sheet example, see Figure 7-2.)

Direct versus indirect costs

You might say that the starting point for any sort of cost analysis, and particularly for accounting for the product costs of manufacturers, is to clearly distinguish between *direct* and *indirect* costs. Direct costs are easy to match with a process or product, whereas indirect costs are more distant and have to be allocated to a process or product. Here are more details:

>> **Direct costs** can be clearly attributed to one product or product line, one source of sales revenue, one organizational unit of the business, or one specific operation in a process. An example of a direct cost in the book publishing industry is the cost of the paper that a book is printed on; this cost can be squarely attached to one particular step or operation in the book production process.

>> **Indirect costs** are far removed from and cannot be naturally attached to specific products, organizational units, or activities. A book publisher's telephone and internet bills are costs of doing business but can't be tied down to just one step in the editorial and production process. The salary of the purchasing officer who selects the paper for all the books is another example of a cost that is indirect to the production of particular books.

WARNING

Each business must determine methods of allocating indirect costs to different products, sources of sales revenue, revenue and cost centers, and other organizational units. Most allocation methods are far from perfect and, in the final analysis, end up being arbitrary to one degree or another. Business managers should always keep an eye on the allocation methods used for indirect costs and take the cost figures produced by these methods with a grain of salt. If we were called in as expert witnesses in a court trial involving costs, the first thing we'd do is critically analyze the allocation methods used by the business for its indirect costs. If we were on the side of the defendant, we'd do our best to defend the allocation methods. If we were on the side of the plaintiff, we'd do our best to discredit the allocation methods — there are always grounds for criticism.

Fixed versus variable costs

If your business sells 100 more units of a certain item, some of your costs increase accordingly, but others don't budge one bit. This distinction between variable and fixed costs is crucial:

>> **Variable costs:** Variable costs increase and decrease in proportion to changes in sales or production level. Variable costs generally remain the same per unit of product or per unit of activity. Manufacturing or selling additional units causes variable costs to increase in concert. Manufacturing or selling fewer units results in variable costs going down in concert.

>> **Fixed costs:** Fixed costs remain the same over a relatively broad range of sales volume or production output. Fixed costs are like a dead weight on the business. Its total fixed costs for the period are a hurdle it must overcome by

selling enough units at high enough margins per unit in order to avoid a loss and move into the profit zone. (Chapter 15 explains the *breakeven point,* which is the level of sales needed to generate enough margin to cover fixed costs for the period.)

REMEMBER

The distinction between variable and fixed costs is at the heart of understanding, analyzing, and forecasting profit, which we explain in Chapter 17.

Relevant versus irrelevant costs

Not every cost is important to every decision a manager needs to make — hence the distinction between relevant and irrelevant costs:

>> **Relevant costs** are costs that should be considered and included in your analysis when deciding on a future course of action. Relevant costs are *future* costs — costs that you would incur or bring upon yourself depending on which course of action you take. For example, say that you want to increase the number of books that your business produces next year in order to increase your sales revenue, but the cost of paper has just shot up. Should you take the cost of paper into consideration? Absolutely — that cost will affect your bottom-line profit and may negate any increase in sales volume that you experience (unless you increase the sales price). The cost of paper is a relevant cost.

>> **Irrelevant (or sunk) costs** are costs that should be disregarded when deciding on a future course of action; if brought into the analysis, these costs could cause you to make the wrong decision. An irrelevant cost is a vestige of the past — that money is gone. For this reason, irrelevant costs are also called *sunk costs.* For example, suppose that your supervisor tells you to expect a slew of new hires next week. All your staff members use computers now, but you have a bunch of typewriters gathering dust in the supply room. Should you consider the cost paid for those typewriters in your decision to buy computers for all the new hires? Absolutely not — that cost should have been written off and is no match for the cost you'd pay in productivity (and morale) for new employees who are forced to use typewriters.

TIP

Generally speaking, most variable costs are relevant because they depend on which alternative is selected. Fixed costs are irrelevant, assuming that the decision at hand doesn't involve doing anything that would change these stationary costs. However, a decision alternative being considered might involve a change in fixed costs, such as moving out of the present building used by the business, downsizing the number of employees on fixed salaries, spending less on advertising (generally a fixed cost), and so on. Any cost, fixed or variable, that would be different for a particular course of action being analyzed is relevant for that alternative.

Furthermore, keep in mind that fixed costs can provide a useful gauge of a business's *capacity* — how much building space it has, how many machine hours are available for use, how many hours of labor can be worked, and so on. Managers have to figure out the best way to utilize these capacities. For example, suppose your retail business pays an annual building rent of $200,000, which is a fixed cost (unless the rental contract with the landlord also has a rent escalation clause based on your sales revenue). The rent, which gives the business the legal right to occupy the building, provides 15,000 square feet of retail and storage space. You should figure out which sales mix of products will generate the highest total *margin* — equal to total sales revenue less total variable costs of making the sales, including the costs of the goods sold and all variable costs driven by sales revenue and sales volume.

Actual, projected, and standard costs

The actual costs a business incurs may differ (though we hope not too unfavorably) from its projected and standard costs:

>> **Actual costs:** Actual costs are based on actual transactions and operations during the period just ended, or going back to earlier periods. Financial statement accounting is mainly (though not entirely) based on a business's actual transactions and operations; the basic approach to determining annual profit is to record the financial effects of actual transactions and allocate the historical costs to the periods benefited by the costs. But keep in mind that accountants can use more than one method for recording actual costs. Your actual cost may be a little (or a lot) different from our actual cost.

>> **Projected costs:** These are future costs, for transactions and operations expected to take place over the coming period, based on forecasts and established goals. Fixed costs are projected differently from variable costs. For example, if sales volume is forecast to increase by 10 percent, variable costs will definitely increase accordingly, but fixed costs may or may not need to be increased to accommodate the volume increase. In Chapter 17, we explain the projection process and forecast financial statements.

>> **Standard costs:** Standard costs are costs, primarily in the area of manufacturing, that are carefully engineered based on a detailed analysis of operations and forecast costs for each component or step in an operation. Developing standard costs for variable production costs is relatively straightforward because most are direct costs. In contrast, most fixed costs are indirect, and standard costs for fixed costs are necessarily based on more arbitrary methods (see the earlier section "Direct versus indirect costs"). **Note:** Some variable costs are indirect and have to be allocated to specific products in order to come up with a full (total) standard cost of the product.

Product versus period costs

Some costs are linked to particular products, and others are not:

>> **Product costs** are attached directly or allocated to particular products. The cost is recorded in the inventory asset account and stays in that asset account until the product is sold, at which time the cost goes into the cost of goods sold expense account. (See Chapters 6 and 7 for more about these accounts; also, see Chapter 9 for alternative methods for selecting which product costs are first charged to the cost of goods sold expense.)

   For example, the cost of a new Ford Bronco sitting on a car dealer's showroom floor is a product cost. The dealer keeps the cost in the inventory asset account until you buy the car, at which point the dealer charges the cost to the cost of goods sold expense.

>> **Period costs** are *not* attached to particular products. These costs do not spend time in the "waiting room" of inventory. Period costs are recorded as expenses immediately; unlike product costs, period costs don't pass through the inventory account first. Advertising costs, for example, are accounted for as period costs and are recorded immediately in an expense account. Also, research and development costs are treated as period costs (with some exceptions).

Separating product costs and period costs is particularly important for manufacturing businesses, as we explain in the next section.

Assembling the Product Cost of Manufacturers

Businesses that manufacture products have several cost problems to deal with that retailers, service companies, and distributors don't have. We use the term *manufacture* in the broadest sense: Automobile makers assemble cars, beer companies brew beer, automobile gasoline companies refine oil, DuPont makes products through chemical synthesis, and so on. Retailers (also called *merchandisers*) and distributors, on the other hand, buy products in a condition ready for resale to the end consumer. For example, Levi Strauss manufactures clothing, and several retailers buy from Levi Strauss and sell the clothes to the public. This section describes costs unique to manufacturers.

Minding manufacturing costs

REMEMBER

Manufacturing costs consist of four basic types:

>> **Raw materials (also called *direct* materials)** are what a manufacturer buys from other companies to use in the production of its own products. For example, General Motors buys tires from Goodyear (or other tire manufacturers) that then become part of GM's cars.

>> **Direct labor and burden** consists of those employees who work on the production line, the wages they are paid, and the burden that is associated with the wages (for example, payroll taxes, workers' compensation insurance, benefits provided to the employees such as paid time off or vacation days, and other costs). As a reference point, it is not uncommon that for every $100 of wages paid to a production worker, another $30 of direct burden is incurred (for a direct burden ratio of 30 percent).

>> **Variable overhead** is indirect production costs that increase or decrease as the quantity produced increases or decreases. An example is the cost of electricity that runs the production equipment. Generally, you pay for the electricity for the whole plant, not machine by machine, so you can't attach this cost to one particular part of the process. When you increase or decrease the use of those machines, the electricity cost increases or decreases accordingly. (In contrast, the monthly utility bill for a company's office and sales space probably is fixed for all practical purposes.)

>> **Fixed overhead** is indirect production costs that do *not* increase or decrease as the quantity produced increases or decreases. These fixed costs remain the same over a fairly broad range of production output levels (see the earlier section "Fixed versus variable costs"). Here are three significant examples of fixed manufacturing costs:

- Salaries for certain production employees who don't work directly on the production line, such as vice presidents, safety inspectors, security guards, accountants, and shipping and receiving workers

- Depreciation of production buildings, equipment, and other manufacturing fixed assets

- Occupancy costs, such as building insurance, rent, property taxes, and heating and lighting charges

Figure 16-1 presents a gross profit report for a business that manufactures just one product. To clearly drive home the concepts in this chapter, our fictitious business is a stand-alone manufacturing company as opposed to our sample technology company that we've used in other chapters. For now, limit your attention to the left side of the report, which lists sales volume, sales revenue, cost of goods sold expense, the four types of manufacturing costs (just discussed), and how total manufacturing costs end up either in cost of goods sold expense or in the increase to inventory. Manufacturing costs are shown both on the total basis for the year and per unit. First, we explain the numbers under the column headed "Base Output Case."

XYZ Fictional Mfg. Company, Inc.
Product Sales & Cost Analysis
for the Fiscal Year Ending
12/31/2020

Gross Profit Report for Year	Base Output Case		Excessive Output Case	
Sales Volume	Units	110,000	Units	110,000
	Per Unit	Totals	Per Unit	Totals
Sales Revenue	$1,400	$154,000,000	$1,400	$154,000,000
Costs of Goods Sold Expense	($760)	($83,600,000)	($690)	($75,900,000)
Gross Profit (aka Gross Margin)	$640	$70,400,000	$710	$78,100,000
Manufacturing Costs Summary for Year				
Production Capacity	150,000		150,000	
Actual Output	120,000		150,000	
Production Cost Components	Per Unit	Totals	Per Unit	Totals
Raw Material	$215	$25,800,000	$215	$32,250,000
Direct Labor & Burden	$125	$15,000,000	$125	$18,750,000
Variable Manufacturing Overhead Costs	$70	$8,400,000	$70	$10,500,000
Total Variable Manufacturing Costs	$410	$49,200,000	$410	$61,500,000
Fixed Manufacturing Overhead Costs	$350	$42,000,000	$280	$42,000,000
Total Manufacturing Costs	$760	$91,200,000	$690	$103,500,000
To Inventory Increase		($7,600,000)		($27,600,000)
To Costs of Goods Sold Expense		$83,600,000		$75,900,000

Confidential — Property of XYZ Fictional Mfg. Company, Inc.

© John Wiley & Sons, Inc.

FIGURE 16-1: Manufacturing costs example.

The $760 product cost equals manufacturing costs *per unit*. A business may manufacture 100 or 1,000 different products, or even more, and it must compile a summary of manufacturing costs and production output and determine the product cost of every product. To keep the example easy to follow (but still realistic), Figure 16-1 presents a one-product manufacturer. The multiproduct manufacturer has additional accounting problems, but we can't provide that level of detail here. This example exposes the fundamental accounting problems and methods of all manufacturers.

Notice in particular that the company's cost of goods sold expense is based on the $760 product cost (or total manufacturing costs per unit). This product cost is determined from the company's manufacturing costs and production output for the period. Product cost includes both the variable costs of manufacture and a calculated amount based on total fixed manufacturing costs for the period divided by total production output for the period.

REMEMBER

The information in the manufacturing costs summary is highly confidential and for management eyes only. Competitors would love to know this information. A company may enjoy a significant cost advantage over its competitors and definitely does not want its cost data to get into their hands.

Classifying costs properly

Two vexing issues rear their ugly heads in determining product cost for a manufacturer:

>> **Drawing a bright line between manufacturing costs and nonmanufacturing operating costs:** The key difference here is that manufacturing costs are categorized as product costs, whereas nonmanufacturing operating costs are categorized as period costs (refer to the earlier section "Product versus period costs"). In calculating product costs, you include only manufacturing costs and not other costs. Remember that period costs are recorded right away as expenses. Here are some examples of each type of cost:

- Wages and associated direct payroll burden paid to production line workers are a clear-cut example of a manufacturing (that is, a product cost) component.

- Salaries paid to salespeople are a marketing cost and are not part of product cost; marketing costs are treated as period costs, which means they're recorded as an expense of the period.

- Depreciation on production equipment is a manufacturing cost, but depreciation on the warehouse in which products are stored after being manufactured is a period cost.

- Moving the raw materials and partially completed products through the production process is a manufacturing cost, but transporting the finished products from the warehouse to customers is a period cost.

The accumulation of direct and indirect production costs starts at the beginning of the manufacturing process and stops at the end of the production line. In other words, product cost stops at the end of the production line — every cost up to that point should be included as a manufacturing cost.

WARNING

If you misclassify some manufacturing costs as operating costs (nonmanufacturing expenses), your product cost calculation will be too low (see the following section, "Calculating product cost"). Also, the Internal Revenue Service may come knocking at your door if it suspects that you deliberately (or even innocently) misclassified manufacturing costs as nonmanufacturing costs in order to minimize your taxable income.

REMEMBER

>> **Allocating indirect costs among different products:** Indirect manufacturing costs must be allocated among the products produced during the period. The full product cost includes both direct and indirect manufacturing costs. Creating a completely satisfactory allocation method is difficult; the process ends up being somewhat arbitrary, but it must be done to determine product cost. Managers should understand how indirect manufacturing costs are allocated among products (and, for that matter, how indirect nonmanufacturing costs are allocated among organizational units). Managers should also keep in mind that every allocation method is arbitrary and that a different allocation method may be just as convincing.

ALLOCATING INDIRECT COSTS IS NOT AS SIMPLE AS ABC

Accountants for manufacturers have developed many methods for allocating indirect overhead costs, most of which are based on a common denominator of production activity, such as direct labor hours or machine hours. A different method has received lots of press: *activity-based costing* (ABC).

With the ABC method, you identify each supporting activity in the production process and collect costs into a separate pool for each identified activity. Then you develop a *measure* for each activity — for example, the measure for the engineering department may be hours, and the measure for the maintenance department may be square feet. You use the activity measures as *cost drivers* to allocate costs to products.

The idea is that the engineering department doesn't come cheap; when you include the cost of their slide rules and pocket protectors, as well as their salaries and benefits, the total cost per hour for those engineers could be $250 or more. The logic of the ABC cost-allocation method is that the engineering cost per hour should be allocated on the basis of the number of hours (the immediate cause, or driver of the cost) that each product requires. So if Product A needs 200 hours of the engineering department's time and Product B is a simple product that needs only 20 hours of engineering, you allocate ten times as much of the engineering cost to Product A. In similar fashion, suppose the cost of the maintenance department is $20 per square foot per year. If Product C uses twice as much floor space as Product D, it would be charged with twice as much maintenance cost.

The ABC method has received much praise for being better than traditional allocation methods, especially for management decision-making. But keep in mind that this method still requires rather arbitrary definitions of cost drivers, and having too many different cost drivers, each with its own pool of costs, is impractical.

Cost allocation always involves arbitrary methods. Managers should be aware of which methods are being used and should challenge a method if they think that it's misleading and should be replaced with a better (though still somewhat arbitrary) method. We don't mean to put too fine a point on this, but cost allocation essentially boils down to an "our arbitrary method is better than your arbitrary method" argument.

Calculating product cost

The basic calculation of product cost is as follows for the base output case in Figure 16-1:

> $91,200,000 total manufacturing costs ÷ 120,000 units production output = $760 product cost per unit

WARNING

Looks pretty straightforward, doesn't it? Well, the equation itself may be simple, but the accuracy of the results depends directly on the accuracy of your manufacturing cost numbers. The business example we're using in this chapter manufactures just one product. Even so, a single manufacturing process can be fairly complex, with hundreds or thousands of steps and operations. In the real world, where businesses produce multiple products, your accounting systems must be very complex and extraordinarily detailed to keep accurate track of all direct and indirect (allocated) manufacturing costs.

In our example, the business manufactured 120,000 units and sold 110,000 units during the year, which is reasonable and not atypical, and its product cost per unit is $760. The 110,000 total units sold during the year is multiplied by the $760 product cost to compute the $83.6 million cost of goods sold expense, which is deducted against the company's revenue from selling 110,000 units during the year. The company's total manufacturing costs for the year were $91.2 million, which is $7.6 million more than the cost of goods sold expense. The remainder of the total annual manufacturing costs is recorded as an increase in the company's inventory asset account, to recognize that 10,000 units manufactured this year are awaiting sale in the future. In Figure 16-1, note that the $760 product cost per unit is applied both to the 110,000 units sold and to the 10,000 units added to inventory.

Note: The product cost per unit for our example business is determined for the entire year. In actual practice, manufacturers calculate their product costs monthly or quarterly. The computation process is the same, but the frequency of doing the computation varies from business to business. Product costs likely will vary each successive period the costs are determined. Because the product costs vary from period to period, the business must choose which cost of goods sold and inventory cost method to use. (If product cost happened to remain absolutely flat and constant period to period, the different methods would yield the same results.) Chapter 9 explains the alternative accounting methods for determining cost of goods sold expense and inventory cost value.

Examining fixed manufacturing costs and production capacity

Product cost consists of two distinct components: variable manufacturing costs and fixed manufacturing costs. In Figure 16-1, note that the company's variable manufacturing costs are $410 per unit and its fixed manufacturing costs are $350 per unit in the base output case. Now, what if the business had manufactured ten more units? Its total variable manufacturing costs would have been $4,100 higher. The actual number of units produced drives variable costs, so even one more unit would have caused the variable costs to increase. But the company's total fixed costs would have been the same if it had produced ten more units — or 10,000 more units, for that matter. Variable manufacturing costs are bought on a per-unit basis, as it were, whereas fixed manufacturing costs are bought in bulk for the whole period.

TIP

Fixed manufacturing costs are needed to provide *production capacity* — the people and physical resources needed to manufacture products — for the period. After the business has the production plant and people in place for the year, its fixed manufacturing costs cannot be easily scaled down. The business is stuck with these costs over the short run. It has to make the best use it can from its production capacity.

REMEMBER

Production capacity is a critical concept for business managers to stay focused on. You need to plan your production capacity well ahead of time because you need plenty of lead time to assemble the right people, equipment, land, and buildings. When you have the necessary production capacity in place, you want to make sure that you're making optimal use of that capacity. The fixed costs of production capacity remain the same even as production output increases or decreases, so you may as well make optimal use of the capacity provided by those fixed costs. For example, you're recording the same depreciation amount on your machinery regardless of how you actually use those machines, so you should be sure to optimize the use of those machines (within limits, of course — overworking the machines to the point where they break down won't do you much good).

The burden rate

The fixed-cost component of product cost is called the *burden rate*. (This is not to be confused with the direct payroll burden we previously discussed.) In our manufacturing example, the burden rate is computed as follows for the base output case (see Figure 16-1 for the data):

> $42,000,000 fixed manufacturing costs for period ÷ 120,000 units production output for period = $350 burden rate

Note that the burden rate depends on the number divided into the total fixed manufacturing costs for the period — that is, it depends on the production output for the period.

Now, here's an important twist on our example: Suppose the company had manufactured only 110,000 units during the period — equal exactly to the quantity sold during the year. Its variable manufacturing cost per unit would have been the same, or $410 per unit. But its burden rate would have been $381.82 per unit (computed by dividing the $42 million total fixed manufacturing costs by the 110,000 units production output). Each unit sold, therefore, would have cost $31.82 more than in the Figure 16-1 example simply because the company produced fewer units. The company would have fewer units of output over which to spread its fixed manufacturing costs. The burden rate is $381.82 at the 110,000 output level but only $350 at the 120,000 output level, or $31.82 lower.

If only 110,000 units were produced, the company's product cost would have been $791.82 ($410 variable costs plus the $381.82 burden rate). The company's cost of goods sold, therefore, would have been $3.5 million higher for the year ($31.82 higher product cost × 110,000 units sold). This rather significant increase in its cost of goods sold expense is caused by the company's producing fewer units, even though it produced all the units that it needed for sales during the year. The same total amount of fixed manufacturing costs is spread over fewer units of production output.

Idle capacity

The production capacity of the business example in Figure 16-1 is 150,000 units for the year. However, this business produced only 120,000 units during the year, which is 30,000 units fewer than it could have. In other words, it operated at 80 percent of production capacity, which results in 20 percent *idle capacity*:

> 120,000 units output ÷ 150,000 units capacity = 80% utilization, or 20% idle capacity

This rate of idle capacity isn't unusual — the average U.S. manufacturing plant normally operates at 80 to 85 percent of its production capacity.

The effects of increasing inventory

Look back at the numbers shown in Figure 16-1 for the base output case: The company's cost of goods sold benefited from the fact that the company produced 10,000 more units than it sold during the year. These 10,000 units absorbed $3.5 million of its total fixed manufacturing costs for the year, and until the units are sold, this $3.5 million stays in the inventory asset account (along with the variable manufacturing costs, of course). It's entirely possible that the higher production level was justified — to have more units on hand for sales growth next year. But production output can get out of hand, as we discuss in the next section, "Puffing Profit by Excessive Production."

Managers (and investors as well) should understand the inventory increase effects caused by manufacturing more units than are sold during the year. In the example shown in Figure 16-1, the cost of goods sold expense escaped $3.5 million of fixed manufacturing costs because the company produced 10,000 more units than it sold during the year, thus pushing down the burden rate. The company's cost of goods sold expense would have been $3.5 million higher if it had produced just the number of units it sold during the year. The lower output level would have increased cost of goods sold expense and would have caused a $3.5 million drop in gross profit.

THE ACTUAL COSTS/ACTUAL OUTPUT METHOD — AND WHEN NOT TO USE IT

The product cost calculation for the business example shown in Figure 16-1 is based on the *actual cost/actual output method,* in which you take your actual costs — which may have been higher or lower than the projected costs for the year — and divide by the actual output for the year.

The actual costs/actual output method is appropriate in most situations. However, this method is not appropriate and would have to be modified in two extreme situations:

- **Manufacturing costs are grossly excessive or wasteful due to inefficient production operations:** For example, suppose that the business represented in Figure 16-1 had to throw away $1.2 million of raw materials during the year. The $1.2 million should be removed from the calculation of the raw material cost per unit. Instead, you treat it as a period cost — meaning that you record it immediately into expense. Then the cost of goods sold expense would be based on $750 per unit instead of $760, which lowers this expense by $1.1 million (based on the 110,000 units sold). But you still have to record the $1.2 million expense for wasted raw materials, so EBIT would be $100,000 lower.

- **Production output is significantly less than normal capacity utilization:** Suppose that the Figure 16-1 business produced only 75,000 units during the year but still sold 110,000 units because it was working off a large inventory carryover from the year before. Then its production output would be 50 percent instead of 80 percent of capacity. In a sense, the business wasted half of its production capacity, and you can argue that half of its fixed manufacturing costs should be charged directly to expense on the income statement and not included in the calculation of product cost.

Puffing Profit by Excessive Production

WARNING

Whenever production output is higher than sales volume, be on guard. Excessive production can puff up the profit figure. How? Until a product is sold, the product cost goes in the inventory asset account rather than in the cost of goods sold expense account, meaning that the product cost is counted as a *positive* number (an asset) rather than a *negative* number (an expense). Fixed manufacturing overhead cost is included in product cost, which means that this cost component goes into inventory and is held there until the products are sold later. In short, when you overproduce, more of your total of fixed manufacturing costs for the period is moved to the inventory asset account and less is moved into cost of goods sold expense for the year.

You need to judge whether an inventory increase is justified. Be aware that an unjustified increase may be evidence of profit manipulation or just good old-fashioned management bungling. Either way, the day of reckoning will come when the products are sold and the cost of inventory becomes cost of goods sold expense or the excess inventory becomes obsolete and can't be sold.

Shifting fixed manufacturing costs to the future

The business represented in Figure 16-1 manufactured 10,000 more units than it sold during the year — see the base output case in the left columns. This isn't unusual. In many situations, a manufacturer produces more units than are sold in the period. It's hard to match production output exactly to sales for the period — unless the business produces the exact number of units ordered by its customers. Anyway, the situation in Figure 16-1 in the base output case isn't unusual and wouldn't raise any eyebrows (well, unless the company already had a large inventory of products at the start of the year and didn't need any more).

With variable manufacturing costs at $410 per unit, the business expended $4.1 million more in variable manufacturing costs than it would have if it had produced only the 110,000 units needed for its sales volume. In other words, if the business had produced 10,000 fewer units, its variable manufacturing costs would have been $4.1 million less — that's the nature of variable costs. In contrast, if the company had manufactured 10,000 fewer units, its *fixed* manufacturing costs wouldn't have been any less — that's the nature of fixed costs.

Of its $42 million total fixed manufacturing costs for the year, only $38.5 million ended up in the cost of goods sold expense for the year ($350 burden rate × 110,000 units sold). The other $3.5 million ended up in the inventory asset account ($350 burden rate × 10,000 units inventory increase). The $3.5 million of fixed manufacturing costs that are absorbed by inventory is shifted to the future. This amount won't be expensed (charged to cost of goods sold expense) until the products are sold sometime in the future.

Shifting part of the fixed manufacturing cost for the year to the future may seem to be accounting sleight of hand. It has been argued that the entire amount of fixed manufacturing costs should be expensed in the year that these costs are recorded. (Only variable manufacturing costs would be included in product cost for units going into the increase in inventory.) Established accounting standards require that *full* product cost (variable plus fixed manufacturing costs) be used for recording an increase in inventory. This is referred to as *absorption accounting* because fixed manufacturing costs are absorbed, or included in product cost.

In the example shown under the base output case in Figure 16-1, the 10,000-unit increase of inventory includes $3,500,000 of the company's total fixed manufacturing costs for the year:

> $350 burden rate × 10,000 units inventory increase = $3,500,000 fixed manufacturing costs included in inventory increase

Are you comfortable with this effect? The $3,500,000 escapes being charged to cost of goods expense for the time being. It sits in inventory until the products are sold in a later period. This results from using the full cost (absorption) accounting method for fixed manufacturing overhead costs. Now, it may occur to you that an unscrupulous manager could take advantage of this effect to manipulate gross profit for the period.

Let us be very clear here: We're not suggesting any hanky-panky in the example shown in Figure 16-1. Producing 10,000 more units than sales volume during the year looks — on the face of it — to be reasonable and not out of the ordinary. Yet at the same time, it's naïve to ignore that the business did help its pretax profit to the amount of $3.5 million by producing 10,000 more units than it sold. If the business had produced only 110,000 units, equal to its sales volume for the year, all its fixed manufacturing costs for the year would have gone into cost of goods sold expense. The expense would have been $3.5 million higher, and operating earnings would have been that much lower.

Cranking up production output

Now let's consider a more suspicious example. Suppose that the business manufactured 150,000 units during the year and increased its inventory by 40,000 units. It may be a legitimate move if the business is anticipating a big jump in sales next year. On the other hand, an inventory increase of 40,000 units in a year in which only 110,000 units were sold may be the result of a serious overproduction mistake, and the larger inventory may not be needed next year.

Figure 16-1 also shows what happens to production costs and — more importantly — what happens to the profit at the higher production output level. See the columns under the *excessive output case* in Figure 16-1. The additional 30,000 units (over and above the 120,000 units manufactured by the business in the base output case) cost $410 per unit of variable manufacturing costs. (The precise cost may be a little higher than $410 per unit because as you start crowding production capacity, some variable costs per unit may increase a little.) The business would need $12.3 million more for the additional 30,000 units of production output:

$410 variable manufacturing cost per unit × 30,000 additional units produced = $12,300,000 additional variable manufacturing costs invested in inventory

Again, the company's fixed manufacturing costs would not have increased, given the nature of fixed costs. Fixed costs stay put until capacity is hit. Sales volume, in this scenario, also remains the same.

But check out the business's gross profit: $78.1 million, compared with $70.4 million in the base output case — a $7.7 million higher amount, even though sales volume and sales prices remain the same. Whoa! What's going on here? How can cost of goods sold expense be less? The business sells 110,000 units in both scenarios. And variable manufacturing costs are $410 per unit in both cases.

The culprit is the burden-rate component of product cost. In the base output case, total fixed manufacturing costs are spread over 120,000 units of output, giving a $350 burden rate per unit. In the excessive output case, total fixed manufacturing costs are spread over 150,000 units of output, giving a much lower $280 burden rate, or $70 per unit less. The $70 lower burden rate multiplied by the 110,000 units sold results in a $7.7 million lower cost of goods sold expense for the period, a higher pretax profit of the same amount, and a much improved bottom-line net income.

Being careful when production output is out of kilter with sales volume

WARNING

In the highly suspect example shown in the excessive output case, the business produced 150,000 units (full capacity). As a result, its inventory asset includes an additional $7.7 million of the company's fixed manufacturing costs for the year as compared with the base output case (see Figure 16-1 again). Its cost of goods sold expense for the year escaped this cost (for the time being). But get this: Its inventory increased 40,000 units, which is quite a large increase compared with the annual sales of 110,000 during the year just ended. Who was responsible for the decision to go full blast and produce up to production capacity? Do the managers really expect sales to jump up enough next year to justify the much larger inventory level? If they prove to be right, they'll look brilliant. But if the output level was a mistake and sales don't go up next year . . . they'll have you-know-what to pay next year, even though profit looks good this year. An experienced business manager knows to be on guard when inventory takes such a big jump.

REMEMBER

Summing up, the cost of goods sold expense of a manufacturer, and thus its operating profit, is sensitive to a difference between its sales volume and production output during the year. Manufacturing businesses don't generally discuss or explain in their external financial reports to creditors and owners why production output differs from sales volume for the year. Financial report readers are pretty much on their own in interpreting the reasons for and the effects of underproducing or overproducing products relative to actual sales volume for the year. All we can tell you is to keep alert and keep in mind the profit impact caused by a major disparity between a manufacturer's production output and sale levels for the year. Managers should understand this point very well. Hopefully, they wouldn't use this tactic to artificially boost profit for the period.

Chapter **17**

Preparing Best-in-Class Forecasts, Projections, and Budgets

et's start this chapter by making an extremely important statement: In today's rapidly changing and evolving economy, all businesses, no matter the size, shape, legal structure, or industry of operation, need to develop business plans. Period! While this statement may appear to be very logical and represent common sense, you would be absolutely amazed at how often businesses simply operate by "the seat of their pants" without a well-developed and structured business plan.

The planning process for most businesses is very broad and includes numerous elements ranging from assessing current market conditions to understanding the macroeconomic environment to evaluating personnel resources to preparing budgets, forecasts, and/or projections. This chapter focuses on one of the most critical elements of the planning process — preparing a financial forecast.

REMEMBER

For the balance of this chapter, the term *forecasts* will be used for consistency purposes, but it should be noted that businesses often utilize other terms including *budgets* or *budgeting*, *projections*, and *proformas* (which basically all mean the same thing). We prefer to use the term *forecasts* because it is broader in scope and helps drive home the all-important concept that business financial forecasting needs to be complete, accurate, reliable, and timely.

Focusing on Key Forecasting Concepts

REMEMBER

Before we delve too deeply into the forecasting process, we want to call out four key concepts to keep in mind:

>> Forecasts *are not* based on the concept of "How much can we spend in our division this year?" Rather, forecasts are more comprehensive in nature and are designed to capture all relevant and critical financial data, including revenue levels, costs of sales, operating expenses, employment requirements, fixed asset expenditures, capital requirements, and the like. All too often, forecasts are associated with expense levels and management, which represent just one element of the entire forecasts.

>> The forecasting process does not represent a chicken-and-egg riddle. From a financial perspective, the preparation of forecasts represents the end result of the entire planning process. Hence, you must first accumulate the necessary data and information on which to build a forecasting model prior to producing projected financial information (for an entire company or a specific division). There is no point in preparing a forecast that does not capture the real economic structure and viability of an entire entity or operating division.

>> Old-school businesses still often rely on the strategy of undertaking budgeting, once a year, to prepare a budget for upcoming fiscal year-end (FYE). For example, a company may be planning for the FYE 12/31/22, including preparing a budget in the fourth quarter of the FYE 12/31/21 to be a road map for the next year. Thirty years ago, this strategy worked well as preparing an annual budget (really an old-school term), and then maybe revising it mid-year (if needed) was sufficient. But we're going to be brutally honest: In today's rapid-paced global tech-driven economy, businesses must develop planning and forecasting systems that can be easily modified, updated, and adapted to market conditions that can seemingly change overnight. As you see in this chapter, we introduce you to concepts and tools to help achieve this objective.

>> We also want to drive home the importance of preparing complete financial information within the financial forecasts. Too often, companies prepare financial forecasts focused on just the income statement and downplay the importance of the balance sheet and statement of cash flows (which may be put on the back burner). The importance of preparing complete financial forecasts is on full display in this chapter, because we include forecasts for both the balance sheet and statement of cash flows. (Flip to Part 2 for details on these statements.)

The bottom line with forecasting (and the entire planning process) is that, without having clearly identified business financial and performance objectives, the business is operating blind. Put simply, it is like flying a plane without having a destination. The need for having clearly identified benchmarks and a road map to reach the benchmarks is essential for every business, regardless of size, shape, or form. Often, the most important question comes down to this: "How are we doing against the plan?"

REMEMBER

Looking at it from a different perspective, a business can't open its doors each day without having a pretty good idea of what to expect. And it can't close its doors at the end of the day not knowing what happened. Recall the Boy Scouts' motto: "Be prepared." A business should follow that dictum: It should plan and be prepared for its future, and it should control its actual performance to reach its financial goals.

Of course, business managers do have the option of waiting for operating results to be reported to them on a "look back" basis and then wing it from there (which is something we strongly advise against). Or they can look ahead and carefully plan for sales revenue, expenses, cash flows, and financial condition to chart the course of the business into the future. Forecasting is a tool of financial planning and control. The business entity's accounting and financial team pull the company's planning details all together and prepare financial forecasts including the financial statements, against which actual performance is compared.

Putting Forecasting in Its Place

Getting into the topic of forecasting puts us in the larger field of management — in particular, management planning and control. This is not a book on management. Goodness knows, enough books on management theory and practices have already been published. In this section, we simply offer a few words regarding how forecasting fits into the broader field of management.

Planning reasons for forecasting

REMEMBER

In previous editions of this book, we made the following statement: "Budgeting is optional for most businesses; the business is not required to do any budgeting." Although this is true, our view has definitely changed because of just how competitive and fast-paced today's business world has become. As previously stated, it's essential that all businesses, organizations, governments, and so on develop well-thought-out business plans that include complete financial forecasts. To emphasize just how important preparing business plans and financial forecasts are, we offer four scenarios:

» **The Business Birth:** We discuss the basics of raising capital in Chapter 18, but we want to highlight just how important it is as it relates to preparing financial forecasts. In the start-up phase of a new business, preparing forecasts is usually indispensable for raising capital and getting the venture off the ground. You simply cannot approach any type of capital source, whether looking to raise equity or secure a loan, without having a well-developed business plan and financial forecast available. Trust us when we say "you will be shown the door you entered extremely quickly" if you attempt to raise capital without a forecast.

» **The Business Pivot:** If the Covid-19 pandemic of 2020 and 2021 taught us anything, it was the importance of how quickly businesses had to adapt to rapidly changing operating conditions. While Covid-19 may be an extreme situation, businesses operating in vastly different industries can often have their operating models upended by any number of events, including government intervention (for example, sanctions placed on foreign suppliers), technological innovation (that makes your products obsolete), and changing sales channel (online/e-commerce shopping, anyone?), just to name a few. When these events hit, businesses must quickly update their plans and revise their financial forecasts to figure out how to survive and how to prosper moving forward.

» **The Business Exit:** Most businesses, in one form or another, will eventually cease to exist after operating for years. In some cases, businesses simply fail as the owners decide to terminate operations or the business is no longer economically viable. In most cases, however, the goal is to build a business and eventually sell it to another party and realize a very handsome "exit." To maximize third-party interest in acquiring a business, it must have a well-developed business plan, including current and relevant financial forecasts. There is simply no way a business owner can approach a potential acquirer and achieve the correct valuation without having this vital information.

» **Business Operations Management:** Forecasting, in the broader management context, is an essential technique for keeping the business on course toward achieving its goals. One purpose of forecasting is to force managers to create a definite and detailed financial plan for the coming period. To construct a forecast, managers have to establish explicit financial objectives for the coming year and identify exactly what has to be done to accomplish these financial objectives. Financial forecasts and their supporting schedules provide clear destination points — the financial flight plan for a business.

The process of putting together a forecast directs attention to the specific things that managers must do to achieve their profit objectives and optimize assets and capital. Basically, forecasts push managers to answer the question "How are you going to get there from here?"

Forecasting can also yield other important planning-related benefits:

>> **Forecasts prompt a business to articulate its vision, strategy, and goals.** A business needs a clearly stated strategy guided by an overarching vision, and it should have definite and explicit goals. It isn't enough for business managers to have strategies and goals only in their heads. Developing financial forecasts forces managers to be explicit and definite about the objectives of the business as well as to formulate realistic plans for achieving those objectives.

>> **Forecasting imposes discipline and deadlines on the planning process.** Forecasting pushes managers to set aside time to prepare a detailed plan that serves as a road map for the business. Good planning results in a concrete course of action that specifies how a company plans to achieve its financial objectives.

Control reasons for preparing forecasts

Many people have the mistaken notion that the purpose of forecasting is to rein in managers and employees, who otherwise would spend money like drunken sailors on shore leave. But forecasting shouldn't put the business's managers in a financial straitjacket. Tying the hands of managers isn't the purpose of forecasting. That said, it's true that a forecasts serves a management control function. *Management control*, first and foremost, means achieving the financial goals and objectives of the business, which requires comparing actual performance against some sort of benchmarks and holding individual managers responsible for keeping the business on schedule in reaching its financial objectives.

By using forecast targets as benchmarks against which actual performance is compared, managers can closely monitor progress toward (or deviations from) the forecast goals and timetable. You use a forecast plan like a navigation chart to keep your business on course. Significant variations from the forecast raise red flags, in which case you can determine that performance is off-course or that the forecast needs to be revised because of unexpected developments.

TIP

For management control, a forecast profit report is generally divided into months or quarters for the coming year. The forecast balance sheet and cash flow statement should also be put on a monthly or quarterly basis. The business shouldn't wait too long to compare forecast sales revenue and expenses against actual performance (or to compare actual cash flows and asset levels against the forecast). Managers need to take prompt action when problems arise, such as a divergence between forecast expenses and actual expenses. In fact, in today's "on demand" tech-enabled global economy, sales revenue and certain expenses are now not just monitored on a weekly or even daily basis but for a number of companies, monitoring sales revenue by the hour or even minute has become the norm.

At a macro level, profit is the main thing to pay attention to, but trade accounts receivable, trade accounts payable, inventory levels, other liabilities, and capital expenditures can also quickly get out of control (become too high relative to actual sales revenue and cost of goods sold expense), creating cash flow problems. (Chapter 8 explains how increases in accounts receivable and inventory are negative factors on cash flow.) A business can't afford to ignore its balance sheet and cash flow numbers until the end of the year.

Exploring Forecasting

REMEMBER

The financial statements included in the financial reports of a business are prepared *after the fact*; they're based on transactions that have already taken place. (We explain business financial statements in Chapters 6, 7, and 8.) Forecast financial statements, on the other hand, are prepared *before the fact* and reflect future transactions that are expected to take place based on the business's financial plan. Detailed financial statement forecasts are generally not shared outside the business as they're strictly for internal management use. However, summarized financial statement forecasts are often distributed to critical external third parties such as investors or lending sources (a bank, for example). These parties have just as much vested interest in making sure the company has a well-developed business plan and stays on course as the internal management team.

The board of directors of a company focuses its attention on the *macro-level forecast* for the whole business: the forecast income statement, balance sheet, and cash flow statement for the business for the coming year. The chief executive officer (CEO) of the business focuses on the macro-level forecast as well, but the CEO must also look at how each manager in the organization is doing on their part of this forecast. As you move down the organization chart of a business, managers have narrower responsibilities — say, for the business's northeastern territory or for one major product line. A macro-level forecast consists of different segments that follow the business's organizational structure. In other words, this forecast is put together from many pieces, one for each separate organizational unit of the business. For example, the manager of one of the company's far-flung warehouses has a separate forecast for expenses and inventory levels for their bailiwick.

The living and breathing business forecast

REMEMBER

Years ago, businesses tended to manage the forecasting process on an annual or maybe semiannual basis. The standard cycle started toward the end of each current FYE (maybe 30 to 90 days prior) as management would get the annual "budgeting" process fired up to plan for the upcoming year. We have no doubt that this annual forecasting process still occurs and is widely used, but based on the economic realities of today's capitalist markets, the forecasting process must be managed as a living, breathing function that should be constantly updated as frequently as critical business information emerges, evolves, and/or changes. This does not mean that preparing updated forecasts needs to be completed weekly (which would be overkill), but trust us when we say that developing forecasting models that have the flexibility to always be rolled forward to look out 12 to 24 months from the end of any desired reporting period is now standard practice.

Understanding that the forecasting process represents a living, breathing function that requires proactive management on a monthly basis, we now turn our attention to some basic concepts to assist with preparing forecasts.

REMEMBER

As you see in the following sections, the concept of CART (complete, accurate, reliable, and timely) is fully embedded in best-in-class business planning and forecasting functions. Companies need to develop and utilize financial forecasting models that are highly flexible and easily adaptable, to adjust to rapidly changing business conditions. Later in this chapter, we provide additional insight on how you can develop more powerful forecasts.

Initial forecasting for a new business

For businesses or professionals that have already prepared prior-year forecasts, this section may not be all that relevant. For first timers preparing a forecast for a new business, you want to become familiar with three acronyms: BOTE, WAG, and SWAG. These stand for back of the envelope, wild-ass guess, and scientific wild-ass guess. You may notice a little humor when referring to these acronyms, but we are being quite serious:

>> The forecasting process needs to start somewhere and often resides with executive management team members discussing a business idea or

opportunity, jotting down some thoughts and basic numbers on the back of a napkin or envelope.

>> This may then evolve into a wild-ass guess where an actual (albeit quite simple) preliminary forecast is prepared using a standard technology tool such as Microsoft Excel.

>> Then, as additional information is obtained and incorporated into the forecast model, it transforms into a scientific wild-ass guess (where key data points and assumptions can be documented and defended).

You would be amazed at how many businesses and forecasts get started with such a simple initial step, but you would be equally amazed at how quickly the forecast model evolves into a very sophisticated management tool.

Initial forecasting for an existing business

REMEMBER

To start an initial forecast for an existing business, you should have a solid understanding of your company's historical financial information and operating results. This history may stretch back three months, one year, five years, or longer, but the key concept is that having sound internal financial information represents an excellent place to start. However, remember that while the financial operating history of a company may provide a foundation on which to prepare a forecast, it by no means is an accurate or guaranteed predictor of future operating results. If the economic environment of a business has changed, then benchmarking off other similar businesses represents an effective means to build a reliable forecast.

Gathering reliable data

The availability of quality market, operational, and accounting/financial data represents the basis of the forecast. A good deal of this data often comes from internal sources. For example, when a sales region is preparing a budget for the upcoming year, the sales manager may survey the direct sales representatives on what they feel their customers will demand in terms of products and services in the coming year. With this information, you can determine sales volumes, personnel levels, wage rates, commission plans, and so on.

While internal information is of value, it represents only half the battle because external information and data is just as critical to accumulate. Having access to quality and reliable external third-party information is essential to the overall business planning process and the production of reliable forecasts. Market forces and trends may be occurring that can impact your business over the next 24 months (that may not be reflected in the previous year's operating results).

Involving key team members

The forecasting process represents a critical function in most companies' accounting and financial department and rightfully so, as these are the people who understand the numbers the best. Although the financial and accounting types produce the final budget, they rely on data that comes from numerous parties such as marketing, manufacturing, and sales.

REMEMBER

You must ensure that all key management team members are involved in the forecasting process, covering all critical business functions, to produce a reliable projection. Just as you would not have a regional sales manager prepare a fixed asset schedule (tracking all asset additions, disposals, and depreciation expense), you would not have your accountant estimate sales volumes by product line during the holiday season (and what prices the products may fetch). Critical business data comes from numerous parties, all of which must be included in the forecasting process to produce the most reliable information possible.

Ensuring consistency and completeness

TIP

The financial forecasts prepared should be both complete and consistent to maximize their value:

>> When we say *complete,* we mean that all relevant financial information should be presented in the forecasts to ensure that the target audience has the proper output and data on which to base economic decisions.

>> Consistency implies that the financial forecasts are prepared in a like format to the periodic financial information provided to the target audience (including all critical financial data points, key performance indicators or KPIs, and so on). There is no benefit to preparing financial forecasts in a format that is different than the periodic internal financial information produced and delivered to the management team (you can imagine the confusion that would ensue). Financial forecast models should be designed to be in sync with critical reporting and utilize the same format for ease of understanding and decision-making.

Considering timing and presentation

As previously mentioned, the annual budgeting process is a thing of the past. While an annual forecast can be produced just prior to the beginning of a new FYE to start the process, management should be prepared, on at least a quarterly basis and for more fluid, high-paced businesses, monthly, to revise and update forecasts as business conditions change.

Presentation-wise, generally the nearer the term covered by the forecasts the more detailed the information and frequency of reporting periods being prepared. If you're preparing a forecast for the coming fiscal year, the monthly financial information should be provided, but if you're looking out three to five years, then providing quarterly financial information should suffice (for years three through five).

Projections as financial models

REMEMBER

Business managers should make detailed analyses to determine how to improve the financial performance and condition of their business. The status quo is usually not good enough; business managers are paid to improve things — not to simply rest on their past accomplishments. For this reason, managers should develop good economic *models* of profit, cash flow, and financial condition for their business. Models are blueprints or schematics of how things work. A financial model is like a road map that clearly marks the pathways to profit, cash flow, and financial condition.

TIP

Don't be intimidated by the term *model.* Simply put, a model consists of variables and how they interact. A variable is a critical factor that, in conjunction with other factors, determines results. A model is analytical, but not all models are mathematical. In fact, the financial models in this book are not mathematical — but you do have to look at each factor of the model and how it interacts with one or more other factors.

Chapter 15 presents a profit model for managers. This profit template is, at its core, a model. It includes the critical variables that drive profit: sales volume, sales price, product cost, and so on. A profit model, such as the one in Figure 15-1, provides the framework for understanding and analyzing profit performance. A good profit model also serves as the platform and the point of departure for mapping out profit strategies for the coming period.

TIP

Likewise, business managers need a model, or blueprint, in planning cash flow from operating activities. (We explain this source of cash flow in Chapter 8.) Managers should forecast the amount of cash they'll generate during the coming year from making profit. They need a reliable estimate of this source of cash flow to plan for other sources of cash flow they'll need during the coming year — to provide the money for replacing and expanding the long-term operating (fixed) assets of the business and to make cash distributions from profit to owners. Managers need a map that provides a clear trail of how the sales and expenses of the business drive its assets and liabilities, which in turn drive the cash flow from operating activities.

Generally, a business should seriously consider preparing all three forecast financial statements based on the appropriate model for each:

» **Forecast income statement (profit report):** A profit analysis model, such as the one in Figure 15-1, highlights the critical variables that drive profit. Remember that this profit template separates *variable* and *fixed* expenses and focuses on *sales volume, margin per unit,* and other factors that determine profit performance. These are the key factors that must be improved to enhance profit performance in the coming period. The highly condensed basic profit model provides a useful frame of reference for preparing the much more detailed, comprehensive profit budget.

» **Forecast balance sheet:** The key connections and ratios between sales revenue and expenses and their corresponding assets and liabilities are the elements in the model for the forecast balance sheet. These vital connections are explained throughout Chapters 7 and 8. The forecasted changes in operating assets and liabilities provide the information needed for forecasting cash flows during the coming year.

» **Forecast statement of cash flows:** The forecast changes during the coming year in the assets and liabilities used in making profit (conducting operating activities) determine forecasted *cash flow from operating activities* for the coming year (see Chapter 8). In contrast, the cash flows of *investing* and *financing* activities depend on the managers' strategic decisions regarding capital expenditures that will be made during the coming year, how much new capital will be raised from debt and from owners' sources of capital, and the business's policy regarding cash distributions from profit.

REMEMBER

In short, forecasting requires good working models of profit, financial condition (assets and liabilities), and cash flow. Forecasting provides a strong incentive for business managers to develop financial models that help them make strategic decisions, do better planning, and exercise effective control.

Increasing the Power of Your Forecasts

We start this section noting that the list of concepts, strategies, and tools overviewed here is not meant to be all-inclusive; rather these topics have been selected to assist with helping make financial forecasts even more useful and powerful. To avoid overkill, we have limited our discussion to summarizing four very helpful planning and forecasting tools in the following sections.

The SWOT

This acronym stands for strengths, weaknesses, opportunities, and threats; it's a business management assessment tool designed to assist the company's management team with preparing a qualitative assessment of the business, helping to keep all parties focused on key issues. The SWOT analysis is often incorporated into a company's planning function but can also be extremely helpful with preparing financial forecasts.

A SWOT analysis is usually broken down into a matrix of four segments. Two of the segments are geared toward positive attributes (strengths and opportunities), and two are geared toward negative attributes (weaknesses and threats). In addition, the analysis differentiates between internal company source attributes and external, or outside of the company, source attributes.

TIP

Generally, the SWOT analysis is prepared by senior management team members to ensure that critical conditions are communicated to management for inclusion in the budget. If used correctly, a SWOT analysis not only can provide invaluable information to support the forecasting process but, more importantly, can help identify what type of management you have in place. The responses you receive provide invaluable information as to whether the party completing the SWOT analysis is nothing more than a front-line manager (a captain needing direction) or a bona fide businessperson (the colonel leading the charge).

Top down or bottom up

Next, we discuss two different forecasting strategies or approaches used by most businesses, *top down* versus *bottom up*:

>> *Top-down* forecasting is exactly how it sounds (that is, the top line for a company, which is sales), as it starts with projecting critical sales revenue data, including sales unit volumes (by all significant product lines or SKUs), pricing by product, any potential sales discounts, seasonality in sales, customer contact to sales timing relationships, and similar data. After this information is incorporated into the forecast model, the balance of the forecast model, including cost of sales, direct operating expenses, business overhead expenses, and other expenses or income (for the income statement), as well as all critical balance sheet assumptions, are incorporated by utilizing relationships or correlations rather than inputting hard data and information.

For example, using a top-down forecasting model, the number of sales representatives required, and any commissions earned would be determined based on X number of product sales at Y price. A relationship for the business might be established that states for every 250,000 units of products sold, one senior sales rep is required and would earn a commission of 5 percent on the sales.

>> Using a bottom-up approach is different because, although certain key correlations or relationships may be incorporated into the forecast model, this approach tends to be much more detailed and includes a large number of hard or firm data points and assumptions being built into the forecast model. For example, in a top-down approach, an expense estimate of $1,000 per month per sales rep may be input to capture all travel, lodging, meals, and entertainment-related (TLM&E) costs. In other words, estimated sales revenue drives the number of sales reps, which drives the monthly TLM&E expense. In a bottom-up approach, an estimate of each type of expense is prepared on a line-by-line basis that then rolls up into a subtotal. Further, sales revenue may be driven by how many sales reps are working or employed; if 10 sales reps are working any given month and, on average, each sales rep should be able to generate $250,000 of sales, total sales for the month would be forecast at $2.5 million.

TIP

Companies often use a hybrid of these two approaches; most financial forecast models utilize some type of correlation and relationship assumptions as well as incorporate hard data for various overhead or fixed costs:

>> The bottom-up approach tends to be better suited for well-established, predictable business models that have a large amount of historical data and operational stability. It also tends to be detailed and static but definitely has use/value within the right business framework, such as when detailed or specific management reporting is required for cost analysis of a bill of material or expense control is a high priority (to track all expenses at a line-item level).

>> The top-down approach is better suited for newer businesses or companies operating in rapidly changing environments where you need to understand important financial results quickly under different or "what if" operating scenarios (see the next section). Top-down forecasting approaches focus on understanding financial correlations and relationships at a macro level to help the management team in evaluating multiple operating scenarios with potentially vastly different outcomes.

To be quite honest, most properly structured top-down forecasting models end up relying on a select few key business drivers or assumptions that really are "make or break" for the company in terms of producing profitable results. Senior-level management members are usually so well versed in understanding their businesses that, when as few as a half dozen assumptions and data inputs that drive sales are known, the senior management team members can usually accurately and quickly calculate what the net profit or loss will be. This is why top-down forecasting models are utilized more frequently at the strategic business planning level (the macro level of big picture), whereas bottom-up forecasting models are utilized actively at the business tactical and implementation level. Under either approach, the goal is to make it easy for team members to participate in the forecasting process and utilize the financial information to assist with improving operating results.

What if?

One concept that is strongly associated with the top-down forecasting approach (see the previous section) is the *what-if* analysis. It should be obvious that the purpose of the what-if analysis is just like it sounds — that is, what will the results or impact be if this situation or set of events occurs? For example, if a company has to implement a significant product price reduction to match the competition, a what-if analysis will help it quickly calculate and decipher the potential impact on its operating results and associated cash flows.

TIP

The reason the what-if analysis is easier to use with a top-down forecast approach is that the goal of this analysis tool is to focus on the macro-level impact (to a business) from a potential material change in key business operating metrics. Thus, by being able to change 6 to 12 key variables or forecast assumptions, a management team can quickly assess the impact on the business (which is one of the key strengths of the top-down forecasting approach). This is not to say that what-if analyses cannot be generated using a bottom-up forecasting approach, but when focusing on macro-level company operating results, starting at the top with sales revenue and watching the waterfall impact on overall operations is a particularly useful and powerful analysis for senior management.

TIP

We would also like to mention that what-if analyses are extremely helpful when preparing multiple versions of the financial forecasts, which most companies do (or should do). It is common practice for companies to produce high, medium, and low versions of the financial forecasts to assist with business planning and evaluate different operating scenarios. Having this information available well in advance allows a business to build different plans to ensure that financial performance targets are achieved. For example, if sales revenue is trending down, management can develop a plan that identifies expenses to cut and by how much and when. Conversely, if the company is having a strong year, this may dictate that additional capital may be needed to support the unanticipated growth (again, allowing management to identify when, what, and how much is needed).

As you see in Figures 17-1, 17-2, and 17-3 later in this chapter, the forecast operating results from our high, medium, and low scenarios are vastly different and indicate that management needs to have proactive plans in place to address potential underperformance issues. By the way, another version of the forecast model that companies have incorporated into their planning process is the "Arm" (which stands for Armageddon) version — or when all hell breaks loose. Companies generally keep a tight lid on this version because whether you are dealing with internal or external parties, nobody wants to entice unwarranted panic.

Rolling forecasts

REMEMBER

Finally, we close this section by discussing the value and benefits of employing *rolling forecasts* (such as 12 months, 18 months, or longer). The purpose of utilizing rolling forecasts is to always have at least one year's (and preferably longer) visibility on your business's operating performance at any point in time. For example, if a business uses a standard FYE of 12/31/20, a 12-month rolling forecast model updated at, let us say, the third quarter ending 9/30/20 would provide visibility for the 12-month period of 10/1/20 through 9/30/21. After each month, the forecast model is "rolled" forward as part of the company's ongoing planning process to provide executive management with the proper business management visibility.

Companies often utilize rolling forecasts to assist with managing their business interests as summarized in the following two examples:

>> **Recast Operating Results:** In our example, a company could combine the actual operating results for the nine months of operations ending 9/30/20 with the updated three months of forecast operating results for the period of 10/1/20 through 12/31/20 to produce recast operating results for the FYE 12/31/20. We use the term *recast* in the context of combining actual operating results with updated forecast operating results to produce revised or recast operating results for a specific time period. Companies often need to provide both internal and external parties with updated outlooks on a periodic basis and utilize recast operating results to achieve this objective.

>> **Operational Pivots:** Companies that may experience an unexpected shock to their operations (such as Covid-19 shutdowns in March 2020) can use rolling forecasts to reset operating targets and objectives for internal management planning purposes. For example, employee commission or bonus plans can be adjusted (based on a revised 12-month outlook) to reflect a new operating norm that was not anticipated. This allows the company to proactively manage difficult environments as well as effectively communicate with the employee base.

TIP

Other examples and benefits of utilizing rolling forecasts could be presented, but the primary purpose remains the same: to provide forward-looking visibility, over the appropriate time period, that is clear, concise, and complete. This forecasting strategy can prove to be invaluable for companies operating in dynamic, rapidly changing, or unstable business environments, which today is more important than ever before.

Seeing a Financial Forecast in Action

Thus far in this chapter, we have covered the topic of forecasts from a conceptual perspective; now we offer examples of financial forecasts for our fictious company. Each figure presents high, medium, and low case forecasts, with Figure 17-1 presenting the income statement, Figure 17-2 presenting the balance sheet, and Figure 17-3 presenting the statement of cash flows. We call out a couple of key issues in each figure to help you understand the importance of preparing multiple forecast versions.

REMEMBER

We could highlight additional issues and findings with the financial information presented in the forecast versions, but these are the points we want to emphasize here:

>> Having complete financial forecasts, including the income statement, balance sheet, and statement of cash flows, is critical for management planning purposes.

>> The power and importance of utilizing the what-if forecasting tool (covered earlier in this chapter) is on full display.

>> Even in a forecast, the all-important concept of realizing that accounting (and finance) is more of an art than a science holds true.

The income statement

Figure 17-1 presents the income statement for our sample company, for which we have elected to provide additional financial information. You see that more detail has been provided with KPIs (key performance indicators), sales revenue, costs of goods sold, and selling, general, and administrative expense. The reason for this is two-fold. First, we want to emphasize the fact that internal company forecasts should provide far more detail and information to develop a proper business plan. Second is that certain performance issues we call out in the low forecast version refer back to this level of detail.

Overall, the operating results in the high and medium versions of the forecast model appear reasonable. Solid sales growth, strong profitability, and key financial ratios, including the current ratio and the debt service coverage ratio (see Chapter 12), are more than adequate. Turning our attention to the low version, significant concerns start to emerge or, in the words of Scooby Doo, "Ruh-roh." On top of the company performing poorly with negative year-over-year (YOY) sales growth and basically operating at a breakeven level, two important ratios need further attention.

Income Statement — Forecast	High — FYE	% of Net Rev.	Medium — FYE	% of Net Rev.	Low — FYE	% of Net Rev.
For the Fiscal Year Ending (All Numbers in Thousands, Except KPIs)	12/31/2021		12/31/2021		12/31/2021	
Key Performance Indicators:						
Revenue Per Full-Time Employee	$626,333		$551,000		$439,000	
Product Sales, Avg. Order Value (Net)	$19,800		$19,800		$12,467	
Macro Level Analysis:						
Year-Over-Year Sales Growth	32.20%		16.30%		−7.34%	
Gross Margin	66.72%		62.34%		57.71%	
Operating Income Margin	17.95%		12.01%		2.01%	
Debt Service Coverage Ratio	10.41		6.42		1.48	
Sales Revenue:						
Software Platform & SAAS Sales	$79,100	84%	$67,800	82%	$56,500	86%
Product Sales	$16,500	18%	$16,500	20%	$11,000	17%
Other Sales, Discounts, & Allowances	($1,650)	−2%	($1,650)	−2%	($1,650)	−3%
Net Sales Revenue	$93,950	100%	$82,650	100%	$65,850	100%
Costs of Goods Sold:						
Direct Product Costs	$9,240	10%	$9,488	11%	$6,600	10%
Wages & Burden	$21,026	22%	$20,637	25%	$20,248	31%
Direct Overhead	$750	1%	$750	1%	$750	1%
Other Costs of Goods Sold	$250	0%	$250	0%	$250	0%
Total Costs of Goods Sold	$31,266	33%	$31,124	38%	$27,848	42%
Gross Profit	$62,684	67%	$51,526	62%	$38,003	58%
Gross Margin	66.72%		62.34%		57.71%	
Selling, General, & Administrative Expenses:						
Advertising, Promotional, & Selling	$12,701	14%	$10,958	13%	$8,965	14%
Personnel Wages, Burden, & Compensation	$6,107	7%	$5,992	7%	$5,597	9%
Corporate & Facility Operating Expenses	$10,950	12%	$10,350	13%	$9,750	15%
Research, Development, & Design & Other Expenses	$14,703	16%	$12,997	16%	$11,096	17%
Depreciation & Amortization Expense	$1,362	1%	$1,301	2%	$1,270	2%
Total Operating Expenses	$45,823	49%	$41,597	50%	$36,678	56%
Operating Income (EBIT)	$16,860	18%	$9,928	12%	$1,325	2%
Operating Margin (EBIT Margin)	17.95%		12.01%		2.01%	
Other Expenses (Income):						
Other Expenses, Income, & Discontinued Ops.	$500	1%	$500	1%	$500	1%
Interest Expense	$263	0%	$263	0%	$263	0%
Total Other Expenses (Income)	$763	1%	$763	1%	$763	1%
Net Income (Loss) Before Taxes	$16,098	17%	$9,166	11%	$562	1%
Income Tax Expense (Benefit)	$5,634	6%	$3,208	4%	$197	0%
Net Income (Loss) After Taxes	$10,463	11%	$5,958	7%	$365	1%

QW Example Tech., Inc.
Unaudited Financial Statements
Forecasts — High, Medium, & Low
for the Fiscal Year Ending
12/31/2021

Confidential — Property of QW Example Tech., Inc.

© John Wiley & Sons, Inc.

FIGURE 17-1: Forecast income statement: high, medium, and low.

First, the company's operating income margin is just 2.01 percent, which basically indicates the company would be operating at a breakeven level. Clearly, this is not desirable and also indicates that the company has no margin for error if it finds itself operating at this level. We should also note that a number of lenders have what are called "minimum profitability" covenants that state the company must generate a profit in order to not be considered in default of the loan agreement. As you can see in the low case scenario, the company would be in trouble with this type of covenant. The same goes for the debt service coverage ratio, which comes in at 1.48 to 1.00; if the debt facility has a covenant that requires this ratio be 1.5 or above (not at all unreasonable for lenders), then again, the company may be in technical default.

Obviously, the company is not in default of these covenants today and does not expect to be in default, because even under the medium case forecast, the company has more than enough breathing room. But for management purposes, having a clear understanding of the operating performance level at which the company does begin to operate under financial stress is extremely helpful, so that if the business does head south, the executive management team can plan for and implement necessary adjustments (for example, expense reductions) to avoid a rather messy situation with the lender.

The balance sheet

We now turn our attention to the balance sheet presented in Figure 17-2. Here again we provide high, medium, and low forecast scenarios for evaluation and draw your attention to a couple of items.

First, you notice that the ending inventory balance in the low version is actually higher than the high version. This may make sense on the surface, because FYE 2021 product sales in the low version are forecast to reach only $11 million versus $16.5 million in the high version (lower sales equals more inventory on hand and a higher value). However, it may also mean that the company's inventory is rapidly becoming obsolete and is becoming harder to sell, raising an all-important question as to whether the inventory is actually worth $2.2 million or whether management should write off a portion of the inventory as worthless (which means the company would have to incur an additional expense and most likely push it from profitability under the low version to a loss — ouch!).

Second, you may ask why the company would pay a dividend when at best it is operating at a breakeven level. This is an excellent question that we explore more in Chapter 18 on understanding the cap table. Basically, what it comes down to is that when the company raised preferred equity, this tranche of equity comes with a guaranteed annual dividend of 8 percent, regardless of the profit level. Hence, the company is required to pay the dividend, and if it does not, it would be in default of the capital raise agreement.

QW Example Tech., Inc.			
Unaudited Financial Statements			
Forecasts — High, Medium, & Low			
for the Fiscal Year Ending			
12/31/2021			

Balance Sheet — Forecast Period Ending (All Numbers in Thousands) Assets	High — FYE 12/31/2021	Medium — FYE 12/31/2021	Low — FYE 12/31/2021
Current Assets:			
Cash & Equivalents	$19,940	$15,935	$10,015
Accounts Receivable, Net	$11,744	$10,331	$9,054
Inventory, LCM	$1,540	$1,779	$2,200
Prepaid Expenses	$322	$283	$226
Total Current Assets	$33,546	$28,329	$21,496
Long-Term Operating & Other Assets:			
Property, Plant, Equipment, & Machinery	$9,537	$9,104	$8,887
Accumulated Depreciation	($5,682)	($5,621)	($5,590)
Net Property, Plant, & Equipment	$3,855	$3,483	$3,297
Other Assets:			
Intangible Assets & Goodwill, Net	$500	$500	$500
Other Assets	$100	$100	$100
Total Long-Term Operating & Other Assets	$4,455	$4,083	$3,897
Total Assets	$38,001	$32,412	$25,393

Balance Sheet — Forecast Period Ending Liabilities	High — FYE 12/31/2021	Medium — FYE 12/31/2021	Low — FYE 12/31/2021
Current Liabilities:			
Accounts Payable	$2,936	$2,583	$2,037
Accrued Liabilities & Other	$543	$533	$517
Current Portion of Debt	$1,000	$1,000	$1,000
Income Taxes Payable	$1,409	$802	$49
Other Current Liabilities	$791	$678	$565
Total Current Liabilities	$6,678	$5,595	$4,168
Long-Term Liabilities:			
Notes Payable & Other Long-Term Debt	$5,000	$5,000	$5,000
Other Long-Term Liabilities	$300	$300	$300
Total Long-Term Liabilities	$5,300	$5,300	$5,300
Total Liabilities	$11,978	$10,895	$9,468
Stockholders' Equity			
Capital Stock — Common	$5,000	$5,000	$5,000
Capital Stock — Preferred	$5,000	$5,000	$5,000
Dividends	($400)	($400)	($400)
Retained Earnings	$5,959	$5,959	$5,959
Current Earnings (Loss)	$10,463	$5,958	$365
Total Stockholders' Equity	$26,022	$21,517	$15,924
Total Liabilities & Stockholders' Equity	$38,001	$32,412	$25,393

Confidential — Property of QW Example Tech., Inc.

FIGURE 17-2: Forecast balance sheet: high, medium, and low.

The statement of cash flows

Finally, we reach the statement of cash flows as presented in Figure 17-3, which also sheds additional valuable information in the low version of the forecast model.

QW Example Tech., Inc. Unaudited Financial Statements Forecasts — High, Medium, & Low for the Fiscal Year Ending 12/31/2021			
Statement of Cash Flows — Forecast For the Twelve-Month Period Ending	High — FYE 12/31/2021	Medium — FYE 12/31/2021	Low — FYE 12/31/2021
Net Profit (Loss)	$10,463	$5,958	$365
Operating Activities, Cash Provided (Used):			
Depreciation & Amortization	$1,362	$1,301	$1,270
Decrease (Increase) in Trade Receivables	($2,861)	($1,448)	($171)
Decrease (Increase) in Inventory	$193	($46)	($467)
Decrease (Increase) in Other Current Assets	$3	$42	$99
Increase (Decrease) in Trade Payables	$1,007	$654	$108
Increase (Decrease) in Accrued Liabilities	($287)	($297)	($313)
Increase (Decrease) in Other Liabilities	$996	$276	($590)
Net Cash Flow from Operating Activities	$10,876	$6,438	$301
Investing Activities, Cash Provided (Used):			
Capital Expenditures	($867)	($434)	($217)
Investments in Other Assets	$0	$0	$0
Net Cash Flow from Investing Activities	($867)	($434)	($217)
Financing Activities, Cash Provided (Used):			
Dividends or Distributions Paid	($400)	($400)	($400)
Sale (Repurchase) of Equity	$0	$0	$0
Proceeds from Issuance of Debt	$0	$0	$0
Repayments of Debt	($1,000)	($1,000)	($1,000)
Other Financing Activities	$50	$50	$50
Net Cash Flow from Financing Activities	($1,350)	($1,350)	($1,350)
Other Cash Flow Adjustments — Asset Impairment	$0	$0	$0
Net Increase (Decrease) in Cash & Equivalents	$8,659	$4,654	($1,266)
Beginning Cash & Equivalents Balance	$11,281	$11,281	$11,281
Ending Cash & Equivalents Balance	$19,940	$15,935	$10,015
Confidential — Property of QW Example Tech., Inc.			

FIGURE 17-3: Forecast statement of cash flows: high, medium, and low.

Reviewing the statement of cash flows in more detail, you notice that the low version of the forecast model produces approximately $301,000 of positive cash flow from operations, compared to required financing payments of $1.400 million, which is comprised of preferred equity dividend payments of $400,000 and debt repayments of $1 million. The good news is that the company has enough cash resources and liquidity to cover this shortfall derived from the guaranteed payments, given its relatively large cash balance forecast to be approximately $10.015 million as of the end of 2021 (see Figure 17-2). But looking closer, this really could become a problem over the long run because in effect the company is using short-term working capital to repay long-term financial commitments (an imbalance that should be avoided).

Rehashing the Value of Forecasts

Chapters 6 through 8 of this book introduce you to the three primary financial statements and the purpose and importance of each one. These were relatively long chapters, as is this chapter on financial forecasting, because all cover a large amount of material. Our goal is not to bury you with too much information (in other words, burying you in the BS), but rather to help you understand just how important complete, accurate, reliable, and timely financial information really is, including forecasts and how top management teams utilize the accounting and finance departments as a competitive weapon (especially with forecasts).

REMEMBER

With this said, we want to rehash some valuable gems and secrets related to financial forecasting that successful business owners, managers, and investors use every day:

>> **Graduate:** Bottom-up forecast models are valuable tools for businesses, but to move up in the executive management hierarchy, you need to graduate and become comfortable using top-down forecasts (both types are covered earlier in this chapter). Top executives usually have such a solid understanding of the economic structure of their business that they can simply change a select number of critical operating assumptions and almost immediate know what the end result will be (for example, a change to top-line sales revenue leads to a bottom-line result). To be an effective executive-level manager, you need to efficiently understand the macro-level impact on your business from economic changing conditions. That is, you "can't see the forest for the trees."

>> **The P&L focus:** Too many businesses focus only on the profit and loss (P&L) when preparing forecasts. It should be clear from this chapter (and this entire book) just how important the balance sheet and cash flow statement are, especially as they relate to cash flow and third-party capital source

management. More than a few companies have failed because they fixated on their P&L performance while neglecting their balance sheet and cash flow statement. Best-in-class forecasts always should include projections for all three financial statements.

>> **External/internal:** Internal financial forecasts include significant amounts of detail and confidential information that should not be distributed to external parties. Not only is the level of detail on a line-item basis excessive, but the high and low versions of the forecast model should not be distributed externally (because these are for internal management use). Again, what a business distributes to external parties is vastly different than what's needed for internal consumption.

>> **Tone it down:** Most companies produce forecasts that derive financial data from multiple internal operating divisions (for example, a company may have a dozen operating divisions that they consolidate to prepare a company-wide forecast). What tends to happen during the consolidation process is that everyone is a bit too optimistic, so when the combined results are produced, the operating results look great (see the high version in Figures 17-1 through 17-3). In reality, somewhere along the line, certain divisions are going to stumble and not perform as well, so although it is fine to set internal expectations relatively high, finalizing a company-wide forecast should be toned down to be more realistic (for distribution to external parties, the company's board of directors, and so on). Nothing is worse than over-promising and underdelivering — and then having to explain yourself.

REMEMBER

One final thought to keep in mind is that at the base or heart of preparing, understanding, and utilizing financial forecasts is the all-important concept of accounting. That is, if you don't have a basic understanding of accounting, then even attempting to prepare and understand a forecast will be next to impossible. This is not a chicken-and-egg question; to master financial forecasts, you must understand basic accounting concepts.

Chapter **18**

Capitalizing a Business: How, When, Why, and What

The birth of almost every type of business organization — small or large, public or private, for-profit or not-for-profit — starts with two simple concepts. First, an idea is needed on which the vision and mission of the business will be based. And second, capital needs to be raised to support the launch of the business. As for the "idea" part of the business, we'll pass on providing any in-depth discussions related to this topic because countless books, publications, articles, and so on have been produced helping the aspiring business owner or entrepreneur launch the next great thing. Rather, in this chapter, we expand on our discussion of raising capital, which was first presented in Chapter 5 and can best be understood by referring to this classic statement: It takes money to make money!

REMEMBER

Before any business can rent a facility, hire employees, develop products, create marketing content, launch advertising campaigns, make the first sale, and actually collect customer payments, the business must do two things:

>> Develop a strategic business plan (even if extremely simple or basic in nature), which acts as a road map to guide the company moving forward. It doesn't matter if you're a small sole proprietorship opening a secondhand clothing store in a 1,000-foot retail location or a conglomerate like Apple that might have an inkling to enter the electronic vehicles automotive manufacturing space, well-developed business plans are an absolute must.

>> Raise capital to implement and execute the business plan. And you guessed it, the foundation of being able to raise capital is an effective business plan that specifically spells out how much, what time, and the amount of capital the company requires to execute the business plan. And here again, whether it's the small secondhand clothing store that is introducing the idea to a family friend to secure $50,000, the next greatest technology cloud-based solution that is being pitched by a group of executives to venture capitalists to raise $10 million, or Apple's board of directors evaluating the opportunities present in the electronic vehicles market and the billions of dollars that will be required, capital must be secured and deployed to execute the business plan.

With these two thoughts in mind, we dive deeper into the capital raising-process and explain exactly why accounting is such an integral part of the process.

Identifying the Elements of a Business Plan

It should go without saying that when either new businesses are formed and launched or an existing business implements a specific strategy (for example, to drive sales growth, improve earnings per share, restructure current operations, and so on), a well-developed, supported, presented, and communicated business plan is an absolute necessity. Business plans provide a road map for company management to implement and execute, because they not only outline the resources that will be required but, more importantly, establish a benchmark on which the company's management team can be evaluated.

Business plans come in all shapes, sizes, and forms, ranging from an entire company-wide plan (for example, laying out how a company like General Motors will transition from making cars with combustible engines to producing electronically powered vehicles over X years) to something as simple as establishing a revenue goal for a group of sales reps who service a specific geographical region. In the following sections, we describe the most important parts of a business plan and provide a few examples.

Capturing the most critical material

Business plans generally include a wide range of information, data, reports, articles, analyses, assessments, and the list goes on and on. The level of detail included in a business plan is usually dependent on the target audience; what might be presented to an external group of venture capitalists or private equity investors (that is, much more condensed with limitations on disclosing confidential information) is significantly different than presenting a business plan to a company's board of directors.

TIP

Also, you may frequently hear the term "The Deck" referenced, which is nothing more than a condensed version of a business plan presented in an easy-to-understand, logical, and appealing format (such as a PowerPoint file or PDF).

A macro-level business plan should cover all relevant and critical material, which can basically be broken down into the following five primary buckets:

>> **Summarize the market environment.** Consider questions such as these: What is the current market opportunity or need? What market or industry characteristics and trends are present? What is the size of the market? What competition is present? On the surface, providing market information should be a no-brainer, yet in practice this is one topic that business plans tend to be weak in addressing, because acquiring reliable and credible third-party market information is much easier said than done.

>> **Overview what resources will be required.** What physical assets will be needed and when? Will new technology need to be developed? What will the organizational chart (org chart) look like? When will personnel need to be hired? What supply chain considerations are present? Again, the potential list of topics is endless, but it should be focused on key operational functions that are critical to the success of the plan.

>> **List the management team.** This is relatively simple and straightforward because there is no way a business plan is going to be executed without a strong, experienced, and committed management team being in place.

>> **Forecast the potential financial return.** Generally speaking, the financial opportunity or return is highlighted with a forecast or proforma income statement that presents multiple years of business operating results (with three to five years of forecast income statements being common).

>> **Summarize the amount and type of required financial capital.** A conclusion should be drawn not just as to the amount of capital investment a company needs to make in order to execute the business plan but, more importantly, what type of capital (debt or equity) will be needed and, even more critical, what the capital structure will be. The financial capital conclusion is often supported by what is referred to as "sources and uses of funds," which outlines total sources of capital and how the capital will be used or deployed.

Condensing this even further, here is what a business plan really is. It answers these questions: What is the opportunity, what resources are needed, who is the management team, what is the potential financial return, and how much capital is needed?

Providing a few examples

The remainder of this chapter focuses on the fifth bullet point in the previous section, related to how much and what type of financial capital is needed; expanding on the first three points would constitute a book of itself (and financial forecasts and projections are covered in Chapter 17). Before we move on with our discussion on exploring financial capital in more depth, we want to remind everyone just how wide the range and scope of business plans can be by providing four very real examples in today's economy:

>> A small family gets together and wants to pool their resources, knowledge, and savings and pursue of the American dream to open a new family-owned restaurant to serve their neighborhood after the local restaurant community was decimated by Covid-19. Although this type of business formation and launch doesn't tend to get much attention from the press or social media, thousands of these types of business "dreams" are launched monthly across the country.

>> Technology start-ups launched by aspiring entrepreneurs are very much in vogue these days. Silicon Valley represents a hub of the technology world and is constantly evaluating and, when appropriate, investing in the next Tesla or Airbnb (hopefully). New start-ups require significant financial capital to launch, with *equity raises* being the most common form of capital.

>> Large, mature businesses operating in industries ranging from finance/banking to technology powerhouses such as Apple have, over the past five-plus years, undertaken strategies to raise capital through issuing "debt," which in turn is used (along with internal cash resources) to buy back their own stock. We cover this Wall Street tactic in Chapter 14, but you should remember that implementing this type of strategy represents just as much of a business plan as a new start-up raising equity capital.

>> To provide another example of a business plan, think about Exxon for a moment. Here is a company that has operated in the oil and gas industry for over 100 years and has had to weather a serious economic correction in this space (most recently with a collapse in the price of oil, starting in 2014) as well as the current threat and opportunity posed by renewable energy sources. You can imagine the business planning that must be undertaken when evaluating the value of billions of dollars of investments in energy properties and what type of capital the company will require to reposition its business in the renewable space.

The point is that business plans and the conclusion on how much financial capital will be needed are vast, complex, and constantly changing and evolving as market conditions change.

Valuing Businesses: A Crash Course in the Basics

Before we get to the meat and potatoes of raising capital in the rest of this chapter, we start our discussion with a brief overview on an extremely important topic of why and how businesses are valued. When raising capital for a business, the "why" part of the equation should be very clear. If your company needs $2 million of equity capital, you can't very well ask for the $2 million without estimating the value of the business. That is, does the $2 million investment get 20 percent ownership in the company (the company would be valued at $10 million after the $2 million investment, owning 20 percent) or 5 percent in the company (the company would be valued at $40 million after the $2 million investment, owning 5 percent)? Obviously, the difference in ownership is substantial, so it should be obvious why businesses need to be valued in order to raise capital.

As a reminder, accounting is often just as much of an art form as a science. The same concept holds with estimating business values; the desired result or objective often influences and dictates the final valuation. As the old accounting adage goes, "What does two plus two equal?" to which the accountant replies, "What does it need to be?"

Why businesses are valued

The why part of valuing a business basically comes down to one of four primary reasons, as you find out in the following sections: raising capital, a liquidity event, business planning and risk management, or estate and personal planning.

We want to offer one comment on a business valuation as it relates to its need or purpose. In the case of valuing a business for a company sale or to raise capital, the primary objective is usually to drive the valuation as high as possible. On the flip side, when businesses are valued for estate taxation purposes or to potentially buy out a pain-in-the-neck partner, lower business valuations may be desired to help reduce potential estate taxes or decrease the amount paid to an exiting partner.

Raising capital

As covered later in this chapter, companies frequently must raise capital to finance ongoing operations and often do this through selling equity. Whether this is done at the private level (for example, a venture capitalist firm investing in a new technology start-up) or at the public level (for example, a company undertaking an initial public offering, or IPO, to raise capital in the public markets), the same concept holds. That is, X percent of the company is sold for $Y, which is dependent on a business value being set. You would never simply invest $Y not knowing how much of a company you would own, thus the reason for setting the valuation.

Be aware that even when a business raises debt to help finance operations, a business valuation may be required. A perfect example of this is with real estate, because a lending institution may require an appraisal (or valuation) to be completed prior to extending a loan. In the real estate industry, this is what is often referred to as loan-to-value ratio.

A liquidity event

It should be relatively obvious that for most (but not all) businesses, there comes a time to achieve a liquidity or exit event (clever names for selling the business). Although companies can achieve a liquidity event through undertaking an initial public offering (IPO) on a large stock exchange such as Nasdaq, this is generally reserved for the largest multibillion-dollar organizations. For most smaller businesses that generate annual sales measured in millions of dollars, outright sales of a business are usually more effective strategies to achieve a liquidity event.

The motivations for business sales vary and may arise for any number of reasons, including business partners wanting to be bought out, early investors looking to cash out, a family-owned business that has reached the end of the line (for example, no further heirs left to operate the business), a group of employees wanting to buy the business from the founders, or a change in market conditions necessitating the sale of a business, to name a few. To achieve a fair and equitable sale of a business, a proper valuation must be established.

Business planning and risk management

Valuations are also extremely helpful in assisting with the management of the business as it relates to supporting various tasks such as ensuring that proper levels of insurance are secured (to protect company assets), establishing benchmarks to evaluate the progress of a business, helping set values for potential equity participation or incentive plans (extended to the company's employees), assisting with evaluating potential business tax obligations or assessments (if business legal forms are changed), and various other management functions.

Estate and personal planning

Valuations are integral and an essential part of the personal financial planning and management process, ranging from estates to gifting to potential marriage dilutions (which all involve protecting accumulated wealth and managing potential taxes that may arise). Estate planning is currently a significant focus area because not only is a massive transfer of wealth about to occur as the Baby Boomers retire and expire (sorry, we all have an expiration date) but also political winds changed in 2020, favoring a much more aggressive position being taken by the U.S. government on levying additional taxes on the wealthy. Increased taxes on the wealthy were a basis of the Democrats' campaign strategy in 2020 and will almost certainly be enacted by 2022. For high-net-worth individuals and families, several of whom own all or a portion of businesses, the need to establish a fair value for these businesses represents a critical element of their estate planning process.

How businesses are valued

REMEMBER

As for the how part of valuing a business, we'll keep this as simple as possible. All business valuations, in one fashion or another, are based on two key variables: the ability to generate positive cash flows (or profits) and the discount rate applied to future cash flows. No matter what valuation model, methodology, logic, concept, technique, and/or principle is used, they all come back to the company's ability to generate future positive cash flow and then discount that cash flow back to "today" to calculate a value. Even when a company is being liquidated, the end value is based on how much cash will be left over for the equity owners after all assets have been liquidated and debts paid. Simply put, cash flow reigns as king when valuing a business.

Throughout this book, we cover the income statement and profit generation, as well as business cash flows or EBITDA (earnings before interest, taxes, depreciation, and amortization) extensively. If you've read the book straight through so far, you should have a solid understanding of these key operating metrics, so we won't go into a detailed explanation of this first variable other than to state the obvious. That is, the higher a company's profit or EBITDA/cash flow, the higher the business valuation tends to be. And with this statement you can see why there is such an emphasis on driving profits and cash flows higher, which generally leads to higher valuations.

REMEMBER

At this point, we want to turn your attention to understanding the second key variable, which is based in the universal concept involving the time value of money (the present value of future cash flows or discounted cash flows). Simply stated, the *time value of money concept* assumes that a dollar in your hand today is worth more than a dollar in your hand next year, two years from today, and so on. Looking back a couple of decades, when interest rates were north of 5 percent and the Federal Reserve Bank had not stepped in to drive interest rates to close to 0 percent, the impact of the time value of money was much more pronounced than it is today. Figure 18-1 shows an example that highlights just how impactful low interest rates can be on a business value.

XYZ DtoC Example, Inc.
Estimated Company Value — Comparison
as of the Fiscal Year Ending
12/31/2020

Summary Income Statement — EBITDA	FYE	Amount $
EBITDA, Actual FYE	12/31/2020	$1,500,000
EBITDA, Forecast FYE	12/31/2021	$1,800,000
EBITDA, Forecast FYE	12/31/2022	$2,160,000
EBITDA, Forecast FYE	12/31/2023	$2,592,000
EBITDA, Forecast FYE	12/31/2024	$3,110,400
EBITDA, Forecast FYE	12/31/2025	$3,732,480
EBITDA, Forecast FYE	12/31/2026	$4,478,976
EBITDA, Forecast FYE	12/31/2027	$5,374,771
EBITDA, Forecast FYE	12/31/2028	$6,449,725
EBITDA, Forecast FYE	12/31/2029	$7,739,671
Net Present Value of Cash Flow Stream @	*4.00%*	$29,800,000
Net Present Value of Cash Flow Stream @	*8.00%*	$23,300,000
Change in Value Based on Discount Rate		21.81%

Confidential — Property of XYZ DtoC Example, Inc.

© *John Wiley & Sons, Inc.*

FIGURE 18-1:
Sample company valuation delta using different discount rates.

Figure 18-1 calculates the value of a business assuming a starting point of $1,500,000 in annual EBITDA/cash flow, which is forecast to grow for the next nine years at a 20 percent compounded growth rate. Assuming a 4 percent discount rate, the company's value is estimated to be roughly $29.8 million. Apply an 8 percent discount rate to the same cash flow stream and the value decreases to roughly $23.3 million (a 21.81 percent decrease).

Note that countless business valuation metrics are in use today that are generally driven by key operating performance standards or targets as established within different industries. For example, the real estate industry bases most valuations on a property's NOI (net operating income) divided by a cap rate — translation, the net operating income or operating profit (cash flow) divided by a capitalization rate (discount rate).

Another example relevant in today's economy is how SaaS companies are valued. For those not familiar with this term, SaaS stands for software as a service and is related to technology companies that sell subscription software services (for example, Shopify, Slack, and so on) to customers who repeatedly use the technology year-in and year-out. Quite often, these companies are valued by applying a valuation multiple on the company's ARR (annual recurring revenue). For example, if a company generates $30 million a year in ARR and receives a five-times multiple on this figure, the company would be valued at $150 million. Again, here is the translation: What most investors know is that a company that produces $30 million a year in SaaS ARR should be able to generate operating profits (positive cash flow) of 25 percent or more on this revenue or $7.5 million. So basically, the valuation has been set at 20 times operating profits, which backs into a discount rate of approximately 4.5 percent (assuming no change in annual operating profits of $7.5 million for a time period of 50 years). The 4.5 percent discount rate may appear low, but in this case, an investor may be "banking" on the company achieving above average revenue and operating profit growth rates translating into higher future positive cash flows.

Surveying Commonly Used Business Valuation Techniques

Countless models exist to value businesses and can get to be rather complex (especially when the Wall Street financial wizards get involved). To avoid overkill, in this section we summarize two business valuation models or techniques that are particularly common and the easiest to understand. One thing you should notice right away is that these business valuation techniques both rely on the same two critical variables described previously: positive cash flow or profits and discount rates applied.

Under either of the following techniques, one fact holds true: When cash flow multiples or price/earnings ratios are higher, the market is effectively "pricing in" a much higher growth rate of earnings over the coming years. Or looking at it from a different perspective, the market is willing to pay much more today for high-growth companies, with significant business upside, that can deliver superior profit and cash flow growth in the future. Of course, anticipated or expected future profits compared to actual delivered or achieved profits are often two very different figures.

Cash flow multiple method

The cash flow multiple method is applicable to most small to medium-sized business operations and is often referred to as the Main Street approach. Under this method, a cash flow multiple is applied to a company's expected/future adjusted cash flow stream. This adjusted cash flow stream is commonly referred to as EBITDA. Cash flow multiples often range from a low end of 3 to over 20 and are influenced by a company's perceived risk and growth factors. In addition, it should be noted that historical cash flow information tends to be used as a basis or starting point when calculating the expected/future "adjusted" cash flow stream. For example, if a company's prior-year EBITDA was $1,500,000 annually and a multiple of 8 is applied, the business's value is approximately $12 million ($1,500,000 × 8).

This business valuation method is more widely utilized by Main Street than the price earnings multiple method (see the next section) due to the nature of how these companies operate (a high volume of relatively small and unsophisticated businesses compared to corporate America as represented by Wall Street).

EBITDA stands for earnings before interest, taxes, depreciation, and amortization. EBITDA represents the basis for determining a business's adjusted cash flow on which to base a business valuation. In addition, this term can be expanded to *EBITDA&O*, which simply adds the term *other* to the end. Several businesses need to add other expenses to this equation to account for various one-time or owner preference expenses and income that are nonrecurring in nature. By accounting for these one-time and nonrecurring items, the calculation of a company's adjusted cash flow stream can be clearly supported (EBITDA updated for other expenses and income that are nonrecurring in nature).

To further your understanding of EBITDA and why it is used, business valuations tend to be based on a company's ability to generate real or comparable operating income and cash flows (between similar companies operating in similar markets). The idea is to identify how much cash flow can be generated from the basic business operation as opposed to how much debt the business has incurred (producing interest expense) and how much has been invested in fixed assets (producing depreciation expense) to support the business.

As an example, interest expense is added back to account for the fact that similar businesses may have been financed differently (one using debt and another using equity). While one of the businesses would have interest expense that would produce lower net profits, the other would not, producing higher profits. External business valuations need to extract the impact of how a company has been financed to properly calculate a real value for the assets being acquired. After the real value has been determined, the parties can then structure how best to finance the potential acquisition.

Price earnings multiple method

The price earnings multiple method is most applicable to larger, publicly traded businesses and is often referred to as the Wall Street approach. Using this technique, a business valuation is derived from taking the net after-tax profit of a company and multiplying it by a market-driven factor. For companies that enjoy the prospects of high growth rates, dominant market positions, significant financial resources, and other positive business attributes — all of which translate into potentially significant higher future cash flow streams — a multiple of 20 or more may applied (and extreme cases of over 100 for companies such as Tesla). For businesses that are more mature with relatively steady cash flow streams, a lower multiple, such as 12 to 15, may be applied. This is one (but certainly not the only) reason why a company such as Microsoft may be valued using a factor of 36 whereas a food company such as Conagra may be valued using a factor of only 18.

This technique is most prevalent with publicly traded companies listed on the New York Stock Exchange, Nasdaq, and other markets. The market quickly and efficiently establishes the total value of the company (its market capitalization) that is readily available at any point in time.

Summarizing the Two Basic Types of Available Capital

With our discussion of business plans and valuations out of the way, we can now turn to the options and strategies available to capitalize a business. To keep this simple, capitalizing a business comes down to one of two types: utilizing debt or equity.

We should note that yes, a business can deploy or recycle internal capital that is available from company-generated profits and positive cash flow, but in effect, this is really the same as utilizing equity; rather than distributing profits via issuing dividends, the company can elect to invest the excess earnings back into or inside the business. Further, larger and stronger companies can often leverage suppliers (by requesting extended credit terms) or customers (requiring deposits or enticing quicker payments) to "mine" cash or capital from key relationships. However, this just represents using a different type of debt as compared to formally structured and documented lending agreements. A perfect example of this is Tesla, which for years has required customers to provide a deposit or down payment in advance of finalizing the purchase of a car (which may take three to six months).

For the purposes of this chapter, we are going to focus our discussion on securing capital from external equity and debt sources. When large amounts of capital are required (relatively speaking to the size of the business), companies need to look to external capital sources such as banks, alternative lenders (an extremely broad group), venture capitalists, private equity groups, hedge funds, and, yes, Wall Street.

TIP

Various forms of capital are available that take on the characteristics of both debt and equity. A perfect example of this is *convertible debt*, a form of a loan. Convertible debt has similar characteristics to the debt discussed next but often has more flexible terms attached (for example, specific assets do not need to be pledged as collateral) in exchange for having the option of converting into company equity if desired (based on a triggering event). Convertible debt is really just a form of equity capital in disguise, but it does offer significant benefits to both the issuing company and the party providing the loan.

TECHNICAL
STUFF

Also, a quick word on other forms of capital, including technology, human, brand or market awareness, and similar types of nonfinancial capital. Needless to say, these are all critical forms of business capital and are essential to the success of any business but are beyond the scope of discussion for this book, because our goal is to keep you focused on understanding financial capital.

Realizing when to raise equity

Raising equity amounts to nothing more than selling a portion of the business to an external party that will own X percent of the business moving forward (and have the right to future earnings). Equity sources of capital are best utilized when a company is operating in a higher-risk environment (for example, new start-up operations or financing high growth, incurring losses) and/or needs to maintain a proper debt-to-equity balance (to avoid becoming overleveraged).

In our sample company, a decision was made to sell 500,000 shares of preferred equity to an outside party for $5 million (refer to Figure 18-2). The 500,000 shares amount to a 33.33 percent (500,000 shares divided by the total common and preferred shares of 1,500,000) ownership stake in the company, assuming all the preferred shares have the same basic rights to earnings as the common shares. The company elected to raise equity to help strengthen the balance sheet as well as to finance a large and potentially risky investment in a future acquisition.

Description	Number of Shares	Invested Amount	Voting Issued & O/S % Owned	Fully Diluted % Owned
QW Example Tech., Inc. **Unaudited Cap Table** **for the Fiscal Year Ending** **12/31/2020**				
Preferred Equity:				
H&H Test VC Firm, Fund V	500,000	$5,000,000	33.33%	30.77%
Subtotal — Preferred Equity	500,000	$5,000,000	33.33%	30.77%
Common Equity:				
Founders, Original	800,000	$2,000,000	53.33%	49.23%
Investors, Various Parties	200,000	$3,000,000	13.33%	12.31%
Subtotal — Common Equity	1,000,000	$5,000,000	66.67%	61.54%
Common Equity Options & Warrants:				
Stock Options Issued & Outstanding	75,000	$0	0.00%	4.62%
Warrants Issued for Common Stock Purchases	50,000	$0	0.00%	3.08%
Subtotal — Common Equity Options & Warrants	125,000	$0	0.00%	7.69%
Total, All Forms of Equity	1,625,000	$10,000,000	100.00%	100.00%

Confidential — Property of QW Example Tech., Inc.

FIGURE 18-2: Sample company capitalization table ("cap table").

REMEMBER

In summary, the pros of raising equity capital are centered in securing much-needed cash, strengthening the balance sheet, and potentially bringing on a valuable long-term capital and strategic partner, among others. The primary cons are centered in having to sell a portion of the company, diluting the current shareholder's ownership stake (in our example, diluting ownership from 100 percent to 66.67 percent) and possibly relinquishing certain management control over critical business decision-making activity.

Knowing when debt is the best source of capital

Raising debt is nothing more than securing a loan from a financial institution (for example, a bank, an asset-based lender, a risk-based lender, and so on) that has set repayment terms and performance requirements. Debt sources of capital are best utilized when a company has assets available to pledge as collateral, can document and support that internal cash flows are adequate to service the debt service debt, has enough strength in the balance sheet to avoid being overleveraged, and for companies that are relatively mature (with stable operations and proven profitability or a defendable business plan).

Referring to our sample technology company, it raised $9 million of debt in the form of a loan in 2018 to refinance existing debt, help finance future asset acquisitions, and support ongoing business operations. As of the end of 2020, the loan balance had been reduced to $7 million, comprised of $6 million of long-term debt and $1 million of current debt; $1 million of debt had been repaid in 2019 and another $1 million repaid in 2020 (see Figure 8-2). You may notice that the total of notes payable, other long-term debt, and current portion of debt amounts to $7.25 million in Figure 7-2, yet our figure here is $7 million. The reason for the difference is that the company has $250,000 of other long-term liabilities that are not part of the loan (and relate to other long-term contingencies that the company is obligated to pay).

In total, our sample company raised $14 million of capital, 36 percent from equity and 64 percent from debt, to support future acquisitions and business growth, leaving excess capital available for other purposes. You may ask why the company raised $14 million of capital when it may only pursue acquisitions of no more than $10 million (a figure we simply include for reference purposes); the answer is simple. The company wanted to make sure it had additional equity capital to invest in new marketing and strategic growth initiatives that are anticipated to take additional time. Translation: It built a cushion to help navigate and manage potential hiccups to its business plan.

REMEMBER

We expand our discussion of debt-based capital in the next section of this chapter, but here we summarize the primary pros and cons of using debt capital:

>> The pros of utilizing debt capital are that it brings in much-needed cash, does not dilute the ownership of the existing investors (an extremely big pro), and helps reduce or limit the potential management influence that may be realized from bringing on new owners.

>> The cons with utilizing debt capital are that the company will generally have to pledge assets as collateral (putting the assets at risk), must adhere to set loan repayment terms (committing future cash flows to repaying the debt), will have to pay interest on the loan, and will most likely have to abide by covenants established by the lender.

Taking a Deeper Dive into Raising Debt Capital

We start our discussion of debt capital by overviewing some basic concepts, strategies, and terminologies to better help you understand debt-based capital at a more granular level.

Maturity and security

REMEMBER

To begin, always keep these two words in mind when thinking about debt: maturity and security.

>> *Maturity* means all debt must be repaid over an agreed-upon period based on the terms and interest rate established.

>> *Security* refers to what assets are pledged and used as collateral or what type of guarantees are provided to support the loan.

Debt sources (loans)

Literally hundreds of different types of financial institutions are willing to provide loans. In fact, the innovation and evolution of lending sources over the past decade has been nothing short of amazing. But in the end, debt sources still generally fall into one of four primary groupings:

>> Traditional banks

>> Risk-based lenders (a very broad group of financing sources, often referred to as shadow banking, that include asset-based lenders, hard-money lenders, lenders disguised as companies providing "advances," and the list goes on and on)

>> Hybrid debt/equity lenders (in other words, convertible debt)

>> Large financial institutions such as insurance companies (that may invest in the bonds issued by a public company)

REMEMBER

To effectively raise debt capital, companies need to clearly understand where they stand in the lender risk appetite food chain. For stronger operating companies that have solid profits and financial strength, banks should be readily available to provide loans (and should also be the cheapest form of debt). For riskier companies that have shaky profits and are highly leveraged, the risk-based lenders would be more logical to approach given their appetite for these types of loans (which also are far more expensive than bank loans). And for the largest publicly traded companies, the public debt or bond markets should be accessible to raise capital (which can offer very inexpensive interest rates in the current environment).

Debt underwriting and costs

The general rule is that when debt sources underwrite a loan, there are several factors:

>> A company's ability to generate positive cash flow (to cover debt service payments)

>> The value of the collateral (in case the collateral needs to be liquidated to repay the loan)

>> Secondary repayment sources that generally fall outside of the company (for example, a personal guarantee, or PG, provided by an owner or a parent entity guarantee)

WARNING

Also, it should be clear that the higher the perceived risk with issuing the loan, the greater the return on the loan needs to be (to the parties providing the loan), which may come from higher interest rates, additional fees, or attaching some type of "equity kicker" (for example, the loan includes an option or warrant to purchase X common shares at a discounted price if desired). However, a word of caution is warranted when raising debt capital: This ocean is filled with sharks, most of which are full of nasty surprises. You would be absolutely amazed at just how expensive debt can be when secured from the risk-based lenders, so do your homework and read the fine print because the devil is in the detail.

Debt structure

The balance sheet provides an important clue related to structuring loans correctly. If you refer to Figure 7-2, you notice that the balance sheet presents the current portion of debt as a current liability and notes payable and other long-term debt as a long-term liability. This means that as of the FYE 12/31/20, our sample company has $1 million of debt due within the next 12 months and approximately $6 million of long-term debt due past 12 months (in our case, over the next three years). And as a reminder, the company has $250,000 of other long-term liabilities present that are not part of the actual loan but, when added to the $6 million of long-term debt, amounts to the $6.25 million figure in the balance sheet.

TIP

When securing debt-based capital, it's important to properly match long-term debt with assets that will generate profits and cash flow over a long-term period (for example, five years), such as property, equipment, and intangible assets, as well as to match short-term sources of debt with current assets such as trade accounts receivables or inventory (that are anticipated to turn into cash relatively quickly). A perfect example of this strategy is securing a short-term loan, which is commonly referred to as a working capital line of credit, that uses a loan advance formula that varies with trade accounts receivable or inventory balances. Companies that have significant seasonality in their business cycles will structure a working capital line of credit that allows them to borrow up to 80 percent of eligible trade receivables (the collateral) to provide liquidity to support customer sales during the high season. As sales and trade accounts receivables increase, the company can borrow against the collateral to provide cash to support ongoing operations, and then when the customers remit payment, the company has excess cash available, which it can then use to repay the line of credit lending facility. The key concept here is to properly match the structure of debt repayment term with the cash generation ability of the asset used as collateral.

Debt covenants

Most loans include lending covenants that provide guardrails (for lack of a better term) to ensure that a company maintains a certain financial performance to support the repayment of the loan. We cover some of these in Chapter 12, including the debt service coverage ratio (DSCR), but we want to point out that lenders will utilize a wide range of other covenants (financial and operational), including maintaining strong current ratios, establishing minimum profitability requirements (the company must generate positive earnings), requiring audited financial statements, and restricting the company from securing other loans, just to provide a few examples of other covenants.

The range of covenants is extensive and varies significantly by type of lender, but the key for the borrower is to clearly understand their company's borrowing needs and market conditions to negotiate the covenants in advance (and as part of the loan underwriting process). For example, if you know your company may have a soft year and struggle to break even, avoid a minimum profitability requirement covenant (at least for the year in question). You should use visibility of your company's financial performance from the forecasting process (covered in Chapter 17) to identify covenants that may be problematic, allowing you to negotiate more flexible and favorable covenants well in advance.

TIP

One final comment as it relates to covenants: in the current economic environment and capital markets, you might come across the terms *cov.-lite* or *no-cov.* loans. These are just as they sound: *cov.-lite* means that a loan is being provided with noticeably light or low levels of covenants, and *no-cov.* indicates that the loan basically has no covenants. Yes, we agree that it is nothing short of crazy for a lender to issue a loan with basically no covenants, but then again, 2020 and 2021 are about some of the craziest markets we have ever seen.

Digging Further into the World of Equity Capital

We've elected to hold our final discussion on raising capital (in the form of equity) to the last section of the balance sheet — owners' or stockholders' equity. This is the section of the balance sheet that appears on the bottom of the right side of the balance sheet (from a horizontal perspective) or at the bottom of the second page (from a vertical perspective). It is no coincidence that we have saved this topic for the last discussion; after all is said and done with learning the what, when, where, and how of financial information, we turn our attention to who owns and controls a business (and why this is so critical, beyond the obvious reasons). We introduce balance sheets in Chapter 7.

REMEMBER

Before we dive into explaining owners' equity in more depth, we want to preface our discussion with highlighting two points:

>> For those readers who are operating a business unit or division of an existing business, our discussion on owners' equity and business capitalization may not appear to be all that relevant (Why bother? The corporate mothership deals with the function of raising capital and managing the owners and creditors). Simple enough, but we should note that the topics covered in this chapter could be useful for you to understand beyond just how your organization is capitalized. It's important to understand clearly that whether you're working with customers, suppliers, strategic partners, or the like, the ownership of any third party can have a huge influence on future decision-making (and your relationship with these parties).

>> Most small businesses tend to be closely held and formed as either partnerships, subchapter S corporations, or simple single-owner limited liability companies (LLCs). For these entities, owners' equity is often an afterthought, because the net equity of these types of businesses is usually just comprised of two components: retained earnings and common equity. For these types of companies, retained earnings are nothing more than a business's cumulative net profits and losses, less any distributions of earnings paid (made over the year). Common equity captures the amount of capital contributed by the owners of the company who generally (and legally) should have the same rights to profits, distributions, voting, and so forth on a prorated basis to their

actual ownership. That is, if one owner invested $20,000 in exchange for 2,000 common stock shares and another owner invested $10,000 in exchange for 1,000 common stock shares, the first owner should maintain rights to distributions of earnings, profits, and voting of 66.67 percent (2,000 shares owned out of 3,000 shares issued in total).

Again, and by reading on, you as a small business owner will gain additional knowledge that may be useful when dealing with third parties or, better yet, if considering raising more complex forms of capital (and their pros and cons).

Our discussion on owners' equity is going to move well beyond smaller businesses and be directed toward more complex business capital structures that involve multiple types of equity and even quasi forms of equity disguised as debt. While all businesses will have retained earnings (as previously discussed) or, in the case of multiple years of losses, accumulated deficits (where cumulative losses are greater than cumulative profits), when companies utilize more complex legal entities such as C corporations or LLCs, they also tend to use a wider range of different types of equity to capitalize their business. In a nutshell, this is what is commonly referred to as the capitalization table or *cap table*.

REMEMBER

The cap table is really nothing more than a table or spreadsheet that spells out exactly who owns what in terms of the equity issued by a company as presented or listed by what type of equity has been issued. On the surface, reading a cap table should be relatively straightforward: It should list various parties and their respective ownership percentage in the company's owner equity. However, as previously discussed, the devil is absolutely in the details when understanding cap tables and the potential impact as to what owners truly control the company and have the most advantageous ownership stakes.

We have laid out the topics covered in this section from the perspective of the equity owner's rights to claims against the company as opposed to the total amount of equity owned in the company. This may seem somewhat convoluted, but as you read through the material, you'll quickly gain an understanding of why it's important to understate rights and preferences in lockstep with total ownership interest. For simplicity, our discussion focuses on three main components of a typical cap table:

>> Risk-based debt (such as convertible notes)

>> Preferred equity

>> Common equity, options, and warrants

Before we dive into these topics in more depth, a quick word is warranted on the primary available sources of equity capital (from the market). Raising equity can be achieved by pursuing different sources of capital ranging from tapping what we like to refer to as FF&CBAs (family, friends, and close business associates), who are often unsophisticated when making investment decisions, all the way through to taking a company public through an IPO (a complex process targeting sophisticated investors).

In between these two extremes is equity capital, which is usually raised from groups that have a keen expertise in providing the right financial capital at the right time and include VCs (venture capitalists), PEs or PEGs (private equity or private equity groups), HNWIs (high-net-worth individuals, sometimes referred to as angel investors), HFs (hedge funds), and other similar types of capital sources. These groups tend to specialize by industry or company stage, usually have significant amounts of capital to deploy, and employ highly qualified management teams to assess the investment opportunities.

Disguising equity as debt

Companies that cannot raise capital from traditional debt sources, such as banks or alternative-based lenders, and that do not want to raise equity capital (over fears of diluting the ownership and control of the company) often use what is commonly referred to as *convertible debt* (a hybrid form of debt and equity that has characteristics of both).

REMEMBER

Convertible debt is a form of actual debt (a loan to the company) that is reported on a company's balance sheet as a liability, similar to a note or loan payable. Most convertible debt is structured to be long term, with common repayment terms of two to five years. The reason for the name is that convertible debt, at the option of the party providing the loan or if a specific event occurs, can be converted into either common or preferred equity of the company. The conversion of the debt may occur for any number of reasons: For example, the company achieved a milestone such as a predetermined sales revenue level being met, the company raised a large amount of equity (the triggering event) and the company is sold, or the due date of the convertible debt is reached and the debt cannot be repaid.

A logical question at this point is why would a company want to raise money using convertible debt, and conversely, why would an external party want to invest in convertible debt? We answer both questions here:

> » **Issuing convertible debt to raise capital:** Raising capital through issuing convertible debt is often used by companies that need to bridge the business (by providing a capital infusion) to get from point D to point F to help substantiate a higher valuation. If a company is worth $X at point D but can see it being worth three times more at point F (based on achieving key milestones), the company can raise equity capital at a much higher valuation and reduce

the risk of ownership dilution. Further, when companies do not qualify for traditional bank or alternative-based loans, it can tap a more junior or subordinated type of debt by raising capital through convertible debt (and if structured correctly by the company, it can avoid providing an actual secured interest in company assets).

Convertible debt, just like traditional bank loans, requires interest payments and set repayment terms the company must abide by, but generally speaking, the repayment terms are structured very favorably for the company. That is, a below-market interest rate is provided, which is accrued monthly and not paid until the due date of the convertible debt. Further, it is not uncommon for convertible debt to not require periodic payments but come 100 percent due at the end of the term. Under this structure, the company has the maximum flexibility to use the capital raised for the longest period of time, because the debt interest and principal will not be due until the very end.

» **Investing in convertible debt to provide capital:** So why would a convertible debt investment be of interest to third parties? Here is your answer:

- Debt has a higher seniority or claim against company assets than equity. Although convertible debt is often structured in a junior position to bank or alternative lender loans (these lenders have a higher claim to company assets in case of a company liquidation or bankruptcy, so they get paid first, assuming cash is available), they sit higher in the "cap stack" as it relates to distributing company assets in the event of an unfortunate or depressed company sale.

- The convertible debt investors can earn a set return on their investments from the interest rate established (such as 6 percent per annum), even though this may not be paid until the due date.

- Maybe most importantly, the convertible debt investors have additional return upside via being able to convert into the company's equity down the road. It is quite common for convertible debt to include a feature that allows the investors to convert into the company's equity at a discount to a future capital raise. For example, the convertible debt investors may be provided a 20 percent discount against the price of company's equity value established in a large subsequent equity capital raise. If the company raised a large amount of capital at $20 per share, the convertible debt investors would be allowed to convert the debt principal and any accrued interest at $16 per share (thus realizing an additional 20 percent return on their invested capital).

Similar to convertible debt, a company may raise capital through issuing a junior tranche of debt that has set repayment terms and interest rates established. But unlike convertible debt, warrants to purchase equity in the company may be attached instead of allowing the debt to convert. For example, if our sample company needed to sweeten the deal to entice the third-party lender to provide the loan of $8 million, it could offer the lender a warrant to purchase 50,000 common shares at $1 per share at the lender's choice. Similar to the 20 percent discount provided to the investors in the convertible debt, the common stock warrant provides for an "equity kicker" to enhance the overall investment return well above the stated interest rate.

REMEMBER

The nuances, details, and specifics surrounding convertible or junior debt are extensive, complex, and well beyond the scope of this book. Our goal with overviewing this form of capital is not to make you an expert on this specific subject but rather to socialize the concept of debt/equity hybrid forms of capital and why they are attractive to both the company raising capital and the investors providing capital. In effect, these forms of capital represent a middle-of-the-road strategy to help balance the use of debt and equity in one type of financial capital. As with all forms of financial capital, there are pros and cons associated with each form, so the trick is knowing when to use each form and, in all cases, making sure you have proper professional counsel to navigate the capital-raising process.

Structuring equity with preferences

We're now going to move further down the cap table and explore the wonderful world of preferred equity. Before we do this, let's look at where we stand in the investor priority list to make sure we understand the basic order of potential claims that creditors, investors, and owners would have against the company (in the event of a company liquidation, dissolution, or bankruptcy), which we touch on in the previous section when referring to the "cap stack."

Figure 18-3 provides a simple summary of the cap stack for our sample company. Earlier in Figure 18-2, we present our sample company's cap table, which emphasizes equity ownership (in other words, who owns what). The cap stack presented in Figure 18-3 emphasizes the pecking order of creditors', investors', and owners' claims against company assets and provides some comments and thoughts on who would get what in a liquidating event. The cap stack can be a very sobering analysis for equity investors; in this case, if the company had to liquidate and received $16.2 million for all its assets because of a forced liquidation proceeding, it would have enough to cover the total liabilities with not quite enough left over to repay the preferred stock owners (leaving nothing for the common stock owners).

REMEMBER

The reason we present the cap stack is to highlight the priority status of the preferred stock owners of being below debt but above common stock owners. This is the first and most critical concept to understand about preferred equity or stock: It almost always has a *preference* to common equity or stock when it comes to not just rights to dividends or earnings (before the common equity) but, more importantly, claims against company assets.

QW Example Tech., Inc.
Estimated Cap Stack
for the Fiscal Year Ending
12/31/2020

Summary of Liabilities & Equity (All Numbers in Thousands)	Priority Status	Amount	Notes/Comments
Payroll, Taxes, & Burden Payable	High	$444	Employee obligations are generally at the top of the list.
Income Taxes Payable	High	$804	Governments make sure they get their money.
Loans & Notes Payable, Secured	High	$7,000	Senior debt/secured against company assets.
Trade Payables & Accrued Liabilities	High/Medium	$2,315	Depending on terms with vendors, could be high or medium.
Deferred Revenue & Other Current Lia.	Medium	$400	Customer advance payments & deposits not secured.
Other Long-term Debt	Medium	$250	Other contingent debt, limited rights to assets.
Subtotal Liabilities		$11,213	
Preferred Stock	Medium/Low	$5,000	Higher preference than common but lower than debt.
Subtotal Liabilities & Preferred Stock		$16,213	
Common Stock	Low	$5,000	Basically last in priority with rights to company assets.
Common Stock Options & Warrants	Bottom	$0	Value dependent on successful company only.
Subtotal Shareholders' Common Equity		$5,000	
Total Liabilities & Equity		$21,213	

FIGURE 18-3: Sample company cap stack.

In our sample company, we previously disclose that the preferred equity has the right to receive an 8 percent annual dividend before any company earnings are returned to common stock owners. The preferred equity investors also negotiated terms in this capital offering that include a 1.5-times preference upon a liquidating event. This means that after all debt is satisfied, the preferred equity investors receive 150 percent of their capital investment (in this case $7.5 million) along with any earned but unpaid preferred stock dividends before the common stock owners receive anything (which is also referred to having a *first out* exit provision; their money is first out of the deal). And just to sweeten the deal further, the preferred equity investors included a provision that allows them to convert their preferred stock to common stock upon a qualified event (for example, a company sale that achieves a specific exit value or a successful IPO).

The second critical concept to understand about preferred equity is that usually the investors demand a certain amount of management control, either directly or indirectly, with the company's affairs. For large, preferred capital raises, it's quite common for investors to demand a seat (or possibly two) on the board of directors. For a company that has five board members prior to the preferred capital raise, the terms of the raise may require that the board of directors increase to seven, of which two will be appointed by the preferred equity investors. There are clear reasons preferred equity investors demand board participation, including the ability for them to monitor their investment more closely, as well as to provide valuable executive management insight they may bring to the table. The point is that board of director participation represents direct strategic management involvement in the company.

Indirectly, the preferred investors can (and usually do) include several negative control provisions that help protect their investment. Examples of negative control provisions include requiring 100 percent board approval to raise capital through another equity offering (so that better terms cannot be offered to the next investors at the expense of the current preferred investors), limitations on how much and what type of loans or notes payable can be secured (without their approval), and 100 percent board authorization and approval in the event the company sells the majority of its business interests. Our examples could go on and on, but by now you should get the picture loud and clear. When capital is raised in the form of preferred equity, the structure of these deals tends to strongly favor the preferred equity investors by providing significant financial preferences (to enhance their return) and management involvement (to protect and control their investments).

HOW UNICORNS ARE INFLATED

The financial community (especially VCs and PEGs) often makes references to unicorns, which are nothing more than start-up or young companies that have achieved an extremely lofty valuation (usually $1 billion or more). The high valuation is derived from the fact that if a $100 million investment is made in a company that values the entire company at $1 billion, then the party (or parties) making the investment owns 10 percent of the company. Okay, simple enough, because somebody invested $100 million for a 10 percent stake in the company (so its value must be $1 billion).

What they do not tell you is that the $100 million investment was made in preferred equity that includes the protections discussed in this chapter. Hence, if the company is successful and sells for $2 billion, the preferred investors can convert their preferred shares into common shares, still owning 10 percent of the company, and sell out for $200 million. Not bad for the investment; this is the story everyone wants to hear and achieve. But in the event the company struggles and is ultimately sold off the scrap heap for $250 million (still a tidy sum), the preferred investors do not get 10 percent or $25 million but rather are protected with a 1-times preference and will get their $100 million back.

Remember this when you hear about unicorn valuations: This is the value the investors hope the company will be worth down the road (not what it is worth now), and if it is not, they can cover their downside by investing in preferred equity with favorable terms. In other words, this is just more financial lingo and terminology to familiarize yourself with to make sure you understand the never-ending flow of bull oozing from the financial community.

There is so much information and knowledge surrounding the subject of preferred equity that an entire book could be written on the terms, conditions, provisions, pros, cons, dos, don'ts, and I-should-have-known-betters. In the nearby sidebar "How unicorns are inflated," we want to leave you with this perspective on preferred equity investments — specifically, how the financial community can put a spin on a company and inflate its value.

Reaching the end of the line with equity capital

REMEMBER

Finally, we reach the end of the cap table and conclude our discussion by briefly discussing common stock ownership and common stock options or warrants. There really is not much to discuss, because the reference to "common" says it all. That is, with common stock, everyone is basically in the same bucket with rights to earnings, voting on company matters, claims against company assets, and similar matters. Larger companies may issue multiple types of common stock with a common feature being that the class A common stock has voting rights and the class B common stock has no voting rights, but this type of equity complexity is generally only found in the largest and most powerful companies (for example, Alphabet, aka Google, Class A and C common stock).

Figure 18-2 presents our sample company's cap table, which now reflects ownership by what type of equity owns what percentage of the company. The items of importance in the cap table are as follows:

» Two columns of ownership percentages have been provided, voting and fully diluted. Voting captures only the equity that is issued and outstanding that has voting rights. Since common stock options and warrants are nothing more than having rights to purchase common stock at a later date, they do not have voting rights (thus the reference to 0 percent ownership in this column). The fully diluted column calculates the ownership percentages of the company if all forms of equity were issued and outstanding and held equal rights.

» The cap table reconciles to the statement of change in stockholders' equity presented in Figure 9-1, but now presents the information in a different format (to help the investors understand where they rank in the cap table and the ownership percentages in the company).

» An item of significant importance is the voting ownership percentage of 53.33 percent controlled by the common equity group referenced as "founders." This indicates that the founders of the company still control a majority of the voting shares (just over 50 percent) and, at least through the most recent preferred capital raise, still retain management control of the company (which is especially important for obvious reasons).

>> Completing a little bit of math, you can calculate that the new preferred equity investors purchased their shares at $10 each compared to the original founders investing at $2.50 per common share and the other common stock owners at $15 per share. In other words, the preferred equity investors are breaking even, the original founders' shares have increased in value, while the other common equity investors are currently holding the bag (with implied losses). Oh well, not every investment turns out to be a winner (at least based on the current valuation), but the other common equity investors are hopeful that management, by implementing its new business plan, can increase the value of the company so that all investors achieve a positive return on their investments.

>> The final item in the cap table captures the issuance of equity incentive grants in the form of common stock options or warrants. Common stock options and warrants are often issued (with the right to exercise at a set price based on a future event) to key employees, board members, strategic third parties, and others to provide an extra monetary incentive to allow these parties to participate in the increase in a company's value (if all goes well). Most large companies utilize these types of incentives to attract top employee talent and keep parties engaged with the business to help build value and achieve a successful exit. If all goes well, everyone makes out, and if it does not, let's just say that more than a few common stock options have turned out to be worthless. Options and warrants may have value to the recipient (eventually), but they only provide an option to purchase so unless the option is exercised, these types of equity have no rights to earnings and cannot vote. Thus, we place them at the very bottom of the cap table, because these (potential) equity owners are truly last in line.

REMEMBER

We've reached the bottom of the food chain as it relates to rights to both earnings and claims against assets. It may seem counterintuitive that the founders and the early other common equity investors along with key insiders (in control of common stock options and warrants), the ones that have poured their blood, sweat, and tears into building the business, stand last in line, but this is the reality of operating a business and building it into something of real value. When you raise capital and ask other parties to believe in your business, you must remember the golden rule: Whoever has the gold makes the rules!

Raising Capital: Tips, Tidbits, and Traps

REMEMBER

Closing our discussion on raising capital, we want to leave you with these words of wisdom:

>> **Cash is king.** Businesses must proactively, appropriately, and prudently manage cash resources, or to paraphrase the words of Warden Norton from *The Shawshank Redemption* (referring to the escape of Andy Dufresne), "Lord, it's a miracle, he just vanished like a fart in the wind." If not responsibly managed and protected, your cash will vanish like a fart in the wind!

>> **Never run out of cash.** It's somewhat easy to discuss a miss or negative variance in the income statement, especially if you have best-in-class information (to explain the miss). But if you run out of cash and must explain this to an investor/lender, get ready to have a rather unpleasant discussion with your capital sources; it's going to be painful and most likely involve some very restrictive and unfavorable terms (if they even consider providing more capital).

>> **When capital sources offer extra cash, take it!** Yes, this may translate into more ownership dilution and/or added interest expense, but the ability to build a liquidity cushion for when a business hits the eventual speed bump (which it will) is invaluable. There is nothing worse than having to raise cash when times are tough.

>> **Timing can be everything.** Companies will look to offer equity when the price is high (to limit ownership dilution). This is a quite common tactic with large, hot companies looking to raise extra cash for use down the road as evidenced by Tesla in 2020 (raising extra capital). You need to pay close attention to economic and market cycles, which can change quickly.

>> **When cash is tight, know your balance sheet and how to squeeze it.** You could incentivize customers to pay early or make deposits (a strategy used by Tesla) or push your vendors a bit (but not too much). You might also be able to work with key lenders or investors to have a bit of a slush fund to tap when needed. The key is to plan proactively, understand your cash flow statement, and communicate effectively.

>> **Most importantly, understand that who you take capital from is often more important than the amount, type, and structure of that capital.** Having the right financial partners that understand your business and timelines and have vast experience and resources can be invaluable. Securing capital from the right source can really help turn a highly stressful process into a wonderful experience. Secure capital from the wrong source, and get ready for hell.

REMEMBER

In summary — and yes, for the last time — we emphasize the importance of understanding and relying on the statement of cash flows (see Chapter 8) and retaining proper levels of liquidity to operate your business in good times or bad. There is nothing worse than having to tap capital markets in a hostile environment because the terms will most likely be ugly (if you get them at all). Also remember the adage about banks: They will lend when you do not need it, and when you do, they are nowhere to be found.

5

The Part of Tens

Check out ten tips to help managers get the most bang for their buck out of the business's accounting system. Think of these ten topics as a compact accounting tool kit for managers.

Discover ten tips for investors regarding what to keep in mind and what to look for when reading a financial report. These tips help you gain the maximum amount of information in the minimum amount of time.

Chapter **19**

Ten Tips for Managers

Financially speaking, business managers have four essential jobs:

» Securing adequate capital from debt and equity sources

» Earning adequate profit on that capital

» Expediting cash flow from that profit

» Controlling the solvency of the business

How can accounting help make you become a better business manager? That's the bottom-line question, and the bottom line is the best place to start. Accounting provides the financial information you need for making good profit decisions — and it stops you from plunging ahead with gut-level decisions that feel right but don't hold water after due-diligence analysis. Accounting also provides the cash flow and financial condition information you need. But in order for accounting information to do all these things, you have to understand and know how to interpret it.

Reach Breakeven and Then Rake in Profit

Virtually every business has *fixed expenses.* These are operating costs that are locked in for the year and remain the same whether annual sales are at 100 percent or below half your capacity. Fixed expenses are a dead weight on a business. To make profit, you first have to get over your fixed-costs hurdle. How do you do this? Obviously, you have to make sales. Each sale brings in a certain amount of *margin,* which equals the revenue minus the variable expenses of the sale. (If your sales don't generate margin, you're in trouble.)

Say you sell a product for $100. Your purchase (or manufacturing) cost per unit is $60, which accountants call *cost of goods sold expense.* Your variable costs of selling the item add up to $15, including sales commission and delivery cost. Thus, your margin on the sale is $25: $100 sales price − $60 product cost − $15 variable costs = $25 margin. Margin is before interest and income tax expenses and before fixed expenses for the period are considered.

The next step is to determine your annual breakeven point. *Breakeven* refers to the sales revenue you need just to recoup your fixed operating costs. These costs provide the space, facilities, and people necessary to make sales and earn profit. Say your annual total fixed operating expenses are $2.5 million. If you earn 25 percent average margin on sales, then in order to break even, you need $10 million in annual sales: $10 million × 25 percent margin = $2.5 million margin. At this sales level, margin equals fixed costs, and your profit is zero (you break even). Not very exciting so far, is it? But from here on, it gets much more interesting.

REMEMBER

Until sales reach $10 million, you're in the loss zone. After you cross over the breakeven point, you enter the profit zone. Each additional $1 million of sales over breakeven yields $250,000 profit. Suppose your annual sales revenue is $4 million in excess of your breakeven point. Your profit (earnings before interest and income tax) is $1 million: $4 million sales over breakeven × 25 percent margin ratio = $1 million profit. The main lesson is that after you cross over the breakeven threshold, your margin goes entirely toward profit.

TIP

Your regular profit and loss (P&L) reports might not separate fixed and variable operating expenses — in fact, we bet that this is your situation. What to do? We suggest sorting operating expenses into fixed and variable groups based on the titles of the expense accounts in your P&L. You'll probably have to make some estimates, but hey, this isn't rocket science. In any case, you should understand the leverage effect on operating profit caused when you exceed your breakeven sales level.

Set Sales Prices Right

REMEMBER

In real estate, the three most important profit factors are location, location, and location. In the business of selling products and services, the three most important factors are margin, margin, and margin. Of course, a business manager should control expenses — that goes without saying. But the secret to making profit is both making sales *and* earning an adequate margin on the sales revenue. (Remember, margin equals sales price less all variable costs of the sale.) Chapter 15 explains that internal P&L reports to managers should separate variable and fixed costs so the manager can focus on margin (although they generally don't, unfortunately).

In the example in the preceding section, your sales prices earn 25 percent margin on sales. In other words, $100 of sales revenue generates $25 margin (after deducting the cost of product sold and variable costs of making the sale). Therefore, $16 million in sales revenue, for example, generates $4 million margin. The $4 million margin covers your $2.5 million in fixed costs and provides $1.5 million profit (before interest and income tax).

An alternative scenario illustrates the importance of setting sales prices high enough to earn an adequate margin. Suppose you had set sales prices 5 percent lower. Your margin would therefore be $5 lower per $100 of sales. Instead of 25 percent margin on sales, you would earn only 20 percent margin on sales. How badly would the lower margin ratio hurt profit?

On $16 million annual sales, your margin would be $3.2 million ($16 million sales × 20 percent margin ratio = $3.2 million margin). Deducting $2.5 million fixed costs for the year leaves only $700,000 profit. Compared with your $1.5 million profit at the 25 percent margin ratio, the $700,000 profit at the lower sales prices is less than half. The point of this story is that here, a 5 percent lower sales price causes 53 percent lower profit!

Don't Confuse Profit and Cash Flow

To find out whether you made a profit or had a loss for the year, you look at the bottom line in your P&L report. But you must understand that the bottom line does *not* tell you cash flow. Don't ever assume that making profit increases cash the same amount.

Cash flow can be considerably higher than bottom-line profit or considerably lower. Cash flow can be negative even when you earn a profit, and cash flow can be positive even when you have a loss. There's no natural correlation between profit and cash flow. If we know the profit number, we don't have a clue about the cash flow number because cash flow depends on additional factors.

Accountants do a lousy job of explaining and reporting cash flow from profit. They don't even call it cash flow from profit; rather, they refer to it as cash flow from *operating activities.* So how do you get from the profit bottom line in the income statement (P&L report) to the cash flow from profit? You could try reading the first section of the statement of cash flows (see Chapter 8). Good luck. The first part of the cash flow statement is written by accountants for accountants. Accountants should be ashamed of how poorly this section helps explain why cash flow differs from bottom-line profit.

If you're a busy manager, our advice is to boil down your cash flow analysis to three main factors that cause cash flow to be higher or lower than net income for the period:

>> Depreciation (plus amortization) expense is not a cash outlay in the period it is recorded, so add this amount to bottom-line net income.

>> Group the three current assets: accounts receivable, inventory, and prepaid expenses. If the total change in these three assets is an increase, deduct the amount from bottom-line net income. If it's a decrease, add the amount.

>> Group the current operating liabilities: accounts payable, accrued expenses payable, and income tax payable. If the total change in these three assets is an increase, add the amount to bottom-line net income. If it's a decrease, deduct the amount.

After doing this jig a few times, the process becomes more or less automatic. Furthermore, you should become more aware of and pay closer attention to the drivers of cash flow from bottom-line profit (net income). You'll be better able to explain cash flow to your banker and investors in the business.

Call the Shots on Accounting Policies

You may have heard the adage that war is too important to be left to the generals. Well, accounting is too important to be left to the accountants alone — especially when choosing which fundamental accounting methods to use. We're oversimplifying, but measuring profit and putting values on assets and liabilities boils down to choosing between conservative accounting methods and more optimistic methods. Conservative methods record profit later rather than sooner; optimistic methods record profit sooner rather than later. It's a "pay me now or pay me later" choice. (Chapter 9 gives you the details on alternative accounting methods.)

We encourage you to get involved in setting your company's accounting policies. Business managers should take charge of accounting decisions just like they take charge of marketing and other key activities of the business. Don't defer to your accountant in choosing accounting methods for measuring sales revenue and expenses. The best accounting methods are the ones that best fit with your operating methods and strategies of your business. As the manager, you know the business's operations and strategies better than your accountant. Finally, keep in mind that there are no "default" accounting methods; someone has to choose every method.

Many businesses choose conservative accounting methods to delay paying their income tax. Keep in mind that higher expense deductions in early years cause lower deductions in later years. Also, conservative, income tax–driven accounting methods make the inventory and fixed assets in your balance sheet look anemic. Recording higher cost of goods sold expense takes more out of inventory, and recording higher depreciation expense causes the book value of your fixed assets to be lower. Nevertheless, you may decide that postponing the payment of income taxes is worth it, in order to keep your hands on the cash as long as possible.

Prepare Accurate Forecasts and Projections

When you hear the word *forecasts* or *projections*, you may immediately imagine a planning system involving many persons, detailed forecasting, negotiations over goals and objectives, and page after page of detailed accounting statements that commit everyone to certain performance goals and use benchmarks for the coming period. In reality, all kinds of projection methods and approaches exist. You don't have to budget like Apple or a large business organization. You can do one-person limited-purpose projections. Even developing small-scale projections or simple forecast models can pay handsome dividends.

We explain in Chapter 17 the reasons for developing flexible and adaptable forecast models — for understanding the profit dynamics and financial structure of your business, and for planning for changes in the coming period. Forecasting forces you to focus on the factors for improving profit and cash flow. It's always a good idea to look ahead to the coming year; if nothing else, at least plug the numbers in your profit report for sales volume, sales prices, product costs, and other expenses, and see how your projected profit looks for the coming year. It may not look too good, in which case you need to plan how you'll do better.

The P&L forecast, in turn, lays the foundation for changes in your assets and liabilities that are driven by sales revenue and expenses. Your profit forecast should dovetail with your assets and liabilities forecast and with your cash flow forecast. This information is very helpful in planning for the coming year — focusing in particular on how much cash flow from profit will be realized and how much capital expenditures will be required, which in turn lead to how much additional capital you have to raise and how much cash distribution from profit you'll be able to make.

Demand the Accounting Information You Want

Experienced business managers can tell you that they spend a good deal of time dealing with problems because things don't always go according to plan. Murphy's Law (if something can go wrong, it will, and usually at the worst possible time) is all too true. To solve a problem, you first have to know that you have one. Managers need to get on top of problems as soon as possible. A well-designed accounting system should set off alarms about any developing problems so you can nip them in the bud.

You should identify the handful of critical factors that you need to keep a close eye on. Insist that your internal accounting reports highlight these factors. Only you, the business manager, can identify the most important numbers that you must closely watch to know how things are going. Your accountant can't read your mind. If your regular accounting reports don't include the exact types of information you need, sit down with your accountant and spell out in detail what you want to know. Don't take no for an answer. Don't let your accountant argue that the computer doesn't keep track of this information. Computers can be programmed to spit out any type of information you want.

TIP

Here are some types of accounting information that should *always* be on your radar:

>> Sales levels, both price and unit volumes

>> Margins — gross, operating, and bottom line

>> Variable expenses

>> Fixed expenses

>> Internal cash flow

>> Overdue accounts receivable

>> Slow-moving inventory items

Experience is the best teacher. Over time, you discover which financial factors are the most important to highlight in your internal accounting reports. The trick is to make sure that your accountant provides this information.

Tap into Your CPA's Expertise

As you know, a CPA performs an audit of your financial report; this is the CPA's traditional claim to fame. And the CPA assists in preparing your income tax returns. In doing the audit, your CPA may find serious problems with your accounting methods and call these to your attention. Also, the CPA auditor points out any serious deficiencies in your internal controls (see the next section). And it goes without saying that your CPA can give you valuable income tax advice and guide you through the labyrinth of federal and state income tax laws and regulations.

You should also consider taking advantage of other services a CPA has to offer. A CPA can help you select, implement, and update a computer-based accounting system best suited for your business and can give expert advice on many accounting issues, such as cost-allocation methods. A CPA can do a critical analysis of the internal accounting reports to managers in your business and suggest improvements in these reports. A CPA has experience with a wide range of businesses and can recommend best practices for your business. If necessary, the CPA can serve as an expert witness on your behalf in lawsuits. A CPA may also be accredited in business valuation, financial advising, and forensic methods, which are specializations sponsored by the American Institute of Certified Public Accountants (AICPA).

WARNING

You have to be careful that the consulting services provided by your CPA do not conflict with the CPA's independence required for auditing your financial report. If there's a conflict, you should use one CPA for auditing your financial report and another CPA for consulting services. And don't forget to ask: Does the CPA have experience in providing the expert services? You might ask for names of clients that the CPA has provided these services to and check out whether these businesses were satisfied.

Critically Review Your Controls over Employee Dishonesty and Fraud

Every business faces threats from dishonesty and fraud — from within and from without. Your knee-jerk reaction may be that this sort of stuff couldn't possibly be going on under your nose in your own business.

WARNING

Without your knowing about it, your purchasing manager may be accepting kickbacks or other "gratuities." Your long-time bookkeeper may be embezzling. One of your suppliers may be short-counting you on deliveries. We're not suggesting that you should invest as much time and money in preventing fraud and cheating against your business as Las Vegas casinos do, but every now and then, you should take a hard look at whether your fraud controls are adequate.

Preventing fraud starts with establishing and enforcing good internal controls, which we discuss in Chapter 3. In the course of auditing your financial report, the CPA evaluates your internal controls. The CPA will report to you any serious deficiencies. Even with good internal controls and having regular audits, you should consider calling in an expert to assess your vulnerability to fraud and to determine whether there is evidence of any fraud going on.

TIP

A CPA may not be the best person to test for fraud — even if the CPA has fraud training and forensic credentials. A private detective may be better for this sort of investigation because he has more experience dealing with crooks and digging out sources of information that are beyond what a CPA customarily uses. For example, a private detective may install secret monitoring equipment or even spy on your employees' private lives. We understand if you think that you'd never be willing to go so far to defend yourself against fraud, but consider this: Someone committing fraud against your business has no such compunctions.

Lend a Hand in Preparing Your Financial Reports

Many business managers look at preparing the annual financial report of the business like they look at its annual income tax return — it's a task best left to the accountant. This is a mistake. You should take an active part in preparing the annual financial report. (We discuss preparing the financial report in Chapter 10.) You should carefully think of what to say in the letter to stockholders that accompanies the financial statements. You should also help craft the footnotes to the financial statements. The annual report is a good opportunity to tell a compelling story about the business.

The owner/manager, president, or chief executive of the business has the ultimate responsibility for the financial report. Of course your financial report should not be fraudulent and deliberately misleading; if it is, you can and probably will be sued. But beyond that, lenders and investors appreciate a frank and honest discussion of how the business did, including its problems as well as its successes.

TIP

In our view, Warren Buffett, the CEO of Berkshire Hathaway, continues to set the gold standard for financial reporting. He lays it on the line; if he has a bad year, he makes no excuses. Buffett is appropriately modest if he has a good year. Every annual report of Berkshire Hathaway summarizes the nature of the business and how it makes profit. If you knew nothing about this business, you could learn what you needed to know from its annual report. (Go to www.berkshirehathaway.com to get the company's latest annual report.)

Speak about Your Financial Statements as a Pro

On many occasions, a business manager has to discuss their financial statements with others. You should come across as very knowledgeable and be very persuasive in what you say. Not understanding your own financial statements does not inspire confidence. On many occasions, including the following, your financial statements are the center of attention and you're expected to talk about them convincingly:

>> **Securing a loan:** The lending officer may ask specific questions about your accounting methods and items in your financial statements.

>> **Talking with individuals or other businesses that may be interested in buying your business:** They may have questions about the recorded values of your assets and liabilities.

>> **Dealing with the press:** Large corporations are used to talking with the media, and smaller businesses are profiled in local news stories.

>> **Dealing with unions or other employee groups in setting wages and benefit packages:** They may think that your profits are very high and that you can therefore afford to increase wages and benefits.

>> **Explaining the profit-sharing plan to your employees:** They may take a close interest in how profit is determined.

>> **Putting a value on an ownership interest for divorce or estate tax purposes:** These values are based on the financial statements of the business (and other factors).

>> **Reporting financial statement data to national trade associations:** Trade associations collect financial information from their members. You should make sure that you're reporting the financial information consistently with the definitions used in the industry.

>> **Presenting the annual financial report before the annual meeting of owners:** The shareowners may ask penetrating questions and expect you to be very familiar with the financial statements.

Chapter **20**

Ten Tips for Reading a Financial Report

You can compare reading a business's financial report with shucking an oyster: You have to know what you're doing and work to get to the meat. You need a good reason to pry into a financial report. The main reason to become informed about the financial performance and condition of a business is *because you have a stake in the business.* The financial success or failure of the business makes a difference to you.

Shareowners have a major stake in a business, of course. The lenders of a business also have a stake, which can be substantial. Shareowners and lenders are the two main audiences of a financial report. But others also have a financial stake in a business. For example, our books are published by John Wiley & Sons, Inc. (a public company), so we look at its financial report to gain comfort that our royalties will be paid.

In this chapter, we offer practical tips to help investors, lenders, or anyone who has a financial stake in a business glean important insights from its financial reports. These tips also help anyone else with an interest in the financial reports of a business.

TIP

In Chapter 12, we explain the basic ratios that investors and lenders use for judging the profit performance and financial condition of a business. We don't repeat that discussion in this chapter, so our first tip is to read or reread that chapter. The following tips assume you know the ratios.

Get in the Right Frame of Mind

So often we hear nonaccountants say that they don't read financial reports because they aren't "numbers" people. You don't have to be a math wizard or rocket scientist to extract the essential points from a financial report. We know that you can find the bottom line in the income statement and compare this profit number with other relevant numbers in the financial statements. You can read the amount of cash in the balance sheet. If the business has a zero or near-zero cash balance, you know that this is a serious — perhaps fatal — problem.

REMEMBER

Therefore, our first bit of advice is to get in the right frame of mind. Don't let a financial report bamboozle you. Locate the income statement, find bottom-line profit (or loss!), and get going. You can do it — especially when you have a book like this one to help you along.

Decide What to Read

Suppose you own stock shares in a public corporation and want to keep informed about its performance. You could depend on articles and news items in *The Wall Street Journal, The New York Times, Barron's,* and so on that summarize the latest financial reports of the company. Also, you can go to websites such as Yahoo! Finance. This saves you the time and trouble of reading the reports yourself. Generally, these brief articles and websites capture the most important points. If you own an investment portfolio of many different stocks, reading news articles that summarize the financial reports of the companies isn't a bad approach. But suppose you want more financial information than you can get in news articles.

The annual financial reports of public companies contain lots of information: a letter from the chief executive, a highlights section, trend charts, financial statements, extensive footnotes to the financial statements, historical summaries, and lots of propaganda. (We discuss the variety of information in financial reports in Chapter 10.) And you get photos of the top brass and directors (whoopee do!). In contrast, the financial reports of most private companies are significantly smaller; they contain financial statements with footnotes and not much more.

So how much of the report should you actually take the time to read? You could read just the highlights section and let it go at that. This might do in a pinch. We think you should read the chief executive's letter to shareowners as well. Ideally, the letter summarizes in an evenhanded and appropriately modest manner the main developments during the year. Be warned, however, that these letters from the top dog often are self-congratulatory and typically transfer blame for poor performance on factors beyond the control of the managers. Read them, but take these letters with a grain of salt.

TIP

Many public businesses release a *condensed summary version* in place of their much longer and more detailed annual financial reports. Apple does, for example. This is legal, as long as the business mentions that you can get its "real" financial report by asking for a hard copy or by going to its website. The idea, of course, is to give shareowners an annual financial report that they can read and digest more quickly and easily. Also, condensed financial summaries are more cost effective.

In our view, the scaled-down, simplified, and shortened versions of annual financial reports are adequate for average stock investors. They aren't adequate for serious investors and professional investment managers. These investors and money managers should read the full-fledged financial report of the business, and they perhaps should study the company's annual 10-K report that is filed with the Securities and Exchange Commission (SEC). You can go to www.sec.gov and navigate from there.

Improve Your Accounting Savvy

Financial statements — the income statement, balance sheet, and statement of cash flows — are the core of a financial report. To make sense of financial statements, you need at least a rudimentary understanding of financial statement accounting. You don't have to be a CPA, but the accountants who prepare financial statements presume that you're familiar with accounting terminology and financial reporting practices. If you're an accounting illiterate, the financial statements probably look like a Sudoku puzzle. There's no way around this demand on financial report readers. After all, accounting is the language of business. (Now, where have we heard that before?)

TIP

The solution? Read and apply the information in this book. And when you're done, consider reading another book or two about reading financial reports and analyzing financial statements. Without undue modesty, we can recommend our book *How to Read a Financial Report*, 9th Edition (Wiley).

Judge Profit Performance

A business earns profit by making sales and by keeping expenses less than sales revenue, so the best place to start in analyzing profit performance is not the bottom line but the top line: *sales revenue.* Here are some questions to focus on:

>> **How does sales revenue in the most recent year compare with the previous year's?** Higher sales should lead to higher profit, unless a company's expenses increase at a higher rate than its sales revenue. If sales revenue is relatively flat from year to year, the business must focus on expense control to help profit, but a business can cut expenses only so far. The real key for improving profit is improving sales. Therefore, stock analysts put first importance on tracking sales revenue year to year.

>> **What is the gross margin ratio of the business?** Even a small slippage in its gross margin ratio (which equals gross profit divided by sales revenue) can have disastrous consequences on the company's bottom line. Stock analysts would like to know the *margin* of a business, which equals sales revenue minus *all* variable costs of sales (product cost and other variable costs of making sales). But external income statements do not reveal margin; businesses hold back this information from the outside world (or they don't keep track of variable versus fixed expenses).

TIP

>> **Based on information from a company's most recent income statement, how do gross margin and the company's bottom line (net income or net earnings) compare with its top line (sales revenue)?** It's a good idea to calculate the gross margin ratio and the profit ratio for the most recent period and compare these two ratios with last period's ratios. If you take the time to compare these two ratios for a variety of businesses, you may be surprised at the variation from industry to industry. By the way, very few businesses provide profit ratios on the face of their income statements — which is curious because they know that readers of their income statements are interested in their profit ratios.

REMEMBER

One last point: Put a company's profit performance in the context of general economic conditions. A down economy puts downward pressure on a company's profit performance, and you should allow for this in your analysis (although this is easier said than done). In an up economy, a company should do better, of course, because a rising tide lifts all boats.

Test Earnings Per Share (EPS) against Change in Bottom Line

REMEMBER

As you know, public companies report net income in their income statements. Below this total profit number for the period, public companies also report earnings per share (EPS), which is the amount of bottom-line profit for each share of its stock. Figure 6-1 shows an example. Strictly speaking, therefore, the bottom line of a public company is its EPS. Private companies don't have to report EPS; however, the EPS for a private business is fairly easy to calculate: Divide its bottom-line net income by the number of ownership shares held by the equity investors in the company.

The market value of ownership shares of a public company depends mainly on its EPS. Individual investors obviously focus on EPS, which they know is the primary driver of the market value of their investment in the business. The higher the EPS, the higher the market value for a public company. And the higher the EPS, the higher the book value per share for a private company.

Now, you would naturally think that if net income increases, say, 10 percent over last year, then EPS would increase 10 percent. Not so fast. EPS — the driver of market value and book value per share — may change more or less than 10 percent:

>> **Less than 10 percent:** The business may have issued additional stock shares during the year, or it may have issued additional management stock options that get counted in the number of shares used to calculate diluted EPS. The profit pie may have been cut up into a larger number of smaller pieces. How do you like that?

>> **More than 10 percent:** The business may have bought back some of its own shares, which decreases the number of shares used in calculating EPS. This could be a deliberate strategy for increasing EPS by a higher percent than the percent increase in net income.

TIP

Compare the percent increase/decrease in total bottom-line profit over last year with the corresponding percent increase/decrease in EPS. Why? The percent changes in EPS and profit can diverge. For a public company, use its diluted EPS if it's reported. Otherwise, use its basic EPS. (See Chapter 12 for details.)

WARNING

In summary, EPS doesn't necessarily move in perfect sync with the profit performance of a business. A deviation in the change in EPS compared with the change in profit can hamper or boost market value or book value per share. Check the percent change in profit against the percent change in EPS, but be warned: You have to do this on your own because neither public nor private companies volunteer this comparison. Most likely, they don't want to call attention to any disparity between the change in profit versus the change in EPS.

Tackle Unusual Gains and Losses

Many income statements start out normally: sales revenue less the expenses of making sales and operating the business. But then there's a jarring layer of *unusual gains and losses* on the way down to the final profit line. (We discuss unusual gains and losses in Chapters 6 and 14.) For example, a business may shut down and abandon one of its manufacturing plants and record a huge loss due to asset write-downs and severance compensation for employees who are laid off. A business may suffer a large loss from an uninsured flood. Or a business may lose a major lawsuit and have to pay millions in damages. The list of extraordinary losses (and gains) is a long one. What's a financial statement reader to do when a business reports such unusual, nonrecurring gains and losses in its income statement?

There's no easy answer to this question. You could blithely assume that these things happen to a business only once in a blue moon and should not disrupt the business's ability to make profit on a sustainable basis. We call this the *earthquake mentality* approach: When there's an earthquake, there's lots of damage, but most years have no serious tremors and go along as normal. Unusual gains and losses are supposed to be nonrecurring in nature and recorded infrequently. In actual practice, however, many businesses report these gains and losses on a regular and recurring basis — like having an earthquake every year or so.

WARNING

Unusual losses are a particular problem because large amounts are moved out of the mainstream expenses of the business and treated as nonrecurring losses in its income statement, which means these amounts do not pass through the regular expense accounts of the business. Profit from continuing operations is reported at higher amounts than it would be if the unusual losses were treated as regular operating expenses. Investment managers complain in public about the special treatment of unusual gains and losses in financial reports. But in private, they seem to prefer that businesses have the latitude to maximize their reported earnings from continuing operations by passing off some expenses as unusual, infrequent losses when, in fact, these gains and losses occur more frequently than you would expect. Check out Chapter 14 to better acquaint yourself with how businesses "massage" the numbers.

Check Cash Flow from Profit

The objective of a business is not simply to make profit but to generate cash flow from making profit as quickly as possible. Cash flow from making profit is the most important stream of cash inflow to a business. A business could sell off some assets to generate cash, and it can borrow money or get shareowners to put more money in the business. But cash flow from making profit is the spigot that should always be turned on. A business needs this cash flow to make cash distributions from profit to shareowners, to maintain liquidity, and to supplement other sources of capital to grow the business.

REMEMBER

The income statement does not — we repeat, does *not* — report the cash inflows of sales and the cash outflows of expenses. Therefore, the bottom line of the income statement is not a cash flow number. The net cash flow from the profit-making activities of the business (its sales and expenses) is reported in the statement of cash flows. When you look there, you'll undoubtedly discover that the *cash flow from operating activities* (the official term for cash flow from profit-making activities) is higher or lower than the bottom-line profit number in the income statement. We explain the reasons for the difference in Chapter 8.

Businesses seldom offer any narrative or footnote explanation of the difference between profit and cash flow. What you see in the statement of cash flows is all you get — no more. You're pretty much on your own to interpret the difference. There are no general benchmarks or ratios for testing cash flow against profit. We couldn't possibly suggest that cash flow should normally be 120 percent of bottom-line profit, or some other such relationship. However, one thing is clear: Growth penalizes cash flow — or more accurately, growth sucks up or consumes cash because the business has to expand its assets to support the higher level of sales.

WARNING

Cash flow from operating activities could be a low percentage of profit (or even negative). This situation should prompt questions about the company's *quality of earnings,* which refers to the credibility and soundness of its profit accounting methods. In many cases, cash flow is low because accounts receivable from sales haven't been collected and because the business made large increases in its inventories. The surges in these assets raise questions about whether all the receivables will be collected and whether all the inventory will be sold at regular prices. Only time will tell. Generally speaking, you should be more cautious and treat the net income that the business reports with some skepticism.

Look for Signs of Financial Distress

A business can build up a good sales volume and have very good profit margins, but if the company can't pay its bills on time, its profit opportunities could go down the drain. *Solvency* refers to a business's prospects of being able to meet its debt and other liability payment obligations on time, in full. Solvency analysis looks for signs of financial distress that could cause serious disruptions in the business's profit-making operations. Even if a business has a couple billion bucks in the bank, you should ask, "How does its solvency look? Is there any doubt it can pay its bills on time?"

Frankly, detailed solvency analysis of a business is best left to the pros. The credit industry has become very sophisticated in analyzing solvency. For example, bankruptcy prediction models have proven useful. We don't think the average financial report reader should spend the time to calculate solvency ratios. For one thing, many businesses massage their accounting numbers to make their liquidity and solvency appear to be better than they are at the balance sheet date (commonly referred to as "balance sheet dressing").

Although many accountants and investment analysts would view our advice here as heresy, we suggest that you just take a quick glance at the company's balance sheet. How do its total liabilities stack up against its cash, current assets, and total assets? Obviously, total liabilities shouldn't be more than total assets. Duh! And obviously, if a company's cash balance is close to zero, things are bad. Beyond these basic rules, things are much more complex. Many businesses carry a debt load you wouldn't believe, and some get into trouble even though they have hefty cash balances.

TIP

The continued solvency of a business depends mainly on the ability of its managers to convince creditors to continue extending credit to the business and renewing its loans. The credibility of management is the main factor, not ratios. Creditors understand that a business can get into a temporary bind and fall behind on paying its liabilities. As a general rule, creditors are slow to pull the plug on a business. Shutting off new credit may be the worst thing lenders and other creditors could do. Doing so may put the business in a tailspin, and its creditors may end up collecting very little. Usually, it's not in their interest to force a business into bankruptcy — doing so is a last resort.

Recognize the Possibility of Restatement and Fraud

A few years ago, the CEO of one of the Big Four global CPA firms testified before a blue-ribbon federal government panel on the state of auditing and financial reporting. He said that one out of every ten financial reports issued by public companies is later revised and restated. Assuming that's true, there's a 10 percent chance that the financial statements you're reading are not entirely correct and could be seriously misleading. An earlier study of financial restatements arrived at a much lower estimate. We're sure future studies will show variation in the rate of restatements. You'd think that the incidence of companies having to redo their financial reports would be extremely rare, but we have to tell you that financial restatements continue with alarming regularity.

REMEMBER

When a business restates its original financial report and issues a new version, it doesn't make restitution for any losses that investors suffered by relying on the originally reported financial statements. In fact, few companies even say they're sorry when they put out revised financial statements. Generally, the language explaining financial restatements is legalistic and exculpatory. "We didn't do anything wrong" seems to be the underlying theme. This attitude is hard to swallow.

All too often, the reason for the restatement is that someone later discovered that the original financial statements were based on fraudulent accounting. Frankly speaking, CPAs don't have a very good track record for discovering financial reporting fraud. What it comes down to is this: Investors take the risk that the information in the financial statements they use in making decisions is subject to revision at a later time. We suppose you could go to the trouble of searching for a business that has never had to restate its financial statements, but there's always a first time for fraud.

Remember the Limits of Financial Reports

There's much more to investing than reading financial reports. Financial reports are an important source of information, but investors also should stay informed about general economic trends and developments, political events, business take-overs, executive changes, technological changes, and much more. Undoubtedly, the information demands required for investing have helped fuel the enormous popularity of mutual funds; investors offload the need to keep informed to the investment managers of the mutual fund. Many advertisements of financial institutions stress this point — that you have better things to do with your time.

When you read financial statements, keep in mind that these accounting reports are somewhat tentative and conditional. Accountants make many estimates and predictions in recording sales revenue and income and recording expenses and losses. Some soft numbers are mixed in with hard numbers in financial statements. In short, financial statements are iffy to some extent. There's no getting around this limitation of accounting.

REMEMBER

Having said that, let us emphasize that financial reports serve an indispensable function in every developed economy. We really couldn't get along without financial reports, despite their limits and problems. People wouldn't know which way to turn in a financial information vacuum. Even though the financial air is polluted, we need the oxygen of financial reports to breathe.

Index

A

absorption accounting, 344

accelerated depreciation, 201, 278

account, 8–9, 58, 61, 62

account function, 86–88

accountability, within external financial reporting, 232–233

accountant, 8, 10–11, 55, 64. *See also* certified public accountant (CPA)

accounting entity, 89

accounting equation, 24, 36, 71, 138–139

accounting manual, 60

accounting methods, changing, 133

accounting software, 78–80, 81, 82–85

accounting systems, 60–68

accounts payable, 124, 131–132, 153, 157, 279–280

accounts receivable

  on balance sheet, 150–151

  conservative accounting methods for, 191

  decrease in, 169

  defined, 125

  financial condition and, 276

  increase in, 169

  sales and, 127–128

  on statement of cash flows, 168–169

accrual basis accounting, 165

accrual basis of accounting, 127

accrued expenses payable liability account

  conservative accounting methods for, 194–195

  financial condition and, 280

  interest within, 155

  overview of, 132

  as spontaneous liability, 157

  unpaid expenses within, 153

accumulated depreciation, 130, 152, 171

acid test ratio, 255

activity-based costing (ABC), 338–339

actual cost, 327, 329, 333

actual cost/actual output method, 342–343

addbacks, 295–296

adequate disclosure, 117, 184

adjusted trial balance, 59

adjusting entries, 59, 65

advertising, 121–122, 214

Amazon, 83

AMC, 35

American Institute of Certified Public Accountants (AICPA), 64, 213

American Institute of Professional Bookkeepers, 64

amortization expense, 153–155, 172

Apple, 35, 59, 280

Arthur Anderson, 214

asset account, 128, 129, 153

assets. *See also* fixed assets

  in accounting equation, 138

  on balance sheet, 23, 37, 38, 89, 149–156

  classification of, 143–144

  current, 139, 143, 144, 145, 281

  debits and credits of, 72

  double-entry accounting and, 70–73

  equation for, 24

  estimates regarding, 297–298

  expenses and, 123–124

  financial, 20, 147

  impairment write-downs of, 203

  intangible, 153–155, 239, 278–279

  long-term, 18, 20

  long-term debt and, 385

  origin of, 9

  profit and, 125

  purchasing of, 38

  revenue and, 123–124

  salvage value of, 175

B

certified management accountant (CMA), 64

certified public accountant (CPA)

  audit process of, 47

  chart of accounts review by, 62

  credential of, 63–64

  expertise of, 405

  report of, 240–244

  role of, 47

  stereotype of, 10

chart of accounts, 60–62

Chartered Global Management Accountant
  (CGMA), 64

chief executive officer (CEO), 27

chief financial officer (CFO), 213

class, 101

classified balance sheet, 139, 141

closing the books, 60

cloud, accounting software on, 78–80

codification, of FASB, 49

collection, internal controls for, 69

common stock shares, 102, 263

compensation, disclosure of, 35

compensation committee, 106

compensatory effects, 224

complete, accurate, reliable, and timely (CART)
  financial information, 15–16, 54, 76

complex capital structure, 262

comprehensive income, within statement of
  changes in stockholders' equity, 186

condensed financial statements, 229–230, 236

condensed summary version, of financial
  report, 411

continuing education, for bookkeepers and
  accountants, 64

contribution margin, 247, 314

control benchmark, 150, 151

controller, 62, 64, 213, 269

convertible debt, 380, 388–389

cooking the books, 52, 73–74, 223, 241

corporate finance, 282

corporation

  board of directors of, 103

  disclosure within, 213

  leadership structure within, 106

  legal structure of, 44

  limited liability within, 100

  management within, 107

  overview of, 99–107

  profit within, 106

  publicly owned, 100–101

  stock shares of, 99, 100–105

  structure of, 48, 186

  taxes of, 100

cost accounting, 304, 325–326, 327

cost center, management responsibility
  within, 305

cost of capital, 329–330

cost of goods sold (COGS)

  additional information within, 61

  on balance sheet, 151–152

  calculating, 195–199

  conservative accounting methods for, 192

  defined, 33, 247, 400

  first-in, first-out (FIFO) method for, 196–197

  on income statement, 119

  inventory and, 128–129

  labor cost within, 122

  last-in, last-out (LIFO) method for, 197–199

  within profit template, 317–318

  reporting of, 330

  sales revenue and, 35

  as variable expense, 312

cost of sales (COS), 33, 35, 247

costing, 18

cost-plus, 327–328

costs. *See also* manufacturing costs

  actual, 327, 329, 333

  allocating, 338–339

  of capital, 329–330

  fixed *versus* variable, 331–332

  importance of, 327–330

  imputed, 329–330

  indirect *versus* direct, 330–331, 338–339

  marginal, 329

  opportunity, 261, 329

predatory pricing and, 328

product, 326, 334, 337–338, 339–340, 341

projected, 333

relevant *versus* irrelevant, 332–333

replacement, 198, 329

sales price and, 327–328

standard, 329–330, 333

types of, 326–327

counterparties, of transactions, 21

covenants, debt, 385–386

COVID-19 pandemic, 75, 78, 183

credit, accounts receivable and, 151

credit card receipt, 56

credit scores, of businesses, 279

creditor, as asset source, 23

crowdfunding, 234

cryptocurrency, 80, 85

current assets/liabilities, 139, 143, 144, 145, 281

current ratio, 145–146, 254

customers, as transaction counterparty, 21

cyber threats, 70

cyber-insurance, 85

D

data entry, 16, 62–63, 76–77, 79

data in, garbage out (DIGO), 76–77

data integrity, 77

data risk, 84

data rooms, changes within, 86–87

debits and credits, 72

debt

advantages of, 157–158

on balance statement, 155

as capital, 381–386

convertible, 380, 388–389

covenants, 385–386

defined, 20, 157

disadvantages of, 158

as equity, 388–390

in the footnotes, 239

interest-bearing, 281–282

maturity, 383

net increase/decrease of, 176

notes payable within, 144

security, 383

for share repurchasing, 257

sources of, 383–384

on statement of cash flows, 42

structure of, 384–385

underwriting and costs for, 384

debt service coverage ratio (DSCR), 264–265

debt-to-equity ratio, 256–257

debt-to-tangible net equity ratio, 257–258

deferred maintenance, 225

deferred revenue, 123, 127–128

depreciation expense

accelerated, 201, 278

accumulated, 277–278

as adjusting entry, 65

amortization expense *versus,* 172

on balance sheet, 152–153

conservative accounting methods for, 193

defined, 277

as fixed, 315

overview of, 129–130, 131

recording, 200–202

on statement of cash flows, 170–172

straight-line, 200–201

diluted earnings per share, 262

dilution effect, 104–105

direct costs, indirect costs *versus,* 330–331

direct deposit, 81

direct labor, as manufacturing cost type, 335

direct materials, as manufacturing cost type, 335

direct method, on statement of cash flows, 163–165

disclosure, 50–51, 184, 213, 215–220

discontinuity, 134

dividends, 47–48, 156, 178

documentation, 62–63, 69

double-entry accounting, 9, 70–73

double-entry bookkeeping, 24

Dropbox, 86

due diligence, 213

E

earnings before interest, tax, depreciation, and amortization (EBITDA), 204, 295–296, 378

earnings management, 223–226

earnings per share (EPS)
  bottom line changes and, 413–414
  defined, 114
  determination of, 106
  overview of, 261–263
  as profit, 294
  rise of, 256

earnings statement, 113. *See also* income statement

earthquake mentality approach, 414

economic value added (EVA) method, 330

electronic payments, 17, 18, 80–81, 82–84

electronic reference, 56

embezzlement, 69, 70, 73–74

employee, compensation to, 17, 21, 124

employee-defined benefits pension plans, 203

end-of-period procedures, 58–59, 65–66

Enron, 68, 214

equity, 20, 380–381, 386–394

equity incentive plans, 203–204

error, 187, 241

estate planning, 375

estimates, for assets, 297–298

Ethereum, 85

events, recording, 21–22

exactitude misconception, 134

exchange traded securities (ETS), 117

exchange-traded fund (ETF), 234

exercise price, for stock option grant, 203–204

expectations gap, 243

expensed fixed assets, 277

expenses. *See also specific expenses*
  analyzing, 286–287
  as asset/liability driver, 150
  cash flow characteristics of, 285
  conservative accounting methods for, 194–195
  defined, 33
  disclosure within, 33

on income statements, 118

management discretion regarding, 225

"other" category of, 116

overview of, 123–124

as profit-making transaction, 20

in service businesses, 35

types of, 61

external balance sheets, 143–144

external control, 81

external financial accounting, 55–56

external financial report, 55, 231–232

external financial statement, 268–269, 270–272

external income statement, 33

external money, 175

external users, 12

extraordinary gains and losses, 292, 293–294, 414

F

financial accounting, 55–56

Financial Accounting Standards Board (FASB), 28, 49, 77, 226

financial assets, 20, 147

financial condition, 272–275, 276–283

financial engineering, 290–299

financial leverage gain, 261

financial literacy, 7

financial management, 282

financial performance, 258–265

financial report
  active reading of, 228–230
  for archival purposes, 229
  changes within, 87
  condensed version of, 229–230
  contract of, 212
  disclosures within, 213, 215–220
  external, 55, 231–232
  features of, 32
  financial statements within, 11
  importance of, 16
  internal controls for, 87
  limitations of, 417–418

models, financial, 356–357
money laundering, 73–74
month to date (MTD), 247
mutual funds, regulations to, 117

N

net income
  on balance sheet, 156
  cash flow variance and, 167–173
  defined, 25, 35, 114, 210, 314
  EPS ratio regarding, 262
  on income statement, 43, 119
net income available for the common stockholders, 260
net income statement, 113. *See also* income statement
net loss, 25
net profit, 41
net working capital, 254–255
net worth, 24, 39, 71
non-accountants, financial reports for, 11
non-cash expenses, 41
nonmanufacturing operating costs, 337–338
notes payable, 56, 144, 145
numbers, manipulating, 220–226

O

object of expenditure basis, 308–309
operating activities
  on balance sheet, 147–149
  cash flow from, 402
  defined, 20, 147, 163
  on statement of cash flows, 41
operating agreement, of LLCs, 93
operating costs, 119–120, 129
operating cycle, 145
operating earnings, 114, 116, 313–314
operating expenses
  accounting rule for, 203
  on balance sheets, 153
  defined, 247

  fixed, 318–319, 321–322
  reporting, 308–309
  in service businesses, 35
  variable, within profit template, 318
operating leverage effect, 321–322
operating liabilities, 38, 172–173
operating margin, 314
operating statement, 113. *See also* income statement
operational pivots, 361
opportunity cost of capital, 261, 329
original entry of financial effects, 57
Other Comprehensive Basis of Accounting, 51
"other" expenses, 116
outputs, of accounting, 55
outside director, 106
outsiders, 12
overhead, as manufacturing cost type, 335
owner, as asset source, 23
owners' equity
  in accounting equation, 138
  on balance sheet, 39
  defined, 23, 71
  example of, 24
  financial condition and, 282–283
  reporting, 26, 185–186
  sources of, 157
  statement regarding, 44
ownership shares, within corporations, 100–101

P

participating preferred stock, 102
partnerships, 91–92, 96–99
pass-through tax entity, 132
payments, forms of, 80–81
payroll, 17, 56, 81
pension plans, 203
period, 58
period costs, 334, 337–338
personal finance, 13–14, 53, 61, 70
personnel, hiring of, 63–65

posting, process of, 58

post-retirement benefits, 203, 239

preconceptions, accounting, 8–11

predatory pricing, 328

preferred stock shares, 101, 186, 260

prepaid expenses, 129, 170

prepaid expenses asset account, 153

price earnings multiple method, 379

price/earnings (P/E) ratio, 263–264

primary capital market, 234

private companies

  audit report of, 240

  financial reporting by, 227–228, 236–237

  financial reporting structure of, 213

  investing in, 234

  standards for, 51

  stockholders' meeting of, 227

Private Company Council (PCC), 51

pro forma operating results, 296

procurement, 18

product costs

  burden rate within, 341, 345

  calculating, 339–340

  defined, 326

  manufacturing costs as, 337–338

  period costs *versus,* 334

product sale, 112, 128–129

production, excessive, 343–346

production capacity, 340–343

product-oriented business, 113–115

professional corporation (PC), 98

professional credentials, 63–64

profit

  assets and, 23, 125

  cash distribution from, 47–48

  cash flow *versus,* 401–402, 415

  challenges of, 303

  defined, 20

  distributions of, 156

  excessive production and, 343–346

  fallout regarding, 10

  fluctuation smoothing of, 223–226

  following breakeven, 400

  gross, 114, 328

  improving, options for, 323–324

  on income statements, 119

  before income tax, 114

  liabilities and, 125

  manufacturing, 297–299

  margin and, 314–315

  misconception regarding, 10, 135

  net income, 114

  operating earnings, 114, 116

  overview of, 9–10, 111, 112, 122–126

  performance, 44–45, 55, 122, 219, 412

  reporting, 25, 307–309

  into retained earnings, 126

  sales revenue and, 121

  scenarios for, 124–126

  of service-oriented business, 115–117

  strategic analysis of, 309–316

  template for explanation of, 315–320

profit allocation, 97–99

profit and loss (P&L) report, 35, 210, 307–308

profit center, 305, 306

profit smoothing techniques, 223–226

profit-making transactions, 20, 147

projected costs, 333

projections. *See* forecasting

property, plant, and equipment. *See* fixed assets

property accounting, 18

proxy statement, 230, 237

public companies. *See also* corporation

  condensed financial statements of, 236

  disclosure within, 213

  EPS figures for, 262

  financial reporting by, 226–227, 236–237

  internal controls reporting of, 214

  overview of, 100–101

  pressure on, 223–224, 227

  standards for, 51

Public Company Accounting Oversight Board, 214

Public Company Accounting Oversight Board (PCAOB), 68

purchase invoice, 56

About the Authors

John A. Tracy (Boulder, Colorado) is Professor of Accounting, Emeritus, at the University of Colorado in Boulder. Before his 35-year tenure at Boulder, he was on the business faculty for four years at the University of California at Berkeley. Early in his career, he was a staff accountant with Ernst & Young. John is the author of several books on accounting and finance, including *The Fast Forward MBA in Finance* and *Accounting Workbook For Dummies*. His son, Tage C. Tracy, joined him as coauthor on *How to Read a Financial Report*, now in its 9th edition. John and Tage have also coauthored *Cash Flow For Dummies* and *Small Business Financial Management Kit For Dummies*. John received his BSC degree from Creighton University. He earned his MBA and PhD degrees at the University of Wisconsin in Madison. He is a CPA (inactive status) in Colorado.

Tage C. Tracy (pronounced "Tog"/Scandinavian descent) has, over the past 25+ years, operated a financial consulting firm focused on offering CFO/executive-level support and planning services to private companies on a fractional basis. These services include providing guidance and support with raising debt and equity capital, completing complex financial analysis, supporting risk management assessments, guiding accounting system designs and structuring, and being an integral part of the strategic business planning management functions. Tage specializes in providing these services to businesses operating at four distinct stages: (1) start-ups and business launches, (2) rapid growth, ramp, and expansion management, (3) strategic exit and acquisition preparedness and management, and (4) turnarounds, challenged environments, and survival techniques.

Tage is also an active author and has been the lead or coauthor for a number of books, including his most recent title, *Business Financial Information Secrets*. Tage has also coauthored (with his father John A. Tracy) *How to Read a Financial Report*, 9th Edition; *How to Read a Financial Report*, Comprehensive Version; *Cash Flow For Dummies*; and *Small Business Financial Management Kit For Dummies*. Tage received his baccalaureate in accounting in 1985 from the University of Colorado at Boulder with honors. He began his career with Coopers & Lybrand (today PricewaterhouseCoopers) and obtained his CPA certificate in the state of Colorado in 1987 (now inactive). Tage can be reached on his website http://financemakescents.com/ or directly at tagetracy@cox.net.

Dedication

Tage C. Tracy: Taking the leading role in revising the 7th Edition of *Accounting For Dummies*, I would like to dedicate this book to, first and foremost, my dad, John A. Tracy, AKA TOP (The Old Pro). It's not often that you see a book dedicated to one of its authors, but in this case, my dad's influence, support, guidance, and dedication to the accounting profession, provided over the past 50+ years, cannot be emphasized enough. I simply can't tell you how much invaluable guidance my dad has provided on the art of writing books when he encouraged me to take over the family business a decade or so ago.

Second, I would like also remember my mom, who passed away in 2017, and express my thanks for "saving my ass" countless times by editing numerous college papers drafted in decades past (a job thankfully taken over by Wiley's editing department). Her commitment, support, and unconditional love showered on our entire family over the decades, including my dad, my four siblings (and spouses), and me, my parents' 12 grandchildren and five spouses (all recently added), and one great-grandchild on the way (as we drafted this book) has always been the rock we all leaned on when life's road took more than a few unexpected twists and turns.

In an era when economic, business, social, and political trust is in such short supply, I can only look back to the foundation my parents laid for everyone in the extended Tracy family with profound gratitude.

Authors' Acknowledgments

We're deeply grateful to everyone at Wiley who, for over 25 years, have helped produce the seven editions of this book. Their professionalism, courtesy, and good humor are much appreciated. It has been a pleasure working with them. Our problem here is that there are too many to thank individually. So we mention only the first person who contacted me, John A. Tracy, about doing this book. The others know how deeply grateful I am for their invaluable help in making the book so successful.

I got a call in 1996 from Kathy Welton, then Vice President and Publisher for the Consumer Publishing Group of the *For Dummies* books. Kathy asked if I'd be interested in doing this book. It didn't take me very long to say yes. Thank you again, Kathy! And a round of applause for everyone listed in the Publisher's Acknowledgments on the next page. The authors get the byline, but these people are "silent partners" who don't always get the credit they deserve.

Publisher's Acknowledgments

Associate Acquisitions Editor: Elizabeth Stilwell

Managing Editor: Michelle Hacker

Project Manager and Development Editor: Georgette Beatty

Copy Editor: Gwenette Gaddis

Technical Editor: Mark Friedlich

Production Editor: Mohammed Zafar Ali

Cover Image: © Umberto Shtanzman/ Shutterstock